ABSTRACTS *from* The OLD NORTH STATE

ELIZABETH CITY
PASQUOTANK COUNTY
NORTH CAROLINA
- 1849 -1850 -

Compiled by:
Raymond Parker Fouts

Southern Historical Press, Inc.
Greenville, South Carolina

This volume was reproduced
from a personal copy located in
the Publishers private library

Please direct all correspondence and book orders to:
SOUTHERN HISTORICAL PRESS, Inc.
PO Box 1267
Greenville, SC   29602-1267

Copyright 1996 by: Raymond Parker Fouts
Copyright Transferred 2023 to:
               Southern Historical Press, Inc.
ISBN #978-1-63914-207-1
Printed in the United States of America

PREFACE

The source for the compilation of these abstracts is North Carolina State Archives Microfilm #ECONS-1, Elizabeth City, Old North State, Weekly May 25, 1841-Dec. 20, 1851. The repository and dates of extant issues are noted at the beginning of each year.

William E. **MANN** became editor and proprietor of *The Old North State* 21 February 1846. He shared editorial duties with Stephen D. **POOL** from 1847 to 1849. In the issue of 8 September 1849, G. M. **WILDER** appeared as assistant editor. He remained in that capacity until the 11 June 1850 issue, when the proprietors were listed as **MANN & GRIFFIN**, with Stephen D. **POOL** as editor. The editors of this paper were staunch Whigs.

Local news items, including deaths, court notices and marriages, are found for nearby counties other than Pasquotank. National news covers items from several of the extant States, including Alabama, California, Maryland, Massachusetts, Tennessee, Texas and Virginia. This information was gleaned from newspapers published in the large American ports, as well as telegraphic transmissions. The printed sources are listed in the "Publications Index." Repetition of earlier advertisements has preserved some from 1847, in accordance with the editor's policy of not discontinuing them until "ordered out." All issues have been included. Advertisements have been recorded only from the first issue in which they appear in legible form.

Each item has been assigned a number, within parentheses. All the indices refer to those numbers, rather than page numbers. All spellings of every surname are indexed. Marshals, Mayors, Postmasters and Sheriffs are indexed under those titles. All references to those persons are also indexed under their individual names. Names of brides are indexed under both maiden and married names, as well as in the "Female Given Name Index." Native-Americans are indexed under "Indians," and African-Americans under "Mulattoes" and "Negroes," the terms used in this newspaper.

Underlined letters emphasize verbatim spelling. "____" denotes missing or illegible letters or words.

31 July 1996
RPF

TABLE OF CONTENTS

1849 -------------------------------------- 1

1850 ---------------------------------- 65

Index ---------------------------------- 129

Female Given Name Index --------- 149

Publications Index -------------------- 151

Location Index ----------------------- 153

ABSTRACTS FROM THE OLD NORTH STATE

ELIZABETH CITY, NORTH CAROLINA

1849-1850

1849 - Filmed from originals in the University of North Carolina Library. The following issues are missing: January 6 through February 17.

(1) *The Old North State.*
Vol. 9. "Error is harmless, when truth is left free to combat it." No. 1.
Elizabeth city, N. C. Saturday, February 24, 1849.
Published every Saturday, by Wm. E. **MANN**, Editor and Proprietor. Terms-Per Annum. To those who have to pay postage on the paper, $2,00 To those who do not, $2,50 Payable in six months after subscribing, or Three Dollars will be charged if payment is delayed until the expiration of the year. No paper stopped until all arreages are paid up, except at the option of the proprietor. Advertisements inserted at $1 per square for the first insertion, and 25 cents for each continuance. Advertisements must be marked with the number of insertions wanted, or they will be charged until ordered out.

(2) Elizabeth-City, Feb. 24, '49. .. Removal. The Office of the "Old North State" has been removed to the *New Office* on North Street, immediately in the rear of the House formerly occupied by Abner **WILLIAMS**, Esq., dec'd, and now by Mr. **SANDERLIN**.

(3) TO OUR SUBSCRIBERS. To-day commences the 9th volume of the "Old North State," and the 4th year of our administration. On the 21st February 1846 we took charge of the "Old North State" and from that time to this have continued to issue it regularly, not even missing *one* publication, a thing never before done in Elizabeth City. Part of the time we have been (as now), both publisher and editor, and have to the best of our ability discharged our duty. For the last two years the paper has been under the editorial management of Mr. S. D. **POOL** he, as announced last week has withdrawn from the field of his late labor and upon us *alone* devolves the responsibility of weekly cateering for the public appetite. ...

(4) ASSAULTS IN WASHINGTON-PICK POCKETS Persons passing along the streets of Washington recently have been ____ and robbed..--Those who attend the Inauguration of Gen. **TAYLOR** would do well to look out for pickpockets in the crowd on that occasion. ...

(5) TO THE MAGISTRATES OF PERQUIMANS COUNTY. Gentlemen! On behalf of ourselves, of our fellow-citizens, and of suffering humanity, we have a petition to make to you--and for it and the facts on which it is grounded, we respectfully solicit your serious consideration. That petition is nothing less than this: That you will refuse to grant any License for the Retail of Intoxicating Liquors in our County during the year 1849. .. We last year made an investigation into the quantity of ardent spirits used in our county in the year 1847. The result of our inquiries developes the fact that 30,000 gallons of whiskey, and probably more were consumed in that single year. This is neither mere assertion nor supposition, but the result derived in most instances from the statements to us of the various merchants throughout the county who are engaged in selling the article. .. Gentlemen of the Magistracy, we beseech you to lend us your aid in arresting the march of Intemperance in our community. ... John R. **WINSLOW**, President. Jeptha **WHITE**, Secretary. Perquimans Friends Society.

(6) LIFE'S UNCERTANTY.--In announcing the death of Captain Augustus L. **SHEPPARD**, of the U. S. Army, which took place recently at Jefferson Barracks, (Mo.,) the *Wheeling Gazette* says: We had the pleasure of serving a campaign in Florida with Captain (then private) **SHEPPARD**. .. Our mess consisted of six individuals; one, Captain **WALKER**, was killed in Mexico, another, Wilson **THOMAS**, shot himself by accident while hunting for pigeons; the 3rd, John H. **PLEASANTS**, was cruelly murdered by the Indians during the Florida war, the fourth, H. **CREMER**, was killed by a decayed tree falling on him in a harvest field,

24 February 1849

(6) (Cont.) the fifth, Capt. **SHEPPARD**, died as above stated, and the sixth, and only surviving member of the mess, is the assistant editor of the *Gazette*, enjoying good general health. Have we not cause to be grateful.

(7) Married. Married, on the 19th instant, at the residence of Mr. Dickie **GALT** in Williamsburg, by the Rev. Chas. **MINIGIRODE**, of Brandon Parish, Col. T. L. **SKINNER**, Esq., of Edenton, N. C., to Miss Eliza Fisk **HARWOOD**, daughter of J. R. **HARWOOD**, dec'd, late a Merchant of Norfolk city.

(8) SALT! SALT! SALT! The subscriber has on hand about 400 Bushels of Salt which he offers for sale. Also 75 sacks Table Salt. C. C. **GREEN**. Feb. 10.

(9) SELLING OFF. The subscriber being about to remove to Tarborough, N. C., offers for sale his entire stock of Goods, consisting of Dry-Goods, Groceries, Hardware, Crockery, Boots Shoes, Hats, &c. &c. .. All persons indebted to the subscriper are requested to come forward and settle up, as he wants all accounts settled. He will also rent his Store and Dwelling after he leaves, for the ballance of the year. Thomas **ALLEN**. Feb. 24.

(10) A NEW ARTICLE. Castor Oil Capsules, a new article for the sick, without taste or smell of the Oil. For sale by L. K. **SAUNDERS**.

(11) Tailoring Business. The subscribers having associated themselves together on the 1st January last, for the purpose of carrying on the Tailoring Business, would most respectfully return their sincere thanks for the patronage they have received, and solicit a continuance of the same. One of the firm, (Mr. **BURGESS**,) is lately from Norfolk, and understands cutting in all its branches as well as the other Partner. .. The latest Northern Fashions regularly received. **BERRY& BURGESS,** John G. **BERRY**, John **BURGESS**,} Hertford, Perquimans Co., N. C., Feb. 24, 1849.

(12) REMOVAL. Solomon **KING**, WHOLESALE DRUGGIST, *Dealer in Paints, Oils, Spices, Dye-Stuffs, Window Glass, Putty, Perfumery, Soaps, Fancy Articles, &c. &c.* No. 1. South Calvert St., Baltimore, Md. Would respectfully inform Country Merchants, Physicians, Druggists and others, that he has Removed from No. 8 to No. 1 South Calvert Street, (nearly opposite to his former place of business) in **JOHNSON** and **LEE**'s large building. A full and fresh stock of every article in his line of business always to be found at this House. ... Jan. 24th, 1849.

(13) GREENSBORO' FEMALE COLLEGE. Guilford County, N. C. The Second Session of the College year, 1848-9, will commence in this Institution on the first Monday in January next. .. Particular attention is invited to the reduced rate of board in the Institution. Expenses. *Board and Tuition for each Session in advance.* Board per Session, at $8 per month, $40 00 Tuition, either in the Classical or English Department, 20 00 Music, 20 00 French or Spanish, 5 00 Painting and Drawing, 5 00 Needle work and Shell work, 5 00 Tuition in the Preparatory Department, 12 to 15 00 Primary Department, 8 00 The College uniform adopted by order of Trustees consists, in Summer, of a plain white dress, in Winter of some suitable material of blue color.

(14) FOR WASHINGTON AND THE INAUGURATION. The steamer Osceola will leave Washington for Norfolk on the following days, at 9 o'clock in the morning: on Friday the 23d of February, Wednesday the 28th, and Tuesday the 6th of March. .. Passage and Fare, to go and return, for both trips to Washington, $6?, with the priviledge of stopping there ten days, and of sleeping on board while at the wharf. After that the Osceola will commence her regular trips to Norfolk, once a week, leaving Washington on Tuesday and Norfolk on Fridays. James **MITCHELL**, Master. feb 24

(15) NEW DRUG STORE, IN ELIZABETH CITY. The subscriber having taken the Store on the corner, under the "Mansion House," lately occupied by S. D. **POOL**, Esq., as a Grocery, intends keeping on hand a general assortment of every thing usually found in a Drug Store. He has just received a fine assortment of Paints, Oils, Drugs, Medicines, Perfumery, Glass, Putty, &c. The above articles are warranted all fresh and no mistake. Lewis **WARROCK**. Jan. 17, '49.

(16) 75 CENTS. Will be opened this morning at the Ladies' Saloon 200 Pairs Ladies' Morocco Slippers, at 75 cents a pair. They were made by Mr. **MC INTOSH**, of Philadelphia. .. For sale at the Ladies' Saloon on Main street near **WALTERS**'s City Hotel. W. H. **ADDINGTON**. Norfolk, Va. Feb. 17

(17) Augustus M. **PRICE**, Wholesale & Retail Fruit Store, No. 183 Market Street, Second door from Light street, Baltimore, Where he keeps constantly on hand a large assortment of Fruits Nuts, and Preserves, together with an extentive Stock of Confectionary of his own Manufacture. All of which are offered at reduced prices. .. aug 1848

24 February 1849

(18) William **MACINTOSH**, Wholesale Manufacturer Of All Kinds Of Ladies Fashionable Boots and Shoes, 71 North Third Street, Philadelphia. North Carolina Merchants are respectfully solicited to give me a call... sept 2.

(19) **MURRAY & CLARK**, Mill Wrights, Pattern and Machine Makers, **CLUFF**'s Wharf Elizabeth City, N. C. The Subscribers are prepared to furnish all kinds of Mill work and Agricultural Machinery, at the shortest notice, viz., Horse Powers, Wheat Machines; Corn Shellers, for hand and horse power, Cutting Boxes, Corn and Cob Grinders, Portable Mills, Wrought & Cast Plows and Plow Irons of all kinds; Wheat Fans, Mill work of all descriptions..all Mills planned and erected by the subscribers warranted to operate well. .. Also large Corn Shellers for Horse Power that will shell from 300 to 700 bushels per hour. We would refer to the following named gentlemen that have them in use: Jas. C. **JOHNSTON**, Esq. Joshua **SKINNER**,} Edenton, N. C. Thos. P. **DEVERAUX**,} Halifax, N. C. Dr. C. M. **FORD**, Woodville, Mr. Joseph **TOMS**, Mr. Francis **NIXON**,} Perquimans Co. Mr. William **GLOVER**, Mr. Jno. C. **BARNES**, Mr. Joseph H. **POOL**, Mr. Wm. H. **DAVIS**,} Pasquotank Co. ... March 20

(20) NOTICE. As the Subscriber intends leaving this place soon he would inform all persons who are indebted to him to come forward and settle up. All having articles at his shop are requested to get them away before he leaves. Joseph N. **BELL**. feb 10.

(21) In Town Again! The Subscriber hereby notifies his old friends and the public generally that he has returned to Elizabeth City, and taken a shop adjoining the Establishment of Capt. Wm. **BURGESS**, where he intends carrying on the Tailoring business in all its branches and sincerely hopes that his old friends will find him when they wish any thing done in that line. ... Henry **KRAUSS**. Dec. 23.

(22) FOUNTAIN HOTEL Light Street, Baltimore. The subscriber would respectfully inform his old customers and the travelling public in general, that he has lately had his house thoroughly put in complete order, and every convenience added for the benefit of those who may patronize him. He has added to his already *Extensive Establishment* several *beautiful Bed Rooms* with *Small Parlors* handsomely furnished attached thereto, for the benefit of families. .. There is attached to the Bar several Oyster Stalls, fitted up in splendid style where can be had at all hours Oysters of every variety. ... Phineas **THURSTON**, Proprietor. Baltimore, March, 1848

(23) Paints, Oils, Glass & Putty. Just received and for sale..pure White Lead..Black Lead..Yellow Lead..Patent Green..Paris Green..Chrome do. Chrome Yellow..Lamp Black..Spanish Brown..Venetian Red..Latharge..Yellow Ochre..Superior Putty..pure Linseed Oil..Porpoise Oil..Pure winter bleached Sperm Oil..Glass 8 by 10, 10 by 12, 12 by 16. The above articles are offered for sale cheap for Cash or its equivalent at the Drug Store of L. K. **SAUNDERS**, On Road street, next door to Z. **CULPEPPER**'s. E. City, January 20th, 1849.

(24) **COCKEY & GAMBRILL**, Grocers & Commission Merchants, No. 59, S. Calvert Street, Baltimore, Will attend to the selling of Lumber, Fish, Shingles & Produce Generally. Commission on all grain One Cent per bushel. References. J. B. **MORRIS**, Pres. of Mechanics Bank. John S. **GITTINGS**, "Chesapeake" Messrs. Henry **REIMEN** & Sons,} Balto. Mr. John H. **FHIEN**, Baltimore. " [Mr.] M. **RUSSELL**, Elizabeth City, North Carolina. " S. S. **SIMMONS**, Columbia, " [North Carolina] August 1847.

(25) STATE OF NORTH CAROLINA. Bertie Superior Court of Law, Fall Term 1848. Harriet **WESTON**, vs Richard **WESTON**.} Petition for Divorce. It appearing to the Court that Richard **WESTON** is not an inhabitant of this State, it is ordered that publication be made for three months in the "Old North State" & "Raleigh Register" for said **WESTON** to appear at the next Term of the Superior Court of Law to be held for the County of Bertie, at the Court House in Windsor, on the third Monday in March next, to plea, answer, or demur to said petition or Judgment, pro confesso, will be entered against him. By order of the Court. R. H. **SMITH**, Clerk. Jan. 20

(26) NOTICE. The Partnership heretofore existing under the firm of Jas. M. **BRUFF** & Co. was dissolved by mutual consent on the 1st inst. Having purchased of my friends in Baltimore, their entire interest in the buisness, I shall hereafter conduct the buisness in my own name and on my own account, hoping to receive a continuation of that patronage which has heretofore been so kindly bestowed upon us. James M. **BRUFF**. .. All persons indepted to us in any shape or form, are particularly requested to call and settle their respective accounts immediatiy, as this is a matter of great importance to me. Jas. M. **BRUFF**. Norfolk, Va. Feb 10

(27) LOOKING GLASSES. The subscriber continues manufacturing Looking Glasses..every variety of Plain and Ornamental Gilt, Mahogany.. Fancy Wood Frames. ... Reuben C. **BULL** No. 63 Liberty-st between Nassau and Broadway New York. Feb.

24 February 1849

(27) (Cont.) 10.

(28) THE DRY GOODS JOBBING BUSINESS, heretofore conducted at No. 283 Baltimore Street, under the firm of George **BAUGHMAN** & Co., will hereafter, at the same place, be carried on by the subscriber, who has purchased the entire interest of all parties concerned, including the Stock in trade, Books, Accounts, and other and all evidences of debt of every kind, pertaining to the business of said late firm. All persons indebted in any wise to said late firm of Geo. **BAUGHMAN** & Co., are hereby notified to make payment to the subscriber ALONE, or his order. Royston **BETTS**. Baltimore, Md., Feb. 10, 1849.

(29) JUST RECEIVED AND FOR SALE. The following articles, to wit: 10 bbls super Flour; 3 Hhds brite retailing Molasses; 1 do, Sugar; 3 do. Whiskey; 3 bbls Swan Gin, 1 do Monongaghala Whiskey..Apple Brandy..Scuppernong Wine..Chewing Tobacco, 1 gross smoking do...Soap..Brooms..Matches, and many other articles usually kept in a retail grocery, Also some of that Good Butter yet and some more expected every day from N. York at T. **ALLEN**'s old stand on the water, corner of North and Front Streets. Wm. **HALSEY**. Jan 17

(30) Private Residence for Sale. The Subscriber offers for sale, the property upon which he now resides near the Town of E. City. This property (including the wharf) consists of four lots which will be sold seperately or together to suit purchasers. The buildings are new and in complete order, and admirably adapted to the comfort of a family. The furniture will be sold, together with the dwelling house, if desired. ... Will. B. **SHEPARD**. August 12, 1848.

(31) A NEW SUPPLY. The subscriber has just returned from the North, where he selected them personally, a fine assortment of mountings for every kind of Harness, Whips of various kinds, sulky and cart Collars. .. He is now prepared also to make Saddles & Harness in the best style. Sulkys, Buggys and Rockaways made up in the best manner and at the shortest notice. All kinds of Repairs in his line done with neatness and despatch. Robert **WATKINS**. Dec. 23, 1848.

(32) Mrs. Ann **SISCO**. No. 95, Baltimore Street, Baltimore, Md. Manufacturer of Odd Fellows, Masonic, and Sons of Temperance Regalia, with jewels Tents, Gavills, Robes, Caps, &c. of every description. Also Banners and Flags constantly on hand and made to order in every variety of style. Also Ladies Dress Trimmings such as Gimps, Fringes, Cords and Tassels, Batteas, with a supply of coach Lace, Bindings, Cords, and every variety of Trimmings which will be sold wholesale and retail ...

(33) GRANDY & HARDY, Grocers And Commission Merchants, Norfolk, Va. C. W. **GRANDY**, H. C. **HARDY**. July 8, 1848.

(34) COME AND SEE. Wm. G. **COOK** would respectfully inform the inhabitants of Elizabeth City, and the adjoining counties, that he has just returned from Baltimore with a complete assortment of Watches and Jewelry... Nov. 4, 1848.

(35) A Fact Worthy to be Known. The subscriber wishes to inform his old Friends and the public generally, that he has recently purchased of Mr. George W. F, **DASHIELL** his entire stock of Goods, and having taken the store formerly occupied by him feels himself prepared to sell upon as good terms, and at as low prices as any..in Elizabeth City. ... Daniel **RICHARDSON**. Feb. 10

(36) NOTICE. The Patent Netting Loom, invented by Mr. John **MC MULLEN**, of Baltimore, Md. is now in full and successful operation, and is producing a most beautiful article of Netting, suitable for fishing nets, seines, fly nets for horses, &c..at a price far below that of a similar article produced by hand, and is in every respect decidedly superior. .. Fishermen, dealers in seins and seine twine, and manufacturers of fly nets..are respectfully invited to call..at No. 74 1/2 **BOWLY**'s wharf, Baltimore, Md. Wm. E. **HOOPER**. Jan. 20

(37) FARMERS INN. The Subscriber having taken the House on the corner, lately occupied by Mr. Geo. W. **KELLENGER**, and nearly opposite the Store of John J. **GRANDY**, Esq., would respectfully inform his old customers..that he has fitted it up with the intention of keeping a House of Entertainment. .. His Table will be supplied with the best that the market can afford. His terms will be moderate--Boarders taken by the day, week, month, or year. ... Robert A. **SAWYER**. Jan. 20.

(38) 1849. All persons Indebted to the subscriber prior to 1849, are earnestly requested to make immediate payments--indulgence neither can or will be given after the first of February ensuing. Wm. D. **ROBERTS**, Jr. Stove Depot, Roanoke Square. Jan. 20.

(39) NOTICE. The co-partnership heretofore existing between Drs. **SPEED & MULLEN** is this day dissolved by mutual consent. Persons indebted to them will please call and settle their accounts. February 3, 1849. Dr. Rufus K. **SPEED** tenders his services to the citizens of Elizabeth City and vicinity. Office on Road Street next door to Zion **CULPEPPER**s Residence, the

24 February 1849

(39) (Cont.) residence of the late Dr. **PERKINS**. E. City, Feb. 3, 1849.

(40) Doctors **CAHOON & MANNING** Having this day associated themselves in the practice of the various branches of their profession, respectfully offer their services to the citizens of Pasquotank County. They may be found in Nixonton at the office of Dr. **CAHOON**, or at their residences, when not professionally engaged. ... Nixonton, Feb. 3rd, 1849.

(41) John A. **GAMBRIL**, Commission Merchant, No. 104, Wall street, New York.

(42) W. J. **NOTTINGHAM**. Market Square, Norfolk, Va. would respectfully announce to the citizens of Norfolk and Portsmouth, that he has just returned from the North with a large assortment of the most approved Fall Styles of Hats And Caps... Also a large assortment of muffs, Ermine, Umbrellas, and Walking Canes on hand. W. J. **NOTTINGHAM**, Fashionable Hatter, market-square. sept 9

(43) For Window Blinds, Window Sash, and Panel Doors. The subscriber having the Agency of a large Manufacturing Establishment in Richmond, Va., will take pleasure in filling orders large or small at a short notice... Samples are kept at my Office in the Store of Messrs. John P. **LEIGH** & Son... Orders to be addressed to A. C. **TOMS**. Norfolk, Va. Sept. 2, 1848.

(44) AMERICAN HOTEL, New York, Broadway, Corner Barclay Street. The Subscribers respectfully inform..that they have taken a lease of this well known Hotel, and have repaired and improved it throughout, and furnished it entirely with New Furniture made expressly to their own order. ... **TABER & BAGLEY**, Proprietors. Job **TABER**, Boston. James **BAGLEY**, Philadelphia}

(45) GREAT ATTRACTION! Christmas & New Year's Goods, For the season of Presents, At J. M. **FREEMAN**'s Watch Maker And Jeweller, Who has just received a general assortment of Fine Gold and Silver Lepine Watches, Jewelry, Clocks, Military Goods, Plated and silver Ware, Hair and tooth brushes, combs, Spectacles and spectacle glasses, With..Fancy Goods... dec 23.

(46) Attention Travellers. The Subscriber having taken the House on the Canal so familiar known as "Major **FARRANGE**s," would respectfully inform the travelling public that he is prepared to accomodate them... Sebastian **WILLIAMS**. dec 16

(47) Brass and Iron Foundry. The Subscriber is prepared to execute to order Iron or Brass castings in all the various forms. Fish and Inspectors brands furnished to order on short notice. The highest cash price given for Old Iron, Brass and Copper in exchange for work. Foundry opposite the custom house, Norfolk, Va. ... Nelson **CORY**. feb 27

(48) LEATHER. The Subscriber has on hand and intends keeping for Sale Shoe and Harness Leather of all kinds. R. H. **BROADFIELD**. nov 24

(49) TO FARMERS. The subscriber having been engaged for some time in making Wheat Thrashers, which experience has shown are adopted to thrashing Peas, Flax, &c., while the same horse power by which the machine is operated..wishes to make known..that he is preparing to furnish Thrashers by next thrashing season, if application be made early, at Fort Landing, north of Alligator River, Tyrrell county, N. C.., or I would deliver them at E. City or Plymouth. My largest size Thrasher has two hoppers... Properly attended, I think it will..thrash 300 to 400 bushels per day. Price $85. I make Thrashers of a smaller size for $55. .. I will also give to purchasers a description of an improved and cheap plan of horse power to work with a rope band, such as David **CARTER**, Esq., of Hyde, and most of the farms of Hyde and Tyrrell counties use. I give below only four certificates out of about sixty that I have from men that have bought Thrashers of me. ... W. R. **PALMER**. N. B. .. Any person wishing to know any thing in regard to thrashing Peas, can call on Louis **MIDYET**, of Stumpy Point, Tyrrell County, N. C. where it is convenient for vessels passing the narrows to call. W. R. **P**. January 13th, 1849.

State Of North Carolina. Tyrrell Couny. This is to certify that I bought of Wm. R. **PALMER** a wheat thrasher of one horse power some three years past, which has proved to be good and will thrash one hundred bushels per day. Joseph **ALEXANDER**. Oct. 27, 1848. State Of North Carolina. Tyrrell County. This is to certify I bought of Wm. R. **PALMER** a wheat thrasher of his own make, and have thrashed one crop of eight hundred bushels... Jessee **MC CLEES**. State of North Carolina. Hyde County. I would say to the public that one of William R. **PALMER**'s machines was used in thrashing my wheat the past summer... Properly attended, I think the machine would..thrash 175 or 200 bushels per day. Richard I. **WYNNE**. February 12, 1847. State Of North Carolina. Hyde County. This is to certify that I have seen several of Mr. William R. **PALMER**'s machines at work, and I believe those machines to be most desirable... I have lived 7 years on Judge **DANNEL**'s Plantations, and experienced the advantages..the use of..improved plan of Thrashers. William **SIMMONS**. Oct 21, 1848.

24 February 1849

(50) Notice. Valuable Farm For Sale. The subscriber being in bad health has determined to offer for sale that well known farm of his lying on **BUTT**'s road, containing about 500 Acres of the richest and most productive land in Eastern Virginia or North Carolina. .. The Farm on which the subscriber lives is also offered for sale. This farm possesses many advantages; contains 3 or 400 acres of land and enough in cultivation to produce 2 or 300 barrels of Corn. There is a Fishery Winter and Spring. Herrings have been caught in a common ware [sic] to the amount of 70 or 80,000 in a season. There is an excellent well of water, a good 2 story Dwelling, large capacious Barns, Stables, and all other necessary out-houses. Any one wishing to buy can finde more information by calling on Wilson **CORPREW**, or the subscriber. .. Possession given at any time when desired. My hands, about 14 or 15 in number, can be hired by the purchaser on reasonable terms. Applications by letter will be promptly attended to, if directed to the subscriber, Land of Promise, Princess Anne County, Va. Thos. B. **GRESHAM**. jan 20

(51) David J. **BURR**, (Late **PATTERSON & BURR**,) Commission Merchant, Richmond, Va. Will give particular attention to sales of FISH, cotton, corn, wheat, &c... References. Dr. Wm. C **WARREN**, Dr. Thos. D **WARREN**. Joshua **SKINNER**, Esq. Thos. H. **LEARY**, Esq. Richard **PAXTON**, Esq.} Edenton. Josiah **WILLS**, Esq. Norfolk, Va. feb 1847

(52) John **WOMBLE** & Co, Successors to John **WOMBLE**, COMMISSION MERCHANTS, No. 100 main street, Richmond, Va. Offers his services to the citizens of North Carolina for the sale of Fish, Bacon, Lard, Corn, Wheat, Cotton, Lumber &c. &c. ...

(53) CASH FOR NEGROES. I Will pay the highest cash price for likely Negroes of both sexes. ... D. D. **RAPER**, near E. City. feb 21

(54) DR. **MARTIN**'s COMPOUND SYRUP OF WILD CHERRY. This Compound is one of the best __edies ever offered to the public in Coughs, whether arising from Colds or the Whooping Cough, or that dreadful malady Consumption. .. The Bishop of the Protestant Episcopal Church of Maryland (the Right Rev. W. R. **WHITINGTON**) has authorized us to say that he has used it __ his own person with decided benefit... The following is from a highly respectable Physician on Kent Island whom we made acquainted with the preparation:

Kent Island, June 22, 1847. Dr. **MARTIN**--Dear Sir, Since my return home, I prescribed your SYRUP OF WILD CHERRY in several cases; one in particular, a case of Asthma, of long standing (about 12 years) a neighbor and patient of mine. .. I do not know that she has had a good night's rest for a long time, but since she has commenced taking your Medicine (and she has only taken one bottle) she is enabled to go to bed and sleep well all night. .. Her husband, Mr. Rederick **EARICKSON**, is a merchant here, and says if you will send him some of it he will act as your agent. Yours, Samuel **HARPER**, M. D. Price 75 cents per bottle. .. **MARTIN & WHITELEY**'s National Tonic. Dr. Geo. T. **MARTIN**, Respected Sir--In justice to you and to the Public..I take this method of making known..the remarkable cure your National Tonic has wrought in my particular case. I had been laboring under an intermitting fever for 15 months..the quinine would stop the chills a day or two, but they would return with double violence until I became weak and emaciated. My stomach swollen hard, my spirits broken..last winter I accidentally saw this invaluable *Tonic*..so I caught at a bottle of your Medicine--commenced taking it, and before I used a *half* bottle my chills left me, my appetite gradually returned..by the time I had finished the one bottle I was, as it were, a new man. Nearly a year has elapsed and I have not had a single chill. ...John **NELSON**. .. Dr. **MARTIN**'s Universal Purgative Pills. .. Revd. Dr. **BOON**'s certificate. G. T. **MARTIN**, M. D. Upper hunting Creek, Caroline Co., Md. Oct. 17, 1846. .. Sir: Having been made acquainted with the composition of your valuable Pill, by yourself, some two or three years ago, I have used them freely in my private practice, with entire success, and shall continue..and now I take great pleasure in recommending such..as a safe and efficient purgative... John E. **BOON**, M. D. Prepared and sold by **MARTIN & WHITELEY**, at their wholesale Drug Store, Baltimore. And for sale by Oliver **FEARING**, E. City. R. J. **SAUNDERS**, Hertford, A. J. **BATEMAN**, Edenton, J. **RAMSEY** & Co., Plymouth, N. C.

(55) $20 REWARD. Ranaway from the subscriber in August last his Negro girl **MARY**. She is about 18 years of age, light complected, about 5 feet 4 inches high, is a large fleshy girl with a very large breast, and has a scar on the calf of one of her legs, caused by the bite of a dog. I will give the above reward if she is delivered to me or confined in any Jail so that I get her. John **BALEY**, Sr. Posquotank Co. N. C. Feb. 3.

(56) NOTICE. The Subscriber wishes to purchase negroes for the ensuing Twelve months of all kinds--for which he will pay the highest CASH PRICE that can be obtained within one hundred miles of this place. ... William **GLOVER**. E. City, Nov. 24.

(57) MERCHANT'S HOTEL! GATESVILLE, N. C. I would inform my friends and public generally, that I am now prepared to accommodate them in the best style, having added 10 new and beautiful sleeping rooms, and a Dining Saloon 20 by 35 feet. I have also added to my Stables 75 stalls, attached to which is a large and convenient lot for the accommodation of Drovers. Board per day, ---- $1,25 T. G. **VAUGHAN**, Gatesville, Gates County, N. C.

24 February 1849

(58) NEW SHIP YARD. The subscribers respectfully inform all owners and masters of vessels, that they have just erected a new set of RAILWAYS on Pleasant Point, at Elizabeth City, N. C., and have prepared themselves with Materials and good Workmen, and are now prepared to take up vessels of any size. **BURGESS & LAMB**. E. City, Nov. 11, 1848.

(59) NOTICE. I would respectfully notify all persons indebted to me by Book account of longer standing than six months to come forward and settle the same. Interest on all accounts due me will be charged after six months from date. Caleb **SYKES**. Oct. 21

(60) Extensive Stock of Fashionable Cabinet Furniture. The subscriber would call the attention..to his present much enlarged stock and assortment of Cabinet Furniture, Chairs, Looking Glasses, &c..on the most accommodating terms. J. D. **GHISELIN**, Piano Forte and Furniture Ware Rooms, next to **BLOODGOOD** & Co,s Main st. Morfolk. Dec. 16, 1848.

(61) A. C. **TOMS**, Commission Merchant, Norfolk, Va References. John P. **LEIGH** & Son, **HARDY & BROTHERS**,} Norfolk, Va. Carl **HEINRICH**, John A. **GAMBREL**,} New York, T. R. **MATHEWS** & Co. Miles **WHITE**,} Baltimore, Md. Jamms P. **WHEDBEE**, Thos. S. **JACOCKS**,} Woodville, N. C. Thomas F. **JONES**, Nathan **WINSLOW**,} Hertford, N. C. J. C. **EHRINGHAUS**, Wm. H. **DAVIS**, Dr. R. H. **RAMSEY**,} E. City, N. C. November 13th, 1847.

(62) H. F. **LOUDON**, Merchant Tailor, Main-street, Norfolk, Va. Respectfully solicits a continuance of the patronage so liberally bestowed on him by his North Carolina friends. Uniforms of all kind made up to order.

(63) James **LITTLE**, Wholesale and Retail Tobacconist, *West Side Market Square, Norfolk, Va.*, Keeps constantly on hand a large supply of all sorts Smoking & Chewieg Tobacco, Cigars and Snuff.

(64) E. R. **HUNTER**, Successor to **WATTS & HUNTER**, *Wholesale and Retail Druggist*, High street, Portsmouth, Va., Keeps constantly on hand a full assortment of DRUGS, MEDICINES, OILS, PAINTS VARNISH, &c.. to which he would respectfully invite the attention of the public generally (at the old stand.) ... aug 7

(65) James **WINSTON**, COMMISSION MERCHANT, RICHMOND, VA. Will make liberal advances on all consignments and will cash sales as soon as closed. An experience of twenty years in the sale of Fish, Corn, Wheat, Cotton and Bacon has qualified him to do great justice to shippers. REFERENCES. **WILLIAMS, STAPLES & WILLIAMS**, Charles H. **SHIELD, HARDY & BROTHER**,} Norfolk, Va.. Miles **WHITE**, Elizabeth City, Nathan **WINSLOW NEWBY's** Bridge, N. C. **JORDAN & BROTHERS**, Gatesville, N. C. James B. **USQUHART**, Southampton, Va.

(66) R. Henry **GLENN**, CIVIL ENGINEER, SUFFOLK, VA. Being provided with a superior set of Surveying, Levelling and Transet Instruments, respectfully offers his professional services to the citizens of North Carolina. He is prepared to survey and divide land on the most approved principles, lay out roads, construct bridges, drain and reclaim swamp lands, select sites for Mills, and furnish drawings for every description of building and Machinery.--Terms moderate. ... August 19, 1848.

(67) NOTICE, The subscriber respectfully invites the attention of the people to his stock of New Goods...he is now fully prepared to make any article embraced in his branch of business, such as Saddles, Harness, Bridles, and Medical Portmanteaus, also the trimming of Buggies and Sulky's. ... Robert H. **BROADFIELD**. E. City. September 23, 1848.

The Old North State.
Vol. 9. "Error is harmless, when truth is left free to combat it." No. 2.
Elizabeth City, N. C. Saturday, March 3, 1849.

(68) Mr. **VATTEMARE**, and his System Of International Exchanges. *Raleigh, N. C., January 8th,* 1849. Mr. Alexander **VATTEMARE**: *Sir,*--We, the undersigned, have the honor to inform you, that we have been appointed by the two Houses of the General Assembly, a Joint Select Committee, for the purpose of inviting you to address the members of the two Houses and the public, on your system of International Litery [sic] Exchanges among the nations of the earth. ... We are most respectfully, &c. &c. K. **RAYNER**, Edw. **STANLY**, J. C. **DOBBIN**, D. W. **COURTS**, H. C. **JONES**,} On the part of the House of Commons. Wm. N. H. **SMITH**, Wm. D. **BETHELL**, W. H. **WASHINGTON**.} On part of the Senate. ...

(69) Elizabeth-City, March 3, '49. .. FACTS RELATIVE TO GEN. **TAYLOR's** FAMILY. A correspondent of the *National Intelligencer*..corrects some erroneous statements in regard to Gen. **TAYLOR's** family, and says: General and Mrs. **TAYLOR** have no children young enough to be "going to school" in Baltimore or elsewhere. They have there a daughter married to Dr.

3 March 1849

(69) (Cont.) **WOOLS**, of the army, and now on that station. Col. **TAYLOR**, the General's brother, whose lady is the daughter of the Hon. John **MC LEAN**, is also in Baltimore, and attached to that station. The public attention and curiosity seem to have been won away by the General entirely from his better half, for his biographers have not told us who she is. Now, for the honor of old Calvert county, in Maryland, be it known that she produced the only person to whom General **TAYLOR** has surrendered. Mrs. **TAYLOR** comes not only from Calvert county, but from, it is believed, the very estate on which Mrs. **ADAM**'s [sic] father, if not she herself, was born--on the shores of..the Patuxent. Mrs. **TAYLOR**'s father was Capt. Walter **SMITH**, an independent and highly respectable farmer, whose estate was situate on the right bank of St. Leonard's Creek, in which Commodore **BERNEY**'s flotilla was blockaded in the late war. She is the sister of the late Major Richard **SMITH**, of the marine corps...

(70) *The Prussian Navy--Compliment to the United States.*--Some time since, a Prussian envoy arrived in the United States, for purchasing sailing vessels and steamers for the organization of a Prussian navy; and we learned at the time that such vessels as might be purchased here would be commanded by Americans, until such time German officers, duly qualified, should be found. An invitation was..extended to some one of our post captains, to visit Prussia, and give the benefit of his experience and knowledge to the Prussian government, in carrying out the project. In pursuance of this invitation, Commodore Foxhall A. **PARKER**, of the United States Navy, obtained leave of absence and proceeded to Germany, a few weeks since... *N. Y. Her.*

(71) DIED, In this place, on Friday, 23d ult., Mr. Wm. B. **ALLEN**, aged about 28 years. Mr. **ALLEN** was a respectable merchant of our town--a very estimable citizen, and for some years a worthy member of the Methodist Episcopal Church.
Communicated. Departed this life on Sunday, the 11th inst. after a short and painful illness, Mr. T. **HATHAWAY**, of Edenton. Mr. **HATHAWAY** was a member of the M. E. Church for some years; he was perfectly resigned to death, and exclaimed on his death bed that he was prepared to meet his God. On Friday, the 11th [sic] instant, after a short illness, Mrs. **HATHAWAY**, aged 77, consort of Mr. T. **HATHAWAY**, deceased. Mrs. **HATHAWAY** was also a member of the M. E. Church for some years, the above was a woman of a meek and mild disposition, and much beloved by all who knew her. ...

(72) "SELLING OFF" AS FAST AS I CAN! The Subscriber not intending to remove to "Tarborough, N. C.," offers for sale his entire stock of Dry Goods... James W. **HINTON**. March 3d. 1849.

(73) SELLING OFF. The subscriber being about to remove to Tarborough, N. C. offers for sale his entire stock of Goods... Thomas **ALLEN**. Feb. 24.

[Issue of 10 March 1849. Only one page remains.]

(74) NOTICE! The undersigned, having duly qualified as Administrator on the Estate of Wm. B. **ALLEN**, Dec'd, will offer for sale at the Store recently occupied by the said **ALLEN**, at Public Auction, on Wednesday, the 21st inst, all his stock of Goods, consisting of Groceries Crockery, Glass and Hardware, and one Horse and Cart. ... Leonard **CHAPMAN**. March 10.

The Old North State.
Vol. 9. "Error is harmless, when truth is left free to combat it." No. 4.
Elizabeth City, N. C. Saturday, March 17, 1849.

(75) Elizabeth-City, March 17, '49. .. IMPROVEMENT. We are pleased to see that there is a spirit of Improvement springing up among our citizens. During the year 1848 there were several new buildings added to our little village, and at this time there are several others going up, while a good many have been altered and repaired which give them the appearance of being new. Among our citizens who have been conspicuous in adding buildings to the town and its suburbs, and also in altering and repairing, we mention the names of Capt. T. **HUNTER**, Col. John S. **BURGESS**, John L. **HINTON**, Esq., Rev. W. W. **KENNEDY**, Joseph H. **POOL**, Esq., G. W. **CHARLES**, Esq., and Oliver **FEARING** Esq. There may be others of which we are not aware. ...

(76) Our Side Walks. While our village has been improving in buildings, some of our side-walks have also been greatly improved, and first and foremost comes the one on North Street, leading from Road Street to our Office. For which, as far as we are individually concerned, we thank our generous neighbort George A. **WILLIAMS**, Esq., and our worthy Commissioners. The former finding the side logs and the latter having them put down... The next improvement is to be seen before the store of our worthy townsman, James W. **HINTON**, Esq.,.. is now paved neatly with some of the best of friend Joshua's Bricks. ...

(77) FISHERIES. Several of our fishermen have put in their Seines. Down at Croatan Mr. Wm. **CHARLES** at the second haul caught 1100 Shad, and some 13,000 Herring. We have not heard of the hauls at any other Fishery. Our friend Wm. **GLOVER**,

17 March 1849

(77) (Cont.) Esq., put in on Thursday last, so we shall see the old familiar Fish Cart daily, as usual, during the season.

(78) We see by the *Baltimore Patriot* that our transient citizen, Miles **WHITE**, Esq., was knocked down in Baltimore the other night by some scoundrel whose object was no doubt to rob him. He was however taken care of in time to prevent the robbery, by some boys, who heard his cries for help, and conveyed by them to the Eutaw House.--What makes the matter worse, the old gentleman was to have been married in two or three days. So much for being rich. ...

(79) Col. Robert T. **PAINE**. It gives us pleasure to learn that this distinguished son of North Carolina, has been assigned an honorable position, as one of the Commissioners to adjust the claims of our citizens against Mexico. He is associated with two other gentlemen of high standing, Hon. George **EVANS**, of Maine, and Hon. Caleb B. **SMITH**, of Indiana. ...

(80) AN INDEPENDENT OFFICE-HOLDER. The *Washington Union* publishes the following, and states that the writer is from the State of Indiana: Washington, March 3, 1849. James K. **POLK**, President of the U. States: Sir: Having opposed the election of General **TAYLOR** to the presidency, and differing with his (the Whig) party in principle, I do not feel disposed to hold Office under his administration, and therefore respectfully resign the situation I have for some years held in the Treasury Department. With great respect, your obedient servant, William H. **ENGLISH**. ...

(81) NOTICE. The undersigned have this day entered into Co-Partnership, under the firm of **SIMMONS & SHUSTER**, for the transaction of a General Commission and Forwarding Business. Any business confided to them will be faithfully and promptly attended to. Daniel D. **SIMMONS**, Jacob P. **SHUSTER**. Norfolk, Va., March 17, 1849.

(82) NOTES LOST. On my way from home to Camden Court House on Monday last the 12th inst., I lost the following bundle of Notes as far as I can ascertain: One note against E. L. **DOZIER** for $526, payable to Ed **FEREBEE**, dated the 15th December 1848. One note against Edwin **FEREBEE** for $200, payable to me, dated Jan. 11th, 1849. One note against the same for $282, payable to S. D. **LAMB**, dated (he thinks) Jan. 1st, 1848. Also an order on the same for $30. One note against Albert **WHITE** for $300, with Charles M. **LAVERTY** security, dated in Dec. 1848. One note against James **SPENCE** for $19, payable to me, dated in January 1848. Two notes against Abner **BERRY**, one of $90, and the other of $77, the first payable to Ed L. **DOZIER**, and the other to me, dated 1st January 1848. One note against Thomas **ETHEREDGE** for $405 payable to W. S. **GRANDY**, dated January 1st, 1849. Two notes against Evan **FORBES**, one of $50 and the other of $39, payable to me, due 1st Jan. 1845. One note against James **FEREBEE**, for $80, payable to Sophia **MEISCHEAU**, or me, I do not recollect which, dated January 1st 1849. One note against Thomas **AYDLETT** for $12, payable to the same, dated the same. Two notes against Wilson **FEREBEE** for $30 each payable to the same and dated one Jan 1st, 1848, and the other 1st January 1849. One note against Wm W. **SANDERLIN** for $18 payable to S. D. **LAMB**, dated 1st January 1847. One note against Sophia **MEISCHEAU** for $50, payable to me, dated October 1848. All persons are hereby forwarned from trading for said notes, as the payment of them have been stopped. Any person returning the bundle to me with all the notes will be liberally rewarded. Miles **LAMB**, Camden Co., N. C. March 17.

(83) WRECK SALE. Was sold by the Commissioner of Wrecks, for the 3d Wreck District of North Carolina on the 20th February last 1900 White Oak Staves, which were picked up along the beach 9 miles north of the Nag's Head Hotel. Any person or persons proving ownership will receive the amount they are entitled to, by applying to the Commissioner. Hodges **GALLOP**, Com. Wrecks, 3d Wreck District, N. C. March 17.

(84) SPRING Supplies.--We are receiving from the Eastern Cities by every arrival, large accessions to our already extensive stock of Hardware, Cutlery and Fancy Goods, and are prepared to offer inducements to our friends who buy to sell again. ... E P **TABB** & Co, Hardware Importers, head of the Square, Norfolk, Va. mh 17

(85) 1000 Cases Boots, Shoes, Brogans, And Travelling Trunks, Spring Stock, 1849. Just received from the manufacturers, and for sale cheap at the Ladies Saloon, on Main street, near **WALTERS'** City Hotel, Norfolk, Va. ... W. H. **ADDINGTON**. mh 17

(86) HORSE FLY NETS. Mrs. A. **SISCO**, No. 95, Baltimore Street, Baltimore, Md. Invites the attention of Merchants and the trade generally to her large assortment of Horse Nets of various patterns, and colours, which she offers 50 per cent less than former prices. mh 17, '49.

(87) Dr. **TOWNSEND**'s Compound Extract Of Sarsaparilla. The most extraordinary Medicine in the World!.. Caution. Owing to the great success and _____ [illegible] sale of Dr. **TOWNSEND**'s Sarsaparilla, a number of men who were formerly our Agents, have commenced making Sarsaparilla Extracts, Elixirs, Bitters, Extracts of Yellow Dock, &c. They generally put it up in

17 March 1849

(87) (Cont.) the same shaped bottles, and some of them have stolen and copied our advertisements, they are only worthless imitations and should be avoided. None genuine unless signed by S. P. **TOWNSEND**.

Principal Office 126 Fulton Street, Sun Building, N. Y. **REDDING** & Co., 8 State street Boston; **DYOTT** & Sons, 132 North Second street, Philadelphia: S. S. **HANCE**, Druggist, Baltimore; P. M. **COHEN**, Charleston; **WRIGHT** & Co., 151 Chartres Street, N. O: 105 South Pearl Street, Albany; and by all the principal Druggists and Merchants generally throughout the United States, West Indies and the Canadas. The genuine for sale by L. K. **SAUNDERS**, Wholesale & Retail Agent for Elizabeth City. Also by his sub-agents. Joseph **ALEXANDER**, Court House, Camden co. Selby **PATRICK**, Little Alligator, Tyrrel County, William **HOOKER**, Tyrrel Co. N. C. E. City, March 17th, 1849.

The Old North State.
Vol. 9. "Error is harmless, when truth is left free to combat it." No. 5.
Elizabeth City, N. C. Saturday, March 24, 1849.

(88) Elizabeth-City, March 24, '49. .. We forgot to mention in our list of Improvements last week, the name of our friend, Wm. W. **GRIFFIN** Esq. who has erected decidedly the handsomest building in our village. Though he did not commence his last year. Our townsmen, Thomas **ALLEN**, and Thomas R. **COBB**, Esqs., have also been putting up buildings, the first named, a large and commodious Store on Road Street, and the last a large Ware House on his lot. Mr. Wm. **MESSENGER** also, we understand is about raising a very large dwelling, while he has also made a great improvement in some of his other real estate. Our neighbor, Maxcy **SANDERLIN**, Esq., is now arranging his house at the corner of Road and North Streets, for a Hotel, which, when completed, will be quite an improvement to this part of the town.

(89) **WASHINGTON** NATIONAL MONUMENT. Mr. William I. **HUNTER**, of Gates County, has been appointed by the Board of Managers as Agent for the **WASHINGTON** National Monument, for this Congressional District, and is now canvassing Pasquotank County for the purpose of soliciting contributors to the same. .. Mr. **HUNTER** has with him two engravings of the design of the Monument--one of large and the other of small size; which is given to each contributor according to the amount subscribed, he has also small and large engravings of **WASHINGTON**, which are disposed of in the same manner. Each person who subscribes, registers his name in a book, also the county and State he lives in, with the amount paid, which book is deposited in the Monument as a future reference. .. The Monument is to be 600 feet high. The corner stone was laid on the 4th July last, and the work is now progressing. ...

(90) We are glad to know that our friend James E. **NORFLEET**, of Edenton, N. C., has been appointed Collector of that Port by Gen. **TAYLOR**.

(91) John **SKINNER**, now editor of *The Plow, the Loom and the Anvil*, is to succeed Edmund **BURKE**, as Commissioner of Patents. Mr. **SKINNER** has filled the office of Assistant Postmaster General.

(92) "HONORABLE" HORACE **GREELEY**. Horace **GREELEY** has published an address to his constituents of the Sixth Congressional District of New York, giving an accout of his stewardship. He does not give Congress a very good name on account of its sins, both of omission and commission.--His closing paragraph..implies that he does not care of the "Honorable!" "In ceasing to be your agent, and returning with renewed zest to my private cares and duties, I have a single additional, favor to ask, not of you especially, but of all; and I am sure my friends at least will grant it without hesitation. It is that you and they will oblige me, henceforth by remembering that my name is simply Horace **GREELEY**."

(93) Married, In Williamston, N. C., on the 15th instant, by the Rev. George **GREGORY**, Mr. William H. **LYON**, formerly of this town, to Miss Barbray Ann **WINDLEY**, of Washington, N. C.

(94) Nag's Head Property for Sale, On Tuesday the 24th day of April next, I shall offer at public sale before the Court House door at Elizabeth City in virtue of a Deed in Trust, executed to me, and duly registered in the County of Currituck, that valuable property at Nag's Head, for several years occupied as a Public House..at the same time I shall sell sundry Household and Kitchen Furniture conveyed to me in the same Deed. ... John C. **EHRINGHAUS**, Trustee. Elizabeth City, March the 24th, 1849.

(95) FOR WASHINGTON. The steamer Osceola leaves Norfolk for the above place on Fridays at 4 o'clock, p. m. returning, leave Washington every Thursday, at 9 o'clock P. M. ... Passage and Fare $5.00. Jas. **MITCHELL**, Capt. mh 24

31 March 1849

The Old North State
Vol. 9. "Error is harmless, when truth is left free to combat it." No. 6.
Elizabeth City, N. C. Saturday, March 31, 1849.

(96) For the *Old North State*. THE BACHELOR'S BRIDE. By Angeline E. **ALEXANDER**. Chapter 1. ...

(97) Elizabeth-City, March 31, '49. .. We have taken up rather too much space in our paper to-day in giving place to the original story of the "*Bachelor's Bride*," written by a young lady of Tyrrel County. We thought first, to put it in, in two papers, but of the urgent request of the fair author to put it *all* in one paper, we concluded to do so, as it is not in our nature to deny the ladies. We would ask of that portion of our readers who are fond of such reading, to give it a perusal, as it is well written.

(98) Surrender For Murder.--A man named **DONALDSON**, charged with the murder of Andrew **MEHAN**, in the streets of New York, one night more than a year ago, surrendered himself in that city last Thursday. A conversation overheard at a house of ill-fame more than six months ago, just gave a clue to the supposed murderer. .. Death Of An Old Citizen.--John **SALMON**, Esq., died at Boston on Thursday, at the age of 83 years. He witnessed the destruction of tea in Boston harbor and the battle of Bunker Hill. .. The Mercury at Lake Lepin, Illinois, on the 8th of January, was at the congealing point, or 40 degress below zero. .. During the last month, there were 60 deaths from cholera at Nashville. .. Col. Jack **HAYS**, of Texas, has arrived at New Orleans on his way to Washington. ...

(99) OFFICIAL. APPOINTMENTS BY THE PRESIDENT. *By and with the advice and consent of the Senate.* Adam **SPEICE**, Postmaster at Dayton, Montgomery county, Ohio, vice Joseph W. **MC CORKLE**, resigned. Appointments By The Postmaster General. George W. **MC CULLOH**, Postmaster at Frostburg, Alleghany county, Maryland, vice John J. **KELLER**.

(100) FOR SALE. A Small Seine about 350 yards long, made for fishing in Newbegin Creek, will be sold a bargain, if early application be made to the subscriber. Jos. H. **POOL**. mh 31, '49.

(101) Ice! Ice!! Ice!!! The Subscriber has filled his Ice House with choice Northern Ice, and is prepared to furnish the public at any time from sunrise till 9 o'clock P. M., at one cent per lb. C. C. **GREEN**. March 31, 1849.

(102) Notice! Drifted ashore on Currituck Beach, District No. 2, near the Great Beach, two Yawl Boats, about 18 feet long. One materially damaged, the other not hurt. Owners will please claim property. Ed. C. **LINDSEY**, C. W. March 31.

(103) MERCHANTS' HOTEL, GATESVILLE, N. C. The Undersigned having recently repaired this Establishment by the additon of 10 new and elegant SLEEPING ROOMS, a DINING SALOON, 35 feet in length by 18 in width, and also having added large accommodations to his Stables, by the building of 75 good and comfortable STALLS, SHEAD, &c., as also having secured that rare article, one of the best Hostlers, is now prepared to offer such inducements to the transient comer, as well as daily boarder, that cannot nor shall not be surpassed by any Establishment of the kind. His Table will at all times be furnished with the best that the Market affords, and his Bar with as good Liquors as can be bought in Norfolk or Baltimore. .. The fishermen can at all times during February and May Courts, be furnished with private and comfortable Rooms to settle with their Hands, a matter heretofore attended with so much inconvenience. Board per day $1 25. Thomas G. **VAUGHAN**. March 31, 1849.

(104) **SANSTON** [sic] & CO., Importers and Wholesale Dealers in Foreign & Domestic Dry GOODS, No. 269, Market St., (between Hanover and Sharp Street, Baltimore. J. A. **SANGSTON**, G. E. **SANGSTON**, L. **SANGSTON**,} Feb. 1849.

(105) Thomas R. **MATTHEWS** & Co., COMMISSION MERCHANTS, No. 10 **BOWLY**s Wharf, Baltimore. Thomas R. **MATTHEWS**, John H. **NEIMYER**, Francis **WHITE**.} REFERENCE, Miles **WHITE**, Elizabeth City, N. C. **WILLIAMS, STAPLES & WILLIAMS, FERGUSON & MILHADO**.}Norfolk, Feb 1849.

The Old North State
Vol. 9. "Error is harmless, when truth is left free to combat it." No. 7.
Elizabeth City, N. C. Saturday, April 7, 1849.

(106) CHEAP PRINTING. While Colonel Alden **SPOONER** printed a paper at Sag Harbor, he was much encouraged by a merchant, who advertised his wares in two long columns, specifying every item of wet and dry goods, shovels, and stationary, and mouse traps. While this was working magically among the villagers, a rival merchant called in one day and asked with a noncha-

7 April 1849

(106) (Cont.) lant air the charge of inserting a couple of lines. He was told fifty cents, and paid the money. He thereupon paraded directly under the long advertisement, I TOO John **THOMPSON**. The joke took mightily, and more particularly as John **THOMPSON** had borrowed his idea from a little squaw, who used to sell her baskets at the Harbor. She had a rival in a larger squaw, with a loud voice, who would cry her baskets with every necessary adjunct of descriptive eloquence. The feeble squaw keeping close at her heels, would squeak out, "I TOO."

(107) Griffin **YEATMAN**, one of the early of the Western Pioneers, died at Cincinnati on the 4th instant. He went to that city in 1793, and was for many years Recorder of the county.

(108) Elizabeth-City, April 7, '49. .. We are authorized to announce the name of the Hon. David **OUTLAW**, of Bertie, as a candidate to represent this Ninth Congressional District in the next Congress of the United States.

(109) NEW PAPER. We have received a copy of a paper published in Windsor, Bertie county, N. C., called "The Gladiator." It is printed by Wm. **EBORN** wsekly at $3 per annum, payable in advance. The paper is very plainly printed, and is Whig in politics. We hope the Proprietor all the success possible, and may he never have cause to regret the starting of the *Gladiator*.

(110) POSTMASTERS APPOINTED IN PENNSYLVANIA. Emanuel **SWOPE**, Leacock, Lancaster Co. Elizabeth **WILL**, McSherrytown, Adams Co. J. J. **SEDWICK**, Butler, Butler Co. John **IRVINE**, **SHAVER**'s Creek, Huntingdon county. G. W. **MC CONNELL**, **POWL**'s Valley, Dauphin county. (new Office.) E. **LEWIS**, Cooperville, Lancaster county. H. D. **HEAGY**, Fairfield, Adams county. J. **SCOTT**, Kittaining, Armstrong county. A. **BRENEMAN**, Elizabethtown, Lancaster county. S. S. **NAGLE**, Marietta, Lancaster Co. J. D. **WARLEY**, York Sulphur Springs Adams county. F. **HUMPHREYS**, Orwell, Bradford Co. Wm. **BUTLER**, Lewistown, Mifflin Co. D. G. **RODGERS**, Bealleville, Washington county. D. R. **STEVENSON**, Cannonsby, S. M. **GRIFFITH**, Hickory. By P. M. General, in New York, since 26th ult. C. **DODGE**, Goveneur, St. Lawrence county, Wm. H. **EDDY**, Mansfield, Cattaraugus co.; Owin **WILCOX**, North Huton, Tompkins co; Peter **FOLAND**, Dunnsville, Albany co.; J. S. **HYNCK**, Rensselaerville, Albany co.; L. **CAPRON**, Broadalbin, Fulton co; William H. **PHILIPS**, Cazenovia, Madison co; Wm. **SEXTON**, Westfield, Chautauque co.; Wm. **STAFFORD**, Waterville, Onedia county.

(111) Oil Contract Taken.--The Government contract for oil was taken to-day by Edward Mott **ROBINSON**, Esq., of New Bedford at 104 3/4 per gallon cash, nearly equal to 104 for spring and 108 for winter.--*Boston Transcript*.

(112) Communicated. On Friday, the 30th of March, Mrs. Louisa **WHEDBEE**, wife of Joshua S. **WHEDBEE**, of this place quietly breathed her last. .. The shaft of death has severed the fond links which had but for one short year connected them. .. She leaves an infant, not however upon the "cold mercies of the world," but she has left him encircled by the warmest affections of a father and the fond embraces of her mother. Poor innocent babe, he however (as the writer of this) will never know a mother's care, the purity of a mother's love. ... G. W. **B**.

(113) NEW FURNITURE. I have just received from New York a most SPLENDID ASSORTMENT of Furniture, consisting in Mahogany, Walnut, Maple and common CHAIRS; Mahogany and other Rocking Chairs of beautiful style. Sofas, Divans, Tables of all kinds, work and candle Stands, Wardrobes, and in fact any and every thing in the Furniture line. ... Call on Caleb **SYKES**. Opposite the Bank. E. City, April 7, '49.

(114) NEW MILLENERY. Mrs. **SYKES** has just received from New York her Spring supply of Millinery, consisting of Bonnets, Ribbons, Fringe, Edgings, Laces, &c. &c. which she will be pleased to make up to order on the most reasonable terms. Esther **SYKES**. April 7, 1849.

(115) I. O. O. F. All transient brethren of the Order are cordially solicited to be present and assist in the celebration of the second Anniversary of Achoree Lodge No. 14, working under the R. W. Grand Lodge of the State of North Carolina, on the first day of May next, in Elizabeth City, N. C. J. W. **HINTON**, J. C. **SCOTT**, W. L. **SHANNON**} Committee. April 7th, 1849.

(116) Notice. I Have this day associated with me Dr. Rufus K. **SPEDD**. The business will hereafter be conducted under the name of L. K. **SAUNDERS** & Co. L. K. **SAUNDERS**. April 1, 1849. N. B. All persons indebted to me are particularly requested to come up and settle their accounts up to April 1st 1849. L. K. **SAUNDERS**. April 7.

(117) Bacon, Lard, Flour, & Butter. The undersigned has on hand and for sale a lot of fine Smithfield Hams,..Carolina do...Lard,.. A lot of Orange County Butter. C. C. **GREEN**. April 7.

7 April 1849

(118) List of Letters Remaining in the Post Office at Elizabeth City, for the Quarter ending March 31, 1849. **ALLEN** John Sen. **BACON** Capt. Joseph **BLANCHARD** John L **BASNIGHT** Benjamin S **BASSETT** William **BUNDY** William **BROSIER** Mrs. Martha **BEEL** Affee **COMMANDER** James **COMMANN** Robert S 2 **COMANN** Rev Wm H **DORCY** Mrs. A **DAVIS** James M **FRENCH** Mrs Emely **HARWOOD** Joseph C **HYDE** Will E **JORDAN** Miss Elenor E **JONES**? Andrew Mc **JARVIS** Thomas C **LAMB** Master William **LEWIS** Durham **MERSER** James B **MC ALISTER** Dr J **MITCHELL** Mrs Sarah **PALMER** Miss Susanna **PAINE** Thomas I? **ROBINSON** Mrs Elizabeth **RUSSELL** Jessee **SAWYER** Robert A **SHEPHERD** Robert **SIMRIL**? M G **TAYLOR** Angus **TRAVIS** William **THATCH** Benjamin W **WESKETT** Capt James **WHITE** Capt H W **WILKINS** Mary **WESCOTT** Mr John **WALKER** Mr C Timothy **GILBERT**, P. M. April 7 Persons calling for any of the above letters will please say they are advertised.

(119) MEN'S BOOTS--Gentlemen will please call up at the Ladies Saloon to see some handsome low priced Boots which have just been received from Philadelphia. We can show you very good calf skin Boots at only $ 1 50 a pair--a better one of that kind at $2, and as good a business Boot as any body can want for $2 50... W. H. **ADDINGTON**. Main Street, Norfolk Va. apr 7

(120) Hoes, Trace Chains, &c. We have just received..from Liverpool..hilling and grubbing Hoes, Casks, trace, halter and back band Chains, Long and short handle Frying Pans..Hinges, A full stock of pad, chest, stock and rim Locks, Enamelled and preserving kettles and sauce pans...tea kettles..curry combs with and with out manes, A full stock of table and small Cutlery..knives, scissors and shears..Files..Best anvils, Smiths vices and hammers, Which we offer at our usual low prices, E. P. **TABB** & Co, Hardware Importers, Head of the Square, Norfolk, Va. apr 7

The Old North State
Vol. 9. "Error is harmless, when truth is left free to combat it." No. 8.
Elizabeth City, N. C. Saturday, April 14, 1849.

(121) *Another of the Old Tea Party Gone.*--Died, at Saco, Maine, on the 23d ult., Benjamin **SIMPSON**, aged 94, one of the party that threw the cargoes of tea from the ships in Boston harbor.

(122) Elizabeth-City, April 14, '49. .. THE FISHERMEN. We are glad to state that since our last issue all the Fisheries then spoken of have been doing a much better business. .. The largest haul of the season, that we have heard of, was made on Sunday last, at the Fishery of Mr. Josiah T. **GRANBERRY**, in Perquimans County, when 90,000 Herrings were landed.

(123) BEAT THIS IF YOU CAN! Mr. Joshua **WHITE**, of Perquimans County, killed on the 16th February last, a hog weighing 700 lbs. This is the largest hog ever raised in the District of Edenton to our knowledge. We regret not to be able to state his age.

(124) NEWSPAPER CASE. In the Supreme Court of Rhode Island, in the case of Jesper **HARDING** vs. Henry **D'WOLF**, for nine years' subscription to the *Pennsylvanian Inquirer*, from 1835 to 1844, it was ruled that the regular mailing of a newspaper for a length of time was at least *prima facie* evidence of its reception, and that receiving a paper for a certain time and not ordering the same discontinued, was sufficient to hold the person liable for the subscription price, notwithstanding he may never have ordered that paper sent. A verdict was accordingly given for the plaintiff.

(125) Still Later from Santa Fe; Col. **FREMONT** and Lieut. **BEALE** on their way to California--extent of the Disaster of **FREMONT**'s Party Mr. J. W. **FOLGER** arrived in this city yesterday from Santa Fe. In company with Capt. **ST. VRAIN**, and others, he left that town on the 24th of February... .. Col. **FREMONT**..left Santa Fe on the 12th ult., on his way to California. Of the dreadful disaster which befel him in the mountains, we have this account.-The published letters from Col. **FREMONT** and his friends left him ascending a mountain and within five or six miles of the summit. But this elevation he never reached. A storm came up, which forced him to retreat, and to seek shelter in the valley below.--Here, it is said, the snow drifted, and accumulated to the depth of thirty or forty feet, and the party lost all their animals, and were compelled to leave their entire outfit. The snow covered the animals, and everything else from view, and Col. F. and his party were driven to seek safety on the sides of the mountains. In this emergency, Bill **WILLIAMS**, a hardy mountaineer, and two others, volunteered to seek succor from the nearest settlements; and it was arranged that they should return in twenty days. As they failed to do so, however, Col. **FREMONT**, and one or two others, resolved upon attempting to reach Taos; and on the sixth day from their leaving camp, they overtook **WILLIAMS** and one of his companions. The other, (Mr. **KING**, of the District of Columbia,) was represented to have died of the exposure and of hunger, and in the extremity to which they were driven, the survivors were forced to eat a part of his body.

Col. **FREMONT** made his way to Taos, obtained aid, provisions and horses, and then set out in search of his

14 April 1849

(125) (Cont.) party.. But more than one third of his men had..died from exposure and hunger; and one or two had given out, and were left to die; when he came up with them. The number who thus perished is stated at eleven, of whom we have the names of only three--Mr. **WISE**, of St. Louis county, and Mr. **KING** and Mr. **PREUSS**, of the District of Columbia. Capt. **CATHCART**, of the English army was among the survivors. ... We learn that L. F. **THURSTON**, Esq., who has filled several offices under the American government in New Mexico, died in Santa Fe during the winter. He was a native of Louisville, Ky.

(126) NEW SPRING & SUMMER DRY GOODS. The subscriber has just returned from the cities of Baltimore and New York with a full assortment of STAPLE AND FANCY DRY GOODS, which are now open and ready for sale. .. He may be found at the first door below the sign of the Big Boot. James W. **HINTON**. April 14.

(127) TAILORING. The subscriber would respectfully inform the citizens of Elizabeth City and vicinity that he has commenced the TAILORING BUSINESS in the above named place, where he intends to do all work entrusted to his care in a style that shall give general satisfaction. .. His shop is next door to the Store of Mr. **TISDALE**, on Road Street. Thomas B. **BROWN**. April 14.

(128) OFFICE CHANGED. Dr. Rufus K. **SPEED** has removed his office to the Drug Store of L. K. **SAUNDERS** & Co., where he can be found at all times when not professionally engaged. Persons wishing his services will please leave their orders at the Drug Store. E. City, April 14th, 1849.

(129) FRESH GROCERIES. COME and buy the following articles which are fresh, and good, and will be sold at a small advance for CASH or something that will command cash, as that is just what I want: ..Whiskey..Gin..Wine..Molasses..Rio Coffee..Rice..Butter..Lard..Sugar..Tobacco..Soap..Candles..Chalk Pipes..Raisins..Chocolate..Crockery..at the old stand on the water. Wm. **HALSEY**. Ap 14.

The Old North State
Vol. 9. "Error is harmless, when truth is left free to combat it." No. 10. 9
Elizabeth City, N. C. Saturday, April 28 21, 1849.

(130) Elizabeth-City, April 21, '49. .. The Weather.--For the last five or six days the weather has been more like the month of December than April. On Sunday night last there was a very severe frost, and since that time there has been one or two others. .. We understand that since the cold spell has set in, the different fisheries on the Albemarle are doing but a poor business. We hear that our friend, Wm. **CHARLES**, Esq., at Croatan, is doing a very good business. Success to him.

(131) Our friend Geo. W. F. **DASHIELL**, has taken the store lately occupied by Wm. B. **ALLEN**, dec'd. where he has opened a general assortment of groceries.

(132) Correspondence of the *Baltimore Patriot*. Washington, April, 15, 1849. Two excellent appointments were made by the President yesterday, to wit: J. Prescott **HALL**, Esq., as District Attorney for the Southern District of New York, in place of Lorenzo B. **SHEPPARD**, Esq., removed; and Philip **HONE** Esq., as Naval Officer for the port of New York, in place of C. S. **BOGARDUS**, Esq., removed. ...

(133) AWFUL TRAGEDY IN WILMINGTON MASSACHUSETTS. A correspondent of the *Boston Mail* gives the following particulars of a cold blooded murder which was committed in Wilmington on the 11th inst.:--"Yesterday morning between the hours of 9 and 10 o'clock, the bodies of Mrs. H. D. **PEARSON** and her twin daughters, 4 years old, were found horribly mangled and lifeless in the house they occupied at Wilmington, about a half a mile from the Andover line. .. A difficulty has existed between Mr. and Mrs. **PEARSON** for a considerable time past, and negotiations were going on for a divorce. He had not lived with her of late, but had been employed in some gentleman's family in Boston as a servant. Report says that he left his place in the city the day before the murder, and has not since been seen." The murdered mother is said to have been remarkably affectionate to her children, and sustained an irreproachable character among the entire community with whom she resided. ...

(134) MEXICAN CLAIMS. The Board of Commissioners appointed for the adjudication of claims of American citizens against Mexico, as stipulated in the late treaty, to be paid by the United States, assembled yesterdey..at the City Hall in this city, Hon. Geo. **EVANS**, of Maine, and Col. R. T. **PAINE**, of North Carolina, being present. The Hon. Caleb B. **SMITH**..is expected to arrive in two or three days, when the Board will be full. ...--*National Intelligencer*.

(135) NEW MILLENERY. Mrs. Joseph N. **BELL**, having taken the house near Zion **CULPEPPER**'s Esq., and lately occupied

21 April 1849

(135) (Cont.) by Dr. **SPEED** has fitted up the front shop as a Millinery Establishment. She has just received her Spring and Summer supply of Millinery, which will be made up to order on the most liberal terms. .. Give a call and judge for yourselves. April 21.

(136) JUST NOTICE THIS! I wish to say to the public that I am now prepared to make up to order all kinds of Cabinet Work in the best and latest styles. I have just returned from New York with a full stock of materials, such as Mahogany, Rose Wood, Zebra Wood, Walnut, Veneers, bird-eye Maple, and ..a lot of Marble Slabs for Bureaus, Stands, &c. &c. ... Caleb **SIKES**. April 21, '49.

(137) NOTICE--Agreeably to our promise we have made other additions to the lot of Children's Shoes worth 75 cents, which we have been selling so rapidly for 37c just because they are old stock--there are some good pickings among them yet, but come quick before they are all gone. ALSO--Misses Bronze Morocco Gaiters to lace up at the side, worth $1 50c. will now be sold off at 75c... The Ladies Saloon is on Main Street, near **WALTERS'** City Hotel. W. H. **ADDINGTON**, Norfolk, Va. ap 21

The Old North State
Vol. 9. "Error is harmless, when truth is left free to combat it." No. 10.
Elizabeth City, N. C. Saturday, April 28, 1849.

(138) POLITICAL. Reply of Will: B. **SHEPARD** to the Communication of the Hon. Edward **STANLY**, published in the *Register* of March 28th. When I published a card in the *Register* some weeks ago, correcting a statement in Mr. **STANLY**'s speech, I did so, solely with the view of exonerating myself from the charge of inconsistency, in voting for Mr. **RAYNER** in preference to Mr. **BADGER**, for the United States Senate. I sincerely hoped my statement would answer its purpose, and that the matter would be permitted to pass into the oblivion which awaited it. The friends of Mr. **BADGER**, however, seem not to be so disposed, and my delinquency in voting against him, is I presume, not to be forgotten.

Mr. **STANLY** thinks it very extraordinary, that I was not aware of Mr. **RAYNER**'s opinions upon the slavery question, because Mr. **RAYNER** was the elector in this District, and frequently addressed the people. Extraordinary as it may seem, the fact is so. I was not present on any occasion when Mr. **RAYNER** addressed the people, and if he discussed or approved of Mr. **BADGER**'s views upon slavery, I never heard it. .. It is not for me to reconcile the absurdity of electing a man to the United States Senate, and then passing resolutions in direct conflict with his opinions. The only excuse for such conduct is, that a large majority of the Whig party in the Legislature, were ignorant of Mr. **BADGER**'s opinion on that subject. Nor was it the first time in the history of the legislation of North Carolina, that gentlemen have been selected to represent the interests of the State, whose feelings were lukewarm, and who rather obstructed than advanced these interests. A similar state of things existed in our Legislature in 1840, which resulted in the loss of Mr. **CLAY**'s land bill; which, if it were now the law of the land, would furnish North Carolina ample means to execute all her cherished works of internal improvements, without restoring [sic] to the precarious resources of taxes, upon an impoverished people. .. When the bill to organize a territorial Government for Oregon was before the Senate, a violent controversy arose between the Northern and Southern Senators, upon that feature of the bill which excluded Slavery; the controversy became so warm, that all moderate men were very much alarmed for the safety of the Union, and with a view of an amicable disposition of the subject, the matter was referred to a committee of eight members, four from the North and four from the South; this committee met and after consultation, reported through its chairman, the Hon. Mr. **CLAYTON**, the present Secretary of State, the compromise bill. ..

It was against this bill, that Mr. **BADGER** voted in company with, (I write from memory) but two other Senators from slave States, viz: Mr. **UNDERWOOD** from Kentucky, who said his State was desirous of getting rid of Slavery, and Mr. **BENTON**, who is known to be peculiar. .. The bill left the slave question, where the Constitution left it; this was the leading feature of the bill, and every friend of the peace and quiet of his country should regret that it did not pass the House of Representatives. ... Will: B. **SHEPARD**. Elizabeth City, April 3d, 1849.

(139) Elizabeth-City, April 28, '49. .. The prospectus for the new administration paper at Washington has appeared. It is to be called the "Republic," and its editors are to be Alex. C. **BULLITT**, late of the *New Orleans Bee and Picayune*, and John S. **SARGENT**, late of the *Boston Atlas* and *New York Courier and Enquirer*. Both are gentlemen of ability and experience, such as to ensure a first rate paper. The first number will appear on the 1st of June. ...

(140) PRESENTATION OF A SWORD TO GENERAL **TAYLOR**.--The *Intelligencer* says:--It gives us pleasure to learn that today is to witness the presentation of a beautiful Sword to General **TAYLOR**, on the part of his native State, Virginia. It was voted to him at the session before the last of her Legislature, and, of course, in communication of the series of his Mexican victories. The deputation that brings this rich and beautiful gift of honor consists of the following gentlemen; Raleigh T. **DANIEL**, Wm. W. **CRUMP**, Henry L. **BROOK**, Lilburn H. **TRIGG**, and John **DANIEL**, Esqs. ...

28 April 1849

(141) A Washington letter in the *N. Y. Journal of Commerce* says--The Second Auditor of the Treasury (Philip **CRAYTON**, Esq., of Georgia,) has recommended to the secretary of the Treasury the dismissal of five clerks and a messenger employed in his bureau, and the substitution of others named. Reasons assigned, incapacity and inattention to business, and interfering in the politics of the adjoining States. The changes will be approved by Mr. **MEREDITH**, to take effect on the 1st of May. It is reported.. that Col. **DONIPHAN**, of Missouri, had been appointed Commissioner of Indian Affairs, vice **MEDILL**, of Ohio.

(142) SINGULAR DISCOVERY. The broken pieces of the original bottle which contained the Attar of Roses, stolen from the Patent Office at Washington, have been received in Philadelphia by the Recorder's Police, together with two skeleton keys, and a quantity of type of various kinds, with fancy borders--These articles were taken out of the cess-pool in the yard of Jacob **SHUSTER**'s alias **HAND**'s residence in that city. They will be conveyed to Washington.

(143) FATAL AFFAIR IN MEXICO. A party of Americans on their way to California, stopped at a city of Irapuato, on the 7th ult., and remained all night. A dispute arose between one of them, Chas. **DUNHAM**, of Connecticut, and the proprietor of the house where they stopped, in regard to three cents of their bill. The matter was referred to the Alcalde, who summoned a guard. One of the men, **CARROLL**, drew a pistol, to use in case of need, when he was knocked down. **DUNHAM** attempted to escape on horseback, but he was shot and killed. The rest of the party were injured, but continued to escape into the cathedral yard. The Alcalde subsequently made numerous protestations of regret, had the wounded cared for, and gave **DUNHAM** a christian burail. The party then resumed their march.

(144) Married, On Thursday evening the 19th inst., by Wilson **SPENCE**, Esq., Mr. Isaac **SAWYER** to Susan, youngest daughter of Mr. Daniel **SPENCE**, all of this County.

(145) NEW STOCK. The subscriber has received a complete assortment of all kind of materials in the Harness and Saddle Line, and is prepared to make up at the shortest notice, any kind of work in his line, with neatness and despatch. .. His Shop is opposite the Mansion House on the corner. R. H. **BROADFIELD**. April 28, 49.

(146) NOTE LOST. A Note given by John **ARMOR**, payable to me, for $48 58 cents has been lost by me. All persons are cautioned against trading for said note as the payment of it has been stopped. John **BURGESS**. April 28, 49.

(147) Keep this before the People, That J. M. **FREEMAN** has just returned from the North with a still more extensive assortment of the most fashionable articles in the way of Watches, Jewelry and fancy goods than he has heretofore offered to the public.. Prices low for cash or good paper. J. M. **FREEMAN**, Norfolk, Va. ap 28

(148) JUST RECEIVED. 25 bbls of fine flour and will be sold cheap for cash. Wm. **HALSEY**. Ap 28

(149) WATCHES AND JEWELRY. Col. William G. **COOK**, Has just received Gold Levers, of M. J. **TOBIAS** & Co..New England Clocks and Time Pieces..Vest and Fob Chains, Seals and Keys, Lockets, Bracelet Clasps; Gold Ear Rings and Pins in sets, Topaz and other stone bracelets... Spectacles. Gold, silver, steel, and German Silver Spectacles with Perifocal Glasses, a new and superior article. ... Ap. 28, 1849.

The Old North State
Vol. 9. "Error is harmless, when truth is left free to combat it." No. 11.
Elizabeth City, N. C. Saturday, May 5, 1849.

(150) Elizabeth-City, May 5, '49. .. What we have long Wanted. We are glad to be able to announce to our citizens and the public at large, that our recent townsman, Thomas B. **STUMP**, Esq., has erected upon his lot on Main street, nearly opposite the Mansion House Stables, a large and commodious "*Livery Stable*," where all in want of *good* Horses and neat Vehicles can always be supplied at the shortest notice. ...

(151) DUEL. A duel was fought at Old Point on Thursday morning, between two young gentlemen of Elizabeth City, Mr. J. P. **JONES** and Mr. J. B. **HOPE**--in which both the combatants were seriously though not mortally wounded.--*Norfolk Herald*. We would inform the public that these two young gentlemen were not from Elizabeth City, N. C., but from Elizabeth City County, Va.

(152) Virginia Elections. The Election for members of Congress took place throughout this State on Thursday, Friday and last. .. As far as heard from the Election stands thus: 1st District--John S. **MILLSON**, Dem. 2 " R. K. **MEADE**, Dem, 4 " Thos. H.

5 May 1849

(152) (Cont.)BOCOCK, Dem. 5 " Paulus **POWELL**, Dem. 6 " James A. **SEDDON**, Dem. 9 " Jeremiah **MORTON**, Whig. 10 " Richard **PARKER**, Dem. 15 " A. **NEWMAN**, Dem. The election of **FLOURNEY**, the Whig candidate in the Third District, is said to be in doubt. ...

(153) Died, On Wednesday the 25th April last at the residence of her son, C. C. **JACKSON** of this County, Mrs. Margaret **TURNER**, relict of the late Col. Alfred A. **TURNER**. Mrs. **TURNER** had entered the fifty-second year of her age. She had been for many years an exemplary member of the M. E. Church. .. She has left several children, and a large circle of friends who feel deeply sensible of their irreparable loss. ...

(154) Scythes Cradled. The subscriber would inform the Agricultural community that he is now prepared to Cradle Scythes with despatch and on accommodating terms. Shop near the residence of Geo. D? **POOL**, Esq. Caleb **CARTWRIGHT**. May 5.

The Old North State
Vol. 9. "Error is harmless, when truth is left free to combat it." No. 12.
Elizabeth City, N. C. Saturday, May 12, 1849.

(155) For the *Old North State*. Pasquotank Co. March 25, 1849. .. Mr. Editor, I here send you the opinion of several distinguished statesmen relative to the **WASHINGTON** National Monument: "A Monument worthy the memory of **WASHINGTON**, reared by the means proposed, will commemorate at the same time a virtue, a patriotism, and a gratitude truly national, with which the friends of liberty every where will sympathize, and of which our country may always be proud. James **MADISON**. Hoping and trusting that this Monument, too long delayed, may be worthy of the great man whose virtues it is intended to commemorate, and that it may stand an enduring memorial of a nations gratitude, to the purest patriots, and noblest of benefactors, until time shall be no longer. Millard **FILLMORE**. While this Monument stands, it will tell the story of his days and deeds, and will invive [sic] his countrymen to imitate his example of patriotism, in whatever public sphere they may be called upon to act. Lewis **CASS**. "One tribute to his memory is left to be rendered. One Monument remains to be reared. A Monument which shall bespeak the gratitude not of States, or of Governments; not of separate communities or of official bodies; but of the people, the whole people of the nation--a National Monument, erected by the citizens of the United States of America. R. C. **WINTHROP**.

(156) A man, named David **WARBLE**, said to be from New York, visited the White House on Tuesday, and created no little alarm among the ladies and gentlemen assembled in the East room, by parading thro' the mansion with a pistol to his head. He did no harm, however, and quietly left the mansion. The next morning he was entering it with a revolver in his hand but was arrested.

(157) Elizabeth-City, May 12, '49. .. We are authorized to announce Lemuel S. **REID** as a Candidate for the Office of Clerk of the County Court. Mr. Editor: You will please announce W. W. **GRIFFIN** as a Candidate for re-election to the Office of Clerk of the County Court. P.

(158) Our thanks are due the Hon. Geo. E. **BADGER** for important Official Documents sent us.

(159) GOLD DOLLARS.--The *Washington Union* states that the Gold Dollar will shortly be issued, that the delay has been occasioned by time necessary to prepare the dies, and that $100,000 are in readiness for stamping and milling.

(160) CALIFORNIA. The *Independence* (Mo.) *Expositor* contains a letter from Mr. T. **MC CLELLAN**; a gentleman of intelligence and veracity, who, with his family, went to California about a year ago. He made the trip out overland in five months and five days... He says: "I brought every species of property I started with, which is worth more here in gold than all I ever was worth put together in all my life. I sold when I landed in the mines, the wagon I bought of **OLDHAM**, and three yoke of oxen, for $1,000 in gold, and was offered $1,200 for the other wagon and oxen, but I would not sell it; it is worth as much to me as a steamboat is to its owner on the Missouri river. I have given it to young **NOTTINGHAM**, who drove it out, on the halves; he hauls from the Embarcados, a town laid out at **SUTTER**'s Fort, forty miles from the mines, and the head of navigation at this time..he hauls from thirty to forty hundred, and the price varies from 20 to $30 per hundred pounds, so that he clears for himself over $50 per day... I sold the pistols I bought of Henry **CHILDS** for $200 and the belt for $75, in gold. I have been in the country some three weeks, and have raised the rise of $3,000 in gold. My litte girls can make from $5 to $25 per day washing gold in pans. So soon as we get ready I expect to ship at this port for Jackson county, Missouri, where I expect to spend the remainder of my days in peace and quietness, and in the enjoyment of family and friends, where of all places I most delight to be. My average income this winter will be about $150 per day, and if I should strike a good lead, it will be a great deal more. .. You know James M. **HARLIN**; he has just bought a

12 May 1849

(160) (Cont.) Mexican rancho, for which has paid in gold $12000 for the stock and land, averaging the stock at $50 per head, and it is thought that he has made at least $12,000 in the operation, which makes him stand monarch of $24,000; but this is nothing. Jessee **BEASLEY** is said to be worth at least $40,000. Governor **BOGGS** has made an independent fortune for all his children. You know **BRYANT**, a carpenter, who used to work for Ebenezer **DIXON**; he has dug out more gold the last six months than a mule can pack."

(161) RECOVERY OF LOST DOCUMENTS. A few days ago information was laid before the Attorney General, which has led to the recovery of an important document, abstracted from the State Archives when, during the attack of the British in 1814, they were removed from Annapolis to a place of greater security. When the papers were brought back and examined, it was found that the roll-book, containing the names of all from the State of Maryland who had served in the Revolutionary War, and were thereby entitled to pensions, was missing. As this was the only record to guard against pension fraud; (for which object the inference would be it had been taken,) several attempts have been made to recover the book, and until the present week all without success.

Upon the information he had obtained, Mr. **RICHARDSON**, the Attorney General, put officer **SNYDER**, on the track; and on Wednesday the officer entered the house of Michael **DUNN**, in S. Paca street, and after a thorough search of the premises, found the roll-book in an old desk. The binding had been torn off, but as yet the leaves appear perfect, and without alteration. .. Officer **SNYDER** met with considerable opposition from the inmates while searching the house, and was compelled to force his way out, when he had got possession of the papers.--*Balt Patriot*, 28*th*.

(162) From the *Phil. North American*. BOLD ATTEMPT AT ASSASSINATION. A most daring attempt was made, last night about nine o'clock, to assassinate Mr. John **MC CANDLESS**, grocer, at the corner of Twelfth and Marion streets, in his own house. An unknown man drove up to his place in a vehicle, and desired to see Mr. **MC C**. The stranger was invited into the sitting room in the second story, when he informed Mr. **MC CANDLESS** that he had called to confer with him in relation to a farm, at the instance of a man living near West Chester. After talking over the matter he endeavored to prevail upon Mr. **MC C**. to get into his vehicle and accompany him to the residence of the owner of the farm, who, he said, only lived a short distance below **GRAY**'s Ferry. Mr. **MC CANDLESS** declined going at night, and after some further conversation, the visitor rose from his seat, and taking a position immediately behind Mr. **MC C**., commenced a murderous attack upon him with a dagger, stabbing him in the neck, face, side and other parts of the body.

(163) Appointments of Post Masters in North Carolina by the P. M. G.--Eli **MURRY**, Dudley, Wayne, vice J. W. S. **WEST**, resigned, (name changed to Everettsville.) R. O. **BENNETT**, Mt. Pisgah, Alexander, vice J. N. **BENNETT**, resigned. John H. **SANDERS**, Oak Ridge, Guilford, vice J. **BENBON**, resigned. W. T. **WHITFIELD**, Weldon, Halifax, vice J. W. **BURTON**. Robt. S. **PARKER**, Murfresboro', Hertford, vice Samuel J. **WHEELER**. B. **MOORE**, Green Plains, Northampton, vice A. W. **MOORE**, resigned. R. **HARRIS**, Luthersville, Rowan, vice John D. **SCHECK**. ---- **HARVEY**, Newbern, vice ----**BRYAN**.

(164) Married, On the 3d instant, by Rev. C. R. **HENRICKSON**, Rev. James **NASH** and Mrs. Sebra **WILLIAMS**, both of this county. On the 10th instant, by the same, John **BURCHER**, Esq., and Miss Casann **SCOTT** all of this place.

(165) State of North Carolina. Camden County. John W. **TORKSEY** vs. Joseph C. **BELL**, et als} In Equity, Spring Term, 1849. Death of Mary **BELL**, one of the defendants suggested, and it appearing that the heirs at Law of said Mary, reside beyond the limits of this State: It is ordered that publication be made in the *Old North State* newspaper, published in Elizabeth City, that Chloe, Jane, John, and Mary **BELL**, heirs at Law of Mary **BELL**, appear at the next Superior Court of Equity to be held for the County of Camden on the 5th Monday after the 4th Monday in September next, and plead, answer or demur or the Bill to be taken pro confesso. Witness, Joseph P. **GORDAN**, Clerk and Master of said Court at office, the 5th Monday after the 4th Monday of March. Anno Domini 1849. Joseph P. **GORDAN**, C. & M. E. Equity Office, Camden Co., May 3d. 1849. May 12th, '49.

The Old North State
Vol. 9. "Error is harmless, when truth is left free to combat it." No. 13.
Elizabeth City, N. C. Saturday, May 19, 1849.

(166) Elizabeth-City, May 19, '49. .. I. O. O. F. We promised in our paper week before last to give in our next a description of the procession, &c. of the Order which took place in our town on the 4th instant..but were unavoidably absent at the time... At about ten o'clock the members of Achoree Lodge No. 14, I. O. O. F. met at their Hall in Elizabeth City to celebrate their Second Anniversary, and after a short time the word was given to form, which being accomplished the word was given to move on, the Band, led by John M. **MATTHEWS**, Esq., struck up one of their splendid tunes, the procession moved from their Hall to Main street--down Main street to Road street--up Road street to South Second street--down South Second street to the Methodist

19 May 1849

(166) (Cont.) Episcopal Church, where they entered, and after a few moments the..ode composed for the occasion by John M. **MATTHEWS**, Esq., was sung by the Order and congregation... After which the Rev. Stephen **FORBES** offered up a prayer to the throne of Grace, when Wm. F. **MARTIN**, Esq., arose and delivered one of the best addresses that it has ever been our fortune to hear. ...

(167) NEW CABINET SHOP. The Subscriber has taken the Shop on Main Street, near the Mansion House, where he is prepared to do all kind of work in the Cabinet Making line in a manner to give satisfaction to all who may favor him with a call. .. He has now made up and offers for sale Bureaus, Sideboards, Wardrobes, Wash Stands, &c. ... D. A. **CLARK**. May 19.

(168) St. Mary's School, Raleigh, N. C. Trinity School, 8 Miles West of Raleigh, Right Rev. L. S. **IVES**, D. D. Visiter. The Summer Term of these Schools will commence on Wednesday, the 6th of June. A punctual attendance of the pupils is requested. For circulars, containing full information as to Terms &c., apply to the subscriber. Aldert **SMEDES**, Rector of St. Mary's School. Raleigh, April 19, 1849.

(169) U. S. Hotel, Edenton, N. C. The subscriber has lately purchased the well known Tavern Stand, known as the UNITED STATES HOTEL, formerly owned by Wm. **MC NIDER**, and more recently by T. C. **WHIDBEE**, but well known as **MC NIDER's** Hotel, for the accommodation of Boarders and Travellers. His TABLE will be supplied with the best the Market affords--his BAR with the choicest Liquors, Wines and Cigars--and his SATBLES [sic] with plenty of Provender and attentive Hostlers. ... James W. **HATHAWAY**. Edenton, N. C. May 19.

(170) Edenton Hotel, AND STAGE OFFICE. The Proprietor, Would beg leave to tender his thanks for the liberal patronage he has had extended to his House for nearly six years past, and would by a continuation of strict attentien solicit a continuance of the same; and would also state, that this well-known and long established Hotel, one door West of the Court House, in Edenton, N. C. has within the last six months, undergone a very great alteration, in having added to it a second story, with nine new and comfortable Bed Rooms, in addition to the former number, gives him thirty-one rooms for the use of the public. His Hoase is large and fronts the South, with a double Piazza, of nearly eight feet. His TABLE is provided with what the Market affords... His STABLES are as good and better than many in this part of the State, and can accommodate nearly 50 Horses, under a good shingle roof, with the attention of a good Hostler. He would also state, that he has Rooms detached, immediately in the rear of the main building, where Ladies or Gentlemen, with or without families can be as private as they would wish. ... Sam'l T. **BOND**, Proprietor Edenton Hotel, N. C. Edenton, May 19, 1849.

(171) Important Sale! By reason of the demise of one of the partners, that valuable FISHERY on Croetan Sound, lately owned and occupied by **WHITLEY & MELSON**, and formerly owned by Mills **ROBERTS**, will be sold to the highest bidder, at the Court House in Edenton, on Tuesday 3d day of July next. With the Fishery will be sold all the fixtures and apparatus belonging to it, including Seine, Batteaus, Stands, cooking materials, &c. At the same time will be sold about 700 bushels Salt, 450 Fish Barrels, 5 Coils new Rope, &c., &c., to be delivered at the fishery in a short time after the sale. Also a schooner called the "Republican" of about 40 tons burthen, will be disposed of at the same time and delivered at Edenton. ... William **MELSON**, Surv. Partner. Henry **WILLIAMS**, Exr. of E. S. **WHITLEY**. Williamston, N. C., May 14, 1849.

(172) Notice! The subscriber having duly qualified at March Court as Administrator of the Estate of Wm. H. **TWINE**, of Pasquotank county, Dec'd, hereby notifies all persons indebted to the Estate to come and pay the same, as no indulgence can be given, and those having claims against the said Estate to present them duly authenticated for settlement, or this notice will be plead in bar of recovery. Simon **MUNDEN**, Administrator. May 19.

The Old North State
Vol. 9. "Error is harmless, when truth is left free to combat it." No. 14.
Elizabeth City, N. C. Saturday, May 26, 1849.

(173) NATIONAL AND PATRIOTIC. The Whigs of Tennessee have nominated for re-election the present excellent Governor, Neil S. **BROWN**, and they expect to carry the State for him very handsomely. ...

(174) Billy **PATTERSON**.--A paper out west announces the decease of this noted individual who has been now *struck* by the hand of death.

(175) PEN AND INK SUPERSEDED BY MACHINERY.--Mr. Oliver T. **EDDY**, of Baltimore, Md., has invented a machine,

26 May 1849

(175) (Cont.) somewhat resembling a very small piano, by touching the springs of which, printed letters are instantly produced upon paper placed for the purpose. There is a key for each letter of the alphabet, the marks of punctuation, figures, &c., and on the depression of a key with the finger, a corresponding letter is printed on the paper. It may be useful as a medium of communication for the blind. The instrument will print with almost the perfection of an ordinary printing press, a single copy of any document, and with about the same rapidity as the document can be transcribed by a good penman--the copying done by the machine, being of course more plain and more easily read.

(176) REMARKABLE LONGEVITY. We learn that there is a rosebush flourishing at the beautiful residence of A. Murray **MELLVANE**, Esq., on the Neshaminy creek near Bristol, Pa., that is well known to be more than one hundred years old. In the year 1742 there was a kitchen built, which encroached on the corner of the garden, and the masons laid the corner stone with great care, saying it was "a pity to destroy so fine a bush." Since then it has never failed to produce a profusion of roses...

(177) Elizabeth-City, May 26, '49. .. We owe an apology to our friend, the Rev. Mr. **FORBES**, for the mistake in his name in our notice of the Odd Fellows Procession in our last paper. It should have been Edward M., instead of Stephen. ...

(178) THEM STRAWBERRIES. On Wednesday evening last we were presented by our little friend, Master John **LAVERTY**, with a large saucer full of that most excellent fruit. We can assure him they were quite a treat to us, and he will please accept our thanks for them. If any other of our numerous friends can beat them sent by John we should like to see it done.

(179) DREADFUL ACCIDENT ON THE NORTH RIVER. Steamer Empire sunk at Newburgh. Great loss of Life. Half Past Seven, A. M. The first serious steamboat casuality upon the North river, which it has been our duty to record this season, occurred last night to the steamer Empire, on her way from this city to Albany. About ten o'clock last evening, and when opposite Newburgh, she discovered a schooner on her starboard bow, loaded with lumber, beating down. The wind was blowing fresh, and the schooner under rapid way, when danger of collision was first apparent. The pilot of the Empire, Mr. Levi **SMITH**, called out to the schooner to luff, but no attention was paid to him. The steamer at the same time backed, and was under a light stern way..when the schooner struck her, near the forward gangway. .. The steamer immediately began to fill. Most fortunately the Rip Van Winkle was directly behind the Empire, and sailed alongside, within ten minutes after the accident occurred. She towed the Empire towards the eastern shore, left her aground, and took off her passengers, part of whom she landed at Newburgh, and the remainder she carried to Albany. .. The bodies of three persons were found upon the boat, who were drowned, all females, one a child... .. The schooner belonged to Deacon **GRANT**, a lumber dealer, of Troy. .. The names of those drowned are not known but the name of Mrs. **NOBLE** is supposed to have belonged to one of the victims.
 THE WRECK OF THE EMPIRE. .. *New York Evening Post*: Newburgh, May 18, 1849--6 o'clock, A. M. .. A schooner had put her bowsprit through the steamer Empire, and she was sinking. .. One family of **LADD**s, from Stonington, Ct., had lost four sons, young lads--no tidings of them last night. .. Wm. **BURDEN**, of Troy, threw a box overboard, got upon it, and was fished up, much exhausted. Mr. **TUTTLE**, of Williamsburgh, was picked up in the river, by David **GARRISON**, a fisherman.

(180) GRAND LODGE I. O. O. F. The Grand Lodge of the Independent Order of Odd Fellows of North Carolina was in session in this City, last week, the attendance, we understand, being much fuller than usual. The following officers were elected for the ensuing year: J. B. **NEWBY**, of Fayetteville, Grand Master. Alex. **BETHUNE**, of Charlotte, Deputy Grand Master. Juslius M. **WILCOX**, of Warrenton, Grand Warden. W. D. **COOKE**, of Raleigh, Grand Secretary. D. **MC MILLIAN**, of Wilmington Grand Treasurer. J. D. **ROYSTER**, of Raleigh, Grand Steward. John H. **MANLY**, of Raleigh, was chosen Representative to the Grand Lodge of the United States, and J. C. B. **EHRINGHAUS**, of Elizabeth City, his Alternate. The Grand Encampment also held its meeting here at the same time. The following are the Officers elected for the ensuing year: T. H. **HARDENBURG**, M. W. Patriarch. Perrien **BUSBEE**, M. E. High Priest. S. G. **SMITH**, W. Grand Scribe. Edw. **YARBROUGH**, W. Grand Treasurer. D. W. **TELFAIR**, Grand Junior Warden. Isaac **PROCTOR**, Grand Sentinel. *Raleigh Times*.

(181) CHOLERA IN NORFOLK. We publish the following from the Board of Health of Norfolk City. We hope our citizens will lose no time in cleansing their lots &c., as the dreadful disease is so near us. BOARD OF HEALTH, Tuesday, May 32. [sic] The Board of Health think it their duty to announce to the public that there have been, since their last report, on the 15th instant, five deaths from cholera... There are now 8 cases under treatment, mostly convalescent. No new case to-day. By order of the Board of Health, T. G. **BROUGHTON**, Sec'y B. H.

(182) DEATH OF GENERAL **WORTH**. A telegraphic despatch to the *Baltimore Patriot*, from New Orleans, announces..that this..distinguished officer of the U. S. Army, died at San Antonio de Bexar, Texas, on the 7th inst., of cholera.

26 May 1849

(183) From the *Raleigh Times*. Revenue Law. We informed our readers in our paper of the 6th April, that "the 7th section of the Revenue Law passed at the last session of the General Assembly has been construed that it does not go into operation until the 1st of April, in the year 1850." We have since been furnished with the following opinion of B. F. MOORE, Esq., Attorney General upon this subject: Raleigh, May 9th, 1849. Sir: You have requested my opinion on the proper construction of the 7th section of the act passed at the recent session of the Legislature, entitled, "An act to increase the Revenue of the State."--The question you present arises on the Proviso, found at the conclusion of that section, and is whether that proviso extends to the whole act; and if not, to how much thereof? I am of opinion that the proviso extends to the entire 7th section and to each and every subject of taxation therein specified, and that it extends to no other part of the act. If the proviso was..intended to be less extensive than the *whole* of the 7th section, I am unable to perceive that intent in the language of the law. Very respectfully, Your obd't servant, B. F. MOORE. C. L. HINTON, Public Treasurer.

(184) DIED, In Perquimans County, on the 18th inst., Mr. Elsbury W. TURNER, son of Nathan TURNER, Esq., of that county, after a lingering illness of Consumption, aged 31 years.

(185) FEMALE CLASSICAL INSTITUTE, Hillsborough Street. The next Session of this Institution will commence on Monday, 25the June. It is desirable that students be present on that day. For further information, address Bennet T. BLAKE. Principal. Raleigh, N. C. May, 1849.}

The Old North State.
Vol. 9. "Error is harmless, when truth is left free to combat it." No. 15
Elizabeth City, N. C. Saturday, June 2, 1849.

(186) MONOCHROMATIC PAINTING. It will be seen by the advertisement of Mr. Wm. G. ANDERSON..that he wishes to get a class in this place. Mr. ANDERSON comes among us well recommended, by many of the first citizens of the State, as a gentleman and an artist. .. We wish him success.

(187) LATER FROM ST. LOUIS. The number of buildings burnt at the great fire is estimated at three hundred, embracing the whole river front, from Locust to Chestnut street, and three squares extending to Main street. .. The conflagration is attended with a serious loss of life. Three persons were killed by an explosion on the steamer Alice, and it is probable that twenty were cut off altogether. Mr. Thomas B. FARGO, an auctioneer, was one of those killed during the fire. He threw a keg of powder into the store of DOENICH & VALLOUX, for the purpose of blowing it up and stopping the progress of the flames at that point, but unfortunately the explosion took place before he could get away from the building. The loss is immense--$4,000,000 to 5,000,000. A single item--the steamboats--runs up to $400,000, of which about half is covered by insurance; and the cargoes $15,000, and freight $50,000 more.

(188) Elizabeth-City, June 2, '49. .. From the *St. Louis Union*. THE GREAT FIRE IN ST. LOUIS. About 10 o'clock last night the steamer White Cloud, lying near the head of the levee, was discovered to be on fire. At the time there was a stiff breeze blowing from the northeast, which soon carried the flames across to the Edwaard Bates, the next boat below; the heat from these set fire to the Eudora, lying above them; the Belle Isle, next below the Bates, then caught fire. .. So intense was the heat arising from this great conflagration..that it set several buildings along the levee..and now while we are writing, one o'clock this morning, the entire block bounded by the levee, Main, Locust, and Olive streets, is wrapped in flames as are those houses in the square fronting the levee between Pine and Olive streets. And various houses on the west side of Main street, from CANTERS & SIMONS, at the corner of Locust and Main sts., to Olive; Mr. John MANDERs large cooper shop at the southwest corner of the levee and st., and also a large two-story brick house...

(189) ARREST AT WASHINGTON. A hostlor named Robert MOORE, was arrested and held to bail at Washington on Saturday, he having been seen, at WALKER & KIMBALL's stables, to pick up a roll of paper, supposed to contain $132 in bank bills, which Rev. Arthur COOPER had dropped. Mr. C. did not miss the money until he got to Georgetown, and the wrapper, a piece of the *Norfolk Beacon*, was afterwards found upon MOORE.--*Balt Sun*, of Tuesday.

(190) LANDSCAPE DRAWING And Monochromatic Painting. Mr. ANDERSON begs leave to call the attention of Parents & teachers and Ladies and Gentlemen of this place to this new and beautiful system of painting, which he proposes to teach in a few easy lessons. .. Private lessons given to Ladies at their own residences where a class of three or four meet together. Edenton, May 24th, 1849. We, the undersigned, patrons and pupils of Mr. W. G. ANDERSON, take much pleasure in expressing our entire satisfaction, in the course of lessons given by him in the beautiful art of Monochromatic Painting. Wm. R. SKINNER, James S.

2 June 1849

(190) (Cont.) JACKSON, James MC COY, Jessee A. WILLIAMSON, M. W. WEBB, J. R. LEMMETT, John M. JONES, A. J. BATEMAN, William BADHAM, Jos. S. JONES, Thos. J. MISKELL, J. W. BILLUPS, Wm. H. WILDER. .. Room over Mr. GRANDY's New Store, open from 8 to 12 A. M. and from 2 to 6 P. M. E. City, June 2d, 1849.

(191) NAG'S HEAD HOTEL NOW OPEN, Mr. Thomas WHITE would call the attention of his friends and the public generally to this establishment, which he has taken and has opened for the reception of visiters. .. Good servants have been engaged... TERMS. When the Proprietor furnishes Rooms $20 00 " Families " " 16 00 By the day, 1 25 By the week, 6 00 Children and servants half price. June 1st, 1849.

(192) Mrs. Esther SIKES Has just received a lot of New and Fashionable Bonnets, together with a most beautiful assortments of Ribbons of all kinds... .. One thing she wishes particularly to inform her customers of; and that is, that she is principled against deceiving the public by palming off "old Bonnets" on them, and at the same time representing them as being "new." And nothwithstanding one of her particular Friends on Road Street (to wit: the wife of a Merchant) has positively declared that her bonnets are neither "New or Fashionable," yet she will prove to the contrary by an examination of her stock. *She has never yet gone so far as to have her old bonnets repaired, and then sell them for new ones.* June 2, 1849.

The Old North State.
Vol. 9. "Error is harmless, when truth is left free to combat it." No. 16.
Elizabeth City, N. C. Saturday, June 9, 1849.

(193) STRANGE, BUT TRUE. Most of our readers recollect that, some months ago, a man named John SCOTT, professing to be deaf and dumb, met with a serious accident in this place. .. By degrees he recovered, until, with the aid of crutches he could walk his room. About this time he was taken with the typhoid fever, which reduced him so low that for a time his life was despaired of. Up to Sunday night there was no change, until some time during the night, when Mr. COVINGTON, at whose house he was staying, was awakened by a noise in the sick man's room. Fearing something had happened him [sic], he went up immediately, and--strange as it may seem--the deaf and dumb man was talking and could hear! as perfectly as any one. Since he began to talk, he says he was about four years old when he lost the power of speech and hearing, and has remained so for 24 years. ...--*Rutherford (N. C.) Telegraph.*

(194) THE OLDEST MAN IN AMERICA. George BUCKHART, living in Harlan Co. Ky., is one of the most extraordinary men of the age, and perhaps is the oldest man now known to be living. He is one hundred and fourteen years old; was born in Germantown, Pa., and has lived for several years in a hollow sycamore tree, of such dimensions as to contain his family, consisting of a wife and five or six children, bed and bedding, cooking utensils, &c. The exploring agent of the Amercan Bible Society, in his travels in Kentucky, recently found him, and also saw respectable gentlemen who have spent one or more nights with him in this singular home. He professes to hold the Lutheran faith, being of a German family, and received the Bible with peculiar manifestations of gratitude. ...--*Bible Society Record* for May.

(195) Elizabeth-City, June 9, '49. .. The Editor, Wm. F. MANN, being too sick to attend to his Editorial duties, must account for any want of Editorial this week.

(196) At a regular meeting of the Rough & Ready Light Dragoons, held in the Court House in Elizabeth City on Saturday, May the 5th, 1849, after parade, Capt. G. W. BROOKS present and presiding as chairman. On Motion of Wm. E. MANN, Resolved that a committee of 5 be appointed, to constitute a committee on the part of this corps whose duty it shall be to conform with any committee appointed by the citizens, and act with such committee, in making all necessary arrangements for properly celebrating the anniversary of our Independence. On motion of Wilson W. WILLIAMS, Resolved that the chair be requested to appoint said committee. Whereupon the chairman appointed, Jos. JENNINGS, Mordecai MORRIS, Martin HARRIS, Davis WHITEHURST, & Charles B. BROTHERS. On motion of James E. WEEKS, Resolved that Capt. G. W. BROOKS' name be added to said committee. There being no further business before the meeting. On motion of Timothy D. PENDLETON the meeting adjourned. G. W. BROOKS, Chm'n. J. Bartlett FEARING, Sec'y.

(197) Mr. Editor: A very respectable number of the citizens of E. City having assembled at the Court-House on Wednesday night last, for the purpose of adopting some suitable plan for the celebration of our approaching Anniversary, the 4th of July. W. F. MARTIN, Esq., was appointed Chairman of the meeting, and Geo. M. WILDER, Secretary. The meeting having been called to order the Chairman proceeded, on motion, to appoint in behalf of the citizens the following gentlemen as a Committee to confer

9 June 1849

(197) (Cont.) with five others appointed by the Rough & Ready Light Dragoons, and make the necessary preparations for the proper celebration of that day. The Committee appointed are: John POOL, Esq. J. M. MATHEWS, A. L. JONES. Dr. S. D. GRICE, J. GLOVER. On motion, the Chairman was added to the committee. The meeting was then addressed very eloquently by Gilbert ELLIOTT, Esq. and by Geo. W. BROOKS in behalf of the Light Dragoons. ... G. M. WILDER, Sec'y.

(198) We learn by reference to the Norfolk papers that Wm. WOODWARD of that city has been arrested on the charge of Forgery, and that upon a preliminary examination before the Mayor, he was committed to stand his trial at the next Term of the Superior Court. The amount of notes forged is about $10,000; all small.

(199) ALABAMA. The Hon. Henry W. HILLIARD has been nominated for re-election to Congress by the Whigs of the District, which he has hitherto represented so ably and faithfully. ...

(200) ACCIDENT. The *Lexington* (Va.) *Gazette* has the following. "On Sunday, the 13th inst., two little negroes, one aged 7, and the other 9 years, went to the pasture of their mistress, Mrs. Elizabeth HULL, on Buffalo Creek, to bring home the cows. The little boy it is supposed tied his sister, the younger of the two, to the tail of one of the cows, and the animal become alarmed, started off kicking, dragging and trampling upon the little sufferer, until it caused her death. ...

(201) FROM WASHINGTON... Washington, June 1, 1849. It is stated upon authority which seems reliable, that the Cabinet have decided to make the following diplomatic appointments: Hon. Abbott LAWRENCE, of Mass., Minister to England. Hon. Wm. C. RIVES, of Va., Minister to France. Ex-Governor GRAHAM, of N. C. Minister to Spain. Bailie PEYTON, of La., Minister to Chili. Hon. Geo. P. MARSH, of Vt., Minister to Berlin or Canstantinople. Col. MC CLUNG, of Miss., charge to New Grenada. Dr. Thomas M. FOOTE, of N. Y., Charge to Bogora or Venezuela. T. L. CRITTENDEN, of K. Y., Consul at Liverpool. Lorenzo DRAPER, of N. Y., Consul at Havre. Ex-Gov. KENT, of Me., Consul at Rio Janeiro [sic]. Elisha WHITTLESEY has entered upon the office of First Comptroller of the Treasury, in place of Mr. MC CULLOCH.

(202) AFFRAY WITH BANDITTI. At 10 o'clock, on the night of the 16th inst. the diligence left Vera Cruz for Mexico with seven passengers, two of whom were ladies. In the stage were Col. A. RAMSAY, formerly of the 11th Infantry, U. S. Army, C. M. BUGBEE, Mr. DOUGHERTY, of St. Louis, Mo., and Mr. JEWELL, of Mexico, and one foreigner. About 1 o'clock at night, the diligence was stopped by four robbers, between Santa Fe and San Juan. They were armed with lances and escopates. The passengers asked them what they wanted, and they answered their money. Upon this they declared they would not give it, and told them to clear out or fight for it. .. Poor BUGBEE, who was formerly connected with your office, was seated on the box with the driver, and on the first check of the horse's speed, he unfortunately dropped his COLT's rifle and was without arms. The driver had got down and opened the door, and the passengers commenced getting out. At this instant the firing was begun by the robbers..and RAMSAY immediately returned the shot and struck one of them, who reeled in the saddle, whereupon the rascals turned and fled. But BUGBEE was wounded severely, three buckshot having entered his hip. He was immediately put into the stage, bleeding very profusely, and carried to San Juan. .. Here it was considered best to leave him until a *litera* could be sent from Jalapa. On the arrival of the stage at Jalapa, a report was made to Mr. CAUX, the excellent agent of the stages, who as soon as possible had one forwarded to him, but on its arrival at Plan del Rio, BUGBEE was no more, having lived until 9 o'clock in the morning in the most excruciating pain. .. I believe Mr. BUGBEE had come out as agent, for the *N. Y. Sun*. BUGBEE had travelled the road upon which he met his death often before, and always under circumstances apparently more perilous than those under which he encountered his fate. He had been shot again and again when riding express for Mr. KENDALL, and was familiar with the hazards of the route. He was from Boston, a young man of spirit and energy, and the stay and support of his family.

(203) GENERAL ITEMS. We are much gratified to learn, says the *Weldon Herald*, that an Agricultural Society was formed in Northampton, at the last Court for said county. For more permanent organization, the Society will meet at Jackson on Monday of June Court, at which time Col. T. Pollock BURGWYN is expected to deliver an address. ...

(204) Mrs. John Quincy ADAMS is rapidly recovering from the paralytic stroke which has kept her confined for some time past.

(205) "HARD TIMES" Occasionally cause persons to do things that in the event prove beneficial to others. I have on hand at present a large lot of fashionable Furniture which I will dispose of at prices that cannot fail to please all who are in want. The following articles may be found at my Cabinet Ware House, to wit: Mahogany Bureaus as low as $10! super Dressing Bureaus, Side Boards, Mahogany Wash Stands..Ward Robes..Work Stands, Candle do., Centre Tables, Pier Tables, Mahogany Dining Tables, Cherry do., French Bed Steads, High Post do, and a few "Matrimonial Fruit Baskets," all of which are manufactured by myself, and warranted to be made up in first rate style. ... Caleb SIKES. June 9, '49.

9 June 1849

(206) JUST RECEIVED, A fresh lot of Family Groceries, Pork, Bacon, Shad, fresh Flour, Lard, Butter, Sugar, Coffee... Wm. **HALSEY**. June 9.

(207) NOTICE. The Partnership heretofore existing in the name and style of **MORRIS & STONE** is this day dissolved by mutual consent. All persons indebted to said Firm, will call on John C. B. **EHRINGHAUS** (or any Agent appointed by him) and settle, as he is fully authorized to collect debts due us and give receipts for the same. **MORRIS & STONE**. June 9, '49.

The Old North State.
Vol. 9. "Error is harmless, when truth is left free to combat it." No. 17.
Elizabeth City, N. C. Saturday, June 16, 1849.

(208) Elizabeth-City, June 16, '49. .. There was a sale of Government steamers at New Orleans on the 4th inst. The New Orleans was bid off by Capt. **TEMPLETON** for $31,000; the Alabama, by Capt. J. J. **WRIGHT**, for $23,000, and the propeller Col. Tompkins, by Jacob **BARKER**, for $2,300. The New Orleans was originally purchased by the Government for $130,000.-- *Patriot.*

(209) Death of General **GAINES**. I. The following official order has been issued by the Secretary of War: OFFICIAL. General Orders, No. 33} *Adjutant General's Office*, Washingt'n, June 9, '49. .. WAR DEPARTMENT, June 9, 1849. With feelings of deep regret and grief, the President announces to the Army the death of Brevet Major General Edmund Pendleton **GAINES**. He died of the epidemic prevailing at New Orleans, on the 6th instant. .. General **GAINES** entered the service of his country on the tenth day of January, 1779, with the rank of ensign. From this humble position he ascended, step by step, to his honorable and elevated rank. Opportunity only hastened that promotion, which his judgment, and courage, and patriotism won. His knowledge was the result of experience. .. He gave not an order in the execution of which he was not prompt to partake of its perils. .. The Adjutant General will direct proper military honors to be paid to the memory of the late Commander of the Western Division of the Army. George W. **CRAWFORD**, Secretary of War. II. As appropriate military honors to the memory of the deceased General, each military post within the Western Division, late under his command, will fire minute guns, (thirteen,) commencing at 12 o'clock M. and and [sic] display the national flag at *half staff* from the same hour till sundown on the day next after the receipt of this order. The officers of the Army will wear the usual badge of mourning for thirty days. By order, R. **JONES**, Adjutant General.

(210) WEEKLY REPORT OF THE BOARD OF HEALTH. Norfolk, June 12th, 1849. The Health Officer reports for the week ending this day, at 12 o'clock, 70 new cases of Cholera, 45 whites and 25 colored, of which twelve terminated fatally--7 whites and 5 colored. T. G. **BROUGHTON**, Sec'y B. H. We understand from private sources that the deaths have been much greater than above stated by the Board of Health.

(211) RELIGIOUS NOTICE. Rev. J. **CULPEPPER**, of S. C. will preach by divine permission at the Baptist Church on Sabbath next at 11 o'clock, A. M.; at candle light, also at Providence at half after 3 o'clock, P. M. E. City, June 16th, 1849.

(212) DIED, Very suddenly in this town on Monday last, Mr. Dempsey **CASEY**, aged about 48 years.

(213) To any Person who wishes to TRAVEL. The subscriber has on hand, one half size GERMAN CAMERA with all appurtenances which he will sell with a knowledge of the art at a reduced price. He has been operating something over two years, which has enabled him to be thoroughly acquainted with the art of Daguerreotyping. .. For further particulars apply to the subscriber at Mr. **SANDERLIN**'s Hotel. Caleb **SANDERLIN**. June 16.

(214) Read the following. The subscriber wishes to inform the public that he is duly constituted an Agent by Doctor D. **JAYNE**, of Philadelphia, for the sale of his "Invaluable Medicines" in this place. .. G. W. F. **DASHIELL**. June 16.

(215) Photographic Notice. The subscriber would respectfully inform the public that he has opened a room over Mr. J. **GRANDY**'s store on Road street where he will be pleased to see his friends and the public. .. Pictures can be had from 2,50 to 7 dollars. Persons desiring pictures will call early as his stay is only two weeks. Geo. W. **TATEM**. June 16.

The Old North State.
Vol. 9. "Error is harmless, when truth is left free to combat it." No. 18.
Elizabeth City, N. C. Saturday, June 23, 1849.

23 June 1849

(216) Elizabeth-City, June 23, '49. ... THE APPROACHING FOURTH JULY. We are glad to learn that the several Committees are making arrangements for the celebration of this glorious day. Our fellow townsman, Capt. William **BURGESS** intends furnishing a Public Dinner, and we sincerely hope *all* will join in the festive board. ...

(217) NAG'S HEAD HOTEL. As will be seen from the advertisement of Mr. Thomas **WHITE**, this House is to be under his management during the approaching season. .. He was the first person who ever kept a Hotel at Nag's Head, and we sincerely hope he will during the approaching season have as many boarders as he can attend to. ...

(218) DEATH OF EX-PRESIDENT **POLK**. We see by the following from the *Baltimore Patriot* that James K. **POLK**, Ex-President of the United States is no more. .. A telegraphic despatch announces the death of Ex-President **POLK**, at his residence in Nashville, on the 15th inst. ...

(219) DOUBLE MURDER. On the 15th inst., while at a public discussion in Madison county, Kentucky, a fight ensued between Cassius M. **CLAY** and Joseph **TURNER**. Pistols were snapped at each other and they came into close quarters with **BOWIE** knives. **TURNER** received a mortal wound in the groin and **CLAY** was instantly killed by a stab through the heart. **TURNER** died shortly after. Another signal vindication of the truth, that the way to destruction is through the unrestrained passions of the human heart.

(220) OFFICIAL. *Appointments by the President*. DEPARTMENT OF STATE. Hon. Daniel M. **BARRINGER**, of North Carolina, Minister to Spain, in lieu of William A. **GRAHAM**, who declines the appointment--the late incumbent, Romulus M. **SAUNDERS**, having resigned. TREASURY DEPARTMENT. James W. **OSBORN**, Superintendent, Branch Mint at Charlotte, North Carolina, vice Wm. J. **ALEXANDER**, removed.

(221) WRITING ON NEWSPAPERS. A neswpaper, bearing the initials of a friend, was received at the post office, Syracuse, directed to a young lady residing in the family of Charles F. **HICKS**. The postmaster, Mr. **TEALL**, demanded letter postage on it, which Mr. **HICKS** refused to pay, but tendered therefore *one cent*, the ordinary newspaper postage, which was refused and the paper retained. The suit was instituted against the postmaster for detaining the paper, and has been carried through all the courts to the Supreme Court of the United States. The *Star* (of Syracuse) says that the Attorney General of the United States, after examining the case, decided that the state courts had no jurisdiction in the case; and that **TEALL** acted legally in charging letter postage on the paper... The costs in this suit will probably amount to at least $400--the amount involved in the original dispute..was *nine cents*.

(222) EXPEDITION TO THE GREAT SALT LAKE. The expedition for a Trigonometrical and nautical Survey of the Great Salt and Utah Lakes and the surrounding country lying in the northern portion of Upper California, was recently organized in St. Louis by Col. J. J. **ABERT**, of the Topographical Bureau, and the command given to Capt. Howard **STANSBURY**, assisted by J. W. **GUNNISON**, of the Topographical Engineers--a corps which may well be called the *working men of the army*. ... --*Balt. Patriot*.

(223) GEORGE **LIPPARD**.--It seems that Mr. George **LIPPARD**, a scurrilous writer of Philadelphia, who left the Locofoco party to support Gen. **TAYLOR** for the Presidency, and who has now turned against the administration, is a disappointed office seeker. The scamp supported the old hero for the sake of office, and now abandons the administration because he cannot get it. ... --*Louisville Journal*.

(224) SUPREME [sic] COURT. The following gentlemen have been admitted to Superior Court practice since our last notice: John Lyon **HOLMES**, Wilmington. J. S. **AMIS**, Granville. T. S. **HAUGHTON**, Edenton. Col. J. G. **MC DOUGALD**, Elizabethtown. Jona. W. **ALBERTSON**, Hertford. Joseph G. **CARRAWAY**, Williamston, Martin county. Wm. F. **CARTER**, Wentworth. E. C. **HINES**, Edenton. *Raleigh Register*.

(225) Communicated. Married, On the 19th inst., at the residence of Thaddeus F. **BANKS**, by George D. **POOL**, Esq., Thomas **GASKINS** to Miss Elizabeth **FRESHWATER**. ...

(226) PUBLIC DINNER. The subscriber intending to furnish a PUBLIC DINNER on the ensuing 4th July, respectfully informs the public that they can procure tickets for the same by calling upon him. Wm. W. **BURGESS**. June 23.

(227) NOTICE. The undersigned has just received the following Goods, which he offers for sale, viz: 4 dozen Jars Preserved Ginger. 2 kegs Tamarinds, 150 Pounds Candies, A lot of Fig Paste, Lemon Syrup. Pickles in glass Jars. C. C. **GREEN**.

23 June 1849

(228) Notice The subscriber having duly qualified at March Court as Administrator of the Estate of John C. BARNES, Dec'd. hereby notifies all persons indebted to the Estate to come and pay the same, and those having claims against the said Estate to present them duly authenticated for settlement, or this notice will be plead in bar of recovery. Wm. CHARLES, Administrator. June 23.

(229) THE FISHERIES. *The American Net & Twine Manufacturing Co.* Wm. STOWE, Agent, No. 56, Commercial-St., Boston, Mass. RESPECTFULLY invite those persons engaged in the Fisheries, to their facilities in manufacturing DRAG NETS, HERRING, SHAD, MULLET, and other descriptions of NETS--Also SEINES, from the smallest to the largest class, made of the first quality of Twine, completed for use and warranted. .. We are pleased to refer to the following gentlemen, who have used Nets and Seines from our Manufactory. John G. WILLIAMS, Esq., Plymouth, N. C. Abner P. NEALE, Esq., Washington, " Geo. F. FISHER, Esq., Newbern, " Lewis LEE, Esq., " " W. H. FINNELL, Esq., Acquin Creek, " ... June 23, 1849.

(230) NOTICE. The Directory of the Dismal Swamp Canal Company, hereby gives notice that on or about the 5th of July, the Water will be drawn off from the South Level of the Canal, for the purpose of make [sic] indispensable repairs to the South Locks, and that Navigation will thereby will [sic] be suspended for some 10 or 15 days. By order James CORNICK, Prest. Dis S C Company. June 23, 1849.

(231) NOTICE. A Yawl Boat 20 feet long was found by the Wreck Master of the 4th Wreck District of North Carolina, and the same sold on the 21st April 1849. All persons having claims are requested to come forward and prove the same, and take the proceeds, after paying necessary expenses. E. B. MIDYETT, Com. of Wrecks, 4th Dis. N. C.

The Old North State.
Vol. 9. "Error is harmless, when truth is left free to combat it." No. 19.
Elizabeth City, N. C. Saturday, June 30, 1849.

(232) Correspondence of the *New Jersey State Gazette's* Reporter. "Six Weeks on the Wing." Passing many thriving towns, we reached Wheeling, 100 miles below Pittsburgh. This place has its name from the circumstance of some Indians cutting off a white man's head and putting it on a pole, to prevent other white men from coming there, *Wheeling* signifying "the place of a head." .. At Wheeling, was the site of old Fort Henry, the heroine of which in 1777, against 500 Indians, is almost unparalled [sic] in warfare. The garrison consisted of 42 men and boys, which was reduced by two stories to 12. They maintained the battle until their ammunition was nearly exhausted and it became necessary to go to a house some distance from the fort for a keg of powder known to be there. It was an expedition of extreme hazard, and the Colonel unwilling to order any one to do it, inquired who would volunteer. A number stepped forward, and among them a young woman of great intrepidity, named Elizabeth ZANE, who insisted that her life was less valuable than a warrior's, and she should be allowed to go. With great reluctance they yielded to her entreaties, and she returned with the powder amid a storm of balls, unharmed. The battle continued all day and night; when the Indians withdrew, Major MC CULLOUGH, while endeavoring to throw succor into the fort, was separated from his men, and surrounded by Indians. They could have killed him on the spot, but they wished to take him alive. He was the greatest hunter of his time, known personally from his wonderful exploits to almost every Indian, and so great was their terror and hatred of him, that any Wyandot chief would have given the lives of twenty warriors to take him alive. Finding himself surrounded, he turned his horse's head, and flew to "Wheeling hill." Reaching the top, he found himself hemmed in on three sides by advancing Indians, while on the fourth was a precipice, 150 feet high, terminating in Wheeling creek. Not a moment was to spare, and lifting his rifle in one hand and gathering the reins in the other, he urged his horse to the leap--the noble steed and daring rider reached the water unharmed, and dashed away to the fort safely. .. It rained heavily all the night and part of the next day, confining us to the saloon in which were Amos KENDALL and other distinguished people. ... B. R. P.

(233) IRON STORES. Five iron stores, says the N. Y. "Scientific American," have been erected on the corner of Murray and Washington streets, in this city, by Mr. E. H. LANG. Each store is 20 by 56 feet long, and they have been erected without dirt, bustle, bricks or mortar, the usual attendants of brick houses, which incommode our streets more than any other thing we know of. Each story is supported by rows of fluted pilasters, the courses between which are completely bolted, and the seams of pannels completely covered and concealed from the view by an ornamental cornice. Thus the walls are in fact one solid iron block, capable of supporting an immense weight. There are about 150 tons of iron in the buildings. .. The cornice and ornaments are made by W. L. MILLER, 40 Eldridge street. The mason work required was done by Messrs. A. & J. WHITE, and the carpenter work by Samuel MARTIN. The entire cost is stated to be about $20,000. They have been put up in the course of two months.

30 June 1849

(234) Correspondence of the *Baltimore Patriot.* I send you for publication an important report, just made by Professor **BACHE**, Superintendent of the Coast Survey. .. OFFICIAL. *Report of the Superintendent of the Coast Survey to the Secretary of the Treasury, relating to Hatteras cove, Hatteras inlet, and Bull's bay, on the coast of North and South Carolina.* Coast Survey Station, Near Annapolis, Maryland, June 11, 1849. Sir: I have received from Lieutenant Commanding J. N. **MAFFIT**, U. S. N., assistant in the Coast Survey, information in regard to the results of reconnoisances made by him, which are of considerable importance to navigators, and which I have the honor to lay before you, with a view to their publication. They relate to a cove which has been formed since 1845, by the extension of Cape Hatteras to the inlet southward and westward of Cape Hatteras, formed in 1846, and to the use of Bull's bay, on the coast of South Carolina as a harbor of refuge. .. 1. *Hatteras cove* lies to the westward of the extreme point of Cape Hatteras, is sheltered from the north east and affords good anchorage in four of [sic] five fathoms water, with a bottom of "soft blue mud." From the anchorage Hatteras light bears NNE., distant about one mile and a half. Since 1845 the SW., spit of Hatteras has made out nearly three-eights of a mile. 2. *Hatteras inlet* is twelve miles to southward and westward of the cape. Twelve feet can be carried over the bar on the ocean side, and there is secure anchorage in five fathoms water. The entrance with a pilot is easy. Lt. **MAFFIT**s statements refer only to the use of the inlet as a harbor of refuge. 3. *Bull's Bay* is about twenty three miles North of Charleston, on the coast of South Carolina. Thirteen feet can be carried across the bar at low water spring tides, the rise and fall of which is six and three quarters feet. .. Very respectfully, yours, A. D. **BACHE**, Superintendent U. S. Coast Survey. Hon. W. M. **MEREDITH**, Sec'y of the Treasury.

(235) Elizabeth-City, June 30, '49. .. We are authorized to announce John M. **MATHEWS** as a candidate for Superior Court Clerk. We are authorized to announce Caleb **SANDERLIN** as a Candidate for Superior Court Clerk. We are authorized to announce William D. **PRITCHARD** as a Candidate for Office of Clerk of the County.

(236) CELEBRATION OF THE APPROACHING FOURTH OF JULY. The citizens of Elizabeth City and the County are requested to assemble in front of the Court House at 10 o'clock A. M. when the procession will be formed under the direction of Wm. E. **MANN**, Chief Marshall of the day. The procession being formed..will march under his order to the Office of John **POOL**, Esq., where the Chaplain, Orator, Reader and Committee of Arrangements will be received and placed in front of the Sons of Temperance. The procession will thence march to the Methodist Episcopal Church, where after singing by the Choir and prayer by Rev. P. F. **AUGUST**, the Declaration will be read by Mr. James W. **HINTON**, and the Oration delivered by Mr. Geo. M. **WILDER**. .. After the services are over at the Church, the procession will return to the Court House where it will be dismissed, by the Marshall, and the command of the Military and the different Orders given up to their respective officers. A Public Dinner will be given by Mr. Wm. W. **BURGESS**, at the Court House, at 2 o'clock P. M. COMMITTEE OF ARRANGEMENTS.

(237) HON. EDWARD **STANLY**. It gives us pleasure to inform our readers, that this champion of Whig principles has lately been nominated by the Whigs of the 8th Congressional District for a seat in Congress. ...

(238) We understand that Capt. Tart **ETHEREDGE**, of Roanoke, has been appointed keeper of the Light Boat stationed off Roanoke Island. ...

(239) Communicated. Married, On the 26th inst., in this County, by S. D. **GRICE**, Esq., Fred **JINNINGS** to Mrs. Patsey **CASEY**.

(240) Died, In this town, on Thursday, the 21st instant, Mr. William **ALBERTSON**, aged about 74 years. Mr. A. was one of our oldest citizens, and has been associated with the town of E. City ever since it was a town, and his absence is missed as one of the necessary appendages of our little village. He was once the Editor of the *E. City Star*, and the Proprietor of an Hotel for a great number of years in this place. After giving up the Hotel he moved to Mississippi where he remained for several years. He arrived back to his native town in 1845, and has been for the last year or so County Register. In this town, on Wednesday last, Robert, infant son of Robert and Cornelia **WATKINS**, aged about six months.

(241) STATE OF NORTH CAROLINA. Pasquotank County. John **PALIN** vs. Edward **DECORMIS**.} Attachment. It appearing to the Court that Edward **DECORMIS** is not an inhabitant of this State, it is ordered that publication be made for six weeks in the "Old North State" for said **DECORMIS** to appear at the next Term of the County Court to be held for the County of Pasquotank, at the Court House in Elizabeth City, on the first Monday in September, to plead, answer, or demur, to said attachment, or Judgment, pro confesso, will be entered against him. By order of the Court. W. W. **GRIFFIN**, Clerk. June 30.

30 June 1849

(242) For Sale or Rent. The Subscriber offers for Sale or Rent for the season on accommodating terms his Nag's Head property, the location is a very healthy one, the lot is well elevated and the aspect towards the Sea and Sound unobstrcted. Address C. G. **LAMB**, Camden Court House, N. Carolina.

(243) NAG'S HEAD PACKET. The Schooner Lizzie G. Russell, Capt. Daniel D. **OWENS**, will commence running as the regular Packet between this place and Nag's Head on Monday next the 2d of July. .. Passage ONE DOLLAR. Meals can be had on board the Packet for 25 cts. each. E. City, June 30, 1849.

(244) NOTICE. The subscriber having duly qualified at March Court as Administrator of the Estate of William B. **ALLEN**, Dec'd, hereby notifies all persons indebted to the Estate to come and pay the same, and those having claims against the said Estate to present them duly authenticated for settlement, or this notice will be plead in bar of recovery. Leonard **CHAPMAN**, Administrator. June 30, 1849.

(245) Attention R. & R. L. Dragoons! You are hereby ordered to attend a parade of the company on Wednesday next-the 4th July, with 10_ rounds of blank cartridges. The company will form at 10 o'clock a. m. precisely on foot before the Court House front, for the purpose of joining the procession. By order of the Capt. J. W. **HINTON**, O. S. June 30.

The Old North State.
Vol. 9. "Error is harmless, when truth is left free to combat it." No. 19?. 20
Elizabeth City, N. C. Saturday, July 7, 1849.

(246) Elizabeth-City, July 7, '49. .. THE ANNIVERSARY. .. Though the rain was falling rapidly, and the streets exceedingly muddy, our citizens turned out in quite a large number and assembled at the place appointed for the oration. And the ladies, regardless of the torrents that fell and the mud that beset the streets, blessed the occasion with their encouraging smiles and the purity of their presence in considerable numbers. The Rough & Ready Light Dragoons formed on foot, and marched to the Hall of the Sons and Cadets of Temperance, when these two Societies, dressed in their handsome regalia and bearing the symbols and tokens of their Orders, joined the procession and proceeded to the office of John **POOL** Esq., when the Chaplain, Orator, and Reader, attended by the Committee of Arrangements were received, and the whole advanced under the Marshal of the day to the M. E. Church. ..

When all had become quietly seated in the Church, the Methodist choir, assisted by members from the Baptist choir, sang a beautiful and touching hymn admirably suited to the occasion... After which was offered a prayer by the Rev. P. F. **AUGUST**--and then came the Declaration by Mr. Jas. W. **HINTON**, prefaced by a few strikingly appropriate and well conceived remarks. Next came the Oration by Mr. Geo. M. **WILDER**, which all unite in praising as able, chaste and well suited. .. A public dinner was served at the Court House, where a number of our citizens assembled and enjoyed the festivity in 4th of July style. ...

(247) MELANCHOLY DISASTER AT NIAGARA FALLS.--The telegraph announces, under the date of last evening, that Miss **LE FORREST**, daughter of one of the most respectable citizens of Buffalo, fell into the stream at the "Hog's Back," on Thursday evening. Mr. Charles C. **ADDINGTON**, a young merchant of Buffalo plunged in to save her but both were carried over the Falls. ... *N. Y. Com.*

(248) COLLEGE OF ST. JAMES, MD. A friend has sent us a "Register of the College of St. James, and the Grammer Schooll; Washington County, Md. for the seventh Session, 1848-49." Among the clases, we find the following young gentlemen from North Carolina: *Senior Class.*--Edward Graham **HAYWOOD**, Raleigh; Louis **HENRY**, do; John **SKINNER**, Edenton; John Creecy **SKINNER**, do. *Freshman Class*--John **DAVES**, Newbern; Henry Martyn **DRANE**, Wilmington; Robert Cochran **GREENE** do.; John Wright **HOLMES** do.; Samuel Walter **LANGDON**, do.; Walker **MEARES**, do.; Geo. **GATLING** Gatesville; William G. **GRANBERRY**, Perquimons Co., Edmund S. **HOYT** Washington; Robert B. **MARTIN**, Elizabeth City. *Grammar School*--David Stone **CHOWAN**, Wilmington; William L. **DE ROSSETT**, do.; Joshua C. **WALKER**, do.; Samuel P. **WATTERS**, do.; Adam E. **WRIGHT**, do.; James A. **WRIGHT**, do.; Frederic S. **MOORE**, do.; Benj. T. **BRYANT**, do.; Edward **GRAHAM**, Newbern William **GLOVER**, Elizabeth City; Durant A. **TILLITT**, Camden Co. In all, during the seventh session, 98.

(249) William B. **TAPPAN**, an American poet of considerable merit, died in Boston of cholera on Monday. He was a Christian and a philanthropist.

7 July 1849

(250) BAUM'S HOTEL. The Subscriber having put his House in complete order will open on the 6th July for the accommodation of all who may favor him with their patronage. .. His table will be at all times, furnished with the best that can be procured and the Bar will be supplied with the best of Liquors, Cigars, &c., and a plenty of that great luxury--ICE. The Terms of board as follows: By the day, $1,00 By the week, 6,00 By the 2 weeks, 9,00 By the 3 weeks, 12,00 By the month, 15,00 Children and Servants half price. Mr. Wm. **WOODHOUSE** will upon application take any passengers across from his dwelling on Narrow Shore to the Hotel.--Passage 37 1-2 cts. Horses taken care of until the return of their owners. A. **BAUM**. July 7, 1849.

(251) THE DISMAL SWAMP CANAL CLOSED. In view of the above event the subscriber has just received 50 Bbls. Superfine Flour, a good article which will be sold for CASH. .. At the old stand on the Water. Wm. **HALSEY**. July 7.

(252) LOOK HERE! The undersign [sic] has just received a lot of large Flat Turnip and yellow Ruta Bega seeds, Butter, Sugar and Water Crackers. C. C. **GREEN**. July 7.

(253) Notice! A general meeting of the subscribers to the Orapeake Canal and Turnpike, will be held at **HARRELL** & Co's Store in the county of Gates, on the 26th day of July next, at 10 o'clock A. M. for the purpose of attending to such business as may appertain to the execution of said work. The books to receive subscriptions, will continue open until the first day of September next; previous to which time, it is expected that all who may feel interested in the work will avail themselves of the opportunity of subscribing. Isaac L. **HARRELL**, John C. **GORDON**, Timothy H. **LASSITER**. Sunsbury, Gates Co., N. C. July 7, 2849.

The Old North State.
Vol. 9. "Error is harmless, when truth is left free to combat it." No. ??. 21
Elizabeth City, N. C. Saturday, July 14, 1849.

(254) *Poetical*. The following curious couplet is painted on a sign-board in Pell street, New York: "Washing, ironing, and going to day's work, Done well and well done, by Louisa **BOURKE**."

(255) Elizabeth-City, July 14, '49. .. A LAUNCH. Our citizens are informed that at the ship yard of our worthy citizen, Capt. Timothy **HUNTER**, this afternoon at about 4 o'clock will be launched a fine Brig.

(256) [*Correspondence of the Washington Union.*] Elizabeth City, N. C. June 22, 1849. Gentlemen: I am very sorry to inform you that our good postmaster Mr. Timothy **GILBERT**, has been removed, and that Mr. W. E. **MANN**, editor of the *Old North State*, has been appointed his successor. The appointment of Mr. **MANN** has caused dissatisfaction among the whigs, (at least part of them,) who think he could have done without the office, as he now has two papers. Mr. **GILBERT** has discharged his duty faithfully; and the whigs begged him to petition to the Pos [sic] Office Department to be retained in the office. .. Mr. **GILBERT** is an old man, and has nine children, who are dependent upon him for support; but we trust that, without an office under the present imbecile administration, he will be able to get a good living. .. I wish also to inform you of the removal of Captain Jas. C. **SCOTT**, from the lightboat. His petetion was signed by all the captains that sail out of this place, certifying that he kept good lights. Two office-holders removed because they were democrats; not that they have not done their duty, but because they did not vote for Zachary **TAYLOR**. We may expect that after August our collector will be removed; but not before then. There are five applicants for that office. Col. David **OUTLAW**; our representative; is afraid to say which one he is in favor of, as the election is not far off. The present incumbent, Mr. **PRITCHARD**, is a very popular man and if removed it would cause great dissatisfaction; for almost every whig is in favor of him. ... A CLAY WHIG.
 We did not see the above until it made its appearance in the *Raleigh Standard*, or we would have noticed it before, and nailed the many *lies* therein contained by this beautiful "**CLAY** Whig" alias-dyed in-the-wool Loco Foco, to the counter. CHARGES . .. The balance of the foul article is taken up in abusing the Administration, and in speaking of the removal of Capt. Jas. C. **SCOTT**--and the contemplated one of Wm. D. **PRITCHARD**, Esq., and also in ascribing to Col. **OUTLAW** a hand in the matter. ANSWERS. .. That we could have done without the office is true, but that we can do a little better with it is equally true, and we suppose that according to Loco Foco logic a man must not accept anything that will in the least better his condition. But we can inform..that because we publish two papers we are not making a great fortune, as we publish one of them by contract, for a religious denomination, and that the contract will not neat us $50 per year. .. But we should like to know how he could say we had two papers under way and tell the *truth*, when his communication is dated *June* 22d, and the *first* No. of the *Baptist Messenger*, did not make its appearance until last Saturday, July 7th, though the paper bears date July 1st. ...

(257) Col. Braxton **BRAGG**, the famous commander of artillery at the battle of Buena Vista, was married in New Orleans on the 7th inst., to Miss Elizabeth B. **ELLIS**.

14 July 1849

(258) DIED, On Tuesday, the 10th instant, in Hertford, N. C., Mary Catharine, infant daughter of Doctor N. Chapman and Caroline **SKINNER**.

(259) STEAMBOAT AT AUCTION. WILL BE SOLD, By order of the Stockholders, on Tuesday, 24th July, at 12 o'clock, at **WALKE**'s wharf, Norfolk, Va., The very commodious and neat steamboat PROPRIETOR, Said boat is about 174 tons, 154 feet long, breadth of beam 19 feet 8 inches, and 32 feet from outside to outside, draught of water 32 inches, Engine 80 horse power and in good order, wrought iron Shaft, Boilers in good order, having been used but 7 months, has recently undergone a thorough overhauling and refitted in a neat style. .. Terms--One-third cash, one-third in 3 months, and one-third in 6 months. ALSO, At the same time and place, between 20 and 3 [sic] cords Pine Wood. H. **FITZGERALD**, Agent. J. H. & J. **NASH**, Auc'trs. July 14.

(260) NOTICE. The Co-partnership heretofore existing between the Subscribers, under the style of **GRANDY & HARDY**, expired at the close of the 30th ult. C. W. **GRANDY** is authorized to use the name of the firm, in liquidation, and will settle all businee [sic] connected therewith. C. W. **GRANDY**, H. C. **HARDY**. I shall continue the Grocery and Commission Business, at the Store, occupied by the late firm of **GRANDY & HARDY**, and solicit a share of patronage from my friends and the public generally. C. W. **GRANDY**. july 14

(261) NORTH CAROLINA Institution for the Deaf and DUMB. The next session of this Institution will commence on Monday, the 16th day of July. Having moved into the new Building, a few more pupils can be received. As pupils will be admitted in their order of application, it is important that application should be made without delay. Any information on the subject will be given by Wm. D. **COOKE**, Principal. july 14.

(262) H. C. **HARDY**, COMMISSION AND FORWARDING MERCHANT, NORFOLK, VA.

(263) Teacher Wanted. Any person wishing the situation of a School Teacher, may do well by applying immediately, to the undersigned committee for the School in Currituck County, Indian Ridge District, as the said District is now without a Teacher. W. T. **COTTER**, C. **BELL**.

The Old North State.
Vol. 9. "Error is harmless, when truth is left free to combat it." No. 22.
Elizabeth City, N. C. Saturday, July 21, 1849.

(264) CONGRESSIONAL DISTRICTS. The following are the Congressional Districts of this State. *First District.* Cherokee, Macon, Haywood, Buncombe, Henderson, Rutherford, Burke, McDowell, Yancy, Cleaveland, Caldwell. *Second District.* Ashe, Wilkes, Surry, Davie, Rowan, Iredell, Catawba. *Third District.* Lincoln, Gaston, Mecklenburg, Union, Anson, Stanly, Cabarrus, Montgomery, Richmond, Moore. *Fourth District.* Stokes, Rockingham, Guilford, Randolph, Davidson. *Fifth District.* Granville, Caswell, Person, Orange, Chatham, *Sixth District.* Wake, Franklin, Warren, Halifax, Edgecombe, Nash, Johnston. *Seventh District.* Cumberland, Robeson, Columbus, Bladen, Brunswick, New Hanover, Sampson, Duplin, Onslow, *Eighth District.* Wayne, Greene, Lenoir, Jones, Craven, Carteret, Beaufort, Pitt, Hyde, Washington, Tyrell, *Ninth District.* Martin, Bertie, Hertford, Northampton, Gates, Chowan, Perquimans, Pasquotank, Camden, Currituck. In the late Congress they were represented as follows: T. L. **CLINGMAN**, Nathaniel **BOYDEN**, D. M. **BARRINGER**, A. H. **SHEPHERD**, A. W. **VENABLE**, J. R. J. **DANIEL**, James J. **MCKAY**, R. S. **DONNELL** and David **OUTLAW**.

CANDIDATES. *First District.*--Hon. T. **CLINGMAN**, whig. *Second.*--Joseph P. **CALDWELL**, whig. *Third.*--Hon. Edmund **DEBERRY**, whig, Hon. Greene W. **CALDWELL**, dem. *Fourth.*--A. H. **SHEPHERD**, whig. *Fith.* [sic]--Hon. A. W. **VENABLE**, dem, H. K. **NASH**, whig. *Sixth.*--W. J. **CLARK**, J. R. J. **DANIEL**, dems. *Seventh.*--Wm. S. **ASHE** and David **REID**, dems. *Eighth.*--Wm. K. **LANE**, dem., Edward **STANLY**, whig. *Ninth.*--Hon. David **OUTLAW**, whig, Thos. J. **PERSON**, dem.

(265) Elizabeth-City, July 21, '49. .. We are authorized to announce Daniel **RICHARDSON** as a Candidate for Superior Court Clerk.

(266) FRESH SHAD. We were presented on Thursday by Alexander **PARKER**, Esq., with part of a fresh Shad caught in one of his nets the night before. It looked very well, being in good order but the natural taste was not there. It was rather soft than shad usually are in their proper season.

(267) 3D CONGRESSIONAL DISTRICT. We are glad that the difllculty heretofore existing in this staunch Whig District by there being three Whig candidates has been amicably settled, and that the Hon. Edmund **DEBRERY** has received the nomination.

21 July 1849

(268) DISMAL SWAMP CANAL NAVIGATION RE-OPENED.--We are requested by the Directors of the Dismal Swamp Canal Company to announce that the water was yesterday let in, and the Navigation of the Canal fully restored.--*Norfolk Herald*.

(269) Married, In E City, on the 17th by S. D. GRICE, Esq. Capt. David THORNTON, to Miss Margret CHALK, all of this City.

(270) DIED, From the *Edenton Sentinel*. In Gates County, on Saturday the 23d ult., Mrs. Martha HINTON, wife of John W. HINTON, Esq., in the 24th year of her age. .. She was a devoted wife, an affectionate mother, and a kind hearted neighbor; but in the midst of so many inducements to live, she was suddenly called to exchange the fond society of husband, sisters, neighbors, and friends, for the silence and solitude of the grave. ...

(271) List of Letters Remaining in the Post Office, at Elizabeth City, Quarter ending 30th June 1849. ALLEN, Mr. Wm. B. ALLEN, Capt. Benj. ALEXANDER, Mr. Benj. BALLANCE, Capt. Hol. BRANT, Mr. John N. 2 BASNIGHT, Mr. Benj. L. BATTLE, Rev. J. A. BANKS, Mrs. Parthnea BACON, Mr. Edward BRIGHT, Big Ephraim BROCKETT, Miss Mary A. BRAY, Mr. Wallis BURKE, Mr. Samuel BANKS, Mr. Wm. C. BUTLER, Miss Jane BURCHER, John Esq. BELL, Mr. J. M. CLARKE, Samuel Esq. COMANN, Rev. Wm. H. CAMERAN, Mr. John A. CARNATHAN, Mr. Davis FISHER, Capt. Wm. D. 2 GRIGGS, Capt. Joseph GRAY, Thaddeus S. GUTHRIE, Capt. Elijah GREGORY, Wm. N. Esq. HAMDEN, Mr. James HARRELL, Mrs. Sally HENDERIXON, Capt. Andrew HARRELL, A. & J. HOWELL, Mr. J. HASKETT, Mr. Henry JACKSON, Mr. Samuel JORDAN, Miss Louisa JAMES, Francis LASTER, Miss Ann LEIGH & Son Messrs. LAIB & LANG Messrs. LABOYTEAUX, John LINDSAY, David Esq. MEADS, Mr. Robert MULLEN, Mrs. Joseph 2 MC KEARY, Henry MITCHEL & ELLIS Messrs. MILLER, Mr. Charles MORRIS, Eason A. MULLER, Mr. L. MARSH, Mr. Bennett PIKE, John PRICE, Mr. Nathan PENDLETON, John F. Esq. REED, Miss Elizabeth 2 ROUTLE, Mr. Wm. R. ROBERTS, Miss Elizabeth SMITH, Mr. Marcellus SAWYER, Mrs. M. SHARBER, Mr. Miles M. STERLING, Capt. John SIKES, Capt. Thomas SPRINGER, Mr. Wm. P. SEWER, Jonathan SKINNER, Miss Ann TRUEBLOOD, Morris 2 TRAVIS, Mr. William TAYLOR, Mr. Argus TOLER, Miss Lydia TOLER, Capt. John THATCH, Benj. W. UMPHREY, Mr. Willis WATCHEL, John WELLS, T. A. 2. WYMAN, Elbridge WHITE, Jara WALKER, Capt. Hugh WOOD, Mr. James WYMAN, Lucy A. WILLIAMS & LIDDEN 2 WINDSOR Capt. John WHITE, Emelia WORF, Wm. WHITSON, James WHITE, Wm. Persons calling for any of the above letters will please say they are advertised. Wm. E. MANN, P. M. july 21.

(272) House and Sign, and Ornamental, Painting. The undersigned having completed his engagements in the country for the present, has returned to Elizabeth City for the balance of this year, prepared to execute, with neatness and despatch, any work in his line of business, with which he may be intrusted. .. Gilbert ELLIOTT, Esq. politely permits a reference to him, who can exhibit a specimen of inside work by Wm. A. BASSETT. All orders left with Messrs. L. K. SAUNDERS & Co., will receive my immediate attention.

The Old North State.
Vol. 9. "Error is harmless, when truth is left free to combat it." No. 23.
Elizabeth City, N. C. Saturday, July 28, 1849.

(273) IN AN AWFUL BAD FIX. Col. NOLAND, editor of the *Batesville* (Ark.,) *Eagle*, tells the following good story of a man being in a very warm and tight place: The late Col. Allen OAKLEY was stopping for the night at a public house. The weather was warm, and OAKLEY, when he retired to bed, divested himself of all his clothes but his shirt. About midnight a terrible fuss was raised in the yard--a catamount had been rustled up, and the dogs were fighting it. After having it around and around for some time they got to the door, which, flying open, in popped the catamount. .. Poor OAKLEY saw no chance to make the door, and sought safety by climbing up the logs to what should have been the loft; but alas! it was deficient of every thing but a cross pole. This he straddled, with the expectation of hearing, if not witnessing the fight going on below. But..he soon had painful evidence that a man can be attacked behind as well as before. He had waked up a wasp's nest something more than a half bushel in size, and they were putting it to him in style. One hand was necessary to hold on with, and the other slapped some. .. Poor fellow! it was not an easy matter for him to ride the next day.

(274) Elizabeth-City, July 28, '49. .. NEW POST OFFICE. There has been a new Post Office erected at the "Corner Gum" in Currituk County, and Wm. E. FEREBEE, appointed Post Master.

(275) PROGRESS OF THE CHOLERA. ... Among the deaths by cholera in New York is Henry VAN WINKLE, who had been employed in the press room of the *Courier and Enquirer* for more than twenty years. ...

28 July 1849

(276) General **GAINES'** Will. We take from the N. Orleans Picayune the following copy of the will of the late Major General GAINES. The document is entirly autograph, and, as the context shows, has been drawn up by himself:--"In the name of God, amen: I, Edmund Pendleton **GAINES**, being now in the enjoyment of excellent health, for which I am duly thankful, but having arrived at that period of life at which it becomes the duty of men to hold themselves ready for disease and death; and, moreover, having this day learned, for the first time in my life, that my late marriage contract will admit of a construction tending to deprive my beloved wife, Myra Clark **GAINES**, of the right of dower to which she would have been entitled without such contract, I do hereby ordain and establish this to be my last will and testament--that is to say:--First--I hereby appoint my wife, Myra Clark **GAINES**, my executrix; and my nephew, Francis S. **LYON**, of Demopolis, Alabama; and my nephew, Francis Young **GAINES**, of Mobile, Alabama; and Vigil **WHITNEY**, Esq., of Binghampton, New York; and my son, Francis Henry Toulman **GAINES**, of Mobile, Alabama; and my son, Edmund Pendleton **GAINES**, Jr., of Memphis, Tennessee, my executors; who are hereby authorized and requested to pay my just debts, and then to divide all the money and property owned by me at the time of my death, equally, between my wife, Myra Clark **GAINES** and my above-named sons, Francis Henry Toulman **GAINES** and Edmund Pendleton **GAINES**, Junior, share and share alike--any thing in the said marriage contract to the contrary notwithstanding. It is, however, to be clearly understood that the above devise shall take effect only in the event of the suits, brought or to be brought, for the recovery of the estate devised by Daniel **CLARK** to his daughter, the above named Myra Clark **GAINES**; as his devisee, or as his heir at law, being decided against her and her husband.

Should the said suits, or any of them, be decided in favor of the said Myra and the undersigned, so as to secure to her the whole, or the principal part, of the said estate sued for, then, in that case, my aforesaid executors and executrix are hereby authorized and requested to make such *equitable* distribution of the estate to which the undersigned may be entitled, as to them shall be reasonable and just. Should they disagree, they are hereby authorized and requested to submit the matter to the arbitration of mutual friends, to be chosen by the said Myra Clark **GAINES** on the one part, and the said executors on the other part. My swords of honor are to be disposed of as follows: The Virginia sword to Henry T. **GAINES**; the Tennessee sword to Edmund Pendleton **GAINES**; and the New York sword to William Wallace **WHITNEY**. A copy of my gold medal to my beloved wife, another to Rhoda, and another to Julia--[his step dughters.] Given under my had [sic] and seal at New Orleans, this 22d day of January, 1845. (Signed) EDMUND PENDLETON **GAINES**. [L. S.]" On the back is the following endorsement: January 22, 1845 10 P. M.--The within is a hasty draft of my last will and testament, which should I live I will, as soon as I have leisue tran_c_ibe and improve. (Signed) EDMUND P. **GAINES**, Maj. Gen. U. S. A., Com'g Western Division. The document was probated in the first District Court, on the 9th instant, by Messrs. **WRIGHT** and **MC MAHON**, attorneys for the executrix. The date of the will shows that the old General's dying words, "My knapsack is packed, and I am ready for the last march, were literally true in every sense.

(277) From the *New York Sun*. A death from starvation and neglect in a city filled as this is with churches and benevolent institutions, with christians and philanthropists, is calculated to strike with astonishment those who do not know how much coldness and hard-heartedness sometimes creeps into our public churches. .. Some five or six months since, a woman named Ann **BURNS**, aged 40 years, from the county of Monahan Ireland, came to this country, with her daughter Catherine **BURNS**, aged 20 years, and her niece, Rose **MORRIS**, aged 19 years, in the ship Gertrude. About the time of their arrival they were taken sick and lay in the Hospital for 15 weeks. On being allowed to come to the city, they had no friends to receive and no acquaintances to assist them; but were allowed by Mrs. **GOODMAN**, a poor woman, to sleep in the premises which she occupied in the basement of No. 49 Leonard street. Though still weak the mother went out to wash and scrub and in this way earned enough to feed herself and the two girls, both of whom had a relapse of fever. They slept together without either bedding or matress on the cords of an old beadstead which was unoccupied. Three weeks ago the mother became so sick that she could not get out of bed. Mrs. **GOODMAN** went to the police office of the 5th Ward, and was told to go to the office of the Commissionars of Emigration. On calling there she was told that the persons wanting assistance must come there, for the Commissioners would not be bothered running after them." She replied that the woman were [sic] too sick to walk, but no attention was paid to what she said. One of the girls becoming worse, Mrs. **GOODMAN** applied again to the Station House, and the girl was carried to the Cholera Hospital. She was kept there two days and then told to go somewhere else, as she had fever not cholera. One of the physicians employed by the corporation called to see the sick mother, and ascertaining that she had fever, and not cholera he refused to attend to her but tried to get Mrs. **GOODMAN** to give him one dollar or even fifty cents, and he would do something for the woman. Mrs. **GOODMAN** had no money, and he went away without doing anything. On Sunday afternoon, at 2 o'clock, the woman Ann **BURNS**, died of starvation and neglect. Mrs. **GOODMAN** went once more to the Commissioners, and after hearing the story they sent *six ship buiscuits* to the sick girl and promised to bury the mother. In the afternoon the body of the mother lay on the cords of the beadstead. One of the girls lay on the floor, and the other sat in the doorway friendless, foodless and hopeless. Whether the Coroner held an inquest on the old woman, or whether the Commissioners of Emigration or our other authorities will do any thing for the girls, we do not know, but there certainly has been a screw loose somewhere. There has been gross heartlessness and neglect of human sufferings.

28 July 1849

(278) Nag's Head Packet. The Schooner Fox, Capt. **RODGERS**, will run as a packet between Hertford, Little River and Nag's Head. She will leave Hertford every Tuesday at 8 o'clock A. M. for Nag's Head. Returning..every Monday for Hertford. She will leave Little River, (Nixonton) every Thursday at 9 o'clock A. M. ... Stephen **RODGERS**. July 28.

(279) $30 Reward. RANAWAY from the estate of John **WOOD**, dec'd., negro man **SOLOMON**. I will give a reward of thirty dollars for his apprehension and confinement in Jail, so that I get him again. **SOLOMON** is a man under the ordinary size, very dark complexion, and rather thin visage, from 30 to 35 years of age. He is well known in Eliz. City, at Mr. **POWELL**'s, on the Canal, and in Portsmouth, Va., as my carriage driver has a wife at Mr. Harvey **DAIL**s, in this County, and mother belonging to Mr. Barney **TISDALE** of E. City. It is probable that he may be lurking about those neighborhoods, and may endeavor to make his way to the Dismal Swamp. An additional Reward of Ten Dollars will be given if taken out of this State. Mary M. **WOOD**, Admintrix. Hertford, July 28, '49.

The Old North State.
Vol. 9. "Error is harmless, when truth is left free to combat it." No. 23. 24
Elizabeth City, N. C. Saturday, August 4, 1849.

(280) CHINA. "China is in a most excited condition, growing out of the probability of a war between this country and England. .. All business is suspended, and robberies by land and water are of every day occurrance. .. "The Preble, with John W. **DAVIS**, Jr., as acting lieutenant, has gone to Japan to release some American sailors that are in prison there."

(281) An Afflicted Family.--We find in the Georgetown, (D. C.) *Advocate*, the following obituary notice: "Died, at North View, near Georgetown, on the 1st inst., Susan Roles, in her 8th year; on the 6th inst., Margaret Adlum, in her 4th year; on the 9th inst. Luke White, infant son, of 5 weeks, and on the 10th inst. Mary Virginia, in her 5th year, all offsprings of Cornelius and Margaret **BARBER**."

(282) STATE OF NORTH CAROLINA. Pasquotank County Court, Spring Term, 1849. J. C. **EHRINGHAUS** adm'r. de bonus non of David **SHARBORO**' To the Court and vs Miles **SHARBORO**, Lowry **DAVIS** and wife, Elizabeth and John **SHARBORO**, and Thomas **SHARBORO**'} Petition to make real estate assetts. It appearing to the Court that Thos. and John **SHARBORO**, two of the defendants in this petition are not inhabitants of this State, it is ordered that publication be made for six weeks in the "Old North State," for said defendants to appear at the next Term of the County Court of Pleas & Quarter Sessions to be held for the County of Pasquotank, at the Court House in E. City, on the first Monday in September next, to plea, answer, or demur to said petition or Judgment, pro confesso, will be entered against them. By order of the Court, Wm. W. **GRIFFIN**, Clerk. Aug. 4.

(283) Elizabeth-City, Aug. 4, '49. .. We would call the attention of our Democratic brethren about here to the following developement lately made by Col. Thomas H. **BENTON**, the wheel-horse of Democracy in the Northern States, and would ask, can they still have the assurance to cry out that the Whigs are the enemies of the South. A slaveholding Democratic President signing a **WILMOT** Proviso Bill, and three of his Cabinet from slaveholding States acquiescing in the matter.
    STRANGE DEVELOPEMENTS.--According to advices by the, *Telegraph*, Thomas H. **BENTON** made the following very extraordinary diselosure in a speech at Lexington, Missouri on the 7th ult. "Col. **BENTON** maintained that he introduced the amendment into the Oregon bill that passed it with a **WILMOT** Proviso attached, and that *it was done to* assert the unlimited power of Congress over slavery in the territories, and *that as a naked absolute, unconditional exercise of the unlimited power of Congress over the whole subject, the Oregon bill, with the anti-slavery clause, received the approving signature of President POLK*, with THE SANCTION OF HIS WHOLE CABINET." The Cabinet, recollect, included Robert J. **WALKER**, John Y. **MASON** and Cave **JOHNSON**.

(284) STILL ANOTHER DEFALCATION. We recorded yesterday the fate of Patrick **COLLINS**, the great Cincinnati Locofoco martyr. We have, regret to say, another case of record, of one who has not been made a martyr, but who has proved his claim to that politicial distinction, by a defalcation, compaired with which, poor Patrick **COLLINS** sinks into insignificance. The case is that of Nathaniel **DEMBY**, late temporary navy agent of the United States at Marseilles, in France. He is a defaulter to the tune of $155,598 4S, and suit has been commenced against him for the amount. Mr. **DENBY** has done well. .. Mr. **DENBY** was a Virginian. He was "known" at Richmond, in the circles frequented by the resolutionists 68... In amount and magnitude, this defalcation is worthy the golden days of the Locofoco leaders, when they did things on a large scale. It would have done honor to a

(284) (Cont.) Wiley P. **HARRIS**, of Columbus. It almost approaches the magnificence of **SWARTWOUT**'s case.

(285) A singular fatality marked the recent death of two brothers in Tishemingo county, Mississippi. One, Elisha H. **RHODES**, having died, the other, Rev. James **RHODES**, went to convey the intelligence to the mother, and on the way was truck [sic] by lightning and instantly killed.

(286) THE GAMBLER'S FATE. A gentleman of the village of Patterson, (N. J. [sic] has shown us [a] five dollar bank-note of the "Northern Bank of New York," upon the back of which is writen the following: "This is my last *five*. God only knows where I will get more. I part with it as though it were my last friend. I started with $450 dollars for California, and got as far as here, and *gambled*. I need not add--*lost*. I now invoke death! Joseph **CROSS**. Fort Independence, March 14, 1849.

(287) We learn that Wm. H. **HAIGH**, Esq., has declined the appointment of District Attorney recently tendered him by the President of the United States.

(288) Married, In Pasquotank County, on 31st ult., by S. D. **GRICE**, Esq., Mr. George **JACKSON** to Miss Phebe **SCOTT**.

The Old North State.
Vol. 9. "Error is harmless, when truth is left free to combat it." No. 25.
Elizabeth City, N. C. Saturday, August 11, 1849.

(289) BURIAL OF THE DEAD. The *New York Tribune* publishes, in the proceedings of the Board of Aldermen, the following revolting description of the mode in which the dead are disposed of in **POTTER**'s field: "A communication was received from F. R. **TILLOU**, Esq., one of the Ten Governors, in relation to the burial place called **POTTER**'s Field, at **RANDALL**'s Island. .. He found that long trenches are dug--not deep, as the stratum of rock will not permit it; that in these trenches the coffins are placed one upon another till they are several feet from the ground when earth is thrown over the top and north side, leaving the south side of the coffins exposed, when another trench, parallel to them is dug, and the coffins piled in as with the others--that when he was there at least 50 coffins were uncovered at the trench on the south side. .. In the year previous to the 1st of June last, there had been 3000 interments at that place, averaging from 30 to 35 a day, and there had been 50 a day during the present month. ...

(290) OLD MEN. There are living, on Spring Creek, in this county, perhaps two of the "oldest inhabitants" in our country. Mr. Wm. **WOODY** is 111 years old, and can now "*wade and split water like a coon*," wading every branch and creek that happens to cross his path; is in good health and of a sound mind. Mr. M. **DAVIS**, his close neighbor, is 103 years old, and we understand is also in good health and spirits. ... *Highland Messenger*.

(291) Elizabeth-City, Aug. 11, '49. .. It will be seen from the advertisement of Mr. George M. **WILDER** in our paper, that he intends opening a school on the 8th October on his own responsibility. We hope he may get as many scholars as he wants. ...

(292) North Carolina Elections. As will be perceived from the *N. S. Whig*, that champion of Whig principles, Edward **STANLEY**, has been elected in the place of the Hon. Richard S. **DONNELL** who declined a re-election. .. Col. **OUTLAW**'s majority would have been still greater had it not been for the election of Clerks of the Superior and County Courts... We publish below the official vote of this District furnished us by Mr. Joshua A. **POOL**. .. **OUTLAW**. .. 4053 **PERSON**. .. 3477.

(293) FROM FLORIDA. MORE INDIAN HOSTILITIES. A ship from the *Sanannah Georgian* brings intelligence of further hostilities by the Indians in Florida.--An express had reached Pilatka, bringing information of the murder of six or seven negroes between Tampa Bay and Charlott's Harbor. .. It is said that previous to the last hostile demonstration, **BILLY BOW LEGS**, one of the principal chiefs, had been met by the United States troops from Tampa, and solemnly disclaimed a participation in the affair, charging it upon a band of outlaws of the tribe. It is said the Indians have a full supply of munitions of war, and provisions, and their numbers have been increased, probably from Alabama. Gov. **MOSELY** has issued a requisiton for a large number of volunteers. .. One hundred men will be mustered into service at Jacksonville, by Col. **PONS** tomorrow, and double that..are in readiness. ...

(294) Major James M. **SCANTLAND**, of Mexican War celebrity, died at the Red Sulphur Springs, Smith county, Tenn., on the 22d inst. Major S., says the *Nashville Union*, gallantly planted the first American flag on the Mexican fort at Monterey, and at Cerro Gordo shot through the head, and at the time, it was thought was impossible for him to survive. He however, partially recovered from the wound which has finally terminated [in] death.

11 August 1849

(295) English & Classical Institute. The Subscriber having now disconnected with the Elizabeth City Academy, the charge of which he has had for four years past, and having been solicited by numerous citizens of this place will open on the first Monday in October next an English and Classical Institute for the instruction of a limited number of Young Ladies and Gentlemen in all the various branches of English and Classical Literature. .. The Principal is determined that the instruction shall be *most thorough*..in such a way as to exercise the understanding of the student, rather than to burden his memory. .. Application may be made to the Principal at Nag's Head Hotel or to J. M. **WHEDBEE**, Esq., E. City, from whom all necessary information may be obtained.

(296) NOTICE. The undersigned having sold out his entire stock in trade, tenders his thanks to the public generally, for the liberal patronage they have been pleased to give him, and recommends to their notice Mr. Wm. B. **BURGESS** his successor in business, in whom they will find the same liberality in trade. The undersigned would further say that he can at all times be found at home ready to receive and settle with those wishing to pay him any balance that may be due from them to him, and being in such a state of health as may make it necessary for him to leave this place, he earnestly solicits their early attention in this matter. Very Respectfully, Zion **CULPEPPER**. Aug 11

(297) Nag's Head Packet. The Schooner FOX, Capt. **RODGERS**, will run certain as follows: From Hertford every Tuesday and Saturday. From Nag's Head for Hertford every Monday and Friday, at 8 o'clock a. m. From Little River every Thursday, and from Nag's Head for Little River every Wednesday at 8 o'clock a. m. Stephen **RODGERS**. Aug. 11

(298) Notice! A general meeting of the subscribers to the Orapeake Canal and Turnpike, will take place at the Store of Isacc S. **HARRELL** & Co., in the County of Gates, on the 23rd day of August next, at 10 o'clock A. M. for the purpose of electing a President and Directors of the Company, and for performining other duties, which may be requisite to carry into execution the above contemplated scheme of improvement. Books will continue open to receive further subscriptions to the work. All persons interested are particularly requested to attend. Isaac S. **HARRELL**, John C. **GORDON**, Burwell **BROTHERS**.} Directors. Gates County, N. C. Aug. 11, 1849.

The Old North State.
Vol. 9. "Error is harmless, when truth is left free to combat it." No. 26.
Elizabeth City, N. C. Saturday, August 18, 1849.

(299) From the *Baltimore Patriot*. PROGRESS OF GENERAL TAYLOR. .. We left Baltimore at nine on Friday morning. In the car specially appropriated by the Baltimore and Su-queanna [sic] Rail Road Company for the accommodation of the President and his company, we noticed Dr. **WOOD** (Gen. **TAYLOR**'s son-in-law.) Mayor **STANSBURY**, Col. **KANE**, also Messrs. **YELLOTT, BARNUM, POUDER, MC CORMICK, HERR** and **COCKEY**, a committee of Directors of the Rail Road Company.--Mr. **MADDOX**, our Post-master, Mr. **FENDALL** of Washington. J. H. Clay **MUDD**, Esq., Col. Wesley **COWLES**, Judge **NESBIT**, R. Taylor **ALISON**, Esq., Messrs. Henry **SNYDER**, Elias **WARE, GRINNELL, WEIRMAN, MC CUBBIN**, and several other gentlemen of our city. .. Messrs. **BARNITZ** and **MORRIS**, of the York Committee of Reception, were also on board. .. At the Pennsylvania Line, we were met by Governer **JOHNSTON**, accompanied by a large number of distinguished citizens of the Keystone State. Byrexues [sic] of Maryland Committee, Coleman **YELLOTT**, Esq. introduced Gen. **TAYLOR** in a brief address, and concluded by "suerendering [sic] him to the hospitalities of Pennsylvania." .. At Wrightsville and Columbia, on the Susquehanna, the General was met by thousands, of both sexes and of all ages. .. The train reached Lancaster about eight o'clock, P. M. Amid the roaring of cannon, strains of martial music and waiving of handkerchiefs, Gen. **TAYLOR** was escorted to **KENDING**'s Hotel. Here the Honorable Thaddeus **STEVENS** welcomed him, in the name of the people of Lancaster. ...

(300) Elizabeth-City, Aug 18, '49. .. NORTH CAROLINA. We are proud to announce now for a certainty, that the *good*, the *glorious* Old North State will return to the next Congress of the United States her six strong and able Whigs. .. The delegation from North Carolina in the next Congress will be composed of District 1--T. L. **CLINGMAN**, Whig. " 2--Jos. P. **CALDWELL**, Whig. " 3--Edmund **DEBERRY**, Whig. " 4--Augustine **SHEPPARD**, Whig. " 5--Abraham W. **VENABLE**, D. " 6--J. R. J. **DANIEL**, Dem. " 7--W. S. **ASHE**, Dem. " 8--Edward **STANLY**, Whig. " 9--David **OUTLAW**, Whig. ...

(301) AFFRAY IN NORTH CAROLINA. The *Danville Register* of Friday learns that a dangerous affray occured at Germantown, N. C. one day during the previous week, which came near resulting in the death of several persons. Some months ago a hoax was sent to the *Greensboro' Patriot*, (and copied from that into the *Register*) representing the marriage of Dr. Madison R. **FONTAINE**, of Germantown, N. C., with a person whose name we have forgotten. Dr. F. was

18 August 1849

(301) (Cont.) speaking of the shameless trick, on one occasion, in the presence of Dr. **WHITE**, residing in the same county, when the latter gentlemen made some remark which induced Dr. **F.** to inflict several blows on Dr. **WHITE**, but the parties were separated without much damage or apprehension as to the consequences. Soon after this occurrence Dr. **WHITE** made a visit to his native county of Appromattox in this State, and while there he received a letter from Germantown, from some friend, reminding him that it was absolutely necessary for him to avenge the insult said to have been received from Dr. **F.** in the first attack. Dr. **WHITE** and his brother then armed themselves and went to Germantown with a vew to cowhide Dr. **FONTAINE**. Arrived at Germantown they alighted and went immediately into the tavern where Dr. **FONTAINE** was seated, and commenced the attack, one holding a revolver to his breast while the other inflicted blows with the cowhide. Dr. **F**, promptly rose and resented the attack, but the bystanders interfered and separated the combatants--Dr. **WHITE** then disappeared and so did Dr. **FONTAINE**, as is supposed in pursuit of his assailant, neither of whom, says our informant, has since been heard from. In the meantime Dr. W's brother was arrested and committed to jail, where he remained several days, but that finally gave bail for his appearance at Court. The news of this difficulty soon reached the ears of Dr. **FONTAINE**'s brothers, Messrs. William and Chas. **FONTAINE**, of Henry, who immediately repaired to Germantown to defend and protect their brother. Arrived at Germantown they found the two doctors were absent, but Mr. **WHITE**, (whom neither of them had ever seen,) still there. At their fist [sic] meeting, however, Mr. Charles **FONTAINE** and Mr. **WHITE** mutually recognized each other by their likeness to their brothers, the doctors; and no sooner had this recognition been made than Mr. **FONTAINE** presented a pistol at Mr. **WHITE**, and was in the act of firing when **WHITE** knocked the pistol upward, the ball penetrating his hand without other damage. **WHITE** then retreated through the tavern, **FONTAINE** bursting three caps at him in his flight. The Messrs. **FONTAINE** were then arrested and held to bail.--Va. Paper.

(302) DEATH OF ALBERT **GALLATIN**. NEW YORK, August 13. The venerable Albert **GALLATIN** died this morning, at the advanced age of 90 years. Thomas G. **WOODWARD**, editor of the *New Haven Courier*, died yesterday at New Haven, Connecticut, age 61 years. He formerly conducted a paper at Charleston, S. C.

(303) Married, by Rev. C. R. **HENDRICKSON**, Mr. John S. **WAUGH** to Miss Sarah E. **HARNEY**, all of this place.

(304) OBITUARY. .. On Tuesday, the 7th inst., at Currituck Court House, about 5 o'clock, P. M. Martha, the daughter of B. T. **SIMMONS**, departed this life after an illness of five days. She had just returned from school with her mind richly stored with useful knowledge, and adorned with all the charms of "sweet sixteen." In her were cherished the hope and delight of a devoted & affectionate father, and relatives. ... Currituck co., N. C., Aug. 1849.

(305) Valuable Farm for Lease. The large and valuable Farm belonging to the estate of Arthur **TAYLOR**, dec'd. WILL BE LEASED, To the highest bidder, for a term of years on Wednesday, the 5th of September, proximo, at the *Beacon* Office News Room, on Wide Water street, in the city of Norfolk, at 12 o'clock. This Farm is beautifully situated near the Village of Kempsville, in this county of Princess Anne, about nine miles from Norfolk City, and about three miles from the Chesapeake Bay... It contains 742 acres of land, 300 well cleared, and has been for the past 8 or 10 years under the masterly management of a skilful farmer. Persons desirous to lease this Farm, will of course visit the premises, before the 5th of September. Further description therefore is unnecessary. Terms will be made known on the day of leasing. Thomas C. **TABB**, Attorney for the Estate of A. **TAYLOR**. Aug. 18.

(306) Family Groceries. The undersigned having taken the store formerly occupied by Zion **CULPEPPER**, Esq., on road street, opposite Mr. T. R. **COBB**'s has, and intends keeping constantly on hand, a large and well assorted stock of FAMILY GROCERIES. ... Wm. B. **BURGESS**. E. City, Aug. 18th, 1849.

(307) Fishery for Lease. The subscriber will Lease to the highest bidder, before the Court-House door in Edenton, on Monday of October Court, (unless previously disposed of by private contract.) His Fishery on the Albemarle Sound, Known as *North Bend*, 12 miles below Edenton, and 3 above Yeopim River. He will at the same time sell the SEINE, BOATS and APPARATUS necessary to conducting the business. Also, 1200 bushels Turks Island Salt, now in the salt-house, and about 300 BARRELS under shelter. The terms will be made known on the day... D. M. **WRIGHT**. Aug. 18

(308) FARM FOR SALE. The subsrciber will sell that well known Farm in **BOYD**'s Neck, called the John M. **SKINNER** farm, containing 310 Acres, with 320 thousand [sic] in good cultivation; with a large and commodious 2 story dwelling and every other necessary building attached to it. It is one of the best located Farms in the lower part of the county, bordering on Little River, and but a very short distance to cart grain. It will be sold a bargain if early application is made to Wm. **SHANNON**, E. City, or the subscriber, Francis **FLETCHER**, **BOYD**'s Neck. Aug. 18, 1849.

25 August 1849

The Old North State.
Vol. 9. "Error is harmless, when truth is left free to combat it." No. 27.
Elizabeth City, N. C. Saturday, August 25, 1849.

(309) From the *Republic* of the 15th instant. The Passport Case. The *Union* joined in the cry of the Abolitionists against the Secretary of State for having "recently refused a passport to a colored man about to visit Europe." Now this falsehood has been exposed and put down so effectually in the northern papers, that even the Abolitionists have nearely ceased to reiterate it. .. They pretended that Mr. **MCLANE** in 1834 had granted one passport to Robert **PURVIS**, and that Mr. **FORSYTH** in 1836 had granted another to the Rev. Mr. **WILLIAMS**, and that they were both colored men. On examining the records of the Department, it was ascertained that they were both represented to the Department and recommended at the time the passports were given, *to be white men*; and the old passport clerks--Mr. **REDDAL** and Mr. **CHEW**, the former the passport clerk under Mr. **BUCHANAN**, and the latter the passport clerk under Mr. **FORSYTH**, and who are still clerks in the State Department..both bear testimony that no passport was ever granted knowingly by any Secretary, within their experience, to any free negro or colored person. .. We have examined a copy of a letter addressed by Mr. **BUCHANAN** to Mr. George D. **COOPER**, of New York city, dated November 6, 1847, in which Mr. **BUCHANAN** refuses passport to William P. **POWELL**, a man "of a mulatto color, but of Indian extraction," and informs Mr. **COOPER** "that the Department can have no authority to issue it." ...

(310) To Drive Away Rats.--Mr. Charles **PIERCE**, of Milton, pounded up potash and strewed it all around their holes, and rubbed some on the sides of the boards and under parts where they came through. The next night he heard a squeaking among them, which he supposed was from the caustic nature of the potash that got among their hair or in their bare feet. They disappeared, and he has not been troubled with them since that time, which was nearly a year ago.--*Boston Cultivator*.

(311) Elizabeth-City, Aug 25, '49. .. California Comforts.--Seth **BRYDEN** writes to the *Newark Advertiser* in this manner: "Some of our party talk of returning, and probably will, if low water does not materially increase our gains. This work is ruinous to clothes, and worse to one's temper. Handkerchiefs and thin clothes are of no account here; the prevailing costume consists of a hat, shirt pants and boots, with a pair of pistols and a rifle, and a blanket to roll one's self in, in the night; we do not shave, of course, and look like a parcel of ruffians. I have, perhaps, given you some idea of our situation though nothing short of actual sight can do it justice."

(312) Peter W. **HINTON**, GENERAL COMMISSION AND FORWARDING MERCHANT, No. 10, Roanoke Square, NORFOLK, VA..

(313) Nag's Head House & Lot for Sale. The subscriber offers for sale his House & Lot at Nag's Head. Also a lot of furniture in the House--Apply to P. W. **HINTON**, Norfolk, Va. aug 25

(314) TO MESSES FITTING OUT. The undersigned are prepared to furnish Messes, with all the various articles in the Hardware and Cutlery Line wanted on shipboard, at..very lowest prices. ... E. P. **TABB** & Co. Head of Market Square, Norfolk, Va. aug 25

(315) COMBS, COMBS. Just received by the subscriber a large assortment of the latest style of fashionable Shell and Tuck Combs. Also, received some new-style Ear-Rings, Pins, Bracelets and Finger Rings, all of which are for sale by J. M. **FREMAN**, Jeweller, Norfolk, Va.

(316) NOTICE. On the 30th Inst. will be sold on the sea beach, opposite Kittyhawk Bay, the Schooner ALGERNON of North Yarmouth, materials and cargo, consisting of Cotton, Nuts and Hydes. Sold by the Commissioner under the direction of the Capt. Isaac **TILLETT**, Ag't. aug 25

The Old North State.
Vol. 9. "Error is harmless, when truth is left free to combat it." No. 28.
Elizabeth City, N. C. Saturday, September 1, 1849.

(317) Elizabeth-City, Sept. 1, '49. .. TO OUR PATRONS. Not having as much time to devote to our paper as we would wish and desire, and not wanting to be behind our brethren of the press in the State, it is with pleasure we inform the patrons of the "Old North State" that we have secured the services of Mr. George M. **WILDER**, (a gentleman well known to our community,) as Assistant Editor. He is a sound and thoroughgoing Whig...

1 September 1849

(318) The Hon. D. M. **BARRINGER**, Minister to Spaine and the Hon. Wm. C. **RIVES**, Minister to France sailed from N. York in the steamer America on the 22d inst. The correspondent of the *Baltimore Patriot*, in speaking of them says: .. Among those who accompanied Messrs **RIVES** and **BARRINGER** to the America and there took leave of them and their families, was the Hon. Abbott **LAWRENCE**, who leaves shortly on his mission to England. Among the passengers of the America were Mr. **CORCORAN**, the Banker at Washington.

(319) The Illinois Senatorship. We learn from the *Missouri Republican* that Hon. Archibald **WILLIAMS**, a learned lawyer and prominent actor in the Constitutional Convention, has given his opinion that Gov. **FRENCH** has the power, and that it is his duty, under the circumstances, to appoint a U. S. Senator for Illinois in place of Gen. **SHIELDS**, and the expense of an extra session of the General Assembly is entirely useless. ...

(320) Capt. Dan Drake **HENRIE** Died at the Hospital of the Sisters of Charity, in St. Louis, on the 16th of August, Inst. He was born at Cincinnatti, and was thirty-five years old at his death. Captain **HENRIE** was one of the most celebrated of the Texas Rangers. The best part of his life was passed in fighting with the Mexicans, either in the quarrel of Texas or of the United States. Having served in previous campaigns, under other officers he was member of the famous **MIER** expedition, in 1842, under General **SOMERVILLE**, and when that leader turned back from the Rio Grande, in compliance with orders from President **HOUSTON**, Captain **HENRIE** was one of those who crossed the Rio Gande, and made the attack upon **MIER**, under General Thomas J. **GREEN**. This attack was as rash and foolish, as it was daring, and the whole expedition was taken captive by General **AMPUDIA**. Some of their companions having been shot, General **GREEN**, **HENRIE**, and others were taken to the city of Mexico, and were afterwards sent to the castle of Perote, where they were imprisoned for a considerable time, and were treated with much rigor.--Their release was effected through the exertions of the American Minister. Soon after the commencement of the war, Captain **HENRIE** was sent into Texas by the Government, to serve in Gen. **TAYLOR**'s division as interpreter. He was ordered to accompany the scouting party of Major **GAINS** and Captain C. M. **CLAY**, which was captured at Encarnation a few days before the battle of Buena Vista.--The escape of Captain **HENRIE** from the Mexican force by which the detachment had been taken prisoners, has often been described, and was one of the most daring feats of the war.--After his escape, **HENRIE** returned to Washington, and was chosen captain of a company in Colonel **HUGHES**'s battalion of volunteers, in which command he served untill the end of the war. Congress, at its last session, passed a bill granting him $2,000 in money and a section of land, partly in consideration of his gallant conduct and partly as compensation for specific services, payment for which was not authorized by previous laws.

(321) DIED, Near Williamston, on the 9th inst., Mrs. Francis H. **ELLISON**, wife of William J. **ELLISON**, Esq. By this sudden and unexpected stroke there has been taken from the midst of a large and deeply afflicted circle of relatives and friends, one, who was tenderly and justly beloved by all who knew her. As a wife, mother, relative and as a friend--she was devoted and warm. ... Williamston, Aug. 15th, 1849.

(322) New Carriage Manufactory. The Subscriber respectfully informs the inhabitants of Pasquotank and adjoining counties, that he has opened a Factory in the Brick Building on Road Street opposite the Mansion House for the Manufacturing of Light Buggys', Rockaways, Phaetons, Sulkies, &c., in the most fashionable styles, and of the very best materials... ... John **DOES**. Sept. 1, 1849.

(323) Elizabeth City Academy. The Fall Session of this Institution will commence on Monday the 16th inst. Those desirous of entering their children would do well to make early application to W. W. **GRIFFIN**, Esq., or to the subscriber as the number of scholars will be limited. Terms. Elementary English Branches, per quarter $5 00 Higher " " 7 50 Latin, French or Spanish 10 00 The Trustees, and parents and Guardians of children are respectfully requested to be present at the opening of the School. S. D. **POOL**, Principal. Sept. 1.

(324) CURRITUCK COUNTY. Court of Equity, Spring Term, 1849. Sarah **HUMPHRIES** vs. David **HUMPHRIES**,} Petition for Divorce. It appearing to the satisfaction of the Court that David **HUMPHRIES**, the defendant in this case is not an inhabitant of this State, and that Subpoenas commanding his appearance before said Court to answer Complainant's Bill have issued twice from this Court, and have been returned not to be found, and proclimation at the Cout House door having been made for him to appear and answer and he having failed so to do, it is ordered by the Court that publication be made in the *Old North State*, a paper published in Elizabeth City, for the space of six weeks, commanding the said David **HUMPHRIES**, to appear at the next Term of this Court, to be held for the county of Currituck, on the sixth Monday after the fourth Monday in September next, to plead, answer, or demur, to Complanant's Bill, or judgment will be taken pro confesso. Witness, B. M. **BAXTER** Clerk and Master of said County, at office, the 6th Monday after the 4th Monday in March. Anno Domini 1849. Sept. 1.

1 September 1849

(325) New & Fashionable Tailoring ESTABLISHMENT. The undersigned being determind to settle in Elizabeth City, and having taken the well known stand on Road Street next door to the store of Mr. Barney **TISDALE**, would most respectfully tender his services to the citizens of Elizabeth City and the surrounding country. He would here state that he has had two years experience as *Cutter in the Large and Fashionable Establishment of H. F. LOUDON*. ... James B. **DYER**. sep 1 1849.

(326) *The Old North State.*
Vol. 9. "Error is harmless, when truth is left free to combat it." No. 29.
Elizabeth City, N. C. Saturday, September 8, 1849.
Published every Saturday, by Wm. E. **MANN**, Proprietor. G. M. **WILDER**, Assistant Editor.

(327) Daniel **WEBSTER**--Marshfield. *Correspondenze of the Cincinnati Gazettt.* Revre House, Boston, July 24, 1849. There is a portion of the Commonwealth of Massachusetts which juts out into the ocean, not unlike a boot in shape, as delineated on maps. This portion of the "Old Bay State" has enduring historical associations... .. With the limits of this "first settlement," and within a few miles of "Plymouth Rock,"..are the Farm And Home Of Daniel **WEBSTER**. .. The "farm" and dwelling place of Mr. **WEBSTER**, is situated in the southeast part of the town of Marshfield, bounded on the east by the ocean, and contains over *fifteen hundred acres of land*. Daniel **WEBSTER** was born in Salisbury, New Hampshire, January 18, 1782, and is, of course, now in the sixty-eighth year of his age; yet he has the physical strength and activity of most men at the age of fifty. .. Mr. **WEBSTER** has but one child living--Mr. Fletcher **WEBSTER**--who has a very fine country residence overlooking the sea, adjoining his father's estate, and about one mile distant from the mansion house. A daughter and son, Mrs. **APPLETON** and Captain Edward **WEBSTER**, died within the past year...

Mr. **CALHOUN** on his Plantation. .. His residence is about four miles from Pendleton, an old town in Pickens district, about 250 miles from Charleston. .. We reached Fort Hill about two o'clock P. M. It was nearly the dinner hour. I was introduced to his family, which at that time consisted of Mrs. **CALHOUN**, his youngest daughter, and the three youngest sons. Mr. **CALHOUN** has seven children--the eldest, Andrew, is a planter in Alabama; the nex [sic,] Patrick, is a captain in the army, and stationed near New Orleans, the eldest daughter is in Europe, the wife of our Charge at Belgium. Mrs. **CALHOUN** is just such a wife as a man like Mr. **CALHOUN** should have, sensible, domestic and industrious..Cornelia, the daughter at home, is a most affectionate companion for the mother. Of the three sons who were at home I must make some mention. John is a physician, and was married shortly after I left to the daughter of a near neighbor; James, the next, is a calm, quiet, thinking young man of 20, and in many respects strongly resembles his father. Willie is the youngest of all Mr. **CALHOUN**'s children, about 18 years of age, and the pet of all. The two last named are students in South Carolina college, and at home during the vacation. .. There are, perhaps, seventy or eighty negroes on and about the place. The largest part of his negroes are in Alabama, where Mr. **CALHOUN** owns a large plantation, which is under the management of his son Andrew..who has the reputation of being one of the best cotton planters in Alabama. .. He has an overseer, Mr. **FREDERICKS**, who superintends his planting interest--a very intelligent and faithful man. The farm is a model farm. It consists of about 1000 acres, 450 of which are in cultivation. .. Mr. **CALHOUN** has some very old slaves on his plantation. One old negress that I saw, Menemin **CALHOUN**, (by the way, all the negroes on his estate are called by his name in the neighborhood,) is over 112 years old. She has 63 living descendants on his plantation, who take care of the old dame. Her husband lived to a very old age; his name was Polydore. Both were brought from Africa, and have lived with the **CALHOUN**s for a century. The negroes on this place pay as much respect to the old negress as if she was a queen.

(328) The *Winchester Virginian* represents that the arrangements for public ceremonies in that town, on Saturday last, in honor of Mr. **POLK**, were sadly frustrated by rain, which fell "from day-light till the afternoon in a steady and unrelenting stream." Mr. Thos. T. **FAUNTLEROY**, however, delivered the eulogy in one of the Churches, and the *virginian* gives his effort high praise.

(329) Elizabeth-City, Sept. 8, '49. .. DENTISTRY. All who wish anything done in the above line, will see from the Advertisement of Mr. J. B. **GODWIN**, that he intends remaining here and in the vicinity for some weeks. We have heard very favorable accounts of the gentleman, as a skillful operator, and wish him success. Dr. E. C. **ROBINSON** will also, (as will be seen by his Advertisement) be in this section in October next. Dr. **ROBINSON** is well known to the public...

(330) EXTENSIVE ROBBERY. A bold robbery was committed at Congress Hall, Rochester, (N. Y.) on Thursday nighs [sic] last by two persons who registered their names as Charles **THOMAS** and W. **ANDERSON**. During the night the rooms of the lodgers were entered and the pockets and trunks of the inmates rifled of their contents. A Mr. **DARRICUTT** was robbed of two gold watches and jewelry belonging to his wife valued at $200. Mr. **VANDENBERG**, a cigar pedlar, had his pockets rifled of money, notes, drafts, &c. $1,200.--The room occupied by Rev. Mr. **SMITH** was entered, and a small sum of money taken. ...

(331) THE GREAT RUSSIAN RAILWAY. The Emperor of Russia is a great despot, but he is a man of enterprise, and has

8 September 1849

(331) (Cont.) engaged in an undertaking which will be of immense advantage to his subjects. It is the construction of a double-track railway, four hundred and twenty miles in length, and intend to connect the great capitals of his empire. It is flattering to American skill and talent that he selected an American (Col. **WHISTLER**) to have the work constructed--and, on the decease of that able engineer, chose a successor from the same country. *The American Railroad Journal* contains various interesting particulars in relation to this great work, some of which were communicated by Mr. William I. **WINANS**, of Baltimore, who was in Russia a short time prior to the death of Colonel **WHISTLER**... *Baltimore Clipper*.

(332) Floogging In The Navy.--A correspondent of the *New York Journal of Commerce*, calling the attention of the public to the necessity of abolishing flogging, and of making the necessary movements to accomplish that object at the next session of Congress, says: The recent letter, published in..our papers, from the pen of "Old Ironsides," as he is familiarly termed, Commodore Charles **STEWART**, is honorble to the head and heart of that brave and able Commander... .. He says, if discipline cannot be preserved without resorting to these cruelties, the wisest policy would be to break up the navy, save the millions drained from the Treasury for its support extinguish its cruelty and oppression, and put an end to a service so wholly and completely artistocratic, that it has not even under monarchy, its equal...

(333) A New Panorama is now under way by Peter **GRAIN**, Sr., which will illustrate the beautiful scenery of the Hudson River, together with that of the James River, Va. Mr. **GRAIN** is one of our finest scenic artists... The Panorama is in a state of forwardness, and will be exhibited for the first time, at the Chinese Museum Monday evening, Aug. 27th. Phil. paper.

(334) UNUSUAL FECUNDITY.--The wife of Job **BURNAP** of the town of Nanticoke in this county, presented her husband on Saturday last with three children, two boys and one girl. This event is owing in part to the auspicious vicinity of the delightful Nanticoke Springs. We have not learned wether they are considered Job's Comforters.--*Binghamton Rep.*

(335) The Governorship Of Oregon Declined.--The *Louisville Courier* learns from reliable authority that the Hon. J. G. **MARSHALL**, of Madison, declines the appointment of Govenor of Oregon, recently tendered him by the President.

(336) J. B. **GODWIN**, Dentist. Having returned to Elizabeth City with the intention of remaining some moths, offers his services to the public, in all the departments of his profession. He will perform all operations on the Teeth, such as Extracting, Filing, Plugging and scaling, and will insert INCORRUPTIBLE ARTIFICIAL TEETH, upon Pivot or plate, from one to an entire set, upon the most improved principle, and in a manner, for beauty and comfort, that cannot fail to please. Particular attention given to regulating all defects in the growth of the Teeth of Children. All operations warranted to remain perfect. He can be found at the office of Dr. S. D. **GRICE**, or at the Mansion House, room No. 5. E. City, Sept. 8, 1849.

(337) E. C. **ROBINSON**, SURGEON DENTIST RESPECTFULLY informs the Ladies and Gentlemen of Camden, Pasquotank and Perquimans Counties that he will visit each county during their Superior Courts in October. Norfolk, Sept. 8th, 1849.

(338) CISTERN PUMPS, LEAD PIPE, We keep on hand a full stock of the Patent Premium Pumps for Cisterns--Also, Lead Pipes of all the sizes, which we sell very low. E. P. **TABB** & Co. Norfolk, VA. sep 1

(339) J. M. **FREEMAN**, Jeweller. Has just been put in possession of a large assortment of GOLD, ENAMEL, TURQUOISE AND STONE SET Belt Buckles... ALSO, Silver, Jet Steel Buckles, Gold Guards, Bosom Buttons, Pins and Ear Rings, together with a new lot of Silver and Shell Combs, all of which will be sold low. Norfolk, Va. sep 1

The Old North State.
Vol. 9. "Error is harmless, when truth is left free to combat it." No. 30.
Elizabeth City, N. C. Saturday, September 15, 1849.

(340) Elizabeth-City, Sept. 15, '49. .. There was brought to our office a day or two since by an individual residing near Cape Hatteras the following..which is said to have come ashore in a bottle. We cannot vouch for its correctness... "The Brig Richmond of Halifax is now in the heaviest gale of wind ever experienced on the high seas. She has lost both masts close off from the deck, and is expected to go down every moment having a hole stove in her bows by the masts bumping against her. We cannot survive more than one hour. .. We have made rafts and intend to try our fate for while there is life there is hope. Hoping this will be received, and our melancholy fate and (that is to be) be reported silently and carefully to our friends; and that you may put this in the paper to let the owners Messrs. **FAIRBANKS** and **ALLISON** known the loss of the vessel." I remain, Your affectionate friend, Capt. George M. **VERNUM**. P. S.--The Sharks are at this moment in numbers about us. ... Good bye, Yours.

(341) *Another Windfall.*--We learn from a south-western paper, that proposals have been issued for a meeting or mass convention at Nashville, Tenn., to be held on the 15th inst., of the heirs of William **JENNINGS**, Esqr., who is said to have died intestate, in Suffolk, England, in 1776, leaving an immense property, now estimated at some $40,000,000--consisting of divers bank and other stocks, mortgages and landed property, &c. still unsettled, and lying in the hands of the Brittish Government, subject to the claim and control of the heirs. Most of the claimants reside in Tennessee, Mississippi, Virginia and Indiana. ...

(342) *Arrest of an American Citizen in Ireland.*--Mr. Charles **WHITNEY**, the elocutionist, has been travelling through Great Britain, delivering lectures on American oratory in Dublin, Belfast and other places. In Dublin his lectures produced much enthusiasm, and on introducing the speech of Patric **HENRY** much excitement prevailed among his hearers. When he came to the words "We *must* fight! I repeat it Sir, we must fight!" An appeal to arms and to the God of Hosts is all that is left for us!" the noted juror on **DUFFY**'s trail [sic], Mr. **BURKE**, stood up and exclaimed, "I'm of that man's opinions," which had the effect of raising the entire assembly enmasse, whose cheering shook the walls of the Rutnuda [sic.] He was subsequently, he says, arrested for sedition, and had his choice to go to jail or give bonds to leave Ireland at once. He did the latter, and is now in England. *American.*

(343) Dissolution of the Union. From the address of Dr. George W. **BETHUNE**, lately delivered at Cambridge, (Mass.) we extract the following paragraph: "Suppose, for one melancolly moment, that this beautiful economy of exchange were broke up; that the Western valleys were shut out from the sea by adverse Government, that those on the cost were hemmed into their own narrow limits by hostile forts along the mountain ridges; that betwen the north and South there were neither commercial nor moral sympathy; that at every State line passports demanded and a tariff set--who must not shrink from describing the terrible consequences; the stagnation of trade, the silence of brotherly counsel; the constant feuds; the multiplication of armies; the Cain-like exterminating war... Oh that those who, for any reason talk lightly of disolving this Union, would consider the immensely greater evils such a rupture would inevitable cause... *R. Times.*

(344) EDUCATION. The undersigned trustees of the Perquimans Academy, located in Hertford, beg leave to announce to the public that having procured the services of efficient and experienced Teachers; this institution will be open for the reception of scholars in both the Male and Female departments on the first Monday of October. Jos. M. **COX**, Francis **NIXON**, Thos. F. **JONES**, Trustees. Sept. 15, 1849.

(345) English & Classical Institute, ELIZABETH CITY, N. C. The Fall Term in this Institution will commence the first Monday in October. The Principal has furnished his School Room with every convenience, and in the most attractive style. .. A few vacancies remain to be filled. Application may be made to the subscriber from whom any information desired may be obtained. G. M. **WILDER**, Principal. Sept. 15, 1849.

(346) O Yes! O Yes! O Yes! *All ye that hunger come and buy if you have the Money.* The following articles are just received from N. York. Fresh and good Butter, Cheese, Lard, Pork, Onions, Codfish, Scotch Herrings 75 cents per box, Rice, Crushed Sugar, Soda Crackers, Pilot Bread, Coffee, Tea, Extra sup. Flour, Cotton, Yarn..Baskets, Oranges, and other articles too tedious to mention in one advertisement. Wm. **HALSEY**. Sept. 15.

(347) Notice! The undersigned would here beg leave to those who owe him, that they would confer a great favor upon him by coming forward and settling the same, as he is desirous of closing his present business this fall as near as possible, at the same time very much in need of the funds to meet liabilities that must be met, therefore do unto me as ye would I should do unto you under the same circumstances. Wm. **HALSEY**. Sept. 15.

(348) NOTICE. The Subscriber has on hand and for sale eight hundred yards of Seine, together with Rope and Cork enough to fit her for hauling. Also two Batteaus and forty excellent fish stands, all of which (except the batteaus) have been used one Spring only. Jos. **COMMANDER**. Sept. 15

(349) Norfolk Female Institute. Principals: Rev. Aristides S. **SMITH**, A. M. Rev. Leondias [sic] L. **SMITH**, A. M. H. **MAGNIN**, A. M., Professor of Modern Languages. .. This Institution will be opened on MONDAY, the first of October, in the large and beautiful establishment commonly known as **RILEY**'s Gardens. The ample graunds attached to this building, and its healthy and retired situation render it admirably suited for a Female Seminary. .. The branches taught are Reading, Writing, Mental and Written Arithmetic, English Grammar, Ancient and Modern Georgeraphy [sic] (with the use of globes,) History, Rhetoric, Botany, Animal and vegetable Physiology, and Chemistry, illustrated by experiments, Astronomy, Geology, Political Economy, Algebra, Geometry, Natural Theology, Evidences of Christianity, Biblical Antiquities, Ancient and Modern Languages, Music on the Harp, Piano and Guitar, Drawing and Painting, and Ornamental Needle Work. TERMS--Per Session of

15 September 1849

(349) (Cont.) Five Months. Tuition, according to advancement, $10 & $25 French, Spanish and Italian (each,) $10 Music on..Harp, Piano & Guitar (each,) $30 Use of instruments (for practising,) $5 Drawing and painting $10 Ornamental Needle Work, $10 Board (including bed, bedding lights and fuel,) $75 Washing, per month, $1 50 Boarders are required to furnish their own Towels, and every article of Clothing must be distinctly marked with the owner's name. Sept. 15, 1849.

(350) IN EQUITY. Malachi **KITE**, per Guardian to the Court, and vs. Joseph **KITE**, et als.} Petition to sell land for Division. It appearing upon satisfactory evidence that Joseph Eamin, and Susan **KITE**, the defendants are not inhabitants of this State, and publication being desired by the petitioners. The said defendants are hereby notified to attend at the next Term of the superior Court of Equity to be held for the County of Camden on the fifth Monday after the fourth Monday in September next, and shew cause if any they have why the prayer of the Petitioners should not be granted, or on failure thereof, Petitioners' prayer will be granted and sale decreed. Joseph P. **GORDON**, Clerk and Master of the said Court at Office at Camden the fifth Monday after the fourth Monday in March, Anno Domini, 1849. Test, Joseph P. **GORDON**, C. & M. sept 13, 1849.--sep 15

(351) Table and Small Cutlery, Direct from **RODGERS** & SONS. SHEFFIELD, ENGLAND. The subscribers have recently opened an invoice of Cutlery from the above celebrated makers, comprising the usual varieties of IVORY, WHITE BUCK, COCOA, AND BLACK HORN HANDLE KNIVES AND FORKS, in setts and dozens, Knives without Forks, Carving Knives and Forks, Table Steels, 1, 2, 3 and 4 blade Pocket Knives, Ladies highly pollished Steel Scissors, Needles, &c. They invite purchasers to examine. E. P. **TABB** & Co. Hardware Importers, head of the Square, Norfolk, Va. sep 1

The Old North State.
Vol. 9. "Error is harmless, when truth is left free to combat it." No. 31.
Elizabeth City, N. C. Saturday, September 22, 1849.

(352) *"THE PLOUGH, THE LOOM, AND THE ANVIL."*--This work, devoted to agriculture, is published monthly in Philadelphia, at $3 for a single subscription, or at $2 for clubs of five and over. The proprietors and conductors of the publication are the Messrs. J. S. **SKINNER** & Son. .. Mr. **SKINNER** has devoted more than thirty years of his active life to unceasing labors in promoting the interest and enlightening the mind of the farmer, and may be truly said to be an able veteran in the cause. He established the first agricultural paper ever published in the country, and..yet, as is the case with most public benefactors, he has not enriched himself. The undersigned, however, make no claims upon the charities of the farmers of Massachusetts..but they do feel constrained, by a desire to aid the cause of agriculture and promote the welfare of their brethren of the plough and the followers of other industrial pursuits, to urge themselves of the light which wisdom and practical experience are shedding upon their path through the pages of *"The Plough, the Loom, and the Anvil."* .. Most earnestly, then, do the undesigned commend to the farmers and manufacturers of Massachusetts and of New England, the perusal and patronage of a work which already begins to show its beneficial influence on public sentiment... Levi **LINCOLN**, President of the Worcester County Agricultural Society. John W. **PROCTOR**, President of the Essex County Agricultural Society. Marsaall P. **WILDER**, President of the Norfolk Agricultural Society. Jos. T. **BUCKINGHAM**, President of the Middlesex Society of Husbandmen and Manufacturers. E. **PHINNEY**, Member of the Massachusetts Society for Promoting Agriculture.

(353) THE SKELETON NEGRO. The *Charleston Courier* gives the following account of a living skeleton now exhibiting in that city: One of the greatest curiosities ever exhibited in human shape, may now be seen at the Hall of the Apprentices' Library, in Meeting st. It is a living skeleton, in the person of a negro, or mestizo, aged about 38 years, and bearing the name of *Wade* **HAMP'ON**.-- To designate him as a living skeleton is no figure of speech, but the literal truth--for he is nothing but skin and bone from his neck down to his extremities. His arms, legs, hand and feet are entirely useless to him; and he occupies a sitting or recumbent posture, being wholly incabable of standing erect. .. Of course he is utterly helpless, and is entirely dependent on others to be fed, dressed and otherwise attended. .. He posseses a pleasant and agreeable visage; his face being fleshy if not exactly full, and in striking contrast with the rest of his outward and attenuated man. Although deprived of the just propottions of humanity..he is intelligent chatty and cheerful; has an excellent appetite, and actually enjoys existence. He says he is one of the sons of temperance, is a member of the Baptist Church, and looks to compensation in Heaven for his stinted allotment of his blessing on earth. .. In his present skeleton state, he has ascribes it to his having taken an over does [sic] of Hippo, or other medicines, and then drenching himself with cold water. He was born in Columbia County, Georgia, about 20 miles from Augusta, and was, at the time of his birth, and still is, the property of a Mr. Humphery **EVANS**, who refuse [sic] to part with him on any terms, and he is now exhibited for the first time. ...

(354) I'M THE OTHER. It appears there are two Legislative members in Maine, of the same name, of whom a correspondent of the *Belfast Journal* tells an amusing incident which happened at Augusta, the other evening. Two gentlemen met, each unknown

22 September 1849

(354) (Cont.) to the other when one asked the other if he knew "where Mr. John **HODGDON** could be found." "You probably mean John **HODGDON** of Arostook, President of the Senate." "No, I'm that John **HODGDON** myself." "*Well, I'm the other one, the representative from Lincolnville.*"

(355) THE SEA SERPENT AGAIN. A correspondent of the *Boston Journal* states that on Saturday, the 25th ult., he saw a monster of the sea serpent.--He says: "We counted *sixteen projections or lumps* upon the surface abaft his head, and should judge his length to have been from one hundred to one hundred and fifty. His body was, I should think, as large round as a common size oil cask, his color a dark, muddy hue. He was in sight about twenty minutes, and did not alter his course from the first time we saw him till he disappeared.

(356) Elizabeth-City, Sept. 22, '49. .. *Forfeiture of Citizenship*.--Marian **RICHARDSON** alias Martan **GLADDED**, a free mulatto woman, was arraigned before the Mayor and required in the penalty of $100 to leave the commonwealth in the space of ten days. It appeard in evidence that Marian had in march last, taken a Northern tour--visiting, among other places, the city of Philadelphia, where she spent a portion of a day, and then returned to this city. The laws of the commonwealth explicitly declare that no free negro or mulatto shall, under any pretext be permitted again to reside within the commonwealth of Virginia, after having gone to any free state in the Union. The trip to Philadelphia coming within the purview of the statute, Marian was commanded to leave the State. *Richmond Times*.

(357) Carriage and Harness. In returning his thanks for the liberal patronage heretofore and continued to be extended to him, the Subscriber with pleasure solicits the attention of his customers and the public..to his newly completed stock of Chariolees, double and single Rockaways, Barouches, Buggies, Sulkies, of the latest and most fashionable styles. His stock of Harnesses, also, is complete, new and of the most recent and approved patterns... Repairs of all kinds..executed with neatness, strength, and despatch, upon reasonable terms. Robert **WATKINS**. E. City, Sept. 22, 1849.

(358) **MURRAY & CLARK**, MILL WRIGHTS, Pattern and Machine Makers, ELIZABETH CITY, N. C. The Subscribers are prepared to furnish all kinds of Mill work and Agricultural Machinery, at the shortest notice, viz., Horse Power, different sizes, Wheat Thrashers, Corn Shellers..Oat Cutters, Corn and Cob Grinders, Portable Grist Mills..Fanning Mills, all kinds Machinery... We would refer to the following named gentlemen that have them in use, viz: Thos. P. **DEVERAUX**, Esq., Dr. Thos D. **WARREN**, Aug. **MOORE**, Esq, Joshua **SKINNER**.} Chowan Co, N. C. Francis **NIXON**, Esq., Benjamin **SKINNER**, Dr. C. M. **FORD**, H. N. **MABANE**, Thomas **NEWBY**, Col. Jas. **LEIGH**, James M. **SUMNER**, Edmund **SKINNER**.} Perquimans Co. N. C. Wm. N. **GREGORY**, Camden County, N. C. Joseph H. **POOL**, Esq., Wm. **GLOVER**, Thos. F. **BANKS**, Mordecai **MORRIS**, Robert **PENDLETON**, Wm. H. **DAVIS**, George D. **POOL**, Thaddeus F. **BANKS**, Mark D. **SAWYER**,} Pasquotank county.

The following Gentlemen have our Fans and other Manchinery of different kinds in use: Jas. C. **JOHNSTON**, Esq., Dr. Thos. D. **WARREN**, Augustus **MOORE**, Joshua **SKINNER**,} Chowan County. Col. Jas. **LEIGH**, James M. **SUMNER**, Thos. S. **JACOCKS**, Dr. C. M. **FORD**, Benjamin **MULLEN**, Jas. P. **WHEDBEE**,} Perquimans County. Wm. **GLOVER**, Esq., Thos. F. **BANKS**. Joseph H. **POOL**, Jas. L. **MULLEN**,} Pasquotank County. Wm. N. **GREGORY**, Esq., Dr. F. N. **MULLEN**,} Pasquotank County. Wm. N. **GREGORY**, Esq., Major **GREGORY**, Wm. R. **ABBOTT**, } Camden County. The *Gladiator* and *Roanoke Republican* will publish to the amount of $5 and charge to this Office. Send one copy to the subscribers. Sept. 22d, 1849.

(359) FEMALE INSTITUTE, SOUTH MILLS, N. C. *A Boarding School for Young Ladies*. The 3d Session of this Institute will be commenced on the first Monday in October, proximo, under the management of a Lady well qualified to discharge her duties, as School Teacher, having had over six years experience, *as such*, in some of the Female Institutions to the North. Terms per Session of five Months--payable on or before the end of each Session. For all the Engligh Branches, usually taught in our best Female Seminaries $8 00 French and Latin, (each) 8 00 Music on the Piano, 20 00 For the use of Instrument, 2 00 Drawing, Painting & Embroidery, 10 00 Board including, Washing &c., as heretofore, will be afforded at six dollors per Month. The subscriber, being engaged in the Education of his own daughters; begs leave to inform Parents and Gurdians, that they may be assured, that no ordinary trouble and expense will be spared by him, in procuring the very best Ladies to conduct his Institution. Wm. **OLD**, Proprietor. South Mills, Camden County, N. C. Sept 22d, 1849.

The Old North State.
Vol. 9. "Error is harmless, when truth is left free to combat it." No. 32.
Elizabeth City, N. C. Saturday, September 29, 1849.

29 September 1849

(360) Elizabeth-City, Sept. 29, '49. .. Mr. Editor: Feeling assured that you are willing and interested, to promote and spread as far as you are able, the means of advancing the cause of education within our State, I take the liberty of calling your attention to a publication..which has for its object the improvement of our Common School system. The publication..is called the *Common School Advocate*, printed at Greensboro', Guilford County, and edited by Dr. Nerus **MENDENHALL**: it is issued Monthly in octavo form, at the small sum of fifty cents a year. I have seen and examined several numbers..and..it is particularly interesting to teachers and the commitees of Common Schools; and the man of science is frequently furnished with interesting matter by its pages. ...

(361) TRIUMPH OF INNOCENCE. St Louis, Sept. 21.--About six years ago, Mr. Augustine **KENNERLY**, the City Collector, was charged with being a defaulter to the amount of $8000. He protested his innocence, said it must be owing to an error in auditing his accounts, and requested that a Committee of Councils should examine his books. This was done, but no error detected--leaving it manifest that he was a defaulter. Disgraced and ruined, Mr. **K.** was dismissed from his office. Yesterday the present Auditor had occasion to overhaul an old day book, where he found that $10,000 was marked posted, though no posting was made. This was the error wich the committee and Mr. **K.** had been unable to ferret out. Thus it will be seen that, instead of..being a defaulter, the city owes him $2000, with six years' interest, which is but poor recompense for his blighted reputation, though it must be indeed a gratification to him to make his honesty manifest, even at this late day.

(362) Notice The subscriber is prepared to repair all kinds of work... Such as Clocks of all kinds, Jewelry, Guns, Pistols, Andirons, Tongs, Shovels, Candlesticks & Snuffers, Tin & Britannia Ware, Still Worms, Umbrellas, Parasols, Whips, Spectacles, Castor Stands, Canes Mounted, &c., &c. The highest price given for old Gold & Silver. Shop next door to Zion **CULEPPPER**s. Joseph N. **BELL**. Sep. 29.

(363) NEW MILLINERY. Mrs. **BELL** would inform the community generally that she has just returned from the North with a complete assortment of Millinery goods..Fashionable Bonnets and Ribbons... All orders..executed at the shortest notice and in the most satisfactory manner at the old stand next door to Zion **CULPEPPER**s.

(364) New Clothing Store IN ELIZABETH CITY. The Subscriber having taken the store on Road Street, next door to J. J. **GRANDY**, intends keeping on hand, a GENERAL ASSORTMENT of every article usually found in a READY MADE CLOTHING STORE, comprising in part of fine and low priced Cloth Dress and Frock Coats, Beaver, Pilot, Cassimere, Broad Cloth and Sattinet business Sack Coats, Cloth Cloaks, Black and Fancy Cassimere and Sattinet Pants..Vests; all made in the best manner and style. Also, fine Linen bosom, and low priced Fancy Shirts, Lamb's wool, Red and Blue flannel Shirts and Drawers, Neck and Pocket Hdk's, Socks, Suspenders, &c. All of which will be sold low. Albert **WHITE**. Sep. 29, 1849.

(365) J. P. **HARTMAN**, MERCHANT TAILOR, No. 163 Baltimore Street between Calvert & Light Streets, Baltimore. Begs leave to inform his friends and customers that having disposed of his stock at his former store on Pratt street,) he has taken the above store where he has opened an entire new and fashionable assortment of CLOTHS, CASSIMERS AND VESTINGS which will be made to order... Should any article sold..not prove as represented the mony will be refunded. ... Sept. 29.

The Old North State.
Vol. 9. "Error is harmless, when truth is left free to combat it." No. 33.
Elizabeth City, N. C. Saturday, October 6, 1849.

(366) Departure of Mr. **LAWRENCE**.--The Hon. Abbott **LAWRANCE**, Minister of the United States to the Court of St. James, sailed to-day in the steamer for England. .. His name is interwoven with all the great improvements which have marked Boston and Massachusetts for the last thirty years. .. Success attend him and a prosperous voyage. *Boston Atlas*.

(367) Elizabeth-City, Oct. 6, '49. .. The subject of Temperance and Moral Reform seem to be making a deep impression in the community throughout the country. Last Thursday night we had the pleasure of listening to a very able discourse from the Rev. C. R. **HENDRICKSON**, before the Sons of Temperance of this place. ...

(368) *From the Pendleton* (S. C.) *Messenger*. THE VIGILANCE COMMITTEE AND THE POST OFFICE. We had quite a stir in our village on Friday last when the Southern mail was delivered. .. Col. William **SLOAN** was among the first to receive his and upon examination he found a printed document post marked Boston, mailed as a letter, charged with ten cents postage, signed Junius, and addressed to the Hon. John C. **CALHOUE** [sic,] of a most malicious, offensive, and insulting character to the Southern people. This document was read by Col. **SLOAN** aloud, and it produced much excitement among the persons

6 October 1849

(368) (Cont.) assembled. A call was made upon the Post Master to know if there were any others in the office, to which he replied that there were 38 in all. The Executive of the Committee of Vigilance and Safety immediately assembled to take action in the matter, and..concluded that it would be better to hold the course to be pursued under consideration until the next morning. .. The next morning the Committee assembled at the office and made a demand for the letters; the Post Master refused to give them up unless to those to whom they were addressed, and the payment of the postage, and urged his duties as an officer of the General Government. The Committee told him they were determined to have the papers peaceably if they could, forcibly if they must, and that resistance would be in vain. They then entered the office, shoved the Post Master aside, and took possession of them, and now have them under lock and key, where they will remain until the meeting of the Committee..on the 29th inst. We should think the above was pretty treatment for a Post Master. .. We think North Carolina is equally jealous of her rights, but we will lay a wager that no where within her borders (not even in Edgecomb) would such high-handed proceedings have taken place under the same circumstances. .. While we are opposed as much as any persons living to the circulation of all such tracts as the Abolitionists of the North are in the habit of sending to the South, we are equally opposed to such measures as the citizens of Pendleton have lately adopted to break up the circulation. It will only fan the fire of revenge...

(369) Col. **CHILDS** and Mr. **POUSSIN**. The following correspondence we find in the *National Intelligencer* of this morning. .. Fort McHenry, (Md.,) Sept. 22, 1849. Sir: In the *National Intelligencer* of to-day I have read with astonishment and indignation the following paragraph, in a communication from the French Minister, M. **POUSSIN**, to the Secretary of State, Mr. **CLAYTON**. "The Legation of France cannot and will not make itself the echo of the reports, more or less well founded, which have been current with regard to Col. **CHILDS** ' conduct in this affair; nor will it press certain facts imputed against him, which it would be perhaps easier to prove that he could prove the charges brought by himself." So long as M. **POUSSIN** confined himself to comments on my evidence before the Board of Commissioners, I felt quite indifferent to his opinions of my testimony; it is on record, and when published will vindicate the court that decided upon the case of **PORT**, the General who approved its proceedings, and the final action of the Government. I deny indignantly the insinuations contained in the quotation, and defy M. **POUSSIN** to establish the remotest point in the dishonorable insinuations that he has made. I feel that is my right to ask, at the hands of the proper authority, that M. **POUSSIN** be requested to make specific and tangible charges; and, whatever they may be, that opportunity be given me to show their falsity. ... Thomas **CHILDS**. Brevet Brig. General U. S. Army. Hon. Geo. W. **CRAWFORD**, Secretary of War, Washington.

WAR DEPARTMENT, Washington, Sept. 24, 1849.} Sir: In reply to yours of the 22d instant, touching the remarks of M. **POUSSIN**, while he was accredited to the Government of the United States, as Minister Plenipotentiary and Envoy Extraordinary of the Republic of France, in relation to claim of M. **PORT**, and your Connexion therewith, I have to state that I cannot comply with your request... The official relation between this Government and M. **POUSSIN** has been severed. .. I cheerfully add that nothing has reached the Department which reflects on your character as an officer and a man. ... Geo. W. **CRAWFORD**, Secretary of War. Brevet Brig. Gen. **CHILDS**, U. S. Army, Fort McHenry, Md.

(370) Correspondence of the *Baltimore Patriot*. WASHINGTON, Sept. 30, 1849. .. Col. Balie **PEYTON**, Minister to Chili, leaves here this evening for New York, where he will take the steamer for Chagres. His daughter accompanies him on his mission, while his two sons will remain in this country and attend an Academy at Alexandria, Va. ...

(371) THE **ASTOR** HOUSE RIOTERS. We have heretofore announced the conviction of the **ASTOR** House rioters, in New York. The following received their sentences on Saturday: E. Z. C. **JUDSON**, (Ned **BUNTLINE**,) was sentenced to twelve months imprisonment in the Penitentiary, and to pay a fine of $250. D. G. **ADRIANCE**, to three months in the Penitentiary. Thomas **GREEN**, one month in the Penitentiary. Thomas **BENNETT**, George **DOUGLASS**, and James **O'NEILL**, eached [sic] sentenced to thirty days imprisonment in the City Prison.

(372) Perquimans Male and Female ACADEMY, Hertford, Perquimans Co., N. C. The Trustees of this Institution are pleased to announce to the public; that they have secured the services of Mr. John **KIMBERLY**, as Principal, and the first session of the school will commence under the most favorable auspices. .. On the last day of every month a Report of the progress and standing of the pupils in their respective studies, together with an account of their department, will be forwarded to the parents and guardians, who are particularly requested to correspond freely with the Principal, and communicate their wishes and suggestions in reference to the pupils. .. The Winter Term will commence on the first monday in October. The Summer Term on the first monday in March. The months of August and September will be given for vacation; and there will also be a short vacation during the Christmas holidays. TERMS FOR TUITION, In the Male Department. For the Elementary course per session, $10 " " English Course, " 15 " " Classical & Mathematial course, 20 IN THE FEMALE DEPARTMENT. For the Elementary course per session, $8 " " higher English Branches, " 12 French and Ancient Languages, each, 5 Music on the Piano & Guitar, each, 15 For use of Instruments, 2 Drawing, Painting and Needlework, 5 Board, including Washing, Fuel and Lights can be obtained in private

6 October 1849

(372) (Cont.) families from $6,50 to $8 per month. ... Thos. F. **JONES**, Jos. M. **COX**, Francis **NIXON**, Trustees. Oct. 6, 1849.

(373) For Rent, The subscriber will rent his Store at **SAWYER**'s Creek to a good tenant, at such a price as cannot fail to suit, taking into consideration the stand for a space of business. .. For further publication apply to James M. **FEREBEE**, of Currituck Co., N. C. Oct 6

(374) The **GRAEFENBURG** Company's Vegetable Pills, Sarsaparilla compound, Green Mountain Ointment, Health Bitters, Children's Panacea, Eye Salve, Fever & Ague Pills, For sale by L. **WARROCK**, Agent for E. City.

(375) A. W. **RAPP**'s Samaritan Ointment. For the cure of Rheumatism, Stiffness of the Joints, Cramps, Sore Throat, and all pains arising from exposure to Cold. The infalliable Sore and Ulser Salve. For sale by L. **WARROCK**. Sept. 6.

The Old North State.
Vol. 9. "Error is harmless, when truth is left free to combat it." No. 34.
Elizabeth City, N. C. Saturday, October 13, 1849.

(376) Libel.--Mr. James C. **CHURCH**, of Fort Hamilton, N. Y., has been mulcted in $2,500 damages, for a libel on Col. **MILLER**, whom he charged with theft in a written notice posted up in his own store.

(377) Elizabeth-City, Oct. 13, '49. .. The *Baltimore Clipper* in enumerating the different articles deposited at the fair of the Maryland Institute puts down the following as lot No. 126. "126 Two Seven Octavo Pianos, made and deposited by J. E. **BOSWELL** of this city. These pianos are both in elegant rose-wood cases--one with a serpentine front; and we have scarcely listened to instruments possessing so much sweetness and fulness of tone. .. Both instruments have a harp pedal, which produces the exact sound of that delightful instrument. ..."

(378) *Corrrespondence of the Baltimore Potriat.* --By Telegraph. Another Visit by the President. WASHINGTON Oct. 10. P. M. President **TAYLOR**, accompanied by the Secretary of the Navy, will leave Washington for Baltimore on Thursday morning, 11th inst. He will remain in Baltimore during Thursday night, leaving..for Philadelphia on Friday morning... The Hon. Reverdy **JOHNSON** is recovering from his recent indisposition. No appointments to-day.

(379) A Proclamation. WHEREAS the General Assembly did, at their last Session, adopt a Resolution in these words: "*Resolved*, by the General Assembly of the State of North Carolina, that the Governor of the State for the time being be directed to set apart a day in every year, and to give notice thereof, by Proclamation, as a day of solemn and public thanksgiving to Almighty God, for past blessings, and of supplication for his continued kindness and care over us as a State and as a Nation." Now, in Compliance with the direction therein given, I do hereby set apart THURSDAY the FIFTEENTH DAY of NOVEMBER NEXT to be observed throughout this State as a day of General Thanksgiving. .. Given under my hand and the great seal of the Sate at the Executive Department in the City of Raleigh, this 1st day of October, 1849, and this 74th year of American Idependence. Charles **MANLY**. By order of the Governor, Langdon C. **MANLY**, Pr. Sec. Raleigh, Oct. _ 1849.

(380) *Correspondence of the Baltimore Patriot.* WASHINGTON, Oct. 5. In the next U. S. House of Representatives the Maryland delegation will be tied and the two parties in the House (should Louisiana and Mississippi be represented as in the last Congress, to wit: by 6 Locofocos and 2 Whigs.) will be pretty nearly tied also. .. But the Free Soil Impractables, headed by Mr. Joshua R. **GIDDINGS**, of Ohio, will hold the balance of power... .. If the Free Soilers choose they can elect Mr. **WINTHROP** Speaker, or the nominee of the Locofoco members. .. Among the Locofocos who are to be candidates for the Clerkship, I have heard named General Hiram **WALBRIDGE**, of New York, and B. B. **FRENCH** and Jas. G. **BERRITT**, Esquires, of this city--all smart, capable men. Jesse E. **DOW**, Esq. intends to run for Sergeant-at-Arms. .. There will be strong opposition to Mr. **DICKENS** and Mr. **BEAL**, the Secretary, and Sergeant-at-Arms to the senate... The venerable Peter **HAGNER**, as I understand, retires from the Third Auditorship at the end of the present quarter, which will terminate on the 15?th inst. Rumor says that John S. **GALLAGHER**, Esq. of Virginia, a good man and a deserving one..to be Mr. **HAGNER**'s successor. Potomac.

(381) List of Letters Remaining in the Post Office, at Elizabeth City, Quarter ending 30th September 1849. **ALDEN** Lt. Com. James **AUSTIN** Bateman **ALVAIADO** Martin 2 **ASHTON** Oscar **ASHBEE** Samuel M. **ALLEN** Wm. **BROTHERS** Miles **BANKS** Jno **BROZIER** Thomas **BUTT** Dr. John 3 **BAILEY** John D. 3 **BELL** James M. **BROWN** Thomas B 2 **BAILEY** Hon S **BOW** Timothy **BACON** Capt Geo W **BURGESS** John **BAILEY** John Jr **BETTS** Capt Wm. M **BROOKFIELD** Capt John **BANKS** Benj F **BANKS** John **CUYLER** Pass'd Mid'n R M **CARMOTH** Mrs. Mary **CASEY** Dempsey **CARTWRIGHT** Marmaduke **CASEY** & **DAVIS CLARKSON** Capt J **CADWORTH** Capt J H **DOLPH?** Jared 2 **DAVIS** J B **DREW** Henry

13 October 1849

(381) (Cont.) **DAIL** Richard **DAVIS** Miles **DUNSTON** Wm **ELLIOTT** Aaron **FEREBEE** Mrs S R **FORBES** Miss Elizabeth **FELTON** Mrs Mary **GORDON** Stephen **GORDON** Francis **GREY** Job **GRANDY** Miss Sarah **HAUGHTON** Tippoo S **HARRISON** Wm S **HOBBS** George **HAMILTON** Zera **HENRY** Dr B **HARNEY** Thomas 3 **HYTER** Henry **JINKINS** Joseph **JONES** J B **JONES** Matilda **JACKSON** John **JACKSON** Barney **JACKSON** William **JACOCKS** Jas G **JONES** Marthana **JENNINGS** Joseph **KNELLER** George **LISTER** Sarah **LESTER** R S **LONG** Wm **LOWRY** Mrs Ann **MULLEN** James 2 **MORRISON** Daniel S **MADIYETT** Edward **MEADS** Stanton **MC KREE** J J **MOORE** Mrs Susan J **MULING** Mointha **MULLEN** James W **MURPHY** William **MC DEAL** Fanny **MURDEN** Benj **MEEDS** Samuel T **NEWBY** Miss Mary **NAINHOUSE** S T **NANTZE** Richard **NASH** James **OWENS** James 2 **OVERMAN** Nathan **OVERTON** Elizabeth Artist to any Dauguerrian **PERKINS** Martin C S **PALMER** W R 2 **POYNER** Capt Jas **PENDLETON** Robert 4 **PERKINS** J Q **PIERSON** Gilbert **PENDLETON** Burgess **PERRY** Cader **PENDLETON** Reuben **PINER** Capt George **PALMER** James **ROUTLE** Wm R **REED** Joseph B 2 **RAILING** Joseph **SUMNER** James M **SIMPSON** Jessee **SYMONS** Miss Synthia A **SMITHSON** Cally **SANDERS** John **SMITH** Murdoc **SHIRDREN** Thomas **SHARBER** Miles **SPRUILL** Miss Sophia **TOWNER** R A **TATEM** Samuel **THOMPSON** John **UMPHREY** Wilson **VOHESS** Geo W **WHITE** Miles 3 **WOOTEN** J C **WHILLON** John **WALKER** Capt Caleb 2 **WALKER & BALLANCE WARCH** Solomon **WHITE** Isaac of color **WHITEHURST** Mrs **WILLIAMS** Barton Persons calling for any of the above letters will please say they are advertised. Wm. E. **MANN**, P. M. Oct 13

(382) Mrs. Esther **SIKES** Has just received from the City of New York the most extensive assortment of Millinary Goods that she has ever offered to the public. Her stock has been purchased with great care and *due regard* to the *various tastes* of the *Ladies*. ... Esther **SIKES**, Road Street. Oct. 13.

(383) VALUABLE FARM FOR SALE. The Subscriber offers for sale his Farm, near Hickory Ground, Norfolk county, Va., upon which he now resides. It contains about 500 acres, about 100 of which is cleared and under cultivation, the balance is well timbered. It has a commodious dwelling in good repair; a large barn, carriage house, kitchen, dairy and other necessary convenient buildings entirely new. Within two miles from the dwelling is situated "Hickory Ground Academy," at which there is a free school kept up all the year under the charge of an able teacher. The situation is considered as healthful as any in the eastern part of the State. Terms will be accommodating for further particulars apply upon the premises to Geo. A. **WILSON**. Oct. 13th, 1849.

(384) $40 REWARD. Ranaway from the subscriber the 25th of August last, two likely negro boys, **GEORGE** & **WASHINGTON**. **GEORGE** is four feet eight or ten inches high, with tolerable stout body and limbs, he is black, with a full face and eyes, has a down look when spoken to. **WASHINGTON** is four feet six or eight inches high, is rather inclined to be spare built, not so black as **GEORGE**, he has sharp face, low forehead, small eyes, and has also a down look when spoken to. They have relations at Dr. **WILLIAMS**'s, who resides near Deep Creek, Va., and are no doubt lurking in that neighborhood, or in the Dismal Swamp. I will give twenty dollars each for the above named boys to any person or persons, who will confine them in Jail in E. City, N. C., or to me, uninjured in any way. Jos. **COMMANDER**, Dry Ridge, Pasquotank Co. Oct. 13, '49.

(385) Sale of Doctor William **MITCHELL**'s Land. Will be sold to the highest bidder, before the Court House door in Hertford, on the 12th of November next (being Court day) the tract of land on which Doctor **MITCHELL** resided at the time of his death. Said land lies 1 1/2 miles from **NEWBY**'s Bridge, contains 170 acres and has on it an excellent dwelling & outbuildings. Persons wishing to purchase can have further information by applying to John R. **WINSLOW** and David **WHITE** Jr. Exect. of Dr. **MITCHELL** It will be sold on credit of six and nine months. The purchasers giving bonds with approved security. Oct. 13 1849

(386) NEW FANCY STORE LADIES BE IN TIME, CHEAP, CHEAPER, CHEAPEST. A. E. **JACOBS** ACCORDING TO PROMISE made the last summer has just returned to E. City and taken the same store lately occupied by him opposite the Mansion House, and has opened an entire NEW and beautiful assortment of GOODS, suited to the Fall and winter trade and which cannot fail to please. ... B. **ISRAEL**, A. E. **JACOBS**, Agt. E. City, Oct. 13, 18498.

(387) NOTICE TO MARINERS. The Light Boat stationed off **WADE**s Point will leave her morrings on Tuesday next the 16th inst. for the purpose of undergoing a thorough repair, and will be absent some 6 weeks or 2 months. G. W. **CHARLES**, Superintendant. Oct. 13.

(388) SOMETHING NEW. Just Received, and first rate, 6 bbls. N. Y. City Mess Beef, 5 bbls. Extra and 5 bbls. Superfine Flour direct from the mills and first rate. No mistake, 13 bbls. Pilot Bread and 1 Firkin Butter. ... W. **HALSEY**.

13 October 1849

(389) Dentist. Dr. C. W. **BALLARD** (successor to Dr. John **HARRIS**) offers his professional services to the inhabitants of Hertford, Elizabeth City, and Edenton as follows. At Hertford during the months of October November and December at Elizabeth City, during January February and March, at Edenton during April, May and June. REFERENCES. Pro. C. A. **HARRIS**, " W. R. **HANDY**, " T. E. **BOND**, Jr. "C. O. **CONE**,} Facilty of Baltimore College of Dental Surgery. Also to the Facilty of the Washington Medical University of Baltimore. Oct. 13

The Old North State.
Vol. 9. "Error is harmless, when truth is left free to combat it." No. 35.
Elizabeth City, N. C. Saturday, October 20, 1849.

(390) Messrs Editors: At a meeting of the Pasquotank Division Sons of Temperance held on the 13th instant, it was *Resolved*, that a copy of the address delivered before the Division by Mr. G. M. **WILDER** on that night be requested for publication in the *Old North State*. The above resolution having been complied with, we present the following remarks, requesting you to give them a place in your paper. John S. **WAUGH**, Recording Scribe. ADDRESS. The present seems to be an age of improvement, enterprise, and invention. Philanthropy, humanity, and benevolence, which are naturally implanted in the heart of man, seem to have been the prime moving cause of the Order of the Sons of Temperance. ...

(391) Female Artists of the West.--One of the finest artists of the West is a lady of this city--an amateur sculptor, some peices of whose modeling in clay have great spirit and beauty. In native genius, perhaps no painter the West has produced surpasses Mrs. **SPENCER**, who has furnished the subject for the engraving of the Western Art Union this year. .. A young lady of Indiana, of whose promise we heard a good deal during her pupilage in this city, is thus spoken of by the *Indianapolis Journal*: "We have seen two portraits painted by Miss Laura M. **BROWN**, of this city, which manifest an unusual degree of talent on the part of the artist. Miss **BROWN** is from Akron, Ohio, and is a pupil of the distinguished western artist, John **FRANKENSTEIN**, of Cincinnati. ... *Cincinnati Gazette*.

(392) Elizabeth-City, Oct. 20, '49. .. We are inclined at all times to recommend to the notice of the people whatever tends to the general prosperity of the country, and particularly what pertains to our own community. .. And we rejoice to see the growing spirit manifested here in the ship-building business. .. We happened a few days since to be in the Shipyard of our townsman Mr. C. M. **LAVERTY**, when we were struck with the busy scene presented there by the industrious Mechanic, refiting vessels for the West India trade. On Thursday we were highly gratified with a visit to the Brig "Hunters," built by our enterprising citizen T. **HUNTER**, Esq., who has displayed a good deal of taste and judgment in her architecture. .. Her cabin will accomodate comfortably ten or twelve persons. .. We are informed that she will carry about one hundred and sixty tons, which constitutes her as large, if not the largest vessel that ever sailed out of this port. She has her cargo, and will sail on Monday for Barbadoes under the command of Capt. Thomas **COOK**; who has for several years been successfully engaged in the trade between Baltimore and Rio Janeiio [sic.]

(393) Col. **FREMONT**. Somebody has started a story that Col. **FREMONT**, who has been appointed the commissioner to run the boundary between the United States and Mexico, had either declined to accept the appointment, or had received the announcement of it with "cool contempt." The *Republic* published the following extract of a letter to show "what the world is given to." It is dated at Puebla, of San Jose, August, 1849. *To the Hon. J. M. CLAYTON, Secretary of State:* "I have had the honor to receive, by the hands of Mr. **BEALE**, U. S. Navy, your letter conferring upon me the post of Commissioner of the United States for the determination of our boundary line with Mexico. I feel much gratification in accepting the appointment, and beg to offer, through you, to the President, my acknowledgments for the mark of confidence bestowed upon me, and which he may be assured is fully appreciated, &c. (Signen) J. C. **FREMONT**."

(394) WASHINGTON NEWS. A correspondent of the *N. Y. Courier*, states that in August last, the second Comptroller of the Treasury examined the accounts of Hon. Isaac **HILL**, late pension agent at Concord, New Hampshire, which examination proved that gentleman a defaulter to the government, in the sum of $13,000. The third Auditor was thereupon instructed to demand of Mr. **HIIL** immediate payment of the amount, and, in case of refusal, to furnish a transcript of his accounts for suit.

(395) Married. In Nixonton on Thursday the 18th inst. By the Rev. P. F. **AUGUST** Mr. Wm. H. **CLARK**, of E. City to Miss Sallie **JACKSON**, of Nixonton. Accompanying the above was the Printers *fee* in the shape of a bountiful supply of Cake. They will please accept our thanks for the same, and may they both long live to enjoy the pleasures of life.

(396) Ten Thousand Dollars worth of Boots, Shoes, Hats, Caps, Trunks and Buffalo Robes, &c., just received at the Store of J. M. **WHEDBEE** & Bro. .. They beg leave to return their most sincere thanks to the public in general for the very liberal and extensive

20 October 1849

(396) (Cont.) patronage they have received, and hope to merit a continuance of the same. ... Oct. 20, 1849.

(397) Attention 1st Regiment N. C. Volunteer Cavalry. The Light Dragoons of Perquimans, Atlantic Guards of Currituck, R. & R. Light Dragoons of Pasquotank and the Camden Guards, are hereby ordered to attend a parade of the Regiment at E. City, on Friday the 2d of November next, in winter uniform, armed and equipped as the law directs, with 10 rounds of blank cartridges. A full turn out of the Regiment is looked for. The Regiment will be formed into line at 11 o'clock A. M. .. The officers of the staff and the Commisioned Officers of each Corps, are hereby ordered to attend at E. City on Thursday afternoon the 1st November, for the purpose of attending a meeting of the Officers of the Regiment, which will take place in the Court House at 7 o'clock P. M. .. The Officers will appear at the meeting in uniform. By Order of the Col. Wm.E. **MANN**, Adjt. Oct. 20.

(398) J. T. **SALTER**, BOTANIC PHYSICIAN. Would respectfully inform the citizens of Elizabeth City and vicinity that he has taken board with Mr. James **BARBER**, where he may usually be found at all hours when not absent on professional business. Dr. **SALTER** courteously solicits the patronage of those who prefer the Reformed or Botanic Medical treatment to any other; also of those who feel disposed to give it a trial, feeling *confident* that since he has had several years experience in this mode of treating diseases he will be able to render entire satisfaction to all who will give him a fair trial. Oct. 20, 1849.

(399) FOR SALE. The subscriber wishing to leave the State, will sell his land upon which he now resides, on the Road leading to **DURANT**'s Neck, and about two miles from Woodville, consisting of 120 acres. About 125,000 [sic] of it is cleared and in a good state of cultivation. Plenty of rail timber and fire wood for the farm. There is on the farm a good two story dwelling house, nearly new, together with all necessary out houses. The above property will be sold at a great bargain. For further particulars apply to James T. **SMITH**. Perquimans Co., Oct. 20.

(400) A Pleasant Country Residence FOR SALE. That fine location in Pasquotank Co. N. C. near the River Bridge, and distant from E. City N. C. about 10 miles, (formerly the property of Peter W. **HINTON**, Esq.) is now offered for sale. The farm now contains six hundred acres or upwards, of high lands and swamp. It is thought that the situation offers high inducements for the location of a Physician, or of a Male and Female Seminary... To those who have never seen the improvements on the said property; it may be proper to state, that they consist of a spacious and neatly finished wood mansion, now stands in perfect repair; and all the out buildings have been built correspondingly with said mansion, are also nearly in the like condition. The wells of good water.. cannot be surpassed in eastern North Carolina. ... Wm. **OLD**, South Mills P. O. Camden County, N. C. Oct. 20, 1849.

(401) TRUST SALE Of Valuable Lands In Princess Anne County, and Other Personal Property. By virtue of a Deed in Trust executed by Edward **LAND**, on the 22d day of November, 1848 (and duly recorded in the Clerk's Office of Princess Anne _ounty Court,) for the purpose of securing the payment of certain sums of money therein mentioned, WILL BE SOLD, On the Farm, now occupied by the said **LAND**, near London Bridge, (16 miles from the city of Norfolk,) On THURSDAY, the 8th day of November next, for cash, The MANOR FARM at the Bridge, containing 300 Acres, together with the STEAM SAW and GRIST MILL thereto attached, and in good order. This Farm is situated near the head of a stream of water which empties into Lynnhaven River, and is navigable for lighters and boats, and convenient for shipment of produce, &c. The improvements are good, and a large portion of the land is cleared. There are also about 430 acres of land adjoining the above tract, of excellent quality, particularly that portion, recently cleared, called the SWAMP LAND. .. Also, at the same time and place, and on the same terms, about twenty VALUABLE NEGROES, viz: **DINEY, CHARLES, SAM, ANTHONY, HANNAH, NED, FRANK, DANIEL, ANNY, NAPOLEON, BETSEY, DENBY, PHILIP, ANNE, SAREY, ANNY, FRANK, JACK, VENUS** and **THADDEUS**, and the increase (if any,) of the females, since the execution of the deed. Also 46 head of Cattle 100 bbls. of Corn, 129 Hogs, 8 Oxen, 7 mules, 6 Horses, 4 Ox Carts, 2 Carrylogs, Wheels and Chains, 4 Horse Carts, 28 stacks of Oats, and all his HOUSEHOLD and KITCHEN FURNITURE of every description, and FARMING UTENSILS and tools of every kind. Sale to commence at 11 o'clock. J. J. **BURROUGHS**, J. W. **STONE**,}Trustees. .. ALSO, By virtue of another Deed in Trust from Edward **LAND**, dated the 23d day of July, 1849, (and also duly recorded in the Clerk's Office of Princess Anne County Court,) to give additional security to John **EWELL** and Wm. S. **COX**. WILL BE SOLD, On the same day, immediately after the above sale, on the same terms, and at the same place, all of said Edward **LAND**'s pressent crop of Corn and Fodder, Oats, Peas, Potatoes and every other article of property, now then in his possession not conveyed by the deed first mentioned. J. J. **BURROUGHS**, Trustee. Oct. 20.

(402) J. B. **GODWIN**, Dentist Having located himself in Elizabeth City offers his services to the *public*, in all the departments of his profession. Office corner of Road & Market streets, in the room formerly ocupied by Wm. **LABOYTAUX** as an ice cream saloon. Persons in town or country prefering it will be waited on at their residence. E. City, Oct. 20, 1849.

27 October 1849

The Old North State.
Vol. 9. "Error is harmless, when truth is left free to combat it." No. 36.
Elizabeth City, N. C. Saturday, October 27, 1849.

(403) Attorney, for Prosecuting Claims at Washington. The subscriber undertakes the collections settlement and adjustment of all manner of claims, accounts or demands against the Government of the U. States, or any foreign State or Country, before Commissioners, before Congress, or before any of the public Departments, at _ashington. The procuring of patents, Army and Navy pensions, bounty land claims, soldiers' dues, drawbacks, all the collection of accounts against the Government, all land claims, and every demand or other business of whatever kind, requiring the prompt and afficient service of an Attorney or Agent. ... Communications must be pre-paid in ALL cases. Charges or fees will be regulated by the nature and extent of the business, but always moderate. H. C. **SPALDING**. Attorney, Washington, D. C. aug 25

(404) Elizabeth-City, Oct. 27, '49. .. Our Superior Court. Our Superior Court, Judge **BAILEY** presiding, has been in session during the week. On Wednesday the Court was occupied all day in the trial of John **JENKINS** of color for the murder of negro boy, **NOAH**, which was committed in the County of Gates in February last. The first witness called for the State was an old negro by the name of **JOE**, and here we would remark, that we never saw negroes in any Court House give in evidence as the negroes in this case did. .. They seemed perfectly at ease and showed none of that fright usually seen in negroes when giving in evidence in a court room. The trial throughout was conducted with the utmost fairness and decorum. .. After the charge, the Jury retired to their room and after the short space of *three* minutes, returned with the verdict of *not guilty*. We omitted to state in the proper place that the defence set up by the consul [sic] for the Prisoner was, that the act of which he was charged was committed when he the prisoner was laboring under an insane mind, and we think the evidence produced proved the thing clearly. .. For the purpose of giving our readers the sum and substance of the evidence we would merely state that the first witness called for the State was an old negro by the name of **JOE**, he swore that the prisoner came to Gatesville on Saturday afternoon about sunset with Mr. **STUMPH**, that he eat very little supper, that he heard no quarrelling going on between him and any other person, that he went out after eating and came in again with boy **MILES**, that he (old **JOE**) went to bed, left him and **MILES** in the room, **MILES** went out and left the prisoner in the room and after an absence of some hour [sic] heard one or two blows given, and heard a deep groan, rushed out and saw the prisoner beating some one down in the fire, he did not know at that time who they were, but thought that it was some one beating the prisoner John **JENKINS**, he did not know when the boy **NOAH** came in the room adjoining, upon seeing the beating going on he run out of the kitchen for help, and as he started out of the front door the prisoner made a lick at him, but did not hit him, he soon brought assistance and had the prisoner secured, saw then for the first time who the parties were, he said the prisoner was hollowing out "good man! good man! Jesus Christ!" and hitting the sides of the kitchen door. The other witnesses corroborated old **JOE**'s evidence in some particulars where they were present with him. The boy **MILES** who old **JOE** went after for assistance brought two white men with him, and he says when he got to the kitchen the prisoner was standing in the back door striking, as if he was striking at something, that he was told by one of the white men Mr. **KING** to go in and seize him, he did so, and threw the Prisoner out at the front door, that all this time the negro boy **NOAH** was laying face downward into the fire. After a while they got him out and he was burned in a most shocking manner--the coals sticking to his face and neck, he heard no quarrelling going on between the prisoner and the boy **NOAH**, that when he went out he left the prisoner and **NOAH** in the room together, that **NOAH** was fast asleep in the chimney corner when he went out, said he had been gone out some hour or so when old **JOE** came after him for assistance. Several Physicians were called in, who swore most positively that they thought, he, the Prisoner was laboring under the *delirum tremens* at the time of committing the deed, and that he was not conscious of what he was doing.

Great credit is due to Mr. Thomas B. **STUMPH**, for the liberal manner in which he provided ample counsel for the prisoner, and who left nothing undone to give him a fair trial. We cannot let this occasion pass without noticing the way and manner that our excellent Solicitor William N H **SMITH**, Esq., conducted the case on behalf of the State. Nothing was left undone that ought to have been brought forward, and nothing was brought forward but what was perfectly fair and just. His style of speaking, so easy, so fluent, and to the purpose, won for him the approbation of all who heard him. The Legislature in electing him..our able Representative, has truly sent us a man, that will fill the station with honor to himself and the State at large.

(405) THE SEABOARD AND ROANOKE RAIRROAD. We have learned from Capt. Jas. **BARNES**, the Engineer of the above work, that the Company have closed their contracts for the whole amount of iron required for laying the entire track of the Road, upon the most advantageous terms, and that the iron will be shipped to this place as fast as vessels can be procured to bring it. In some two or three weeks, we may therefore confidently expect to see this enterprise going forward with all the spirit and activity which its great importance demands. *Portsmouth Pilot.*

(406) His excellency D. M. **BARRANGER**, Envoy Extraordinary and Minister Plenipotentiary of the United States of America to her Catholic Majesty, with his family and suite, arrived in Paris on Thursday, *enroute* for Madrid...*--Paris paper, Sept. 23.*

27 October 1849

(407) THE PANAMA RAILROAD. The *New York Journal of Commerce* has the following article on this subject: "We are happy to learn that the Panama Railroad Company have put under contract that portion of their railroad across the Isthums which lies between the Chargres river and bay of Panama, about twenty-one miles--the whole distance from Panama to Limon by being forty-six miles. The contractors are Messrs. **TOTTEN** and **TRAUTWINE** whose proposals were the most favorable, and who posssess the great recommendation of having been employed for the last four or five years in the territories of New Granada, in constructing a canal ninety miles long, to connect two branches of the Magdalene river. .. The construction will be carried on under a new organization. Col. **HUGHES**, of the old Topographical Corps..has resigned his place as chief engineer, and returned to the duties of his profession. .. William H. **SIDELL**, esq., his principal assistant on the Isthmus, has been appointed to succeed him. Mr. **SIDELL** graduated with distinction at West Point, and, immediately afterwards turning his attention to civil engineering, has been employed on some of the most important public works of the country, and gave up the charge of one of the most difficult sections of the Erie, for the Panama Railroad. ..."

(408) Married. In this place on Thursday Evening last by the Rev. E. M. **FORBES**, Mr. Thomas B. **STUMPH**, to Miss Mary G. **LEWIS**, both of Elizabeth City. .. On Thursday evening last, by Rev. C. R. **HENDRICKSON**, Mr. Newton **SAWYER** to Miss Susan **TRUEBLOOD**, both of this county.

(409) DIED, In this place on the 20th instant Samuel **MATHEWS** son of William P. and Sarah G. **MATHEWS** age 5 years and 11 days. Thus we see that death is no respecter of persons. ...

(410) Lands and other Valuable Property for Sale. The Subscriber, intending to leave the State, offers for Sale on accommodating terms, his Lands in Currituck County as follows, viz: The Juniper Ridge Tract containing 800 acres of which 300 are cleared and 200 deaded. On the premises are four good tenant houses, a large barn, with other necessary buildings, and the Lands are in a good state of cultivation, also the John **LAMB** Tract of 450 acres, 200 cleared, with good dwelling and out houses, also the **CAMPBEL** Ridge Tract of 150 acres, 180,000 in cultivation and of very superior quality. Also eleven fine mules, four houses and a quanity of Stock of other descriptions. Also a good four horse power, **SINCLARE**s patent, Wheat Machine and Corn Thresher, one double Rockaway and Harness, and farming utensils of all kinds. Persons anxious to purchase can doubtless be suited as to terms by calling on James M. **FEREBEE**, Currituck County, N. C. Oct. 27.

(411) More New Goods. RECEIVED this morning, from Mr. **FREEMAN**, who is now visiting the principal Northern cities and factories, a splendid lot of RICH AND BEAUTIFUL JEWELRY..which will be sold low, by J. M. **FREEMAN**, Jeweller. oct 27

The Old North State.
Vol. 9. "Error is harmless, when truth is left free to combat it." No. 37.
Elizabeth City, N. C. Saturday, November 3, 1849.

(412) AMERICAN CASSIMERES. We have seen the sample cards of Fancy Cassimeres referred to in the annexed certificate of one of the Committees appointed at the recent Fair held in this city. They are as beautiful goods of the kind as have ever come under our notice, and will successfully compare in fabric, style and finish with any foreign manufacture. .. Owing to an inadvertance, which is much to be regretted, a card of samples of Fancy Cassimeres made by the Broadbrook Manufacturing Company of Connecticut, was not received in time to be acted upon by the judges of the wollens at the late Fair of the Mechanics' Institute. They however cheerfully concord [sic] in the following notice of them by the *Philadelphia Pennsylvanian*, of the 10th inst., they then being on exhibition at the Fair of the Franklin Instituttute of that city. James **HARVEY**, John M. **OREM**, R. MC **ELDOWNEY**, } Committe on Wollens. "Nothing in the Fair surpasses the Broadbrook goods. They are the best finished Cassimeres ever brought into the Institute, and are well worth the examination and consideration of our whole community."--*Balt. American.*

(413) INTERESTING FROM THE CAMANCHE NATION.--We learn from the *National Intelligencer* that accounts has been received at the War Department respecting an important National Council recently held by the Camanche Indians. This council lasted ten days, and its object was to elect a new chief to rule the nation, in place of the one recently deceased,) and the individual thus honored glories in the name of *BUFFALO HUMP*. On being installed into office, after the Indian fashion, this head chief called upon his subordinates freely to express their opinion upon all matters of importance connected with the affairs of the nation; whereupon many speeches were delivered. They were generally of the most friendly character, but none more so than that delivered by the newly elected chief himself. He maintained that his people had formerly made war upon Texas when it was "feeble and alone," and had gained nothing; and he gave it as his opinion that if they now continued to make war upon Texas, since it had become a part of the United States, the result would be their utter destruction as a nation. He also expressed his

3 November 1849

(413) (Cont.) determination to do all in his power to put a stop to the thieving depredations which had been committed by a portion of his people against the white inhabitants, and expressed a hope that his efforts would be successful. The prominent members of the Council having agreed to the advice of *BUFFALO HUMP*, two subordinate chiefs were appointed to communicate in person the result of the Council to Capt. **STEELE**, of the 2d dragoons, at Fredicksburg, by whom a report was made to Gen. **BROOKE**, commanding in Texas, who forwarded it to the War Department.--*Balt. Patriot*.

(414) Elizabeth-City, Nov. 3, '49. .. LAUNCH. A fine schooner was launched from the Ship Yard of our townsman C. M. **LAVERTY**, on Saturday last. As she glided into her native element the bottle of wine was broken and John A. Gambril was the name pronounced. She is a very large vessel and will do well for the West India Trade. .. This speaks well for E. City, for less than three months, three fine vessels, two of them of large size and intended for the West India trade and the other for the Canal, has been launched from the ship yards of E. City. One the "Huntres" from the yard of Capt. T. **HUNTER**, and the John A. Gambril, from the yard of C. M. **LAVERTY**, Esq., and the Samuel D. Lamb, from the yard of Messrs. **BURGESS & LAMB**. ...

(415) The brig Richmond, of Halifax, arrived there on the 15th instant, safe and sound, without the loss of a spar or the stranning [sic] of a rope-yarn. This is the vessel concerning which fears were entertained, from a notice published in the papers some time since, of a bottle being picked up near Elizabeth City, N. C., containing a note which stated that the brig at the time was in a heavy gale of wind, had a hole stove in her bow, both masts gone, and expected to go down every moment. The perpetrator of such a miserable hoax deserves the execration of all mankind. *N. Y. Express*.

(416) From the *Republic*. APPOINTMENT BY THE PRESIDENT. John S. **GALLAHER** to be Third Auditor of the Treasury, vice Peter **HAGNER**.

(417) Married. On the 22d inst., at the Hotel of Mr. S. **WILLIAMS**, on the Canal, by A. **CHERRY**, Esq., Mr. Wm. R. **JONES**, of Norfolk, Va., to Miss Ann **REY**, formerly of Bertie Co. North Carolina. On the same day and place, and by the same Justice, Mr. John **ARMSTEAD** of Mathews Co. Va., to Miss Clarissa **BURNUM** of the same county.

(418) Patent Netting Machine, INVENTED BY JOHN **MC MULLEN** OF BALTIMORE. FISHING NETS and SEINES, made on the above machine, can be supplied to dealers in and consumers of the article, at the low price of 30 cents per pound for inch meshes. .. Persons wanting seines, are invited to call and examine a specimen of the work at the office of the "Old North State." Manufactured and for sale by Wm. E. **HOOPER**, **BOWLEY**s Wharf. Baltimore, Md. Nov 3.

(419) FARM FOR SALE, Containing 200 acres near the forks of the Road in the upper part of Pasquotank county, N. C., adjoining the lands of William **OLD** and John L. **HINTON**, Esqrs. For further particulars apply to P. W. **HINTON**, No 10 Roanoke Square, Norfolk, Va. Nov. 3

(420) SALT FOR SALE. The subscriber has in store a beautiful article of TURKS ISLAND SALT which he will sell at 27 CENTS CASH per bushel, in any quantity, from one to one thousand bushels. Call at the store on the Water, near the Market. Wm. **MESSENGER**. nov. 3.

(421) LAND FOR SALE. The plantation that I purchased of Mathew **CLUFF** whereon William T. **BRYANT**, now resides, being in the Immediate vicinity of E. City, Pasquotank County N. C. Containg [sic] 138 acres, about 85 acres cleared and in a good State of Cultivation, is now offord for Sals on Libarel [sic] terms. .. Mr. **BRYANT** my authorised agent, will take pleasure in showing the Land to any person that may wish to purchase, and is at Liberty to bargan and sell the said Land. If not sold before the 20th day of December next will on that day be sold at publick auction on the premises, and at the same time and place will be sold all the Corn, Fodder, Pease, Potatoes, Oats, Horses, Cattle, Hogs, Carts, and Farming Implements together with all the Household, and Kitchen Furniture. Terms liberal and made known on the day of sale. Russell **KINGSLOW**. Oxford, N. C. Nov. 3.

(422) Just as you might have expected. The undersigned has just received from the Northern Cities an extensive stock of every thing connected with the cabinet buisness [sic], not only ready made articles, but all the materials requisite for making up anything connected with his line of buisness. ... Caleb **SIKES**. Nov. 3.

(423) NEW STORE AT THE WATER. The subscriber having taken the Store near the water formerly occupied by Thos. **ALLEN**, Esq. has just received and opened a well assorted stock of Dry Goods and Groceries also Ship Chandlery of every description. Boots, Shoes, Hats, Caps, &c. of the best quality and at prices that cannot fail to suit. ... Thos. W. **KNIGHT**. Nov. 3.

10 November 1849

The Old North State.
Vol. 9. "Error is harmless, when truth is left free to combat it." No. 38.
Elizabeth City, N. C. Saturday, November 10, 1849.

(424) VERMONT LEGISLATURE. We have before us a printed list of the members of our present Legislature, with the place of residence, birthplace, politics, business, age, and number of years each has been a member of either branch of the General Assembly...... The oldest member is Joseph **HENRY**, esq. of Halifax, whose age is seventy four; and the youngest member is Mr. **RANDALL**, of Eden, whose age is twenty-six. ... *Brattleboro 'Eagle.*

(425) The first divorce in Minesota Territory has just been made by the Legislature--that of Lewis **LARAMMINE** from **WA-KAN-YE-KE-WING**, an Indian woman.

(426) PRINTERS AND PRINTING. J. T. **BUCKINGHAM**, esq., in his series of reminiscences, in course of publication in the *Boston Courier*, speaks of the importance of the printer to the authors, as follows: "Many, who condescend to illuminate the dark world with the fire of their genius, through the columns of a newspaper, little think of the lot of the printer, who, almost suffocated by the smoke of a lamp, sits up till midnight to correct his false grammar, bad orthography, and worse punctuation. ..."

(427) It is said that the Hawaiian Government is desirous of negotiating a treaty with the United States on a fair and equitable basis, and also to secure a modification in the clauses of the treaties of England and France, by which the King's independence is still trammeled. Mr. James J. **JARVES** of Boston, long resident at the Sandwich Islands, has been deputed by the King to effect these desired ends. *N. Y. Sun.*

(428) The editor of the *Hartford Times* has recently visited Groton, where he was introduced to Mother **BAILY**, the heroine of the Stonington fight. She is still hearty and affable, though in her 92d year. She lived with the husband of her youth 70 years, (she says) "without a word spoken in anger." Charles E. **HORN**, the great musical composer, died at Boston on Monday, in 63d year of his age.

(429) A calculation made by William **DARBY**, esq., the Geographer, goes to show that if the National Monument at Washington be elevated to five hundred feet, its apex will be visible at a distance of twenty-seven and a half miles.

(430) AMERICAN TALENT IN DEMAND ABROAD. The *New York Mirror* States that Major Thompson S. **BROWN**, late Engineer to the Erie Rail Road, will soon leave this country for a five years' engagement with the Emperor of Russia from whom he is to receive a salary of $12,000 per annum.

(431) At the Bourbon, (Ky.) Agricultural Fair, held a short time since, Mrs. Chapman **COLEMAN**, daughter of Gov. **CRITTENDEN**, received the premium, a $100 cup, for the best silk quilt, made with her own hands.

(432) Mr. E. G. **SQUIER**, our Charge d'Affaires to Central America, in a paper read at a meeting of the Ethnological Society in New York, stated that he had discovered a city about 150 miles from Leon, that was buried beneath a forrest, and far surpassing in architecture the ruins of Palenque.

(433) Elizabeth-City, Nov. 10, '49. .. EARLY SNOW. We understand by a gentleman by the name of **PALMER**, that there was a slight fall of snow in Tyrell county, on the 31st October last.

(434) Appointments by the President. *Washington*, Oct. 31, P. M.--John C. **CLARK**, of Va., 1st Auditor, has been appointed Solicitor in the Treasury department, vice R. H. **GILLETT**, removed; and Thos. L. **SMITH**; formerly Register, as 1st Auditor, vice John C. **CLARK**.

(435) The National Hotel at Washington was opened on Thursday, under the auspices of the experienced and enterpising host, Mr. E. D. **WILLARD**. The papers speak in highly commendatory terms of the interior arrangements...

(436) FOR SALE. One fourth part of the first class Canal Boat Corfu, one year old, of fifty-five tons, carrying three thousand bushels, and well equipped in every respect. Any proposal personally, or by letter post paid, will be attended to. John B. **SKINNER**. E. City, Nov. 10th, 1849.

10 November 1849

(437) $100 REWARD. RANAWAY from my plantation, in Chowan County, on the 16th of May, 1849, my negro man **HENRY**. Said boy **HENRY** is 21 years of age next August--is about five feet eight inches high, yellow complexion, and has a down-cast look when spoken to--has a small scar on one of his rists. The above reward..will be given if taken out of the State and confined in any jail, so I get him--or Fifty Dollars if taken in the State and delivered to me or confined in jail. All persons are forwarned from employing or harbor- [sic] said negro under the penalty of the law. Thomas **GREGORY**. Nov. 10

(438) Notice. On the first day of January next, under a decree of the Court of Equity passed at Fall Term 1849, I shall offer before the Court House in the Town of Elizabeth City, the tract of Land and improvements late of Thomas **ELLIOTT** senior dece'd, and on which he resided at the time of his death. ... John C. **EHRINGHAUS**, Clerk & Master Pasquotank Court of Equity. E. City, Nov. 10, '49.

The Old North State.
Vol. 9. "Error is harmless, when truth is left free to combat it." No. 39.
Elizabeth City, N. C. Saturday, November 17, 1849.

(439) THE CHEROKEE NATION. The *Tahlequah Advocate* of the 8th inst. contains the proceeding of the National Council, which met the previous week. Hon. James **KELL**, of Delaware district, was elected President of the National committee, or Upper House of the legislature, and the Hon. **SIX KILLER**, of Going Snake district, Speaker of the Council. .. The message of John **ROSS** the principal chief, was received and read... .. The Indian Mission Conference of the Southern Methodist Episcopal Church was to meet at **RILEY**'s chapel, two miles from Tahlequah, on the 24th ult., and Bishop **PAINE** was expected to preside.

(440) Elizabeth-City, Nov. 17, '49. .. Latest from California. .. The Hon. Thomas Butler **KING** was still at San Francisco, slowly recovering from his illness; and was to leave in the steamer of 1st November, for the States. He was about starting for the valley of Sonoma, in the hope of a more rapid recovery.

(441) THE CONVENTION. The most important intelligence is the action of the Convention convened at Monterey, pursuant to the proclamation of Gen. **RILEY**, to frame a constitution preparatory to the admission of California into the Union as a State. The Convention met at Colton Hall on the 1st of September, and on the 3d, the San Francisco delegation having arrived..proceeded to business. The following delegates were recognised by a vote of the Convention as duly elected, and took their seats: San Diego--Miguel **DE PEDRORENA**, Henry **HILL**; Los Angeles--S C **FOSTER**, J A **CARILLO**, M. **DOMINGUEZ**, A **STEARNS**; Santa Barbara--P **LA GUERRA**, San Luis Obispo--Henry A **TEFFT**, J M **COBARRUVIA**; Monterey--H W **HALLECK**, T O **LARKIN**, C T **BOTTS**, P **ORD**, L S **DENT**; San Jose--**ARAM**, K H **DIMMICK**, J D **HOPPE**, A M **PICO**, E **BROWN**; San Francisco--E **GILBERT**, M **NORTON**, W M **GWIN**, J **HOBSON**, W M **STEUART**, W D M **HOWARD**, F J **LIPPITT**, A J **ELLIS**; Sonoma--J **WALKER**, R **SEMPLE**, L W **BOGGS**, M G **VALLEJO**; Sacramento--J R **SNYDER**, W S **SHERWOOD** L W **HASTINGS**, J S **FOWLER**, W E **SHANNON**, J A **SUTTER**, J **BIDWELL**, M M **MC CARVER**; San Joaquin--J Mc H **HOLLINGSWORTH**, C L **PECK**, S **HALEY**, B S **LIPPINCOTT**, T L **VERMUILE**, M **FALLUN**, B F **MOORE**, Walter **CHIPMAN**.
    The following were then elected officers: President--Robert **SEMPLE**. Secretary--william G. **MARCY**. First Assistant Secretary--C. **LYONS**. Second Assistant Sec'y--J. B. **FIELD**. Translator--W. E. P. **HARTNELL**. Assistant Translator--H. **HENRIQUEZ**. Sergeant-at-Arms--J. S. **HOUSTON**. Doorkeeper--Cornelius **SULLIVAN**. Gen. **RILEY**, military governor of California, who was presented, was invited to a seat within the bar. .. Padre **RAMIREZ** and the Rev. S.H. **WILEY** were the chaplains of the body. ...

(442) Correspondence of the *Balt. Patriot*. Philadelphia, Nov. 13--P. M. Henry **CLAY** visited the Walnut Street Theatre last evening, by invitation of the manager, Mr. **MARSHALL**, to witness the personation of Lady Macbeth, by Miss Charlotte **CUSHMAN**. The box appropriated to him was draped with flags, and when he entered, attended by Hon. Richard **BAYARD**, Col. **SWIFT**, and others, the audience rose up and saluted him with six cheers. ...

(443) Dr. William **HODGES**, Dentist. Having located himself at Elizabeth City, respectfully offers his Professional Servises to such as may require them, in the surrounding country. He may be found at the office of Dr. **BAXTER**. REFERENCES. NORFOLK, C. F. **MARTIN**, D. S. W. M. **MC KENNEY**, D. S. Jno. N. **ANDREWS**, M. D. Wm. **WILSON**, M. D. Wm. **MOORE**, M. D. B. **BAYLOR**, M. D. E. CITY, O. F. **BAXTER** M. D. S. D. **GRICE**, M. D. G. J. **MUSGRAVE**, M. D. J. C. **EHRINGHAUS**, Esq. Rev. C. R. **HENDRICKSON**

24 November 1849

The Old North State.
Vol. 9. "Error is harmless, when truth is left free to combat it." No. 40.
Elizabeth City, N. C. Saturday, November 24, 1849.

(444) Most Extraordinary and Startling Disclosures in Texas. *The Confessions of one of a Banditti, composed of Men in high and low life from Missouri to Mexico.* The following confessions of one of the banditti, who for a year have been the terror of the inhabitants of the northern portion of Texas, and who was arrested some time since near Natchez, Miss., we copy from the *San Augustine Union*:--I was born in the State of Alabama; my parents moved to Texas when I was very young. My father and my mother always stood fair, and were regarded as honest people. At a very early period of my life, I disobeyed the instructions of my parents, and took my own course, or rather the plan and course of my eldest brother, William **SHORT**. Almost as far back as I can recollect, my brother William would pick up little matters, which I kept concealed from my father and mother. About the time my brother married, he broke into a store in company with several others, and one of the articles which my brother took was a pair of ladies' stockings, which he presented to his intended wife; from time to time William went on, step by step, stealing small articles, until he got so he could take a horse, or trade for a horse that he knew was stolen. I was gradually initiated into the secret of stealing, and particularly of the necessary item of hiding well. During this time, one of my sisters married Mr. **SANSUM**, who became a member of the party. Some time ago, Mr. **SANSUM** took off the irons that were on a Mr. **JACKSON**, convicted for rape in Fayette county. At or near the same time, William **SHORT**, Mr. **SANSUM**, James **CROOK**, James **MC LAUGHLIN**, and Alfred **O'BAR** decoyed and run two negroes, one the property of Dr. **ADKINSON**, of Lagrange, Fayette county, the other negro the property of Mr. **CLEVELAND**, of Travis, Austin county, and a fine horse, of Mr. **NORTON**; after the sale of the negroes and in the divide **MC LAUGHLIN** and William **SHORT** fell out and quarrelled with **CROOK**, he **CROOK**, had a league of land they wanted, which **CROOK** refused to let them have, and, in the quarrel, **CROOK** threatened to disclose on them. This alarmed the party, and especially **SHORT** and **MC LAUGHLIN**. After a conversation, it was arranged to kill **CROOK**, who made his home at William **SHORT**'s, John **MARSHALL** and John **RICH** were to be the murderers. **SHORT** sent me after John **MARSHALL** and John **RICH** to let them know the time. The night appointed, **CROOK** was not at home but stayed in the neighborhood.

In the morning, **SHORT** sent his wife to Mr. **CAROTHERS**, that she might not witness the transaction. **MC LAUGHLIN** was fearful **CROOK** would not return, and rode some distance in the course that **CROOK** would come, and as soon as he ascertained from a neighbor of **SHORT**'s that **CROOK** had gone home..returned in time to give the finishing touch to **CROOK**. I was then instructed how and what to prove, if anything was done at law. I was a witness before the Justices' Court; I was excused in the District Court. Suffice it to say, **MC LAUGHLIN** and **SHORT** were cleared, and **RICH** and **MARSHALL** never tried. Divers thefts and outrages were perpetrated from that time, until the party arrested have broken a link in the chain that extends from Missouri to Mexco.

Major **MOORE**, of Crockett, deals in counterfeit coin. Rev. Nathan **SHOOK** makes land certificates; he has the seal and everything necessary for the same. I saw Parson **SHOOK** making out some land papers at **SHORT**'s; he then went out on the Guadaloupe, where Mr. **MC PETERS** stole a fine mare belonging to Mr. **ESTILL**, and swapped her to Parson **SHOOK** for a likely gray mare, also stolen property. **SHORT** went to Guadaloupe with **SHOOK**, and they returned together, **SHOOK** slept till midnight, and left my brother's, since when I have not seen him. At or near Crockett, are three **LONG**s. At or near the same place are two **PEARSON**s. These men receive and trade in stolen horses, and asssist in harboring and running off negroes. Nathaniel **GREER** often applied to Wm. **SHORT** to be a full partner, and with **SHORT** and **MC LAUGHLIN** made arrangements to steal, run off, and sell a lot of mules belonging to a gentleman of Brenham. I never heard of James **COX** stealing any property, nor do I believe he would steal more than a gun-barrel but **COX** has been consulted in all deep planning. I learned from **SHORT** that **COX** could sell land patents to great advantage abroad, and could pass half-eagles without suspicion. It is said he passes as "Parson **COX**." .. Thomas **IRVIN** went to A. J. **GRIGG**, near Jacksonville, with William **SHORT**, and in justice to Mr. **IRVIN** I will here state, he had claim against one of the Messrs. **JACKSON**, that served to keep down suspicion. **SHORT** informed me that **IRVIN** and himself had made a fine saddle, and that **IRVIN** had agreed to harbor and secret any negroes that **SHORT** would send him, until the time arrived to run them off. James **MC LAUGHLIN** was the father of all and every kind of stealing, passing counterfeit coin, and murdering. He says he commenced early in life, and run many risks of life. **MC L.** informed the party, that whenever they went into a general negro stealing they would be detected. His prediction has been fulfilled; justice has overtaken them, and **MC LAUGHLIN**'s race has been run. I learn he was anxious that some honest man should raise his children.

Enos **COOPER** hired and paid to Wilson **SMALL** a $100 horse to kill a Mr. **ELKINS**, who married a sister of Beverly **POOL**, (formerly Mrs. **HAWK**.) **COOPER** sold some of Parson **SHOOK**'s land certificates, and I was informed assisted in starting Mr. **HILL**'s negro; also in stealing Robert **MOORE**'s mare fore the negro to ride. I am sure he is one of the clan. Mr. **GRIGG** gave me the name of **CARMEAN** as being one of the party, but I do not believe it.

Mosey **BOREN** aided and gave comfort and lodging to the party, and would do anything James **COX** asked him to do. **BOREN** occasionally exchanged for stolen horses. Louis **BOREN** and Orlando **SAP** passed counterfeit money and stole horses;

24 November 1849

(444) (Cont.) they are the men that received Mercer **HILL**'s negro from A. J. **GRIGG**, William **SHORT**, and Enos **COOPER**, and brought said negro boy **JOE** to me at the Star Hotel at Galveston, where I was in company with **AGERY**, our general agent for Texas. **AGERY** and John **FORD** came to Wm. **SHORT**'s, at La Grange, and proposed a general association, by connecting certain points and carrying on a general negro and horse stealing and counterfeit money passing arrangement. Brother William **SHORT** informed them that Col. **TAYLOR**, being near the Round Top House, would start shortly to Alabama, and that he would take about seven thousand dollars with him to buy negroes, and that **BOSTICS**, himself and one or two other gentlemen, would have him killed for the cash, which would enable the company to organize and go into active operations; but in case **TAYLOR** did not start in a short time the company would steal, run, and sell a few negroes, in order to have funds to start on. My brother William was to keep the Star Hotel; Mr. **AGERY** was to run a schooner on the Gulf, between Galveston and New Orleans: and a Mr. **JONES** was to be general agent at New Orleans, was to keep a boarding-house and run a boat on the Mississippi river; **MC LAUGHLIN** Wm. **SHORT**, A. J. **GRIGG**, **GREER**, and **COX** were to arrange the plans, and decoy the negroes. **BOREN**, Sap **WHITELY**, **O'BAR**, **CROWNOVES**, and several others, were to run negroes from the interior to Glaveston, and at a proper time, Mr. **AGERY**, with his schooner, would convey them to New Orleans, and deliver them to Mr. **JONES**, who..would send them up the Mississippi river, and have them sold; all of this was to be done through their own line, in order to evade detection. Alford **O'BAR** was cosidered a poor hand to sell negroes, as he had run the boy **SAM**, belonging to a German gentleman, near the Colorado river, by land to Red river, thence he took water, and went up to the mouth of the Ohio river. The boat had freight to discharge on the Ohio side, and while discharging freight, **SAM** stepped of [sic] the boat, learning his foot was on free soil.

Some time last season, a Mr. **CARRINGTON**, overseer for Mr. **HILL**, carried off a woman slave and two children to Mexico; he said the children were his own. About the first of may, **CARRINGTON** was in the Colorado Bottoms, and it was believed he was after more negroes. Brother William informed me that James and Samuel **MILLER** passed counterfeit money, traded for stolen horses, and occasionally stole a few cattle. They live on the road leading from Bastrop to Caldwell, Burleston county. Judge **JELSAW** lives on or near the Guadaloupe, and stands fair in the community. He had the promise of wagon master and pay-master in Gen. **WORTH**'s division to El Paso del Norte; our company were to furnish him with counterfeit gold to pay of the teamsters, and he was to divide the profits with our agents. The judge is quite conversant with all the plans of the company, and assists in carrying out our measures.

Joe **BARRINGTON** follows gambling, picks up a horse occasionally, passes counterfeit gold with considerable dexterity, sells **SHOOK**'s land certificates, and is in possession of all the plans of our party. Bird **SMITH** is a constant associate with **BARRINGTON**, and engages in the same acts... William **SHORT**, my poor unfortunate brother, has engaged in every species of crime, led a miserable life, died a disgraceful death, and thus far I learn his body has been exposed a prey to wild wolves and vultures. He led me into stealing, and after I had commenced, could not withdraw for fear of my own life, as death was the penalty for disclosure. Mr. **SMITH**, on the Gaudaloupe, is an associate with **MC PETERS**, and engages in every species of crime common to the party. **HALEY** lives on the Beedi near the Trinity river, and engages in every species of crime to which human beings are accessible. .. **MC LAUGHLIN** said Beverly **POOL** would do to depend on, was acquainted with all the ropes, but was too lazy to engage in active operations. ...

I learned the location of two mints for counterfeiting gold coin, one fifteen miles above Brownsville, on the Rio Grande, where coin can be had at fifty cents on the dollar, to change off and trade to the Mexicans. The other mint is fifteen miles from Crockett, in a cane brake on a thicket bottom, and Moss **MORE** general agent; he furnishes the coin at fifty cents on the dollar. The present coin are eagles and half-eagles, well executed, the engraving is elegant, equal to any of the genuine American coin; one acquainted, may tell it from the color being a shade brighter than pure gold; the weight corresponds, or nearly so, there is only from one to two grains difference in the half-eagle; the eagles are the precise weight, and will and have deceived many; and a good many have gone into the banks at New Orleans; they resist the tests of acids, being a plate of pure gold: but in order to apply the plate correctly, the plate is partially changed. The quickest way to detect them is to examine the edge, where a line or division may be discovered in the centre of the edge. .. About the 1st of May last, I called at **MC LAUGHLIN**'s, on my way to Galveston. I asked.. for a horse to ride the trip; he told me he would loan me a horse until I could find one, and that I was a poor rogue if I could not find a horse. I started..early in the morning, and soon found a large bay horse. .. I rode the horse to Houston, and sold him for $15. I then went to Galveston, where I met **AGERY** and **FORD**; I went to inform them that **JOHNSON** and **SMITH**, alias **BOREN** and **SAP** would be there soon with Mercer **HILL**'s boy, **JOSH**. The next day, **AGERY** wrote me a bill of sale, purporting to be from William H. **RICE**, of the town of Gennaros, county of Gonzales, to William **SMITH**. I objected to taking the bill of sale under the name..but the negro did not know my true name when I left home. .. When I arrived at New Orleans, I stopped at **ROBINSON**'s boarding-house. The next day **AGERY** arrived, and stopped at another place. He then sent me to sell the negro, but the police kept such a watch, **AGERY** thought best to send me up to Natcez; encouraged me by informing me that he had sold many, and that people of Natchez were so eager to buy young negro men that they would scarcely ask my name. Encouraged by so smart a man as **AGERY**, with a tongue well fitted for a boy of 18 years, I consented to go, but when I learned the amount of cash he could start I was near backing out. .. When the time arrived for me to go, six dollars was all the cash we both had, barely enough to pay our way deck passage, (rather low for a negro trader.) I arrived at Natchez in the night, and went to **WHITE**'s tavern, under the hill. The

24 November 1849

(444) (Cont.) next day I offered the boy for $750, to **WILSON**; he said if he liked the boy when he had talked with him, he would give me my price. Just as I dreaded and expected, I was betrayed in a few moments. I was waited on by officers, my bill of sale asked for, my name, my residence, and a thousand of other questions, and a polite invitation to walk to the court house; my face, my actions all embarrassed, soon told the tale for me. I was informed I had stolen a negro.

The next day I called for paper, and wrote to Texas; my letter was intercepted, though I did not know it. I looked for assistance; I heard strange voices without--the door opened--I recognized the face of Dr. **WIER**, and with it I received the information that the whole party was disclosed--one **GRIGG** arrested, **BOREN** and **SAP** were pursued, and I could take my choice to stay at Natchez for trial, or go to Brenham. I readily consented, provided I could have a trial at law. Dr. **WIER** and Mr. **FERRELL** pledged their honors that such should be my case; and now, reader, I am in irons in Brenham jail, guilty and depending on the sympathies of the community, from whom I deserve none. Taomas **SHORT**.

(445) **BAIN**'s TELEGRAPHIC MACHINE. We perceive that Alexander **BAIN**, the inventor of the Electro-Chemical Telegraph, is about to visit Europe. He designs to return to this country with his family in the Spring. .. Other experimentalists bent their energies to the invention of Electro-Magnetic telegraphs, and seemed to suppose that all other electrical forces, except that of the Electro-Magnet, were useless for telegraphing; but Mr. **BAIN** left the beaten road, and turned his attention to the sciences of Electricity and Chemistry for the purpose of making a telegraphic agent. .. We think this machine superior to any other invention. Some recent improvements made by Mr.**BAIN**..are deserving of especial notice: By an ingenious contrivance, he has made a combination of two powers which regulates the Electric movements, and times them so that 500 machines scattered over the Union may be made to make a perfect synchronous movement; and a dot or line made in New Orleans, may at the same moment be made in Louisville, and at all intermediate stations. .. By the new arrangement, the operator composes the message and transmits it at the rate of 1000 [letters] per minute without the agency of the type cutting machine. .. The inventor of this instrument was notified in September, by **MORSE, KENDALL** & Co., that a motion would be made at the October term of the Kentucky District Court, for an injunction against his machine, as an infringement upon the rights of the owner of all Celestial Electricity--S. F. B. **MORSE**. The question was never argued, the motion having been abandoned by Mr. **KENDALL**. .. He is about to bring his family to this country though he may be restrained from doing so by the fear, as is said in the *Louisville Courier*, that Amos **KENDALL** will claim his wife and children as inventions of Professor **MORSE**, or perhaps Amos **KENDALL**. *N. Y. Express*.

(446) TUNNEL UNDER A CITY.--Somebody in N. York has started a project to tunnel Broadway for an underground railway, with openings and stairways at every corner, from Bowling Green to Union Square. This subalterranean passage is to be brilliantly (!) lighted with gas laid down with a double track, the cars to be drawn by horses, and a "trottoir" to be made on either side for foot passengers, the names of the streets to be placed at every stairway, so the travellers can be apprized of their locality--and the cars to stop ten seconds at every opening, to let the wayfarers go out and get in.

(447) Elizabeth-City, Nov. 24, '49. .. The Brig Huntress, Capt. Thomas **COOK**, which sailed from this port a short time since destined to Barbadoes, when about 300 miles from Hatteras, experiencing a heavy gale sprung a leak and put into Norfolk in distress. We understand that the gale was so severe, and that there was so much water in the hole of the Brig, that it was only by the faithfulness and skill of the captain and crew that she was saved from sinking.

(448) APPOINTMENT. We learn from the *N. Y. Enquirer* that Nixon **WHITE** of Perquimans County has been appointed Purser on board the sloop-of-war Falmouth, in place of W. B. **HARTWELL** deceased.

(449) We have received a number of the *Wilmington Aurora*, a new Democratic Semi-Weekly paper just issued under the Editorial management of Henry I. **TOOLE**, Esq. It is printed on good paper with good type, and presents a very attractive appearance. ...

(450) The steamboat Georgia, of the Baltimore line has again taken her position upon the route. Since the accident that befel her last summer, she has been thoroughly overhauled and put in complete order, and under her experienced commander Capt. **CANNON**, and obliging Clerk, Mr. Loyd **PARKS**, she cannot be surpassed either in safety or comfort.

(451) *Correspondence of the Baltimore Patriot*. WASHINGTON. The national capital is fast filling up with strangers, and a few members of Congress. The Hon. George **EVANS**, of Maine, has returned to the city and resumed his chair, as President of the Board of Commissioners to settle claims against Mexico. Colonel **PAINE**, one of the Commissioners..is laboring under an indisposition which deprives the Board of his presence. .. Colonel **WEBB**, of the *New York Courier and Enquirer*, is in town, looking remarkably well, and..has been tendered, and has accepted, the post of *Charge des Affaires* to Austria, *vice* Mr. **STILES**, of

24 November 1849

(451) (Cont.) Georgia, who has just returned from Vienna to the United States. This post..was formerly a full mission, but was cut down to its present grade, by Congress, some five or six years ago, about the time of the appointment, by Mr. **TYLER**, of Mr. George H. **PROFFIT**, as Minister to Austria. The Hon. John W. **FARRALLY** is in town..and will tomorrow morning enter upon his duties as Auditor of the Post Office Department. ...

Why the Hon. John C. **SPENCER**, who had the reputation of being a dictatorial, cold, austere head of a Department--but who never had a superior, as Secretary of the Treasury, except, perhaps, Alexander **HAMILTON**--remarked to the writer of this, on one occasion: "Sir, the appointing power over the clerks in the bureaus of the several Auditors of the Treasury, belongs by law to the Secretary of the Treasury; but the Secretary always pays great deference and respect to the suggestions and recommendations of the Auditors..." .. The Hon. James **BROOKS**, M. C. and editor of the *New York Express*, is in town for a day or two, looking out for a house and winter quarters. It is pretty certain that the Hon. Thos. Butler **KING** will not be able to get here, from California, by the opening of Congress. It is understood that the Hon. William J. **BROWN**, of Indiana, is sick at his home, too feeble to travel; and that the Hon. Mr. **SWEETZER**, of the Columbus District, Ohio, has sickness in his family, which may deter him from being here at the opening of Congress . .. Senator **BENTON** has arrived from Missouri, and..Mr. **VINTON** from Ohio, and Mr. **DUER** from New York. The Hon. Richard W. **THOMASON**, member of the last Congress from Indiana, is in town. ...

(452) DIED, In this county on Saturday morning last, Mr. Joseph R. **BRADSHAW**, aged about 28 years. He was buried by the "Rough & Ready" Light Dragoons of which corps he was a member, and an exemplary one at that, always at his post, ready and willing to do his duty. He has left a disconsolate wife and one child to mourn their irreparable loss. In the death of this young man how true the adage that "in the midst of life we are in death," for it was only on the Thursday previous, that we saw and conversed with him, and he appeared to be enjoying his usual health. But alas, forty-eight hours had not sped their rapid flight before he was called to that "bourne from where no traveller returns. Peace be to his ashes.

(453) NOVELS, MAGAZINES &c. Just received a large variety of Novels, cheap Publications, &c. .. We shall be receiving something new every week and any work not on hand, will be ordered if wanted. Call and examine for yourselves at the Drug Store of L. K. **SAUNDERS** & Co., on Road street. Nov. 24, 1849.

(454) WRECK SALE. Will be sold on Saturday the 1st day December, at 12 o'clock, at Hatteras Beach, Hyde county, for the benefit of the owners, underwriters & all others concerned, the Schr. Lydia Jane, as she now lies stranded on said Beach, with all her Sails, Rigging, &c. By order of the Master, John S. **FRIEND**. Nov. 24.

(455) NEW STOCK OF GOODS. The undersigned have taken the old stand occupied by John J. **GRANDY**, Esq., where they have opened, an entire new stock of DRY GOODS & GROCERIES which they are offering to the public on reasonable terms--all kinds of produce taken in exchange for goods. **PRITCHARD & NASH**. Nov. 24.

(456) **KELLY**'s for Sale. The subscriber from recent misfortune and inability to give personal attention to it, will sell on accommodating terms, this well known Farm, situated in Norfolk County, containing by estimate, two hundred and thirty acres, more or less. It is half a mile from the city by land, and one mile by the Elizabeth river. It is also bounded on one side by a Creek, which it is thought, will make a good tide mill, and may be dammed at a trifling expense. The place has been recently limed and much improved, and will make a handsome garden and dairy farm, doubly Valuable on account of its contiguity to the city market, and Baltimore boat. If not sold prior to the twentieth of December next, it will leased [sic] out for ten years. Arrangements will be in progress, until the farm is disposed of, for an early spring garden. Persons wishing to purchase will apply to Nathaniel **WILSON**, **BRIGG**'s Point, All communications with regard to the above property will be promptly attended to. nov 24.

(457) Riddicksville Seminary, NEAR SUNSBURY, GATES CO., N. C. The next Session of this flourishing English and Classical Academy, will commence on the first Monday in January, and continue without interruption till the last Friday in July.-- August and September will be set apart for vacation. TERMS: Board and Tuition, including room rent, wood and washing, per session of ten months, In the English Department, -- $110 " " Classical " -- 120. Books and Stationery furnished at a reasonable rate. Boys are fitted for any College in the Union or for active buisness. For further particulars, address Henry **RIDDICK**, Esq., the Proprietor, or S. J. **LEARNED**, A. M. Principal. Sunsbury, Nov. 24.

(458) $50 REWARD. A REWARD of fifty Dollars will be given for the apprehension and delivery to me, in Gates Co. of my negro man **PETER**. He is about 5 feet 8 inches high, has a very great impediment in his speech; has a scar on his breast, as if burned, and has lost a toe from one of his feet. He has a sister at the late Mrs. Jos. H. **SKINNER**'s, in Chowan County, and one in Elizabeth City, I think at Mrs. **MC MORINE**s. H. E. **RASCOE**. Nov. 24

24 November 1849

(459) J. B. **GODWIN**, DENTAL SURGEON. Having *permanently* located himself in E. City offers his services to the *public*, in all the departments of his profession. Office corner of Road & Market streets, in the room formerly occupied by Wm. **LABOYTAUX** as an ice cream saloon. Persons in town or country prefering it will be waited on at their residence. J. B. **GODWIN**, has the pleasure of refering to the following named gentlemen. S. D. **GRICE**, M. D., George J. **MUSGRAVE**, M. D., R. K. **SPEED**, M. D., Gilbert **ELLIOTT**, Esq., Gen. J. C. B. **EHRINGHAUS**, Hill **BURGWIN**, Esq., John **BLACK**, Esq., James W. **HINTON**, Esq., William E. **MANN**, Esq., of Elizabeth City, N. C. E. City, Nov. 24, 1849.

The Old North State.
Vol. 9. "Error is harmless, when truth is left free to combat it." No. 41.
Elizabeth City, N. C. Saturday, December 1, 1849.

(460) Original Letter of General **WASHINGTON**. Annexed is the letter of Gen. **WASHINGTON** to his wife..which was found among the papers of the late Hon. Hugh **NELSON**. The reader will observe that it begins abruptly. The first part of the letter, including the date, &c., is gone; but it is evident from the remainder, that it must have been written a [sic] Cambridge in the beginning of the Revolutionary struggle. The reader cannot but be struck with the calm self-possession, the conscientious adherence to duty, the caution and discretion so characteristic of Gen. **WASHINGTON**, which are strikingly prominent in this letter. It is also made evident, by this document, if there were no other proof, that Gen. **WASHINGTON** entered the Revolntionary struggle from no motives of personal ambition. .. We may add, that a copy of the letter had been placed in the hands of Hon. W. **RIVES**, who intended to present it to the Virginia Historical Society. That gentleman is now, however, absent at a foreign post. We have been authorised to publish the letter, and shall also comply with pleasure with Mr. **NELSON**'s request to place the manuscript in the hands of the Virginia Historical Society: * * * * "to sow the additional supply of hemp and flax seed, which Mr. **MIFFLIN** has procured for me in Philadelphia, and which I hope will be with you before this letter. For obvious reasons, you will not sow it on the island, nor by the water side. But I hope you will have a good account of your crop on the Ohio. If **BRIDGEY** continues refractory and riotous, tho, I know you can ill spare him, let him by all means be sent off, as I hope Jack **CUSTIS**'s boy **JOE** already is, for his sauciness at Cambridge. .. Suffice it that, I say, what I have often before told you, that, as far as I have the controul of them, all our preparations for war aim only at peace. Neither do I, at this moment, se [sic] the least likelihood of there being any considerable military operations this season, and if not in this season, certainly in no other. It is impossible to suppose, that in the leisure and quiet of winter quarters, men will not have the virtue to listen to the dictates of plain common sense and sober reason. The only true interest of both parties is reconciliation, nor can there be a point in the world nearer than that both sides must be losers by war, in a manner which even peace cannot soon compensate for. We must at last agree and be friends; for we cannot live without them, and they will not without us, and a bystander might well be puzzled to find out why as good terms cannot be given and taken now, as when we shall have well nigh ruined each other by the mutual madness of cutting one another's throats.--For all these reasons, which cannot but be as obvious to the English Commissioners and ours, as they are to me, I am at a loss to imagine how any thing can arise to obstruct a negotiation, and of consequence a pacification. You, who know my heart, know there is not a wish nearer to it than this is; but I am prepared for every event, one only excepted--I mean a dishonorable peace. Rather than that, let me, tho' it be with the loss of every thing else I hold dear, continue this horrid trade, and by the most unlikely means, be the unworthy instrument of preserving political security and happiness to them, as well as to our selves. Pity this cannot be accomplished without fixing on me the sad name, Rebel. I love my king, you know I do; a soldier, a good man, cannot but love him. How particularly hard, then, is our fortune, to be deemed traitors to so good a King! But I am not without hope that even he will yet see cause to do me justice; posterity I am sure will. .. I see my duty, that of standing up for the Liberties of my Country, and whatever difficulties and discouragements lie in my way, I dare not shrink from it, and I rely on that Being, who has not left to us the choice of duties, that whilst I conscientiously discharge mine, I shall not finally lose my reward. If I really am not a bad man, I shall not long be so set down. ..

Let me rely that your answer to this will be dated in Philadelphia. If am not very busily engaged, (which I hope may not be the case,) perhaps I may find ways and means to pay a visit of a day or two; but this I rather hint as what I wish, than what I dare bid you expect. If you still think the fragments of the set of greys I bought of Lord **BOTTETOURT** unequal to the journey, let Lund **WASHINGTON** sell them, singly, or otherwise, as he can to the best advantage, and purchase a new set of bays. .. I beg to be affectionately remembered to all our friends and relations, and that you will continue to believe me to be Your most faithful and tender husband, G. **W**.

(461) Elizabeth-City, Dec. 1, '49. .. *From the Pittsburg Advocate.* Married, In St. Andrew's Church, on Thursday, the 22d inst. by Rev. Wm. **PRESTON**, Mr. H. **BURGWIN**, of N. C., to Miss. Mary, daughter of late Maj. A. **PHILLIPS**, U. S. A.

(462) DIED, Mr. Zion **CULPEPPER**--the subject of this Obituray [sic] bade adieu to the sorrows and afflictions attendant upon human life on Thursday, 29th inst. For several months past Mr. C. has been lingering as it were upon the very threshold of time,

1 December 1849

(462) (Cont.) just ready to enter into boundless, endless eternity. For some time prior to his death he appeared to look forward to the moment of his dissolution, with deep interest and anxiety. He had no fears of death, for his peace was made with God. .. The writer of these lines would willingly speak of the merits of Mr. **CULPEPPER**, but is conscious of his entire inability to do justice thereto. Suffice it to say that his general treatment towards those with whom he had to do, was of such nature, as always to command their respect and esteem. The needy and dependant around him always had a ready passport to his kindness and benevolence. He was for several years previous to his death engaged in the Mercantile business, by which he succeeded in acquiring a handsome property. Mr. **CULPEPPER** has left a disconsolate wife and four little children, to lament his death. ...

On Thursday, the 16th inst., after a short illness, Mrs. Sarah **HOOD**, aged 34 years, leaving a husband and three children to mourn their loss. ...

(463) $50 Reward. Ranaway from the subscriber in August last, my negro boy **BOB**, aged about 18 years. He is a very likely boy, thick set, and very black, speaks quick when spoken to, and in walking he leans over in front. I will give the above reward if secured in any Jail so that I get him. W. W. **WILLIAMS**. E. City, Dec. 1, 1849.

(464) VALUABLE FARM FOR SALE. The subscriber being desirous of leaving the County, offers for sale the plantation whereon he now resides. The farm is situated in a pleasant part of the county, and the soil is well adopted to the culture of Corn, Wheat and Potatoes, and being situated on Little River, but little trouble is necessary to deliver the produce. This farm contains about 225 acres, 150 of which is under a good state of cultivation. There is upon the farm a good comfortable dwelling house and all necessary farm houses. Persons wishing to purchase, will please make application to the undersigned--any information respecting the farm can be obtained by applying to him or Jeptha **WHITE**, of Perquimans County.--Terms will be made reasonable to the purchaser. Morris **TRUEBLOOD**. Dec. 1, 1849.

The Old North State.
Vol. 9. "Error is harmless, when truth is left free to combat it." No. 42.
Elizabeth City, N. C. Saturday, December 8, 1849.

(465) TWO SCENES IN THE PROGRESS OF COL. **BENTON**. The *Democratic Banner*--anti-**BENTON**--furnishes the following sketch of a scene at the meeting in Bowling Green, Pike county, to hear Col. **BENTON**'s appeal: At the conclusion of his speech, Mr. Robert **ALLISON**, a very respectable citizen of this county, and personal acquaintance of Col. **BENTON**, offered him a written question in the following words, to wit: "Senator **BENTON**: Owing to the difference of opinion among the citizens of this vicinity, in regard to your position on the question of the **WILMOT** proviso, we respectfully submit..the following question...: "Are you in favor of or opposed to the principles of the..proviso, as applied to the territories of the United States?" This question had been previously drawn up and signed by some of the oldest and most prominent citizens of the county, viz: James L. **TEMPLETON**, James H. **HUFFORD**, Hezekiah **ODEN**, Nathan **VANEY**, Mathew **GIVENS**, Harmon **HAWKINS**, Thomas **STANFORD**, James **TURNER**, James D. **MC ELWEE**, John **SOUTH**, Adam G. **GOURLEY**, William **LUCE**, Chamness T. **SMITH**, Mormon H. **EIDSON**, Robert **FULERTON**, James A. **MACKEY**, Jos. **PUGH**, Thomas R. **VAUGHAN**, John B. **HENDERSON**, P. **CARR**, and Enoch **MARTIN**; but instead of giving it a respectful consideration, he insultingly refused to receive it, and treated with scorn and contempt him who offered it. ... [*Missouri Repub.*, 2d.

(466) THE GREAT SHOPPING STORE OF AMERICA. The city editor of the *New York Evening Post* gives the following elaborate description of **STEWART**'s magnificent establishment, which is, beyond a doubt, the first in America. His marble store in Broadway, is one of the curiosities of the great city; and it appears that he is already about enlarging his extensive premises: "Few instances, in our city, of what may be achieved by well directed and unremitting energy, stand out more prominently as indicative of its triumphant results, than the career of Mr. **STEWART**. Some twenty-two years since, he laid the foundation of his immense business, which has already become the most conspicuous, and systematically the best conducted in this country, though he has not yet passed the meridian of life. His mercantile career was commenced with a compartivaly [sic] limited capital, yet, by judicious use of his resources, which were subsequently argumented, by some accessions derived from his connection with the Lispenard **STEWART** estate, he is at present, it is believed, possessed of a fortune of between two and three millions of dollars. .. He was the first here to introduce the system of adhering to fixed prices. By this method of inspiring public confidence he has accumulated a business that now defies competition. ..

The interior, which consists of five stories, is decorated in the mast beautiful style of art; the first floor, or retail department, being devoted to the sale of silks, cashmeres, shawls, delaines, lace, hosiery, merinoes and mourning goods; there are three upper stories, in which the wholesale business of the establishment is carried on. These are reached by a broad flight of stairs, the entrance of which is on the south wing of the building. The basement is reserved as a depot for the sale of carpets and upholstery goods. The entire cost of the edifice is estimated at a little within $300,000; and the contemplated additions, which will

8 December 1849

(466) (Cont.) extend the range of building from Read to Chambers-st., will probably cost $200,000 more. ...

(467) A MISER ROBBED. A letter in the *New York Commercial*, from Carlisle, Schoharie county, N. Y.; says that on Tuesday last and aged Dutchman, named Peter **BECKER**, who has been hoarding for years all the specie he could get, was robbed of all he had, (nearly $4000.) About 2 o'clock on the morning above mentioned three men in disguise broke open the outside door with a large stone, and entering the house, one of them seized a son of Mr. **BECKER**, and throwing him on the bed, held him by the throat, threatening both him and his wife with instant death if they persisted or made the least noise. The other two then proceeded to rifle the chest containing the money, which was mostly gold and silver, deposited in small tin trunks and canisters. These they emptied into bags..and after threatening the inmates..with death, if they attempted to alarm the neighbors, made their escape with the rich booty.

(468) Elizabeth-City, Dec. 8, '49. .. MELANCHOLY SUICIDE. The *Buffalo Courier* contains the following account of the suicide of a daughter of Hon. John **NORVELL**, of Detroit, formerly U. S. Senator from Michigan: Niagara Falls, Nov. 27--8 1/2 P. M. .. The train of cars yesterday morning brought hither a young woman of fine personal appearance, and about 35 years of age, having with her two bright-looking boys, 4 and 6 years old. After taking rooms at the Eagle Hotel, she called for writing materials, and nothing more was known of her until this morning. Between 7 and 8 o'clock the bell of the room she had occupied was rung by the little boys. They were inquiring for their mother.

Upon the table were found three letters--one directed to Major **MILLER**, U. S. A., and one to Hon. John **NORVELL**, Detroit, Mich., and one to the proprietor of the Eagle Hotel, (a copy of which I send you,) also the ringlets of one side of her head, her gold watch, two trunks of clothing, a silk purse containing some gold and silver coins, and her wedding ring. The children state that their mother had bid them good bye and kissed them, after they had gone to bed--that they had last come from Winchester, Virginia, and that their father was in Florida. .. *9 1/2 o'clock, A. M.*--Enough has been found to warrant the belief that the unfortunate lady leaped from the Bridge that leads to Goat Island and was swept over the Falls. .. Her father has been telegraphed, and the children have been kindly taken charge of by Hon. Augustus **PORTER**. [The following is a copy of the letter..to Mr. **WHITE**, of the Eagle Hotel:] .. My mind is made up: I have no wish to live any longer. I shall go where my body will never be recovered. .. Please take care of my two little boys till they can be sent to Detroit, where their grandparents reside. They are the sons of Major **MILLER** of the Army, now in Florida, and grandsons of Hon. John **NORVELL**, Detroit, Michigan. Please forward my letters and protect my children till some of their relatives can come for them. Mrs. J. G. **MILLER**.

The *buffalo Commercial Advertiser* of the 28th copies the above, and says: It is reported here that a lady, answering to the description of Mrs. **MILLER**, left this city for the East in the express train yesterday morning, and that there are circumstances leading to the belief that the apparent evidences of suicide are *only* apparent. .. The *Buffalo Republican* says in reference to the above occurrence: "We have learned that there is every reason to believe that Mrs. **MILLER** is still alive, having eloped with a friend from Philadelphia... .. On Thursday last a man, who registered his name as "Henry **BLAKEMER**, Philadelphia," stopped at the Exchange Hotel, in this city. .. On the arrival of the Sunday morning train, he was observed by the porter of the depot, with a lady with two children. The lady, who was afterwards ascertained to be Mrs. **MILLER**, took lodgings at the Exchange, where she remained until Monday morning, when she took the 9 o'clock train for the Falls. On the afternoon of Monday, Mr. **BLAKEMER** went to the livery stable of Mr. **MILLER**, on Washington street, and hired a horse and buggy to go two miles below Tonawanda. He returned about three o'clock on Tuesday morning with a lady believed to be Mrs. **MILLER**, leaving her at the railroad depot, when he brought the horse back to the livery stable. He then called at the Exchange for his baggage, and, accompanied by Mrs. **MILLER**, took the last train which leaves here at half past 5, purchasing tickets for Cayuga Bridge. This **BLAKEMER** is about five feet eight inches high, light complexion, dark hair and beard, which had not been shaved, apparently, for three or four weeks, and from twenty-five to thirty years of age.

(469) J. Nevitt **STEELE**, Esq., has been appointed charge d'affaires to Venezuela.

(470) Horrible Affair in Boston. *Supposed Murder of Dr. George **PARKMAN**--Arrest of Dr. **WEBSTER**, of the Medical College--Great Excitemen--the Military ordered out by the Authorities.* About a week ago we announced the mysterious disappearance of Dr. George **PARKMAN**, a well known and much respected gentleman, of Boston. The event produced the greatest excitement in that city and vicinity, and the utmost efforts were made to find him. They were without success, till Friday evening, when the half-cousumed remains of a human being, supposed to be those of the unfortuneate man, were reported to have been found under the private room of Professor **WEBSTER**, in the Medical College, in Grove st. Soon after the disappearance of the Dr. his brother-in-law, Robert G. **SHAW**, Esq., published the following notice in the newspapers: $3000 REWARD. DR. GEORGE **PARKMAN**, a well known citizen of Boston, left his residence No. 8 Walnut street, on Friday last; he is 60 years of age; about 5 feet 9 inches high, grey hair, thin face; with a scar under his chin; light complexion, and usually walks very fast. He was dressed in a dark frock coat, dark pantaloons, purple silk vest, with dark figured black stock and black hat. As he may have wand-

8 December 1849

(470) (Cont.) ered from home, in consequence of some sudden aberration of mind, being perfectly well when he left his house; or as he had with him a large sum of money, he may have been foully delt with. The above reward will be paid for information which will lead to his discovery, if alive; or for the detection and conviction of the perpetrators, if any injudry may have been done to him. A suitable reward will be paid for the discovery of his body. Information may be given to the City Marshal. Robert G. **SHAW**. Boston, Nov. 26, 1849. Two or three days after this, no trace having been discovered of the missing man, Mr. **SHAW** published the following notice: $1000 REWARD Whereas, no satisfactory information has been obtained respecting DR. GEORGE **PARKMAN**, since the afternoon of Friday last, and fears are entertained that he has been murdered, the above reward will be paid for information which leads to the recovery of his body. ROBERT G. **SHAW**. Nov. 29. .. The entire police force of the city were constantly engaged in endeavoring to ferret out the affair. .. The search continued through Friday afternoon till evening, when the mutilated remains of a human body were discovered in the Medical College attached to the Massachusetts General Hospital, in Grove and Allen streets, Boston. This discovery led to the arrest of Professor **WEBSTER**, of that institution.
      TELEGRAPHIC. .. Boston, December 1--4 P. M. The excitement in the city, growing out of the arrest of Professor **WEBSTER**, charged with the murder of Dr. **PARKMAN**, is very great. About the furnace of the accused have been found a jaw-bone, some buttons, and some gold. The discovery of the remains was first made by Mr. **LITTLEFIELD**, a porter in the College, who broke through a brick wall into the private vault, to which none but Mr. **WEBSTER** had access. .. The inquest will commence on Wednesday next. ...

(471) Notice The firm of L. K. **SAUNDERS** & Co., is this day dissolved by mutual consent. All persons who are indebted to the said firm are requested to make payment to Rufus K. **SPEED**, who alone is authorized to settle all business of the concern. Rufus K. **SPEED**, L. K. **SAUNDERS**. Dec. 8, '49

(472) English & Classical Institute, ELIZABETH CITY, N. C. The next Term in this Institution will begin on the 2d of January next. Students are thoroughly and practically intrusted [sic] in all the sciences partaining to an English and Classical Education. G. M. **WILDER** Principal. Dec. 8

(473) Samaritan Salve, For the cure of every description of sore and ulcer, Credentials and certificate of its infallible efficacy, will be presented to every applicant gratuitously: SAMARITAN OINTMENT. This ointment has been in use for the last 60 years, but not for sale. It is now for the first time, presented to the world as infallible in every instance, for rheumatic complaints, and for the cure of every pain arising from cold or wet weather. .. Warranted to contain no particle of mineral substance.
      Norfolk, Va. Sep. 26, 1849. I with pleasure add my testimony to the efficacy of the "Samaritan Ointment" in affording me almost immediate relief from an attack of Rhuematism. S. T. **SAWYER**. Elizabeth City, N. C. Oct. 1 1849. This is to certify that I was troubled with rheumatism in my feet and ancles so bad that I could not put my feet to the ground in 9 months, and was prevailed on to try some of Dr. **RAPP**'s Samaritan Ointment, and in 18 hours after the first application I was able to stand without pain--and now I can walk as well as ever. I confidently recommend it to those troubled with the above disease. Arthur **JONES**. I have used with decided good effect Mr. A. W. **RAPP**'s Rhuematic Ointment in Inflammatory Rheumatism in my left arm and hand, and although I am opposed to popular nostrums, I take pleasure in recommending this preparation as an excellent one. J. W. **FAUQUIER**. The genuine for sale by L. K. **SAUNDERS**, who is the only agent for E. City, N. C. Dec. 8

(474) VALUABLE PROPERTY FOR SALE. Will be sold, on Tuesday the 18th of DECEMBER next, at the residence of the late Edmund B. **SKINNER**, near **HARVEY**'s Neck, Perquimans County, ALL THE PERSONAL AND CHATTEL PROPERTY. BELONGING TO THE ESTATE consisting of the Crop of Corn, Fodder and Peas, Horses, Mules, Work Oxen, Beef Cattle, Cows and Calves, Sheep, fatted and other Hogs, ox and mule Carts, Carrylog and Chains, and all other articles for farming operations. ALSO, ALL THE HOUSEHOLD & KITCHEN FURNITURE. At the same time will be Rented for one year, the PLANTATION --and the NEGROES hired out for the same term. Terms made known on the day of Sale, BY THE EXECUTORS. Dec. 8th, 1849.

(475) Notice! The Subscriber being desirous to enter into some other business offers for sale on accommodating terms the farm on which he resides, known as the "Hickory Farm," lying on the public road from Woodville to Hertford, and within three miles of a navigable stream, containing 225 acres, most of which is first rate land. There are (2) hundred thousand of it now cleared and in a fine state of cultivation--Twenty thousand in wheat which will be sold with the farm if desired. It has on it a new two-story dwelling forming an ell 36 by 16 each way; and all necessary out buildings, which are mostly new, having been built during the present year. There is a good water cistern attached, holding from 5 to 6000 gallons. There is another piece of land containing 107 acres adjoining this which can be purchased upon fair terms. .. All requisite information can be had through the Post Office at Woodville, or from the subscriber on the premises, or from Joseph M. **COX**, Esq., at Hertford. If no opportunity offers for selling the above property, it will be rented for the ensuing year. All the farming utensils and a stock of provisions, corn, fodder &c. &c., sufficient to supply the farm for the ensuing year, and also his stock of cattle, hogs and horses, will be sold on accommodating

8 December 1849

(475) (Cont.) terms if early application be made. Matthew O. **JORDAN**. Hickory Grove Dec. 8, 1849.

(476) BLOCK TIN WARE. We have in store, of our own importation, a full stock of: Best English _lanished Tin Dish Covers Coffee Urns, Coffee and Tea Pots, Plate Heaters, Plate Covers, &c., which we are prepared to sell very low. E. P. **TABB** & Co., Hardware Importers. Norfolk, Va. Dec. 8

The Old North State.
Vol. 9. "Error is harmless, when truth is left free to combat it." No. 43.
Elizabeth City, N. C. Saturday, December 15, 1849.

(477) DESCRIPTION OF **BILLY BOW LEGS** THE SEMINOLE CHIEF. **BILLY** is thus described by an eye witness who was present at an interview recently between this distinguished personage and General **TWIGGS**, on the coast of Florida. The Chief is a fine looking warrior, about forty years old, with an open, intelligent expression of countenance, totally devoid of that wild look which so frequently characterizes the inhabitant of the forest. His figure is about the ordinary height, and well proportioned, with a pleasing deportment, and evincing much self possession in his manners. His head was enveloped in a read shawl, surmounted with white feathers, encircled with a silver band, with cresents of the same metal suspended from his neck, to which was appended a large silver medal, with a likeness of President **VAN BUREN** on its face; his throat was richly covered with strands large [sic] blue beads; he also wore bracelets of silver over the sleeves of decorated huntining shirt. A broad showy bead belt passing over his breast, suspending a beautiful headed rifle pouch under his left arm, and red leggings with brass buttons, which were richly ambroidered with beads where they covered the upper part of the moccasins, completed the costume.

(478) Elizabeth-City, Dec. 15, '49. .. MAMMOUTH TURNIP. There was sent to our office the other day a turnip which grew on the plantation of James **NASH**, Esq., weighing seven pounds and a quarter, and in a good state of preservation. ...

(479) Married. In this County on the 6th instant, by Francis **BROTHERS**, Esq., Mr. Thos. **REED** to Miss Marenda **TRUEBLOOD**, all of this county. At Baudon Chowan Co. N. C. Nov. 14, by Rev. Samuel I **JOHNSTON**, Dr. Richard B. **BAKER** to Miss Nannie T. daughter of Charles E. **JOHNSTON** Esq.

(480) DIED, In Tuscumbia, Alabama, on Monday the 26th inst., after a few hours illness, William F. **REID**, Esq., a native of Pasquotank County, N. C., in the 44th year of his age.

(481) Lost!! A red Morocco pocket book, containing $32, and receipt; it also had in it a broken finger ring. Any person returning it to the subscriber, will be liberally renumerated [sic.] Henry **CULPEPPER**. dec 15

(482) EXECUTORS NOTICE. Having qualified at the last term of Pasquotank County Court, as Executor for Zion **CULPEPPER**, dec'd., all persons indebted by account, note or otherwise to the estate of Mr. **CULPEPPER** are hereby called upon to make immediate payment, as no indulgence can be given, and all persons having claims against said estate, are requested to notify me of the same within the time prescribed by law, or this notice will be plead in bar of their recovery. G. W. **BROOKS**, Executor. Dec. 15, 1849.

(483) NOTICE. Will be sold at public sale on the first day of January next, on the premises--the lot of Land with Store and other improvements formerly belonging to W. B. **ALLEN**, dec'd., and now occupied by Geo. W. F. **DASHIELL**. Terms to be made known on the day of sale. And at the same time and place three likely negro slaves on a credit of six months. Leonard **CHAPMAN**. dec 15

(484) NOTICE. Will be sold on the first day of January, 1850, before the Court House in E. City, the negroes belonging to the estate of Chlotilden **JACKSON**, dec'd., for the purpose of a division. There are four negro men, one boy and four women. A credit of six months will be given, by the purchasers giving their notes payable in the Bank of E. City, with interest from date. Sold by the Administrator. Dec. 15, 1849.

(485) NOTICE Is hereby given to creditors, &c., that letters of administration on the estate of Thos. Wilson **BUTLER** deceased, were granted to the subscriber December Term, 1849, of Pasquotank County Court. Susan **BUTLER**. Dec. 15, 1849.

The Old North State.
Vol. 9. "Error is harmless, when truth is left free to combat it." No. 44
Elizabeth City, N. C. Saturday, December 22, 1849.

22 December 1849

(486) Elizabeth-City, Dec. 22, '49. ... For the purpose of giving those who are employed in our Office an opportunity of participating in the Christmas festivities, no paper will be issued next Saturday. We take this occasion to renew our thanks for the liberal support of our patrons and wish them a happy and merry Christmas. ...

(487) DREADFUL ACCIDENT. We regret to state that Mr. Agustus C. **SAUNDERS**, of Hertford N. C. was thrown from his horse near that town on Monday last and killed. Mr. S. was a young man beloved by all who knew him, and his sudden death has caused a gloom over the whole community in which he lived.

(488) Dr. **PARKMAN**--Verdict of the Coroner's Jury. The Boston papers of Friday contain the verdict of the Coroner's Jury which held the inquest over what were supposed to be a part of the body of Dr. **PARKMAN**. The *Atlas* says: Coroner **PRATT** stated that in accordance with the opinion expressed by the Attorney General of the Jury, in which vote he concurred, the evidence before the inquest would be kept secret from every body until laid before the Grand Jury. He remarked that the inquest had been in session 10 days, and examined a large number of witnesses, and that the evidence occupied over eighty large foolscap pages of writing paper. He then said that the verdict which had been agreed upon would be made public, and accordingly the Secretary of the Inquest, Mr. **ANDREWS**, was directed to read the verdict as duly recorded..in the following language: An inquisition taken at the city of Boston, within the county of Suffolk, thirteenth day of December, in the year of our Lord one thousand eight hundred and forty-nine before Jabez **PRATT**, Esq. one of the Coroners of said county, upon the view of sundry parts of the body of a dead man, viz: thorax, kidneys, perlvis, two thighs, left leg, and sundry, bones , there lying dead, by the oaths of Osmyn **BREWSTER**, John L. **ANDREWS**, Pearl **MARTIN**, Thomas **RESTIEUX**, Lewis **JONES** and Harum **MERRILL**, good and lawful men, who being charged and sworn to inquire for the Commonwealth, when, how and by what means the said dead man came to his death, upon their oaths do say--that they all have been demonstrated to be parts of one and same persons--that these parts of the human frame have been identified and proved to be the remains and parts of the dead body and limbs of Dr. George **PARKMAN**, late a citizen of said Boston, aged about sixty years--that he came to his death by violence, at said Boston, on the twenty-third day o [sic] November last, or between the hour of one and a half of the clock, in the afternoon of that day, (about which time he entered alive, and in good health, into the Massachusetts Medical College building, situate in North Grove street, in said Boston,) and the hour of four of the clock in the afternoon of the thirteenth day of November last, (when a portion of the said remains were found concealed in and under the apartment of Dr. John W. **WEBSTER**, of Cambridge, in the county of Middlesex, in said college building,) in which the residue of said remains were afterwards discovered that he was killed in said college building by a blow or blows wounded or wounds, inflicted upon him with some instrument or weapon to the jurors, unknown, and by means not yet known to said jurors, and that said blow or blows, wound or wounds, were inflicted upon him, and said means were used by the hands of said Dr. John W. **WEBSTER**, by whom he was killed. In witness whereof the said Coroner and Jurors to this Inquisitoin have set their hand and seals, the day and year above said. Jabez **PRATT**, Coroner, [seal.]   Osmyn **BEWSTER**, Foreman, [seal.] John L. **ANDREWS**, Secre. [seal.] Pearl **MARTIN**, Thomas **RESTIEUX**, [seal.] Lewis **JONES**, [seal.] Harum **MERRILL**, [seal.]
    The *Post* says: .. Prof. **WEBSTER**'s time is wholly employed in reading and epistolary correspondence with his friends. Although it is is understood that Hon. Franklin **DEXTER** has declined to act as counsel for defence, he is still admitted at the Jail as such, in common with Edward D. **SOHIER**, Esq.

(489) Married. In this place on the 13th inst., by the Rev. E. M. **FORBES**, Dr. Josiah T. **SMITH**, of Perquimans County, to Miss Josephine C. B. **HOLSOM**, of this place. On the Canal, on the 5th inst., at the residence of S. **WILLIAMS**, Esq., by A. **CHERRY**, Esq., Mr. Wm. B. **GRAY**, to Miss Eliza **CHAPMAN**, all of York County, Va.

(490) At Home Again! NEW JEWELRY STORE. The Subscriber has removed to E. City, where he has opened a handsome assortment of GOODS, consisting of Gold patent and detached Levers, Silver patent, Detached, Cylender and Verge Watches, with hunting and other cases--all made by the best makers, and warranted to perform well. He has also a handsome aasortment of Ladies bosom and velvet pins and bracelets, latest style. ... Call at the sign of the *big Watch*. J. M. **POOL**

(491) Persons indebted to the late firm of L. K. **SAUNDERS** & Co., are requested to call and settle their accounts with the subscriber, on or before the 15th day of January 1850, as no longer indulgence can be given. All claims not adjusted prior to that will be placed in the hands of an officer for immediate collection. Rufus K. **SPEED**, Trus. Dec. 22

(492) LOOK AT THIS! All persons indebted to me for Beef, &c., will please come forward and settle the same. The year being near the close I wish to have a clear settlement with all, so as to be able to commence the new year all straight. I would here inform my customers that I shall expect a settlement at the expiration of each month for the coming year, and in no case will this rule be deviated from. I hope all of my customers will like this mode of settlement as it will prevent long accounts from being contracted. Samuel **CARTWRIGHT**. Dec 22

22 December 1849

(493) WIDOW'S SON LODGE, CAMDEN COUNTY, N. C. The brethren of the above Lodge, respectfully invite members of adjoining Lodges, and all transient brethren, to join them on the 27th inst., in celebrating St. John's day. By request of D. B. **MORRISETT**, W. M. Camden Co., N. C., Dec. 22, 1849.

(494) Perquimans Male and FEMALE ACADEMY. John **CINTEELY**?, M. A. Principal. The exercises of this Institution will be resumed after the Christmas vacation, on Monday, the 31st inst. The pupils and those intending to join the School, are requested to be punctual in their attendance at its opening, as the classes in the languages will then be formed for the year. Hertford, N. C., Dec. 22, 1849.

(495) STATE OF NORTH CAROLINA, GATES COUNTY. *Court of Please & Quarter Sessions, November Term,* 1849. Sarah **BABB** and others, vs. Dempsey **RUSSELL** & others,} Caveat to the will of William **BABB**. A paper writing, purporting to be the last Will and Testament of William **BABB**, deceased, is produced in open Court, and offered for probate, when Dempsey **RUSSELL** and wife, John B. **MARCH** and wife, and Blake **BAKER** and wife appear, by their attorney, and enter a caveat--whereupon an issue is directed to be made up whether the said paper writing is the last Will and Testament of the said Wm. **BABB**, and so executed as to pass real and personal estate. It appearing to the Court that Miles **COLLINS** and wife Jane R., James B. **BABB** and John E. **BABB** are not inhabitants of this State. It is therefore ordered that publication for four weeks be made in the "Old North State," for them to appear at the next Term of this Court, to be held for the County of Gates, at the Court House in Gatesville, on the third Monday of February next, and "see proceedings" continued. Witness, John **RIDDICK**, Clerk of said Court, at Gatesville, the third Monday of November, Anno Domini, 1849. John **RIDDICK**, Clk. Dec. 22, 1849.

(496) STATE OF NORTH CAROLINA, GATES COUNTY. *Court of Please & Quarter Sessions, November Term,* 1849. Benjamin **BROWN** and others heirs at law of Sam'l **BROWN**, versus. Benjamin **WILLIAMS** & others heirs at law of Sarah **WILLIAMS**.} Petition for petition [sic] of Land. In this case, it appearing to the satisfaction of the Court, that the defendants, Benjamin, Allen, Jordan, Robert, Betsy, Sophia, Nancy, Louisa and Martha **WILLIAMS** and others, if any, whoever they may be, heirs at Law of Sarah **WILLIAMS**, deceased, are not residents of this State. It is therefore ordered that publication be made for six weeks in the "Old North State," notifying the said non-residents to be and appear at the next Term of this Court, to be held at the Court House in Gatesville, on the third Monday of February next, then and there to answer or demur to the said petition; otherwise judgment will be entered against them, and this petition heard, ex parte as to them. Witness, John **RIDDICK**, Clerk of our said Court, at Gatesville, the third Monday of November, Anno Domini, 1849. John **RIDDICK**, Clk. Dec. 22, 1849.

1850 - Filmed from originals in the University of North Carolina Library.

The Old North State.
Vol. 9. "Error is harmless, when truth is left free to combat it." No. 45.
Elizabeth City, N. C. Saturday, January 5, 1850.

(497) **MASON** and **DIXON**'s Line. The survey of the section of the boundary line of Pennsylvania, Delaware and Maryland, authorized by the Legislature of the respective States, under a joint commission, was completed day before yesterday.--Col. **GRAHAM**, and Lieut. **THORN** of the U. S. Topographical Corps, were the Engineers, having been assigned to the duty by the War Department at the request of the Governors of the three States. This section comprises a small part of the celebrated **MASON** and **DIXON**'s line; and it is interesting to know that it was surprisingly accurate. Most of the monuments were found entire. Of these, every fifth stone, at distances of five miles, is ornamented on one side, with the sculptured arms of Lord **BALTIMORE**, and on the other, with those of the **PENN** family. The stones are of granite, and the engraving was doubtless executed in England. .. To revert to the..line--it is a gratifying circumstance that the location of it was committed, by the English Government, to such able hands.--Charles **MASON** was, indisputably, one of the most accomplished and scientific men of his times; and was, for some years, attached to the Royal Observatory. ... *Phil. N. American.*

(498) Elizabeth-City, Jan. 5, '50. .. Lyman **RAYMOND**, of Lowell, Mass., has recovered $9975 from the corporation of that city; as compensation for a broken knee-pan, causing premanent lameness, which he got by stumbling over a grate in the gutter, which stuck up some two inches above the curb stone.

(499) HON. EDWARD **STANLY**. The Washington correspondent of the *Boston Atlas* writes in the following handsome terms of Mr. **STANLY**, the Representative in Congress from the Newbern district: "Among the ablest and best men in Congress is Hon. Edward **STANLY**, of North Carolina. Mr. **STANLY** is a bold, vigorous and energetic speaker. He is a true, earnest man--modest and amiable in every relation in life, but one who speaks his sentiments with freedom and boldness. .. He is of a small stature,

5 January 1850

(499) (Cont.) a very expressive face, which is "sickled over with the pale cast of thought." He is now, I should say, about 43 years of age, and of light com-complexion [sic.] He is one of the favorites of the Whigs, and his name and character are as well known and appreciated in New England as in Carolina. Mr. **STANLY**, though a Southern man, and imbued with Southern views upon the slavery question, is nevertheless no disunionist, and is far from possessing that narrow, proscriptive view of public affairs that would inhibit a New England man from an election to Speakership. ...

(500) CASSIUS M. **CLAY** ACQUITTED. The *Richmond* (Ky.) *Chronicle* says that the Grand Jury of Madison county, after an investigation of the Foxtown recounter, in which Cyrus **TURNER** was killed by Cassius M. **CLAY**, failed to find an indictment in the case.

(501) Married, At Fort Landing, Tyrrell County, N. C., on Dec. 13th, by Justice **MC CLEESE**, Mr. Chas. C. **HOPKINS**, to Miss Mary F. **PALMER**.

(502) NEW DRUG STORE, AT THE OLD STAND. The subscriber has recently purchased the stock of Goods owned by the late firm of L. K. **SAUNDERS** & Co, and intends keeping up throughout the year a full and well assorted stock of Drugs, Medicines, Paints, Oils, Window Glass &c. &c. .. He hopes by strict and constant attention to business, to deserve, and procure the patronage of the public. Two years experience in the sale of Drugs has amply fitted him for carrying on the business. All are particularly requested to call at the store opposite Thos. R. **COBB**'s, formerly occupied by L. K. **SAUNDERS**, & Co. John E. **DEFORD**. Eliz. City, Jan. 5, 1850.

(503) Elizabeth City Academy. The exercises of my School will re-commence Monday the 7th inst. The Trustees of the Academy, Parents and Guardians of the Children of my school, and all others who feel an interest in the Subject of Education, are respectfully invited to call, at any time, and listen to the recitations of the pupils. At the commencement of the second Session (February 25th,) the Female Department of the school will be placed almost exclusively under the control of Mrs. C. S. **POOL**. Stephen D. **POOL**, Pirn. [sic] Jan. 5, 1850.

(504) NOTICE. Sealed proposals will be received at the Custom House, Elizabeth City, N. C. on Monday the 14th inst. for the purpose of ascertaining who will furnish Good Winter Strained Lamp Oil to the Light Boats stationed off **WADE**s Point and Roanoke Island and at what price for one year from date of first account. George W. **CHARLES**, Superintendant. Jan. 5.

(505) Valuable Lands FOR SALE. The undersigned wishing to remove to the West offers for sale the Farm on which he now resides, lying one and a half miles from Elizabeth City, on the road leading through Pool Town; containing 60 acres of good kind land; about 35 of which is cleared, and under a good state of cultivation. Situated upon it, is a good two-story dwelling house and all necessary out buildings. Also an other tract nearer town situated on either side of the road at the brickkiln; containing a little the rise of 100 acres. Upon this tract are two comfortable one-story dwellings, and three log houses which rent for 18 or 20 dollars each annually. 50 acres of this land is cleared, and under a good state of cultivation. Terms reasonable, and will be made accommodating to the purchaser. For further information, inquire of the subscriber on the premises. Joshua **TRUEBLOOD**. 1st mo (January) 1850.

(506) Concord Male and Female *CLASSICAL INSTITUTE*. South Mills, Camden County, N. C. The subscribers beg leave to inform the citizens in the vicinity of South Mills and the surrounding country that they will open for the reception of pupils--both an English and Classical school--on the 15th January next, and continue without interruption until 15th December following, vacation included. The scholastic term will embrace two sessions of (5 months each) the first commencing the 15th January, and ending 15th June. The citizens of South Mills and its vicinity having long felt the need of a permanent school and deeming this to be a healthy location--in the midst of a fashonable, moral and intelligent community--have resolved on establishing an Academy upon which its patrons can look with pride and delight. .. The Principal flatters himself as he has associated with him a gentleman of high, intellectual attainments--having graduated in one of the best Colleges of the U. States, viz. University of Pennsylvania--that his exertions will be crowned with success. For himself he asks no favours, but what the success of four year's experience in teaching will warrant. TERMS, For the Common English Branches, (of 2 ses.) $16.00 " Higher, " " 20,00 " Latin and Greek, 20,00 " French, 10,00 Each of the above Languages, or for all, 30,00 Board can be obtained in respectable and moral families for $6 per month. ... J. W. **HOLLAND**, Prin. O. B. **YOUNG**, M. D. Asst. South Mills, Jan. 5, 1850.

(507) NEW JEWELRY STORE IN EDENTON, N. C. The Subscriber has taken the Store on Main St., next door to the store of Messrs. **WOOD & BROTHER,** where he has opened a handsome assortment of GOODS, consisting of Gold patent and detached Levers, Silver patent, Detached, Cylender and Verge Watches... J. M. **POOL**. Edenton, Jan. 5.

12 January 1850

The Old North State.
Vol. 9. "Error is harmless, when truth is left free to combat it." No. 46.
Elizabeth City, N. C. Saturday, January 12, 1850.

(508) Elizabeth-City, Jan. 12, '50. .. We are informed that an inquest has been held on the body of a Mr. **PUGH** lately killed in this County by George **FOX**. We have not been informed as to the particulars of the case any farther than, that, an examination of the body was made by Dr. **GRICE**, on whose testimony the jury of inquest decided that the deceased came to his death by a blow inflicted on the head with a stick. **FOX** the perpetrator of the deed has escaped from justice by absconding...

(509) SUDDEN DEATH. We regret to state that the wife of Mr. Joshua **MC COY**, of Edenton was taken suddenly ill at the tea table on Sunday Evening last, and expired in about 8 hours. The Physician who attended her we understand pronounced it a case of Cholera. Our citizens will better know her, when we state, that she was, previous to her marriage with Mr. **M**. the widow of Mr. Joseph **SAWYER** late of Columbia, Tyrell Co., she was married to Mr. **MC COY** on Christmas night last.

(510) THE **PARKMAN** MURDER.--*Important Discovery.*--It will be remembered that during the excitement attendant upon the arrest of Prof. **WEBSTER**, charged with the murder of Dr. **PARKMAN**, it was stated that the Professor had received from Mr. **SAWIN** a large quantity of grape vine cuttings. It was at first reported that those were bundles of faggots to be used for the purpose of kindling fires, &c., but when the nature of the wood became known, it was supposed that the Professor had merely ordered them to be sent to his laboratory for some chemicle experiement. It has since been ascertained, by burning flesh with grape wine cuttings, that *the effluvia arising is entirely concealed.* This is an important discovery in science, and may not have been known to the Professor. We also learn that Dr. Alex. **HOUSTON** called at the house of Dr. **PARKMAN** on the day of, or day after his disappearence, and was informed by a member of Dr. **PARKMAN**'s family that he had left the city and would not return for several days. Our readers can draw their own inference. *Boston Herald.* Dec. 27.

(511) Married. In Gatesville, at the Merchant's Hotel, on Thursday 20th Dec., by Wm. G. **DAUGHTY**, Esq., Mr. D. W. **WHITEHEAD**, to Miss M. J. **DANNIEL**, both of Nansemond County, Va.

(512) List of Letters Remaining in the Post Office, at Elizabeth City, Quarter ending 31st December 1849. **ARONHOUSE** Brooks Artist to any Dag. **AYERS** Miss Cassindra **AYDLOTT** Wm. D. **ARMOUR** Mrs. Mary **BUCHANAN** David 2 **BUTLER** Mrs. Susan 2 **BRAY** Ambrose W. **BANKS** Geo W **BUTLER** James **BELL** Major 2 **BUTT** Mrs Jane G **BANKS** Wm C **BELL** Mrs Affey **BALANCE** Holaway **BANKS** John **BRYAN** Sidney **BUNDY** Elizabeth Ann **COMMANDER** Miles 2 **CLAYTON** T G **CRANK** Caleb T **CARTWRIGHT** M **DAVIS** Isaac **DELONG** Harvey 3 **DAILEY** John **ETHEREDGE** Josiah **ELLIOTT** Aaron **FLETCHER** Francis **FORD & PERRY GALLOP** Miss B **GODFREY** Mary **GIBSON** Nathan **GRAY** Wesley **HEATH** Thos C **HITER** Henry **HENLEE** Capt N W 2 **HOLLAND** James W **HALEY** John **HINTON** P W **KIRBY** Rodgers 5 **LISTER** Wm **LORY** Wm **LOVETT** Miss M J **LONG** Miss Martha S **LEWIS** James R **LAMB** C G **LUTON** David 2 **MC DOUGAL** G **MURDEN** Benj **MURDEN** Mrs Sophia **MULLEN** Dr Francis N **MARSH** Bennett **MORRIS** Thomas O **MEADS** Alfred **MARCHANT** Dr G C **MARCUM** John **OLD** Wm **OXLY** Elizabeth **OVERTON** Elizabeth **POULE** Wm **PIERCE** John **PURDY** Mary **PERKINS** Dr J Q **REID** Wm **RHODES** Miss Liddy **ROGERS** Capt Wm **RUTTER** William **STONE** Mrs Alicent **SMITH** J H **SANDERS** Wm **STOUGH** Alfred 2 **SYMONS** Jacob **SHANNON** John **SIMMONS** Capt Josiah **STEVENS** Charles H **SCOTT** John **STONE** Geo W **WILCOX & WOOD WADE** Abigal **WHITE** Osborne **WHITE** Thomas 2 **WHITEHURST** Davis **WALKER & BALANCE WOOTEN** Messrs J C & Co Persons calling for any of the above letters will please say they are advertised. Wm. E. **MANN**, P. M. Jan 12

(513) The Aeolian Minstrels CONSISTING OF MISS E. M. **SMITH**, MR. J. W. **SMITH**, " C. H. **SMITH**, " WM. B. **THOMPSON**, WILL GIVE A Vocal & Instrumental Concert, At E. City on Monday Evening, Jan'y 11th. On which occasion they will give a varied collection of Pieces, original and selected, which they are happy to say, have been most flatteringly approved of by the "Lovers of Music," in most of the cities and towns in the U. States and Canadas. .. Doors open at 6 1/2 o'clock--Performance to commence at 7 o'clock precisely. Tickets 25 cts to be had at the Post Office and at the Door. ... Jan'y 12, 1850.

(514) REVOLVING PISTOLS. We have just to hand a full supply of "**ALLEN**'s" SIX BARREL, REVOLVING, & SELF-COCKING PISTOLS, which we are prepared to sell at the lowest prices. ... E. P. **TABB** & CO. Hardware Importers, head of the Square, Norfolk, Va. jan 12.

(515) NOTICE! I hereby forbid any person's crediting my wife on my account, as I shall pay no debts of her contracting. Wm. **JONES**. Jan. 12, '50.

12 January 1850

(516) REGALIA, REGALIA, &c, &c. Newly established Regalia Store. I keep constantly on hand, and am able to supply the different Orders with Regalia, Jewels, Banners &c, in as fine style and at as low prices as any establishment in the Union. Members of Encampments, Odd Fellows, Masons, Red-Men, Temples of Honor, Sons of Temperance, Recab__, Cadets of Temperance, &c, are invited to call..or send their orders. .. Seals neatly engraved on Wood to order. I respectfully solicit a call, from those in want of the above articles at the Millinery Store of Mrs. E. F. **MURPHEY**, east side Church street 4 doors from the corner of Main street Norfolk Va., or direct their order to Wm. H. **MURPHEY**, Regalia and Insignia Agent, Norfolk Va. Jan. 12.

(517) NOTICE. Was found, and sold on Bodys Island Beach on the 22d of Sept. 1849, 3 bales of cotton, marked T. **B**. Also 10? pieces of pine timber no marks. Sold by E. B. **MIDGETT**, C. Wrecks, 4th W. D., N. C. Jan. 12

(518) FOR SALE. The House and lot on which I now reside will be sold on reasonable terms, if early application be made. The House is within 3 hundred yards of the town. MARTHA H. **IVES**. E. City, Jan. 12, 1850.

(519) JOHN **WOMBLE** & CO, COMMISSION MERCHANTS, No. 100 main street, Richmond, Va. Offer their services to the citizens of North Carolina, for the sale of Fish, Bacon, Lard, Corn, Wheat, Cotton, Lumber &c. &c. .. For any information respecting us and our manner of attending to business, we refer to our friends in North Carolina, which includes nearly all engaged in Fisheries, and to Messrs. **DICKSON, MALLORY,** & Co., and **HARDY & DELK,** Norfolk, Va.

(520) English & Classical Institute, ELIZABETH CITY, N. C. The next Term in this Institution will begin on the 2d of January next. Students are thoroughly and practically instructed in all the sciences partaining to an English and Classical Education. G. M. **WILDER,** Principal. Dec. 8

The Old North State.
Vol. 9. "Error is harmless, when truth is left free to combat it." No. 47.
Elizabeth City, N. C. Saturday, January 19, 1850.

(521) Elizabeth-City, Jan. 19, '50. .. We owe an apology to the present Mayor and Commissioners of our Town for not mentioning their election before. .. The list is as follows: JOSEPH H. **POOL**, Esq., Mayor. Geo. A. **WILLIAMS**, Esq., Capt. Wm. **SIMMONS**, John **BURCHER**, Esq.} Com.

(522) From the *Baltimore American.* NEW YORK, Jan. 10. *Important News from California--The Elections*. Bayard **TAYLOR**, Esq., the private correspondent of the *New York Tibune*, just before the steamer Unicorn was leaving San Francisco for Panama, put a letter on board dated San Francisco, December 1st. [So the despatch reads, but it is evidently a mistake, as the last previous advices from San Farncisco were to the 1st Dec., at which time the Unicorn was advertised to leave on the 10th.] .. The State election is over, and 15,000 votes were cast. Peter H. **BURNETT** has been elected Governor, and John **MC DOUGAL** Lieut. Governor. George W. **WRIGHT** and Edward **GILBERT** have been elected Representatives to the United States. They are all democrats. There is nothing yet decisive as regards U. S. Senators. ...

(523) Married, On Thursday evening 17th inst., by Rev. C. R. **HENDRICKSON**, Mr. Robert **RAPER**, *printer*, to Miss Elizabeth N. **TRUEBLOOD**, both of this County.

(524) Land and Negroes for Sale, On Saturday the 16th day, of Feb. next, I shall offer for sale, pursuant to an order of the County Court, on a credit of 1 and 2 years, interest from date. The Farm lying in Perquimans County within one mile of Hertford, formerly owned by Micajah **BUNCH**, dec'd., containing about 500 acres. There is a very good Dwelling and out-houses on the same; some 250 thousand in cultivation and will produce 5 to 6_0 barrels of corn. Any person desiring to purchase can examine the same or apply to the subscriber for further information. Also on Tuesday 12th of the same month, at Hertford, will be offered some 10 to 15 likely young negroes, belonging to the Estate of said **BUNCH**; some for cash and others on a credit of 6 and 12 months. Further particulars on the day of Sale. Joseph **MARDRE**. Perquimans Co. Jan. 19th 1850.

(525) $50 Reward. Ranaway from the subscriber on Monday the 7th of this month, negro man **MOSES**. He is about twenty one or two years old, about six feet high, is rather over ordinary size, has a dark complexion, a high forehead and long projecting eyebrows. He wore when he left a blue blanket overcoat, and a new black wool hat. His father belongs to Mr. Benjamin **BERRY**, in Ballahack, and his mother belongs to Mr. Richard **FELTON**. The above reward of Fifty Dollars will be paid to any person who will apprehend said negro, and deliver him to me, or confine him in Jail so that I get him. Grizell P. **JACOCKS**. **DURANT**'s Neck, Perquimans County, N. C., Jan'y 19th, 1850.

19 January 1850

(526) ETHERIAL OIL OR GASS, TO BE HAD AT THE OLD STAND. I have this day received 25 gallons of the above article which is cheaper and the best now in use, better for Families and Stores. Also a variety of Fresh Medicines; just received at the Drug Store of J. E. **DEFORD**. Jan. 19.

The Old North State.
Vol. 9. "Error is harmless, when truth is left free to combat it." No. 48.
Elizabeth City, N. C. Saturday, January 26, 1850.

(527) Elizabeth-City, Jan. 26, '50. .. DISSOLUTION OF THE UNION. The subject of dissolution seems to be agitated in Congress to such a degree that we are led to inquire into the cause. .. The whole cause of the angry discussions and personalities between the members of Congress is the subject of slavery. We have noticed carefully the spirit with which this subject is discussed both by the Northern fanatics and the ultras of the South; and we are forced to believe, that the motives..are mostly political, for party purposes, and to overthrow and defeat the Administration. ...

(528) EXACTLY RIGHT. In the House of Delegates of Virginia on Saturday last, the Governor, having laid before that body the insulting and fanatical resolutions of the Legislature of Vermont, Mr. **SYME** of Petersburg, offered the following resolutions, accepting as an amendment that part which says that "the Legislature of Virginia know their Constitutional rights, and mean to maintain them": Resolved, by the General Assembly of Virginia, That the resolutions from the State of Vermont; on the subject of slavery, be returned to the Governor of this Commonwealth with the request that they be returned to the Governor of Vermont, and that the Governor of Vermont be informed that the Legislature of Virginia *understand their Constitutional rights and mean to maintain them.* The ayes and noes having been ordered on the above, it was passed unanimously. Mr. **BURWELL**, of Bedford, offered the following resolution: Resolved, by the General Assembly, That it be and is hereby recommended to the people of Virginia, not to import, purchase or consume, any articles, the produce or Manufacture of the State of Vermont--or of any other State of the Union, which shall address to Virginia the language of menace or reproach. It was adopted without dissent, and referred to the Select Committee, having under consideration the **WILMOT** Proviso and other kindred subjects.

(529) The *Baltimore Sun* states that letters from Paris announce the death of George Washington **LAFAYETTE**, son of General **LAFAYETTE**. He died about the 1st of December at Lagrange the family seat. Once an adopted member of the family of **WASHINGTON** himself, he never forgot the republican principles he there imbibed; and in all the relations of life he is said to have enjoyed in a high degree the esteem of his countrymen.

(530) Auction Sales. Auction at my store to night. Come one--Come all. A. E. **JACOBS**, Auct. jan. 26.

(531) New Store. The subscriber respectfully informs the Lady's [sic] and Gentlemen of E. City, and the country, that he has taken and fitted up the house (next door to the Dry Good House of J. J. **GRANDY**, Esq.,) for the sale of Confectionaries, Fruits, Books, Stationary, Fancy articles, &c. He has just returned from Baltimore with a full assortment of the above, and will continue to receive something new and nice every week. ... Wm. J. **KELLINGER**. Jan 26, 1950 [sic.]

(532) OUR HOUSE. The subscriber has taken the House, near the Court House, lately occupied by Timothy **GILBERT**, Esq., where he intends keeping a public House of Entertainment. He has also attached an elegant Bar, and intends to keep it furnished with the best of Liquors, Cigars, &c. He intends keeping Oysters during the oyster season, and will have them served up in any style and at the shortest notice. Families furnished with Oysters whenever on hand. Meals furnished at any hour of the day, or until 11 o'clock at night. Juries can be supplied with meals whenever wanted. He respectfully solicits the patronage of the public. Robt A. **SAWYER**. Jan 26

(533) Notice. The subscriber is prepared to repair all kinds of work in his line of business at the shortest notice... Such as Clocks of all kinds, Jewelry, Guns, Pistols, Andirons, Tongs, Shovels, Candlesticks & Snuffers, Tin and Brittania Ware, Still Worms, Umbrellas, Parasols, Whips, Spectacles, Castor Stands, Canes Mounted, &c., &c. .. He has removed to a new Shop immediately in the rear of the office lately occupied by Dr. **MUSGRAVE**, and also can be found in the front part of the same Office, now occupied by Dr. **SALTER**. Joseph N. **BELL**. Jan 26

(534) J. T. **SALTER**, BOTANIC PHYSICIAN. Would respectfully inform the citizens of Elizabeth City and vicinity that he has rented the Office recently occupid by Dr. **MUSGRAVE**, where he can usually be found at all hours of the night as well as the day when not absent on professional business. .. A full assortment of *pure* Thomsonian and other Botanic preparations of Medicines can be obtained at his Office. Jan. 26, 1850.

26 January 1850

(535) Attention R. & R. L. Dragoons. You are hereby ordered to attend a parade of the Company and a regular Court Martial on next Saturday the 2d Feb. Punctual attendance is ordered, as all fines heretofore laid will be acted on. By order of the Capt. Jas. W. **HINTON**, O. S. Jan 26

The Old North State.
Vol. 9. "Error is harmless, when truth is left free to combat it." No. 49.
Elizabeth City, N. C. Saturday, February 2, 1850.

(536) A new invention for the propulsion of Steamboats, by the application of power at the stern, has been successfully tested in Philadelphia. It is called the "single blade propeller;" and was invented by Mr. Alexander **BOND**, of Philadelphia. The principle is that of the "scull."--The propeller is said to be peculiarly applicable to canal navigation, inasmuch as three feet of water, the inventor contends, are sufficient entirely to submerge the propeller of a three hundred ton boat, and, at the same time, to afford ample resistance to obtain a speed of eight miles an hour, while the whole propelling surface is contained in a single blade, thus insuring the most perfect resistance from the water with least possible amount of surface. It is contended that its economy in the cost of construction, by the substitution of a simple blade for the cumbrous and expensive wheele hitherto used, must eventually overcome the principle obstacles to the successful navigation of canals by steam.--*Balt. American.*

(537) ITEMS OF NEWS. We observe that Mr. **CLAY** has presented in the U. S. Senate a memorial from Wm. A. **SEELY**, a lawyer of New York, who was instrumental in recovering the crown jewels of Holland, stolen from the Prince of Orange many years ago, and brought to this country. ...

(538) Elizabeth-City, Feb. 2, '50. .. The attention of our Whig friends, is particularly called..in reference to the nomination of the next Governor of North Carolina. We say "the next Governor," for if the Whig party will work together as they ought, nothing is more certain. .. There are plenty of talented and high minded Whigs, who would fill the Chair of State with honor to themselves and to their State. Among the number from this section of the State we would mention the names of the Hon. Wm. B. **SHEPARD**, Hon. Kenneth **RAYNER** and the Hon. Edward **STANLY**...

(539) *Correspondence of the Baltimore Patriot.* Washington, Jan. 29, 1850. .. As the press had heretofore suggested, Mr. **CLAY** to-day offered his compromise resolutions upon the slavery question. .. Some of the ultra-Southern Democrats protested against the resolutions of Mr. **CLAY**. Among them was Mr. Jefferson **DAVIS**. He started out, with books and documents in hand, to show that Mr. **CLAY** had changed his position, since '38, upon the question in discussion, but lo! and behold! when he come to read from the journal of that time, a totally different result from the one he expected came to pass! The opinions of Mr. **CLAY** were precisely those he had ever held. A smile of charitable pity for the young Senator passed over the countenances of those present. Mr. **DAVIS** behaved gallantly in Mexico, but the Senate is not the place for him. ...

(540) Married. In the Methodist Episcopal Church, in the town of Edenton, on Sunday Evening last, by the Rev. Mr. **DOLL**, Mr. Charles E. **ROBINSON** to Mrs. Martha A. **SWAIN**, both of Edenton. May they long live to enjoy the blessings of life.

(541) Feb. 14th, St. Valentines Day. I have just received the hadsomest lot of Valentines that ever was in E. City, both sentimental and comic. .. I have also some very fine Note paper, Envelopes, Cards, Fancy Mottoes, Steel Pens, Quills, Stamps, &c., for sale by Wm. J. **KILLINGER.** Feb 2

(542) Tin Ware and Sheet Iron MANUFACTORY. The subscriber would inform..that he has taken a Shop near Mr. Wm. **SHANNON**'s residence, and will carry on the above business in all Its various branches and forms, and will keep for sale and manufacture any Tin or Sheet Iron at the shortest notice. Tin gutters for houses, Bathing Tubs, Oil Stands, Lard do. of all sizes, Stove pipe, and a general assortment of Coffee pots, Buckets, Pans, Wash Basins, Milk Buckets and Strainers. All work neatly repaired at the shortest notice. Thos. J. **MISKELL.** Feb. 2d.

(543) Valuable Property for Sale. The subscriber being desirous of devoting his time to farming alone, proposes to sell on accommodating terms his well known Toll Road leading from his house across Pasquotank river to Jno. L. **HINTON**'s. The said road is in good order and may stand for years without further repairs. .. There is a new store house recently erected--built of good materials, which together with the lot will be sold with the road if desired. It being situated at the junction of said road and the river renders it more desirable to men of business. .. It is necessary to state that the charter for said road embraces ninety-nine years--and that the charter for the contemplated road between Parksville and the aforesaid Turnpike will be transfered to the purchaser. For further particulars apply to Wm. R. **ABBOTT.** Camden County, N. C., Feb'y 2d, 1850.

9 February 1850

The Old North State.
Vol. 9. "Error is harmless, when truth is left free to combat it." No. 50.
Elizabeth City, N. C. Saturday, February 9, 1850.

(544) The following from a Boston letter of the 19th, to the *New York Herald*, may possibly be true: "Mrs. **PARKMAN**, the widow of the victim, will be spared the pain of testifying at Dr. **WEBSTER**'s trial, as her brother, R. G. **SHAW**, can positively identify the remains. ...

(545) Elizabeth-City, Feb. 9, '50. .. HALIFAX JANUARY 15, 1850. DEAR SIR, The want of a better outlet from Albemarle Sound to the Ocean, has been long felt and deeply deplored, by a large, intelligent, and wealthy portion of the people of North Carolina, but strange as it may be, no combined, energetic and efficient effort, has yet been made by those most deeply interested in this very desirable object. It is true, the attention of the General Government has been repeatedly called to this subject, from time to time, by the members who have represented the Edenton District in Congress, and under authority of that government, various surveys and examinations have been made, to ascertain the most eligible point at which to open this communication; the mode, and manner of constructing the necessary works; the probable expense thereof, and whether its importance and utility, would justify the expenditure likely to be incurred. .. The question then naturally occurs, why has this needful work been neglected, why has nothing been done in its behalf by Congress? The appropriate answer..will probably be found in the fact, that this measure involving a heavy expenditure has been left alone, to the unaided efforts of the representative in Congress from the Edenton District, and that he has not been properly sustained by openly avowed public sentiment. Full confidence is reposed in the present able and patriotic representative from that district..but his efforts should be sustained by the whole people residing on Albemarle Sound, and all that district of the country whose water courses empty therein. To this end we propose that a convention of the people be held at Plymouth on Thursday the 14th day of March next, for the purpose of talking [sic] such action on this important subject, and of making representations to Congress in favor of the work, as may seem just and proper. .. It is respectfully suggested, that the people of the several counties interested, be called together, and that a large delegation from each be appointed to the convention. Thomas P. **DEVEREUX**, Whitmel H. **HILL**, Whitmel H. **ANTHONY**, H. K. **BURGWYNN**, Colin M. **CLARK**, James N. **SMITH**, A. **JOYNER**, Richard H. **SMITH**, John H. **FENNER**, Wm. R. **SMITH**, T. P. **BURGWYNN**, John **DEVEREUX**.

(546) The *Southern Democrat* says that "Butcher **EWING** deserves to be stamped with the mark of Cain." We understand that the editor of that paper has first and last, been stamped with the marks of at least a dozen *canes.--Louisville Journal*.

(547) DIED, In this place on Tuesday morning, Feb'y the 15th, Mrs. Nancy **MORGAN** the wife of James M. **MORGAN** and daughter of Maxcy **SAUNDERLIN**, in the 22d year of her age. The funeral will take place on the 17th instant, in the Baptist Church in E. City.

(548) The most Fashionable and Decidedly the Cheapest Gentlemens Clothing Depot ever Established in this Place! The subscriber has the pleasure to announce to the public, the interesting fact that he has opened, at the store formerly occupied by Wm. A. **HARNEY**, and on the corner of Water and Main Sts., opposite the Market House, a well selected assortment of Ready Made Clothing for Gentlemen, Boys and Children. ... M. **GOLDSMITH**. Feb. 9, 1850.

(549) Plows! Plows! Plows! My assortment of Plows is very large and complete, numbering over 2000, and embracing a large variety of the most and [sic] approved and improved patterns, for one, two, three and four horses... S. **MARCH**. Norfolk, Va., Feb. 9.

(550) Men Wanted to Travel as Agents, for the History of the Mexican War. The subscriber is now publishing the HISTORY of the MEXICAN WAR, including Biographical Sketches of the lives of Generals **TAYLOR**, **SCOTT**, **WORTH**, **WOOL**, **TWIGGS**, **QUITMAN**, and several others of the most distinguished officers.--Illustrated by numerous engravings and portraits. By John **FROST**, L. L. D. A number of enterprizing and intelligent men of good character, are offered profitable employment, in circulating by subscription the above work in Pasquotank County and other Counties in the State of North Carolina. ... H. **MANSFIELD**, Bookseller and Publisher; 134 York st. New Haven, Connecticut. Feb 9, 1850.

(551) STATE OF NORTH CAROLINA, Gates County. William G. **DAUGHTRY**, Administrator of Hiram **HURDLE**. vs. Joseph T. **HURDLE** and others. } In Equity to Spring Term 1850. It appearing upon the affidavit of the complainants, in this cause, on file in my office, that the defendants, Isaiah **CARTWRIGHT**, Isabella **CARTWRIGHT**, Sophia **CARTWRIGHT**, Mahaly **CARTWRIGHT**, and Reuhamy **CARTWRIGHT**, children of Penina **CARTWRIGHT**, reside

9 February 1850

(551) (Cont.) beyond the limits of this State. The said Isaiah, Isabella, Sophia, Mahaly, and Reuhamy **CARTWRIGHT**, and all and every other person claiming any interest in the estate of the said Hiram **HURDLE**, under or through the said Penina **CARTWRIGHT**, are therefore hereby notified to be and appear, at the next Court of Equity, to be held for the County of Gates aforesaid at the Court House in Gatesville, on the first Monday, after the fourth Monday in March next, then and there, to answer plead or demur to the said plaintiffs bill of complaint, otherwise the same will be taken pro confesso, and heard ex parte, as to them. Witness, William J. **BAKER**, Clerk and Master in Equity in the County of Gates. W: J. **BAKER**, C. M. E. Feb 9, 1850.

The Old North State.
Vol. 9. "Error is harmless, when truth is left free to combat it." No. 51.
Elizabeth City, N. C. Saturday, February 16, 1850.

(552) Elizabeth-City, Feb. 16, '50. .. NEW BARBER SHOP. We neglected to notice last week, that Mr. A. E. **JACOBS** had secured the services of a barber (not James) and hereafter all who wish anything done in that line can have it done in order by calling at the Shop, on the right hand side as you go in to the "Saloon" of Mr. Wm. W. **BURGESS**'.

(553) PUBLIC MEETING IN BEHALF OF NAG'S HEAD. According to notice given, the citizens of Pasquotank met at the Court House last Saturday, when on motion of George W. **BROOKS**, Esq., Dr. R. H. **RAMSAY** was appointed President, Seth **MORGAN** Esq., Vice President, and Geo. D. **POOOL**, Esq., Secretary of the Meeting. The object of the meeting was fully explained by the President. After which the Hon. Wm. B. **SHEPARD** being respectfully called upon made a very affective speech, and concluded by moving that the President of the Meeting appoint fifty delegates to attend the Convention to be held at Plymouth, in March next, whereupon the following persons were appointed: Hon. Wm. B. **SHEPARD**, Dr. **SPEED**, Gen. **EHRINGHAUS**, Jos. H. **POOL**, John **POOL**, Capt. Wm. **SIMMONS**, Wm. F. **MARTIN**, Dr. **GRICE**, Wm. **SHANNON**, Addison **WHEDBEE**, Dr. R. H. **RAMSAY**, Seth **MORGAN**, Geo. D. **POOL**, Mark S. **SAWYER**, John A. **WARROCK**, John C. **EHRINGHAUS**, Wm. H. **DAVIS**, Jr., Jos. R. **PARKER**, Thos. **GASKINS**, Gilbert **ELLIOTT**, Joshua A. **POOL**, G. W. **BROOKS**, Thomas **HARVEY**, Jos. **MULLEN**, Thos. D. **KNOX**, John **BLACK**, Wm. E. **MANN**, Job **CARVER**, Wm. S. **HINTON**, Geo. W. **HINTON**, Jos. **PRITCHARD**, Elias **CARVER**, Edgar L. **HINTON**, Jos. B. **REED**, John F. **BUTT**, John **SMALL**, Jas. E. **WEEKS**, Francis A. **BROTHERS**, Dr. O. F. **BAXTER**, Daniel **SAWYER**, Caleb L. **WHITEHURST**, Stephen D. **POOL**, Willet **HERRINGTON**, Thaddeus F. **BANKS**, Robt. **PENDLETON**, James **BANKS**, Doctrine R. **PERRY**, F. S. **PROCTOR**, Geo. A. **WILLIAMS**, Shadrach D. **CARTWRIGHT**, Jas. L. **MULLEN**, W. W. **GRIFFIN**, John L. **HINTON**, John J. **GRANDY**, Arthur **JONES**, and John **THOMPSON**.

(554) THE BEAUTIES OF DUELLING. And Kentucky is the only country where no man has ever been punished for giving, accepting, carrying a challenge, or killing his antagonist in a duel. What inroads have been made in the family of A. **POPE**, my old friend, with whom I practised law until he died by the duelling propensities of those two young men, Henry and Fountain **POPE**. One was killed in Arkansas, and the other near Louisville, without any cause, if the parties had understood each other. The parties fought at the distance of thirty yards with shot guns. Did I not know while in Boston, **BARRON** and **DECATUR**, two of the first men at that period in America, came up in mortal array, within sixteen feet of each other, because one was near sighted, and the rule was, that both should take deliberate sight before the word to fire was given. They both fired, and fell with their heads not ten feet from each other, and before they were taken from the ground, each expected both to die; they spoke to each other, and a reconciliation took place. They blessed each other, and declared there was nothing between them. There was the case also of **MC CARTY** and **MASON**--own cousins--who fought one of the most murderous duels on record, because **MC CARTY**, voting for another man, **MASON** being a candidate felt aggrieved and challenged his vote on the ground of not being 21. .. **MC CARTY** has told me that the duel was forced upon him by one of **MASON**'s seconds. Such are the scenes which illustrate this bloody code of honor, as it is styled.--*Ben HARDIN's Speech in the Kentucky Legislature.*

(555) DIED, In this County on Monday last, Mr. Jonathan **BANKS**, aged about 38 years. Mr. **BANKS** was one of our best farmers. He was a good neighbor, a kind and generous master, and in his domestic circle every thing went on as pleasant as heart could wish. He has left an affectionate family and a large concourse of relatives and friends to mourn their irreparable loss.

(556) Good Things, Just received 200 lbs. Fresh Candy assorted, Preserved Limes, Guavai Jelly, Citron, Currants, Oranges, Lemons, Apples, Almonds, Raisins, Filberts, Butter Nuts, Pea Nuts, &c. All of which are fresh and good, at the Curiosity Shope, of W J **KELLINGER**. Feb. 16.

(557) FARM FOR SALE. The subscriber offers for sale a Farm, about 1 mile from the Great Bridge, containing 103 acres, more

16 February 1850

(557) (Cont.)or less. The said Farm has on it a two story Dwelling House, 26 by 28 feet, two Rooms and a Passage below, and three Rooms and a passage above; a Kitchen, Smok-house, Crib and Stables. There is land enough cleared to make about 50 bls of corn. The cleared is high and sandy, and the uncleared land good Oak and Gum land, and easy to drain. There is plenty of Rail Timber on the said land for fencing, and has a most excellent range for Cattle and Hogs. As the said farm lies about 7 miles from the subscriber, he would sell it low, and on accommodating terms. An adjoining farm of 80 acres can also be purchased should it be wanted. James G. **MARTIN**. Mount Pleasant, Norfolk County, Va. Feb 16 1850

The Old North State.
Vol. 10. "Error is harmless, when truth is left free to combat it." No. 1.
Elizabeth City, N. C. Saturday, February 23, 1850.

(558) Elizabeth-City, Feb. 23, '50. OURSELVES. To-day commences the 5th year since we have been re-engaged in the Printing line. We took the sole charge of the Press on the 21st February, 1846, and from that time to this have not missed a publication--a thing never before performed in Elizabeth City, by any other printer since we have known the place. .. We are also under many obligations to our kind patrons, who have come forward and paid us up their dues so as to enable us to meet our pecuniary matters. Nevertheless there are yet a great many in arrears and we hope they will lose no time in coming forward and paying up. .. It is our purpose to start to Baltimore on Monday after our County Court, for the purpose of arranging our Office matters in that City, and to get our semi-annual supply of paper, and hope all our Subscribers who may owe us..will "fork over." ...

(559) ANOTHER VESSEL LOST. The schooner Atlas, of Plymouth, Capt. **AINSLEY**, went ashore on **WADES'** Point Shoal on Thursday night 14th inst., and immediately after grounding she commenced going to pieces. She was loaded with tar and staves and bound for Baltimore. .. Two of the crew were drowned, and the captain after working very hard to save the vessel gave up and died in about 5 minutes after stopping work. One negro and a dog was taken off the next morning by Capt. **MERCER** of the **WADES'** Point Light Boat. .. A jury of inquest was held over the body of the captain and one of the crew on Saturday last, the other person drowned has not yet been discovered. ...

(560) We have been shown the first number of a new paper published at Wadesborough, by F. M. **PAUL**, called the *Cadet of Temperance*. The object of the paper seems to be, not only the support of the Order of Cadets, but the encouragement of youth in virtue and integrity. .. We wish the Editor success ..and hope he will be liberally patronized from this section of the State.

(561) From the *Baltimore Patriot*. MUTINY AND MURDER AT SEA. Captain **RHODES**, of the barque Montezuma, arrived at New York from Demarara and St. Thomas. He left the latter place on the 6th inst., and reports that the schooner J. B. Lindsey, **RIGGS**, of Norfolk, bound to Trinidad, had just arrived, with the captain sick from wounds received in conflict with some of his crew. .. Since the above was put in type we have been put in possession of the following letter to Capt. Wm. **SIMMONS**, one of the owners of the J. B. Lindsay:--Saint Thomas, Feb. 8th, 1850. Capt. Wm. **SIMMONS**, Elizabeth City, N. C. Dear Sir:--This will inform you of my arrival in this Port, on Monday last, from Trinidad, which place I left on the 27th ult. and on that night about half past 10 o'clock after I had turned in, two of my crew Mutinized [sic] and killed my mate and also a passenger I had from Trinidad. Upon my running up on deck, they attacked me, shooting me in the throat, but I am happy to say not seriously; after which I fired at them and shot one of them alongside the nose, the ball passing across the roof of his mouth, after which they somewhat stopped. I was obliged to take to the cabin, where they kept me confined for three days, when they finding they could not succeed in getting any money, they determined to take the boat and scuttle the schooner and leave us, but as they were alongside in the act of doing so one of the men who they had confined in the forecastle, broke out and cut off the painter, letting them go adrift, when we got clear of them. I am happy to say I am now here where I shall be obliged to spend a few days to heal my wounds and recover somewhat from the loss of blood &c., as well as to refit a little after my escape, as they let every thing go adrift while they had me in durance. I am in hopes that in the course of a few days to be able to pursue my voyage. You will please let my wife hear of me that I am still in the land of the living, and doing as well as can be expected after what has happened. The particulars I will more fully explain, when I reach home, in the mean time, I Remain, Your Ob't Servant, Solomon S. **RIGGS**, Pr. N. **CARRINGTON** & Co.

The J. B. Lindsay sailed from this port on the 18th December last, with the following named persons as her crew: Solomon S. **RIGGS**, of E. City, N. C. Capt. John **HEENEY**, of Boston, Mate, aged 22 years, 5 feet 7 1/2 inches high. Thomas **COSTLEE**, of Portland, Me. Seamen, Thomas **REED**, of Hudson, N. York, do. Edward **CLEMENS**, of Platsburg, N. Y. do. Daniel S. **SMITH**, of Charleston, S. C. Cook. ...

(562) For the *Old North State*. The citizens of Gates County, feeling deeply interested in common with the citizens generally the [sic] northeastern part of the State, in the opening an outlet to the Sea from Albemarle Sound, held a meeting in the Court House,

23 February 1850

(562) (Cont.) in Gatesville, on Monday the 18th inst., for the purpose of appointing delegates to attend the Convention, proposed to be held in Plymouth on Thursday the 14th day of March next. Whitmel **STALLINGS**, Esq., was called to the Chair, and William G. **DAUGHTERY**, Esq., appointed Secretary. On motion, the following persons were appointed delegates to attend said Convention: Willis F. **RIDDICK**, Wm. J. **BAKER**, Geo. B. **GORDON**, Mills H. **EURE**, Henry E. **RASCOE**, Riddick **GATLING**, John **WILLEY**, John D. **PIPKIN**, Dr. **LEE**, Nathaniel **EURE**, David **PARKER**, Dr John **GATLING**, Timothy H. **LASSITER**, Wm. H. **HARRELL**, Jos. **RIDDICK**, Henry **RIDDICK**, John C. **GORDON**, Dr. Chas. E. **BALLARD**, Isaac H. **HARRELL**, James K. **COSTEN**, Henry **WILLEY**, Barney **GOODMAN**, Simon **WALTERS**, Wm. H. **CROSS**, Benjamin **SAUNDERS**, Mills **ROBERTS**, Tim. **WALSTON**, Dr. Sam'l J. **LOUTHER**, A. S. **JORDAN**, Jesse R. **KEE**, Rob't H. **BALLARD**, John **RIDDICK**, William L. **BOOTHE**, John M. **MATTHEWS** and James **CARTER**. The Chairman and Secretary were also appointed delegates. W. **STALLINGS**, *Chm'n.* Wm. G. **DAUGHTERY**, Sec'y. Gatesville, Feb. 19th, 1850. *Edenton Sentinel* will please copy.

(563) FOR SAN FRANCISCO. We take the following from the *North State Whig* of last week. PORT OF BEAUFORT--SAILED. Ship Louisa Bliss, of Beaufort, Captain Authur **MC PHAILS**, for San Francisco, California, loaded by Wm. C. **BELL** & Co. with the following cargo: 242 M P P Lumber; 70 M of which is in House Frames; 245 M Shingles; 30 M Bricks; 500 barrels of Merchandise, and the following passengers from Beaufort, and vicinity: Dr. James L. **MANNEY**, Brian H. **RUMLEY**, super cargo, James **BUSK**, Wm. F. **HATSEL**, Charles **WHITEHURST**, Wm. Penn **HELLEN**; Leroy **PIVER**, Sam'l **GILLICHEN**, James **RUMLEY**, Jr., Wm. D. **NOE**. This ship started from her anchorage, with a light breeze head tide--and only about 1/3 of her canvass spread, and was at Sea in *forty* minutes. She drew 16 feet water when she went to sea. We submit the question to the sovereign People of North Carolina, is not the Harbour of Beaufort the best Eastern terminus of the great Central Rail-Road: J. **MANNEY**.

(564) Washington, February 18, 1850. SENATE. A large number of petitions were presented, one of them by Mr. **CLAY**, from James A. **DELACOUR**, of Baltimore, praying that the Senate should rebuke the spirit of dissolution by expelling the first Senator who would dare to propose it; and a large number of reports on private bills were made.

(565) Sons of Temperance. The Pasquotank Division S. of T. will celebrate their first Anniversary on the 5th March next, when the Rev. Samuel **PEARCE**, the agent appointed by the Grand Division for the State will be present. .. A procession will form at the Odd Fellow's Hall and proceed to the Baptist Church where an address will be delivered before the Order by the State agent. ... C. R. **HENDRICKSON**, J. W. **HINTON**, J. M. **WHEDBEE**,} Com. Ar'ments.

(566) Elizabeth City Academy. The 2d Session (3d Quarter) of this school will commence Monday next, 25th instant. The Female Department will then be placed in charge of Mrs. S. D. **POOL**. The number of pupils in the two Departments will be limited to sixty; of this number, fifty are already engaged. I can assure parents and Guardians that no exertions will be spared on the part of my wife and myself to give to the children entrusted in our care a *thorough, practical and moral Education*. TERMS, PER QUARTER 11 WEEKS. Primary, English Branches, $5.00 Higher, " " 7.50 Latin, French or Spanish, 7.50 Book keeping (single or double entry) 2.50 ... S. D. **POOL**, Prin. FEB 23, 1850

(567) NOTICE. There came to the farm of the Subscriber, about 3 months since, a Steer of the following description: in color, red--with a slit and under square in the left, and upper keel in the right ear. There being no Ranger in the County to report to, the owner will call on me, prove proper [sic,] pay charges and take him away; or he will be dealt with according to law. G. W. **CHARLES**. Feb 22,

(568) JUST RECEIVED. I have this day received direct from the Manufactory, 50 gallons of pure Etherial Oil. Also a lot of beautiful Lamps of a dozen different patterns of the most improved style. The above articles are very cheap, and can be had at the Drug Store of J. E. **DEFORD**. Feb 23

(569) French and Spanish Languages. F. **LE BARBIER**, who has been engaged for many years, in several Institutions of the United States and of the Island of Cuba, give lessons of French (his native language) and Spanish, either in classes or in private families. .. Apply to him every morning before 10 o'clock, or in the afternoon between 2 and 4, at Mr. **MASON**'s Mansion House. Best reference can be given. Feb 23

(570) NOTICE. When I resided in town, some one borrowed the first volume of *MOSHIEM's Ecclesiastical History*, belonging to me--I forget who borrowed it, and most respectfully request the borrower, or whoever may now have it, to return it to me, as I doubt very much whether it has been read. If he will not return it, he can call and I will give him the other volume. The gentleman

23 February 1850

(570) (Cont.) who borrowed my copy of *AINSWORTH's Latin Dictionary* the quarto London edition, has used it long enough--he will much obliged me by returning it, as I know he has no longer any use for it. F. S. **PROCTOR**. Feb. 23

The Old North State.
Vol. 10. "Error is harmless, when truth is left free to combat it." No. 2.
Elizabeth City, N. C. Saturday, March 2, 1850.

(571) SIR JOHN **FRANKLIN**.--The Washington correspondent of the *Philadelphia North American* says: A liberal and praiseworthy proposition has been submitted to the Secretary of the Navy, through Moses H. **GRINNEL**, Esq., of New York, to equip and furnish two suitable vessels for the prosecution of the search after Sir John **FRANKLIN**, upon condition that the Government will lend its countenance to the noble enterprise, by appointing naval officers to conduct the exploration. ...

(572) The **WASHINGTON** Manuscript.--The original manuscript of **WASHINGTON**'s Farewell Address was purchased at the sale, in Philadelphia, for James **LENNOX**, Esq., of New York. Mr. **LENNOX** has a fortune which yields $120,000 per annum. He is a bachelor, and a man of most princely liberality and benovolence. It is said that his charitable contributions amount to $60,000 per annum--one half of his income.-- *Balt. Pat.*

(573) LONGEVITY.--The *Port Tobacco Times* records the death of a colored man named **VINCENT**, aged 106 years, the property of Mrs. Ann **MILLS**. He retained his memory and sight perfectly unimpaired up to within a few days of his death. He delighted to speak of his participation in our Revolutionary struggle, having been present at sevesal battles, among them the battle and surrender of **CORNWALLIS** at Yorktown, as servant to Col. **REED**; and said he had frequently seen General **WASHINTGON**.

(574) ITEMS OF NEWS. Hon. Neil S. **BROWN**, ex-governor of Tennessee, is announced in the *New York Tribune* as minister to St. Petersburg, in place of Mr. **BAGBY**.

(575) THE UNION.--The following was one of the regular toasts at a dinner lately given to the Hon. Garrett **DAVIS**, of Kentucky by the members of the Louisville Bar. "The Union: Entire, indivisisable [sic,] and sacred; the strength and glory of the Republic. Next to our maker, it challenges our highest reverence. We pledge our lives, our fortune and our sacred honor to maintain it."

(576) Elizabeth-City, March 2, '50. .. THE GREAT WESTERN CIRCUS. As will be seen from an Advertisement in our paper to-day the *Great Western Circus* of **STONE & MC COLLUM**, will exhibit in this place on the 18th and 19th of this month. .. Among the numerous troupe of good performers stands the renowned Dan **RICE**, of whose acting every paper speaks in the highest terms.

(577) We are informed that the Cadets of Temperance belonging to the Ark of Safety No. 1 Old North State, will assemble on Tuesday next 10 1/2 o'clock A. M. before the residence of I. **FEARING** Esq., when a splendid banner will be presented to the members of the Ark by Miss Virginia **FEARING**. After which they will join the procession of the S. of T. in the celebration of their Anniversary.

(578) CALEB **SIKES**, Manufacturer of "**ANTHONY** and **EMERSON**'s Patent Double Acting Rotary Churn." The attention of Farmers and Dairymen is particularly invited to this the most excellent of all churns extant. The subscriber has purchased the exclusive right for selling this article in the Counties of Perquimans, Pasquotank, Camden & Currituck, and is at present engaged in making up a large supply of them for the accommodation of the public. The prices of these churns will vary from $3, to $5; capable of Churning from 1 1/2 to 5 1/2 gallons of milk or cream. ... Caleb **SIKES**, Road street E. City, opposite the Bank.

(579) Barber's Notice. Circumstances of a pecuniary and domestic character, have recently made it obligatory on the part of "The Barber" to absent himself from his family and customers for a few week; [sic] During which time many of his kind patrons have been subjected to inconvenience in *getting shaved*. He is now happy to advise them, and the generous public, that his office is again prepared for their reception, and his fingers cleansed preparatory to taking his friends gently by the nose. He would also take advantage of the present opportunity to remind, in the most respectful manner, his debtors in small sums, that eight shillings make one dollar; and that although sixteen out of twenty feel not a sixpence each, a dollars is most acceptible to one afflicted with chill penury. In all probability, if his friends and his own exertions avail, he will not be a *shaver* in "the good Old North State" longer than three or four months--yet in the mean time he most respectfully solicits a share of patronage, and most humbly requests a reconciliation between debit and credit. The obedient servant of The shaving community, Stephen **RELFE**, The Barber. March 2d, 1850.

2 March 1850

(580) Notice All persons indebted to the estate of W. B. **ALLEN**, dec'd, either by note or account, are requested to come forward and settle the same, as further indulgence cannot be given. March 1, 1850, Leonard M. **CHAPMAN**, Admr.

(581) **STONE & MC COLLUM**'s GREAT WESTERN CIRCUS COMPANY, WILL EXHIBIT AT ELIZABETH CITY ON MONDAY & TUESDAY, MARCH 18th & 19th, for two days only. The Corps of performance of this Company are without parallel. Having among this extensive establishment, Four Performers, the World cannot Produce their Equals, viz: T **MC COLLUM**, Acknowledged the best TWO HORSE RIDER and general Performer living. T. **NEVILLE**, THE BEST SINGLE HORSE EQUESTRIAN. John **SMITH**, The unrivalled negro delineator and the original and inimitable Dan **RICE**, Surnamed the ORATOR, the JESTER, the JOKER, the POET and CLOWN; this gentleman is one of the four bright Stars in the Equestrian Firmament, assisted by his brother Clown G. B. **JOHNSON**: With the celebrated Equestrians, D. W. **STONE**! **LIPMAN**! **BATCHELOR**! **FISHER**! **EDGAR**! **REYNOLDS**! **BROWN**! Masters **JEAN, BURT, & CORNELIUS**. With a host of others. **GAULS**' Brass Band, With its Celebrated Leader, Will Discourse the most Fashionable Music--and will enter Elizabeth City, on Monday March 18th, seated in their Band Chariot drawn by 20 Horses and driven by Mr. John **ALLEN**, from *BATTYS' Royal AmphiTheatre*, London. Doors will open at 1 1/2 and 6 1/2 o'clock. Commence at 2 and 7 o'clock P. M. Admittance. Box 50 cents. Pit for Colored Persons 25c. A performance on Monday & Tuesday afternoon at 2 o'clock, for families living in the Country, and those unable to attend the night exhibition. To Exhibit at Edenton, on Thursday & Friday, March 14th & 15th. " " " Hertford, Saturday 16th. Elizabeth City, March 2, 1850. G. L. **EATON**.

(582) **NIEMEYER & WHITE**, Commission Merchants, AND GENERAL Produce Brokers, Portsmouth, Va. Offer their services to the Shipping, Planting, Trading and Manufacturing Interests. We will give strict attention to selling or shipping Tobacco, Cotton, Flour, Grain, Provisions, Lumber and Naval Stores; for forward Merchandize with dispatch. Henry V. **NIEMEYER**. James C. **WHITE**. March 2, 1850.

(583) Notice! Having sold out my stock of goods, and being determined on removing from this place to Norfolk, I most urgently request all indebted to me, to come forward and settle the same without any difficulty. John J. **GRANDY**. March 2.

(584) Strayed or Stolen. From the stable in E. City, on Saturday night last, a small Bay horse, without any mark, except a *white* place on the right side, near his weathers, caused by the saddle. Any person who will deliver him to me or give information where he can be found shall be reasonably rewarded. Henry **CARL**, At Capt. **BAKER**s. March 2d.

The Old North State.
Vol. 10. "Error is harmless, when truth is left free to combat it." No. 3.
Elizabeth City, N. C. Saturday, March 9, 1850.

(585) WHIG MEETING IN WAKE. At a large and respectable meeting of the Whigs of Wake County, at the City Hall in the city of Raleigh, on Wednesday afternoon, the 20th inst. on motion of Maj. **HINTON**, Johnson **BUSBEE**, Esq was called to the chair, and Leonidas B. **LEMY** appointed Secretary. H. W. **MILLER**, Esq., explained the object of the meeting to be, the appointment of Delegates to the Whig State Convention, &. whereupon, the following gentlemen were appointed a Committee to report resolutions for the action of the meeting, viz. Messrs John H. **BRYAN**, M. W. **MILLER**, Ch. C. **RABOTEAU**, G. W. **HAYWOOD** and Seaton **GALES**. The Committee having retired, a call was made upon Sion H. **ROGERS**, Esq. who responded in a speech full of Whig patriotism and spirit. After which, the committee returned, and Mr. **BRYAN**, their Chairman, reported the following preamble and resolutions, which were unanimously adopted, viz: Whereas, it is proposed to hold a Convention of the Whig party of North Carolina, in the city of Raleigh, for the purpose of nominating a suitable person as the Whig Candidate for Governor of the State--1. *Resolved*, That this meeting approve of said Convention. 2. *Resolved*, That we have undiminished confidence in the ability, integrity, and patriotism of the present incumbent; do cordially approve his administration; and heartily recommend his re-nomination: nevertheless, we are prepared to sacrifice all personal preferences, and to support, by all fair and honorable means, whomsoever may be selected by the Convention. 3. *Resolved*, That the Chairman of this meeting appoint thirty delegates to represent this County in the Convention, and that they be earnestly requested to attend. 4. *Resolved*, That, as a deversity of opinion seems to exist relative to the proper time for holding said Convention, we recommend Wednesday the 8th of May, as a suitable and convenient day therefor, and ask the concurrence of the Whigs of the State. 5. *Resolved*, That we have the most unbounded confidence in the integrity, ability, and patriotism of General **TAYLOR**, and feel assured that his administration will be conducted in such a way and upon such principles, as will advance the interest and honor of the country--protect the rights of each and every section of it, and preserve the integrity of the Union. .. The Chairman then appointed the following Delegates to the Convention for Wake County: H. W. **MILLER**, Stephen **STEPHENSON**, Gov. **IREDELL**, Wm. H. **HOOD**, Jacob **MORDECAI**, C. G. **ROOT**, Dr. C. E. **JOHNSON**, Sion **ROGERS**, Senr. Sam'l. P. **NORRIS**, John **LIGON**, G. W.

9 March 1850

(585) (Cont.) HAYWOOD, Alfred JONES, John MC CULLERS, Ch. C. RABOTEAU, John H. BRYAN, Needham PRICE, Allen ADAMS, Richard HINES, Seaton GALES, T. R. DEDMAN, T. J. LEMAY, Dr. H. W. MONTAGUE, Maj. W. D. JONES, Col. Wm. LAWG?, Anderson PAGE, Adam G. BANKS, Willie H. FULLER, Peleg ROGERS, Dr. R. B. HAYWOOD, Col. J. H. MANLY, Sion ROGERS and C. C. BATTLE. On motion the name of the Chairman and Secretary were added. On motion of C. C. BATTLE, the Chairman appointed the following committee, should the Convention meet in Raleigh, to make the necessary arrangements, and publish the same, viz: Messrs BATTLE, MILLER, HINES, G. W. HAYWOOD, PRIMROSE, W. H. H. TUCKER, R. W. HAYWOOD, E. B. FREEMAN, and ROOT. Gov. IREDELL moved that these proceedings be inserted in the city papers, with a request for the other papers of the State to copy the same. Johnson BUSBEE, Ch'n. J. B. LEMAY, Sec.

(586) Elizabeth-City, March 9, '50. .. Such is Life. By the assistance of a generous and accommodating public, I intend pursuing the same buisness, in which I have been engaged for some time. My sincerest thanks are due the public for the very liberal and extensive *practice* which I have heretofore received. The *old papers* have all recently been received and I am now ready for going ahead with *renewed* energy. All claims that are put in my hands for collection, will be prosecuted as ordered without fear, favor or affection. .. I will also attend public sales and sell property in any part of the county. ... Arthur JONES. march 9, 1850.

(587) Military Notice. The commissioned officers of the Atlantic Guards, Camden Guards and Pasquotank R. & R. L. Dragoons, are hereby ordered to attend a Court Martial of the Regiment, at Elizabeth City, on Tuesday the 23d April next, equipped as the law directs. All persons having business before the said body are hereby ordered to attend, as judgment final will be entered up against all that were fined *ni si* at the last Court Martial; without they attend and offer such an excuse as will be accepted by the Court Martial. By order of the Col. Wm. E. MANN Adj't. March 9th 1850

(588) For the Nags Head Convention, AT PLYMOUTH ON 14*th* MARCH. The Steamer General Taylor, Capt. TRIPPE, will ply between Edenton and Plymouth during court week leaving Plymouth for Edenton as follows: Tuesday, March 12th, at 2 P. M. Wednesday, " 13, at 11 A. M. & 5 P. M. Thursday, " 14, at 11 A. M. & 4 P. M. EDENTON FOR PLYMOUTH. Monday, 11th, March at 8. A. M. Wednesday, 13 " at 8. A. M. & 3. P. M. Thursday, 14 " at 8. A. M. & 2. P. M. Marshalk PARKS Agent. Norfolk & Roanoke Steam Boat Line.

(589) NOTICE. The subscriber offers for sale the tract of land on which he now resides, containing 90 or 100 acres. Also several other tracts--one containing 30 acres--one containing 3 acres (the folly land) and one containing 22 acres of cypress swamp. He also offers at private sale the stock of the Farm viz: Horses, Hogs and cattle, together with Household and Kitchen furniture, and 2 sets of Cabinet makers tools and two work benches--nets and Bateaus. For information apply to Wm. H. MC DONNELL, Near Newbegin creek, Pasquotank Co. March 9th 1850.

The Old North State.
Vol. 10. "Error is harmless, when truth is left free to combat it." No. 4.
Elizabeth City, N. C. Saturday, March 16, 1850.

(590) Elizabeth-City, March 16, '50. .. For the *Old North State*. At a meeting of the citizens of Camden County, held at the Court House, on Monday the 11th inst., to take into consideration the propriety of sending delegates to a proposed Convention to be held at Plymouth the 14th inst., on the subject of the re-opening of Nagg's Head Inlet, A. BERY, Esq., was called to the Chair, and J. W. BURFOOT, appointed Secretary. On motion of D. FEREBEE, Esq., a committee of 8 was appointed by the chair to select 8 delegates from each Captains District to attend said convention, who retired to consider the same. In the interval the meeting by request was forcibly addressed by D. D. FEREBEE, Esq., Gen'l J. C. B. EHRINGHAUS, and John P. JORDAN, Esq. The committee then reported the names of 50 delegates which upon motion were adopted, and the meeting adjourned. A. BERY, Chm'n. J. W. BURFOOT, Sec'y.

(591) Heavy Bank Robbery--$100,000 Stolen.--A telegraphic dispatch was yesterday received from R. R. CUGLER, President of the Central Railroad Banking Company, Savannah, Georgia, dated the 4th inst., stating that one hundred thousand dollars of the notes of that institution had been stolen. The supposed thief is described as being about forty-five years of age, medium size, dark hair and eyes, dark complexion, black beard, fine teeth, speaks low and soft and steps quick. A reward of five thousand dollars is offered for the recovery of the money and the arrest of the thief.

(592) Latest from California. .. The Georgia brings the mails of the California and Panama steamers of the 15th of January and 1st February... A man named Henry PULLEN, of Providence, R. I., died on Sunday morning week, just before the steamer entered

16 March 1850

(592) (Cont.) Havana, and was buried at sea. .. The most interesting civil trial which has occupied our Courts lately was the suit of Mrs. **FARNHAM** against Capt. **WINSOR**, master of the ship Angelique. Captain W. left the plaintiff at Valparaiso, after having contracted to convey her to San Francisco. For this Mrs. **FARNHAM** claimed $15,000 damages, but the jury gave their verdict in favor of the defendant. On the motion of a new trial, the judge said that he should grant it, because the plaintiff is a woman and her character has been aspersed. In the meantime Capt. **WINSOR** has sailed on a foreign voyage. Capt. **SUTTER** is in town. He came to meet his family--wife, daughter and two sons, who arrived in the last steamer from Panama. Capt. **SUTTER** has been absent from his family seventeen years. His residence is at Hook Farm, on Feather river. Gen. P. F. **SMITH** is also in town Col. **HAYES** came up from San Diego a few days ago. ...

(593) Names in Boston Two Hundred Years ago.--A gentleman who was lately looking over the record of births in the Boston city clerk's office, which occurred about the year 1650, was so struck with the singularity of some of the names he met with, that he sent a few specimens to the *Transcript*, for the amusement of its readers. They are as follows: Grace **BEAMSLEY**, Mercy **BEAMSLEY**, Dick **BEAMSLEY**, Deliverance **BECK**, Strange **BECK**, Free Grace, **BENDALL**, Reform **BENDALL**, Hope-for **BENDALL**, Seaborne **COTTON**, Fathergone **DINLEY**, Return **GRIDELY**, Believe **GRIDLEY**, Hope **HAWKINS**, Constance **MILNA**.

(594) English & Classical Institute, ELIZABETH CITY, N. C. The next Term in this School will comence March the 25th. .. All who are interested in the subject of education are invited to call and observe the course of intellectual training pursuits. Tuition the same as heretofore. G. M. **WILDER**, Prin. March 16th.

(595) Singing School. All persons, who are desirous of receiving instruction in Vocal Music will leave their names with J. M. **MATHEWS**. Mr. **THOMPSON**, the teacher, will commence giving lessons in this place, on, or about the first of April, if a sufficient number of scholars can be obtained. Terms--$3 for twenty lessons. Three lessons per week. March 16, 1850.

(596) Odd Fellows and Sons of Temperance Regalia. The undersigned is the authorized agent of Mrs. A. **SISCO**, Baltimore, Md., for the sale of all kinds of Regalia appertaining, either to Odd Fellows or Sons of Temperance. .. Any Regalia, Badges or Jewels peculiar to the Masonic Order can be obtained by giving due notice and timely warning to the subscriber. Jas. W. **HINTON**, March 16, 1850.

The Old North State.
Vol. 10. "Error is harmless, when truth is left free to combat it." No. 5.
Elizabeth City, N. C. Saturday, March 23, 1850.

(597) TO ALL WHOM IT MAY CONCERN. We would most respectfully commend to the notice of those who are ambitious to be delegates to the contemplated Nashville Convention, the following extract from the *Franklin* (Tenn.) *Review*, Feb. 15th. "The rulers of the "kingdom" of South Carolina have already appointed delegates to come up to Nashville, and hatch out their disunion treason on the soil of Tennessee. Nobody in Tennessee invited them here, and on such a mission nobody will sympathie [sic] in their action, against the Union, but such abhorrent Abolitionists as Davy **WILMOT** and Wm. Loyd **GARRISON**. Their object is, professedly, to show their devotion to the interests of the slave States, but in reality their whole efforts will be to sow the seeds of treason, and to that it was done in Tennessee. We tell them that Tennessee is no harbor for treason--no refuge for a clan of bankrupt politicians whose sole object it to dissolve the union, that they may personally profit by the calamity. ...

(598) A Shirt for Poor Prince **ALBERT**.--We copy the following extraordinary paragraph from the *St. Louis Republican*: "We examined yesterday some beautiful specimens of needlework, which have just been finished in this city, and are intended as a present for Prince **ALBERT** and his youngest son, of England. They were two shirts--one designed for the father, the other for the son--made of the finest linen which could be obtained, and the needle work exquisitely wrought. Some idea may be formed of the labor bestowed upon these articles, when it is stated, that there are 152,217 stitches upon the large, and 65,154 stitches on the small garment. .. They were made by Mrs. Mary E. **HICKS**, formerly of Connecticut, and Miss Elizabeth **HAWKINS**, late of Toronto, Canada, but both now of St. Louis--the latter doing all the hemming.--They are to be sent to the British Minister at Washington, by whom it is expected that they will be transmitted to the Prince."

(599) The *Charleston Courier* states that a sea monster, of remarkable appearance, was seen last week off the coast south of that city, by the passengers in the steamer William Seabrook. It is represented to be about a hundred and fifty feet in length with a body of enormous bulk, and a head about the size of a hogshead, and resembling, in appearance, that of the alligator. The monster was not at all "like a whale."

23 March 1850

(600) LONGEVITY. The following article is taken from a Norwick (Conn.) paper, printed some 14 years since: "There is now living in this town a man in the 85th year of his age, who was born on Sunday, his wife on Sunday, and his first child on Sunday; they had a child born on every day of the week, the first on Sunday morning and the last on Saturday night. He is the eldest of four genetions [sic,] all born on Sunday, all bearing the same name, and now living, and all present at a family reunion a short time since." We are enabled to say that the same man is yet living in good health, and has just entered his 99th year. He was in New York some two years since and on visiting Wall-st., pointed out the spot where he stood and witnessed the inauguration of the immortal **WASHINGTON**. He was for a great number of years U. S. Surveyor of the Port of Norwich. He is now the patriarchial head of five generations, the last one having religiously observed the family rule of coming into the world on Sunday. The name of this ancient man is Erastus **PERKINS**. Several of his descendents reside in this City; among them a grandson, James H. **PERKINS**, of "Odd Fellows' Hall."--*N. Y. Tribune*.

(601) Elizabeth-City, March 23, '50. .. PLYMOUTH. In the absence of official proceedings of the Convention, we will merely state that the convention met according to previous notice. All the counties of this Congressional District were represented except the County of Currituck. Also several counties in the 6th and 8th Districts. After a few preliminary remarks by Josiah **COLLINS** Esq., the convention was called to order by appointing John A. **ANDERSON** Esq., of Hertford Co., as President, and Gen. H. G. **SPRUILL**, of Bertie, Secretary. The counties were then called over and the list of delegates handed in to the Secretary. When on motion of Josiah **COLLINS**, Esq., the following Resolution was adopted: *Resolved*, That a committee of one Delegate from each County, represented in this Convention, be appointed, by the President pro tem, whose duty it shall be to propose proper officers for the Convention. The President then appointed the following persons: Josiah **COLLINS**, Dr. J. H. **BURNETT**, C. L. **PETTIGREW**, James N. **SMITH**, A. L. **DOZIER**, R. K. **SPEED**, John P. **JORDAN**, Stark **SHARP**, Willis F. **RIDDICK**, J. R. **GILLIAM**, H. K. **BURGWYN** and B. **HATHAWAY**.

The committee retired, and in a short time returned and reported the following Gentlemen, as proper officers for the Convention, viz: For President, Col. Andrew **JOYNER**, of Halifax County. For Vice Presidents, J. C. **NORCUM** of Washington County, Thomas P. **DEVEREUX**, of Halifax County, J. H. **LEARY**, of Chowan County, and Thomas F. **JONES**, of Perquimans County. For Secretary, H. G. **SPRUILL**, and J. MC **BOYLE** of Washington County. The report of the committee was concurred in, and the officers were conducted to their seats by Josiah **COLLINS**, and Joseph **HALSEY**, Esqrs. .. The convention was addressed by several gentlemen; among the number were Josiah **COLLINS**, Wm. J. **ELLISON**, Aug. **MOORE** and William D. **VALENTINE**, Esqr's, Gen. J. C. B. **EHRINGHAUS**, and the Hon. Wm. B. **SHEPARD**. .. Those who spoke showed conclusively that the work was a practicable measure, and only needed the exertions of the citizens of this section of the State to carry the point. .. We cannot overlook the great interest taken in the proceedings by Josiah **COLLINS**, Esq. Reports, Maps, &c., running back for a century were produced by him for the information of the Convention. .. We shall lay the contents of the ancient map there presented by him, before our readers soon, or at least, that portion of it, that take in Nagg's Head and the surrounding country. This we look upon as the most valuable of all information, as it was engraved by the British Government, for the benefit of the English Navigators. ...

(602) HORRIBLE MUTINY AND LOSS OF LIFE ON BOARD THE SCHOONER J. B. LINDSAY. We are under the painful necessity of publishing to-day the facts in reference to the Mutiny, as related to us by Captain **RIGGS**, and which took place on board the J. B. Lindsay, owned by William **SIMMONS**, Esq., of this place, on the 27th January last, when one day out from Trinidad on her passage to this port. .. The first day the J. B. Lindsay left Trinidad when in latitude 11 north, and at about 2 o'clock P. M., a pistol was fired in the forward part of the vessel, which was the first intimation of a mutiny with the exception of a slight suspicion which the captain had entertained of two of his crew Thomas **REED** and E. **CLEMMONS** while in St. Thomas. On hearing this noise the Captain went on deck and asked the Mate what it meant, who replied that he did not know, but would go and see. He went forward and the captain thinks demanded the pistols of **REED & CLEMMONS** who were, as it has since been proved the only two mutineers on board. They told the mate they would give the weapons to him soon; and in a short time he returned to the captain with two pistols. All seemed to be quiet till about 10 o'clock at night..when he was awoke by a noise on deck and heard the mate calling for mercy. He went on deck and with a pistol in each hand proceeded to the mate who was laying by the wheel in the last agonies of death, and who made no reply to the captain's interrogatories but faintly said "good bye." The mutineers retreated forward on the approach of the captain, who then tried to get the mate into the cabin; but they again approached him, both being armed. The captain seeing them coming made an effort to jump into the cabin, when **REED** fired at him, the ball striking him in the throat, cutting away the flesh and a part of the windpipe so that he breathed through the wound swallowing much blood. .. The captain having succeeded in getting into the cabin bound up his wound so as to prevent it bleeding. .. The next the captain saw of **REED** was on the left side of the house. Here **REED** presented his pistol to the captain, and the captain at the same time presented his. They both fired. .. **REED** fell on deck. .. The captain loaded again, during which time **REED** got up. From this time the captain sat by the aft door of the cabin till nearly morning when he went into the after cabin with the steward (Daniel **SMITH**.) They remained there till after the light of day when they went into the other cabin. During the whole time

23 March 1850

(602) (Cont.) one of the crew by the name of **COSTELLOW** who was a faithful friend of the captain, was kept on deck under the power of the mutineers, and prevented from rendering any assistance to the captain. During this time a passenger by the name of **WALKER** had been killed on deck, at what exact time the captain does not know. .. After this **CLEMMONS** again asked if he could have the boat, to which the captain replied that he could if they would go away and leave him. .. This being done they brought it to the starboard side of the vessel, and put into it their baggage, the salis [sails,] and whatever provisions they could get. **REED** now got into the boat and **CLEMMONS** ordered **COSTELLOW** to follow him which he did. After **CLEMMONS** had descended into the boat, **COSTELLOW** jumped on the deck..when **CLEMMONS** asked him where he was going; to which he replied, after the ax... He found the ax with which he endeavored to cut the painter and let the boat go adrift..he cut the boat loose, and run for the hold. .. Feeling now free from danger the captain, **COSTELLOW** and the cook sewed the mate up in a hammock, tied some bags of sand to his feet and buried him according to the usual custom, by throwing his body overboard.

We take the following from a St. Thomas paper of the 2nd inst. The U. S. Commercial Agent of this place informs us that he is in receipt of a letter from the American Consul at Laguayra, announcing the arrest, at that port, of Thomas **REED** and Edward **CLEMENS**; the late mutineers on board the schooner J. B. Lindsay. .. They are to..take them to the U. S. for trial.

(603) DIED, On the 16th instant, after a very sudden illness, and on her 16th birthday, Martha **MC MORINE**, youngest daughter of the late John **MC MORINE**, Esq., of this place. ...

(604) Important to Country Merchants and all others. New Queensware, China and Glass WAREHOUSE, CHINA HALL, No. 8, Main Street, Norfolk, Virginia. R. Q. **DRUMMOND**, & Co., have recently fitted up the commodious Warehouse..and have now in store an extensive stock of China, Glass, and Queensware... R. Q. **DRUMMOND** & Co. China Hall, Norfolk, Virginia. March 22, 1850.

(605) For Sale. 900 Bushels Turks Island Salt, a beautiful article for Fish, at the lowest cash price. .. Also, 20 bbls yellow planting Irish Potatoes for sale low for cash, at the old and well known stand formerly occupied by Wm. B. **ALLEN**. Wm. **HALSEY**. E. City, March 23, 1850.

(606) STATE OF NORTH CAROLINA. PASQUOTANK COUNTY SPRING TERM 1850. The heirs of Newton **EDNEY**, To The Court.} Petition to divide land. It apppearing to the satisfaction of the Court, that Edward **EDNEY** and Cartwright **EDNEY**, are non-residents of the State, it is ordered that publication be made for six weeks in the "Old North State," for the said Edward and Cartwright **EDNEY**, to appear at the next term of our Court, to be held for the County of Pasquotank, on the first Monday in June next, to show cause why the prayer of the petitioners should not be granted. Witness Wm. W. **GRIFFIIN**, Clerk of our said Court, at Elizabeth City, the first Monday in March, A. D., 1850. Wm. W. **GRIFFIN**, Cl'k. March 23d 1850.

(607) Attention R. & R. L. Dragoons. You are hereby ordered to attend a parade of the company on Saturday the 6th of April. Punctual attendance is requested as the Election of Officers takes place and other business will be brought before the company, By order of the Capt. Jas. W. **HINTON**, O. S. March 23

(608) FLAGSTONE of the best quality, about 3 to 4000 feet, all 4 feet one way and various lengths, will be sold low if called for immediately. Robert **DALRYMPLE**, Norfolk Va. March 23, 1850.

The Old North State.
Vol. 10. "Error is harmless, when truth is left free to combat it." No. 6.
Elizabeth City, N. C. Saturday, March 30, 1850.

(609) Proceedings of the Nag's Head Convention, Held AT PLYMOUTH, ON THE 14TH MARCH, 1850. In pursuance of a proposition made by several Gentlemen of Halifax and Northampton Counties, that a Convention, be held in the Town of Plymouth, N. C. on the 14th day of March 1850, to be composed of Delegates from the Counties interested, in opening an Inlet at or near Nags Head; and to adopt such measures, as they may deem proper, for accomplishing that object. .. The convention was called to order by Josiah **COLLINS**, Esq., who moved that, for the temporary organization of the convention John A. **ANDERSON**, Esq. of Hertford county be appointed President pro tem, and Gen. H. G. **SPRUILL**, Secretary pro tem-- The counties were called over, and the following counties were represented by the following Delegates. Northampton county, H. K. **BURGWYN**. Bertie county--Samuel B. **SPRUILL**, Dr. John R. **GILLIAM**, P. H. **WINSTON**, H. B. **HARDY**, J. H. **ETHRIDGE**, Josiah **WHITE**, Wm. D. **ETHRIDGE**, Noah **GREEN**, John B. **FREEMAN**, John **HENRY**, H. A. **GILLIAM**, James **GILL**, Wm. J. **MITCHEL**, John **DEVERAU**, L. S. **WEBB**, and W. G. **CLARY**. Hertford county--John A. **ANDERSON**, Abner **HARRELL**, William **HANES**, William D. **VALENTINE**, Col. Starkey **SHARP**, Dr. R. H. **SHIELD**, J. A. **JACKSON**, Maj, W. L **DANIEL**, Joseph J. **SCULL**, Watson **LEWIS**, Jr. Starky **HARRELL**, Dr. S. J. **WHEELER**, W. N. H. **SMITH**. Gates county, Willis F. **RIDDICK**. Chowan, Augustus **MOORE**, Col. Jas. C. **BOND**, E. C. **HINES**, Joshua

30 March 1850

(609) (Cont.) **SKINNER**, Thos. W. **HUDGINGS**, Thos. J. **MILLER**, Charles G. **MANING**, J. H. **LEARY**, Wm. D. **LOWTHER**, Jr. John **COX**, R. R. **HEATH**, Thos. H. **LEARY**, Jr. Jno. W. **SKINNER**, B. W. **HATHAWAY**, George W. **BRUER**, James N. **FLOYD** R. R. **FELTON**, John **BADHAM**, Wm. R. **SKINNER**. Perquimans county--Thos. F. **JONES**, James M. **SUMMER**, Chas. M. **FORD**, John P. **JORDAN**, Edward F. **SMITH**, James L. **BUNCH**, Wm. **SUMNER**. Pasquotank county--Gen. J. C. B. **EHRINGHAUS**, S. D. **GRICE**, Dr. R. K. **SPEED**, A. **JONES**, Thomas **KNOX**, Jos. **MULLEN**, Wm. J. **KELLINGER**, Hon. Wm. B. **SHEPARD**, M. S. **SAWYER**, Thos. **HARVEY**, Wm. E. **MANN**, J. E. **WEEKS**, John **SMALL**, A. **CURRAN**, J. B. **GODWIN**, Thad. F. **BANKS**. Camden county,--Thos. S. **GRANDY**, Willis S. **GRANDY**, Abner L. **DOZIER**, C. G. **LAMB**. Halifax county,--Col. Andrew **JOYNER**, Thomas P. **DEVEREUX**, James R. **SMITH**, Richard **SMITH**. Martin county--S. S. **SHEPHARD**, Clayton **MOORE**, D. W. **BAGLEY**, Wm. J. **ELLISON**, A. C. **WILLIAMS**, Dr. J. H. **BURNETT**, G. L. **MOORE**, D. C. **GUYTHER**, S. C. **BENJAMIN**, J. W. **GLASS**, P. P. **CLEMENTS**, P. W. **YARREL**, N. B. **FAGAN**, F. W. **TATEM**, John B. **WHITEAKER**. Washington County--Josiah **COLLINS**, R. B. **DAVIS**, H. W. **DAVENPORT**, J. J. **LINDSEY**, Wm. D. **DAVENPORT**, Franklin **SNELL**, Henry **DOWNING**, John B. **CHESSON**, E. W. **JONES**, Asa. **JOHNSTON**, A. F. **GARRETT**, Jos. C. **NORCOM**, John B. **BEASLEY**, Dr. B. F. **FESSENDEN**, Thos. E. **PENDER**, H. G. **SPRUILL**, T. B. **NICHOLLS**, Saml. **KISSAM**, John **MC BOYLE**, Charles **LATHAM**, W. W. **MIZELL**, G. J. **CHERRY**, F. F. **FAGAN**, Thomas S. **JOHNSTON**, Wm. L. **ARNOLD**, Abram **NEWBERRY**, Thomas S. **ARMSTEAD**, Dr. Wm. **ARMSTEAD**, Joseph **DOWNING**, Doctrine P. **DAVENPORT**, H. H. **WATERS**, H. B. **SHORT**, Jehu **NICHOLLS**, Thomas **BECKWITH**, B. J. **SPRUILL**, and Dr. J. F. **GAYLORD**. Tyrrel County,-- Joseph **HALSEY**, Solomon **HASSELL**, R. **DAVENPORT**, James F. **DAVENPORT**, Charles L. **PETTIGREW**, John T. **SPRUILL**, J. R. **STUBBS**, Jos. **MC CLEES**, Silas **DAVENPORT**, S. H. **SAMPLE**, T. L. **HASSELL**, B. J. **SIKES**, W. D. **CARSTARPHEN**, S. H. **MC REY**, Thomas **SWAIN**, J. B. **DAVENPORT**, R. B. **KNIGHT**, George W. **DAVENPORT**, Dr. R. S. **HALSEY**, Wm. C. **DAVIS**, J. D. **ARMSTRONG**, B. A. **SPRUILL**, Thos. **CLAYTON**, J. D. **BRABBLE**; Wm. B. **ETHERIDGE**.

Mr. **COLLINS** introduced the following Resolution, viz. *Resolved*, That a committee of one Delegate from each County..be appointed, by the President pro tem, whose duty it shall be to propose proper officers for the Convention. The Resolution was adopted, and the President appointed the following gentlemen..Josiah **COLLINS**, Dr. J. H. **BURNETT**, C. L. **PETTIGREW**, James N. **SMITH**, A. L. **DOZIER**, R. K. **SPEED**, John P. **JORDAN**, Starky **SHARP**, Willis F. **RIDDICK**, Dr. J. R. **GILLIAM**, H. K. **BURGWYN** and B. W. **HATHAWAY**. The committee retired, and in a short time returned and reported the following Gentlemen, as proper officers for the Convention, viz. For President, Col. Andrew **JOYNER**, of Halifax County. For Vice Presidents, J. C. **NORCUM** of Washington County, Thomas P. **DEVEREUX** of Halifax County, J. H. **LEARY**, of Chowan County, and Thomas F. **JONES**, of Perquimans County. For Secretary, H. G. **SPRUILL**, and J. McC. **BOYLE** of Washington County. .. Mr. **BURGWYN**, offered the following Resolution. *Resolved*, That a committee, to consist of one delegate from each county be appointed, to prepare subject matter for the consideration and action of the convention. The resolution was adopted, and the president appointed the following committee, viz: Messrs. H. K. **BURGWYN**, Richard H. **SMITH**, D. W. **BAGLEY**, Joshua **SKINNER**, Willis F. **RIDDICK**, John A. **ANDERSON**, James L. **BUNCH**, J. C. B. **EHRINGHAUS**, Thos. F. **GRANDY**, Jos. **HALSEY**, Jos. B. **CHERRY**, Thos. E. **PENDER**. The committee retired and in a short time returned, and reported the following resolutions... *Resolved*, That a committee to consist of one Delegate from each county..be appointed..to draw up a memorial and lay the same before this convention, setting forth, all matters, in relation to the reopening of Roanoke Inlet at or near Nag's Head. *Resolved*, That the convention appoint a committee to consist of _____ members, to whom the memorial shall be put in charge, and that they proceed to Washington city, and deliver the same to each and every one of our Senators and Representatives in Congress, and call upon them, to use every proper effort to enforce the same. The Resolutions were adopted. On motion of S. B. **SPRUILL**, the blank in the second Resolution, was filled with one from each county. Mr. **COLLINS** proposed that those Gentlemen who had maps, documents &c., relating to the subject of an inlet at Nag's Head, be requested to lay them on the Secretaries table which was agreed to. Charts and documents, were presented by Josiah **COLLINS**, J. C. B. **EHRINGHAUS**, and J. C. **BOND**. The President appointed the following gentlemen to compose the committee under the first Resolution... Messrs. Wm. B. **SHEPARD**, Josiah **COLLINS**, Augustus **MOORE**, H. K. **BURGWYN**, Wm. J. **ELLISON**, Joseph **HALSEY**, Thomas F. **JONES**, Cornelius G. **LAMB**, Richard H. **SMITH**, P. H. **WINSTON**, Wm. D. **VALENTINE**, and Willis F. **RIDDICK**. The Convention then adjourned until 3 1/2 P. M. The Convention met according to adjournment. Hon. Aug. **MOORE**, moved that a committe of 5 be appointed to open subscriptions to meet the expenses of printing &c, and Lithrographing **WIMBLE**s map, laid on the table by Mr. **COLLINS**. The President appointed the following..committee, viz: Messrs. Aug. **MOORE**, Dr. Benajmin L. S. **WEBB**, C. **LATHAM**, P. P. **CLEMENTS**.

Mr. **ELLISON**, introduced the following resolution, viz: *Resolved*, That a committee of 2 from each county, be appointed by the President, to report to this convention, (for the use of the committee appointed, to draw up a memorial to Congress) the amount of tonage passing through Croaton Sound, and the Dismal Swamp Canal, and other statistical information, of the amount of Produce exported from the Albemarle Sound, and its tributaries. The resolution was adopted and the following gentlemen were appointed to compose the committee, viz: Messrs. Wm. J. **ELLISON**, D. W. **BAGLEY**, H. K. **BURGWYN**, S.

30 March 1850

(609) (Cont.) T. WHEELER, W. L. DANIEL, J. H. SMITH, J. Mc C BOYLE, C. L. PETTIGREW, James F. DAVENPORT, Abner HARREL, James F. DEVEREUX, L. S. WEBB, Starkey SHARP, Willis F. RIDDICK, John COX, John H. LEARY, Wm. E. MANN, Jos. MULLEN, C. M. FORD, E. F. SMITH, Willis GRANDY, Abner L. DOZIER. .. On motion the Convention adjourne [sic] until tomorrow morning 10 o'clock.

Friday, March 15th, 1850. The convention met according to adjournment. Dr. R. K. SPEED introduced the following Resolution, viz: *Resolved*, That a committee of 3 persons be appointed to have printed the memorial..and to distribute copies thereof. *Resolved*, That a committee of ___, be appointed for each county..and for the county of Currituck, whose duty it shall be to procure subscribers to said memorial, and transmit them to the members, representing the 7th 8th and 9th Congressional Districts. *Resolved*, that the committee appointed to superintend, the printing of said memorial, send copies of the same to such persons in our large commercial cities and elsewhere; as they may deem proper, and urge the several persons, to whom the same may be sent, to co-operate with us in our effort, to obtain a better outlet to the ocean. On motion of Dr. SPEED, the blank in the second Resolution, was filled with 'six from each county.' The President appointed the following gentlemen to compose the committee under the first resolution, viz: Hon. Wm. B. SHEPARD, Dr. R. K. SPEED, Gen. J. C. B. EHRINGHAUS. The President appointed the following gentlemen to compose the committee of six in each county, under the second Resolution. For Northampton County,--H. K. BURGWYN, Samuel CALVERT, John RANDOLPH, M. SMALLWOOD, C. W. BARNES, and E. JACOBS. For Bertie County,--L. H. WEBB, W. A. FURGERSON, W. P. GURLEY, Priston PERRY, T. B. HARDY and R. H. COX. For Gates County,--Whitmel STALLINGS, Henry MILLER, Reddick GATLING, George B. GORDON, Charles E. BALLARD, and Wm. J. BAKER. For Hertford County,--Col. Starkey SHARP, J. A. JACKSON, A. P. YANCY, W. L. DANIEL, R. G. COWPER, and G. C. MOORE. For Chowan County,--Wm. D. LOWTHER, jr., John M. JONES, James C. BOND, R. R. FELTON, James L. ROBERTS, and Jas. J. CANNON. For Perquimans County,--Dr. FORD, Thos S. JACOCKS, Edmund C. BLOUNT, Jeptha WHITE, Edward F. SMITH, and Joseph WHITE. For Pasquotank County,--Dr. R. K. SPEED, Dr. S. D.GRICE, Wm. E. MANN, A. JONES, James E. WEEKS, and Mark S. SAWYER. For Camden County,-- C. BARCO, Wm. G. WILSON, C. G. LAMB, E. L. DOZIER, A. BERRY, and Wm. R. ABBOTT. For Currituck County,--B. T. SIMMONS, John BARNARD, E. C. LINDSEY, John B. ETHEREDGE, J. B. LINDSEY, and Tully L. DOZIER. For Halifax County,--Wm. R. SMITH, W. J. HILL, M. FERRALL, H. J. HARVEY, James SIMMONS, and Dr. W. L. LONG. For Martin County,--Clayton MOORE, G. L. MOORE, D. W. BAGLEY, B. BENNETT, Wm. K. WILLIAMS, and Dr. S. C. BENJAMIN. For Tyrrel County,--Jos. HALSEY, Jno. MC CLEES, Charles MC CLEES, C. L. PETTIGREW, Jos. MC CLEES, and J. F. DAVENPORT. For Washington County-J. B. CHESSON, Charles LATHAM, A. J. MIZELL, Dr. H. HARDISON, Henderson B. PHELPS, and Wm. L. RHODES.

Hon. Wm. B. SHEPARD, Chairman of the Committee appointed to draw up a memorial..reported a memorial, which was adopted. .. Hon. Wm. B. SHEPARD introduced the following Resolution, viz: *Resolved*, That this convention do highly approve of the publication of a N. C. Gazetteer by Dr. WHEELER of Murfreesboro', and recommend the delegates..to furnish such aid, as may be required in the completion of said work. On motion of Mr. COLLINS. *Resolved*, That the Convention now proceed to the appointment of one delegate in each county and an alternate delegate under the second resolution reported yesterday , from the committee reporting subject matter for the convention. The Convention appointed the following..viz: Northampton-- H. K. BURGWYN--D. A. BARNES, alternate. Bertie--Lewis THOMPSON--S. B. SPRUILL, alternate. Gates--Whitmel STALLINGS--H. WILLIE, alternate. Chowan--James C. JOHNSTON--Dr. T. D. WARREN, alternate. Hertford--Hon. Keneth RAYNER--G. C. MOORE, alternate. Perquimans--J. P. WHEDBEE--Dr. C. M. FORD, alternate. Pasquotank--J. C. B. EHRINGHAUS--Dr. GRICE, alternate. Camden--Willis S. GRANDY--D. D. FEREBEE, alternate. Currituck--B. T. SIMMONS--Tully L. DOZIER, alternate. Halifax--A. JOYNER--R. H. SMITH, alternate. Washington--Josiah COLLINS, J. C. NORCOM, alternate. Tyrrel--C. L. PETTIGREW--Jos. HALSEY, alternate. On motion Resolved unanimously that Hon. Wm. B. SHEPARD be added to the list of Delegates to Congress. On motion of Mr. HALSEY, *Resolved*, That when this Convention adjourn it adjourn to meet in Edenton on Thursday after the 1st Monday in November next. On motion of Hon. Wm. B. SHEPARD, *Resolved*, That the President..be requested to transmit to the several Boards of Trade in our commercial cities, a copy of the memorial of this convention, and request their co-operation in accomplishing the object. The Convention adjourned until 3 1/2 P. M. ... Andrew JOYNER, President. J. C. NORCOM, T. P. DEVEREUX, J. H. LEARY, T. F. JONES} Vice Presidents. H. G. SPRUILL, J. Mc C. BOYLE,} Secretaries. I hereby certify that the foregoing is a true copy, from the Journal of the Convention in my possession. H. G. SPRUILL, Sec'y. Plymouth, March 15, 1850.

(610) Mr. A. W. DESSANER, a merchant of Weston, Missouri on his way to the East, lost a belt at St. Louis containing $13,000, in gold and paper.

(611) Elizabeth-City, March 03 [sic,] '50. .. *Correspondence of the Baltimore Patriot*. WASHINGTON, March 24, 0850. .. The present administration has been mindful of the services of the press. A majority of the Chargeships have been given to editors. E. G. SQUIRES, Charge to Central America, was formerly an editor in Hartford, Connecticut, and afterwards in Chillicothe, Ohio.

30 March 1850

(611) (Cont.) Thomas M. **FOOTE**, Charge to Bogota, was and is editor of the *Buffalo Commercial*. Col. **WEBB**, Charge to Austria, is editor of the *New York Courier and Enquirer*. Mr. **KINNE** si [sic] now pretty certain of a similar appointment. The speech of Truman **SMITH** was very long. It was after 5 o'clock, Saturday evening, before he got through. When printed, it will be a powerful vindication of the President's course in appointing to office. .. John **BELL**, of Tennessee, has the floor on this subject. It was taken for him, on Saturday, by Mr. **SEWARD**, of New York. ...

(612) *From the Rockingham* (Va.) *Register.* THE GENERAL CONVENTION OF THE **JENNINGS** FAMILY OF THE UNITED STATES. *To be held in Charlottesville, Va. May 15th* 1850. Upon mature deliberation and consultation with a great number of persons of several branches of the **JENINGS** [sic] family in different parts of the United States, it is deemed important, for the interest of all concerned that one general convention of the entire **JENNINGS** family in the United States, be held at Charlottesville Virginia, on the 15th day of May, 1850, for the purpose of examing [sic] the claims of all, in the estate of William **JENNINGS**, who died intestate in 1798, in Suffolk, England, leaving an immense property, still unsettled, and in the care of the British Government, subject to the claim of the true heirs. Although a report has been set on foot, and industriously circulated, that the estate has long since been distributed, which report was doubtless designed to discourage and prevent those interested from a further investigation of their claims, yet it is known that the property is still open to claimants. And, further, it is known that no act of limitation will cut off claimants in this case, for several years to come; and the government of England will not, and her statutes cannot, interfere with claims based upon proper legal *data.* ... Many **JENNINGS**es. March 6th, 1850.

(613) TERRIBLE STEAM BOAT ACCIDENT.--The Steam Boat Orline St. John, bound from Mobile to Montgomery, with a large number of passengers on board, took fire at 5 o'clock in the afternoon of the 5th inst., two miles above Bridgeport, Ala., and so quickly was she enveloped by the flames, that between forty and fifty souls, men, women, and children, perished, either by being burnt to death, or drowned in the river after jumping overboard. .. Mrs. **HULL** and daughter, of Augusta, Ga., and Mrs. and Miss **VAUGHAN**, and Mr. J. R. **MC KAIN** and mother, of Camden, S. C., are mentioned as among those lost. ...

(614) Blankets were first made at Bristol, in England, about the year 1338, by a poor weaver, whose name was Thomas **BLANKET**, and who gave his name to his peculiar manufacture of woollen cloths.

(615) The trial of Dr. **WEBSTER** which is now going on in Boston, for the murder of Dr. **PARKMAN** is creating great excitment in that City. The Court Room is crowded daily... The evidence, as we learn from the *Boston Advertiser*, has as yet all been on the part of the State, and not at all favorable to the acquittal of Dr. **WEBSTER**. A Boston correspondent of the *New York Commercial* has the following remarks upon the evidence given on Thursday: The cross examination of Dr. Charles T. **JACKSON** in no degree invalidated the clear, intelligible evidence given in his testimony for the prosecution. Dr. **CROSBY**, his assistant, was scarcely less lucid in his testimony. The testimony of Dr. **KEEP** followed. His evidence was considered to be of great importance, and the prisoner evidently listened to him with painful interest. The alarm of fire, given while Dr. **KEEP** was on the stand, caused a recess of the Court, during which Prof. **WEBSTER** held some conversation with his friends and with Dr. **JACKSON**. At the reassembling of the Court, Dr. **KEEP**'s examination was continued, the witness being frequently affected to tears while giving his evidence. The production of the bones, and other fragments of the body, by Dr. **WYMAN**, created deep sensation in the Court. The prisoner, however, seemed entirely unmoved, and evinced no other feeling than that of an unconcern [sic] spectator. The Government have thus far..examined fourteen witnesses, and have seventy two men to examine, of whom at least eight are medical men. The counsel for the prisoner are rather tame in cross-examination, do not show their hand, and seem to rely rather on the weakness of the Government than on their own strength. ...

(616) MANUFACTURES IN NEWBERN. It is with deep felt gratification that we announce to our readers that Newbern has taken another step..towards establishing Domestic Manufactures within her borders. The establishment of the Sash Factory on Union Point and the large Tannery at Linden, we regarded as the initiatory steps. By reference to our advertising columns, it will be seen that Dr. J. A. **GUION**, and Mr. E. R. **STANLY** are about establishing a Woolen Factory within the limits of the Town. The building is to be erected on the vacant lot back of the residence of Dr. P. **CURTIS**, and is to be 125 feet in length, by 50 feet in breadth, and the machinery to be worked by steam. .. They design we understand to employ white labour, and to give the preference to our own population of the Town and adjoining country.--*Newbernian.*

(617) J. E. **DEFORD**, Apothecary and Druggist, And Wholesale and Retail dealer in Drugs, Medicines, Chemicals, Paints, Oils, Glass Ware, Dye Stuffs, Brushes, Perfumery, Fancy Articles, &c. The subscriber has recently received from New York and Philadelphia, a large and valuable addition to his stock of the above articles... J. E. **DEFORD**. March 30, 1850.

(618) Land and Negroes for Sale. The subscriber being desirous of leaving this state, offers for sale the following property. A

30 March 1850

(618) (Cont.) farm in the lower part of the county, containing 250 acres; 160 of which is in a fine state of cultivation, it produces fine crops of corn and and is surrounded by land of excellent quality, most of which can be bought so as to form a large plantation. The improvements are all new, and within one mile of the mouth of little river. Terms liberal, possession given on the first of next January. A small farm of 170 acres, near the town of Nixonton, 100 of which is in cultivation. Also a lot in Nixonton. .. Several likely negroes, stock and farming utensils. The above property can be seen by applying to the subscriber in Nixonton. J. B. **SKINNER**, March 30th, 1850.

(619) Union Hotel. Union Street, Norfolk, Va. The subscriber, who has been a steamboat Captain for the last 21 years, and who has as he believes, given general satisfaction to the public, now having taken charge of the above Hotel..is prepared to accomodate all who may be disposed to patronize him with neat and comfortable lodgings. ... Jas. **HENDERSON**, Agent. March 30.

(620) New Milinery Establishment. Mrs. Lucinda **RUTTER**, would most respectfully inform her old friends and the public at large, that she has just returned from the North, where she selected with great care, a beautiful assortment of every article used in the Millinery Line. .. All orders will be thankfully received and promptly attended to. Her establishment is nearly opposite the dwelling of Mr. Elisha **NASH**, and about 50 yards from the store of Mr. James **LONG**, on the same side. Lucinda **RUTTER**. March 30th, 1850.

The Old North State.
Vol. 10. "Error is harmless, when truth is left free to combat it." No. 7.
Elizabeth City, N. C. Saturday, April 6, 1850.

(621) The *Philadelphia Inquirer*, in mentioning the death at Naples on the 22d ult. of Passed Midshipman Charles Carroll **BAYARD**, says--His death was occasioned by a wound received from a stone thrown from the crater of Vesuvius, while he was standing in company with other officers on the side of the mountain. ...

(622) Elizabeth-City, April 6, '50. .. The trial of Dr. **WEBSTER** for the murder of Dr. **PARKMAN** has, after a long and critical examination of witnesses on both sides, been brought to a close; and he has been found guilty of murder in the first degree. ...

(623) We regret to learn that John C. **CALHOUN**, U. S. Senator from South Carolina, died at his residence in Washington on the 31st ult. The country has lost a statesman and patriot...

(624) CALIFORNIA--MR. **KING**'S REPORT.--The Washington correspondent of the *N. Y. Journal of Commerce* writes that Mr. Thomas Butler **KING**'s Report on California was read to the President and Cabinet on Monday, and occupied two hours and a half in reading. It will of course be soon presented to Congrss. ...

(625) LIONISING. Jenny **LIND** must be a very sensible woman. She has evidently heard of the American penchant for lionizing, and she is determined not to be made a victim of it. .. The last accounts say that she stipulates with **BARNUM** to be private when not on the stage. ...

(626) New Millinery Goods. Mrs. Ann **BELL** respectfully informs her friends, the Ladies of E. City and surrounding Country, that she has just returned from the North with a beautiful and complete assortment of every article in her line, and is now prepared to have them made in the best and most fashionable manner. .. She is also prepared to execute Mantua-Making in the most fashionable styles. Shop next door to Z. **CULPEPPER**'s dec'd. E. City, April 6th, 1850.

(627) NEW GOODS, &c. &c. The Subscriber has just received from Baltimore a variety of articles, among which are Brushes of all kinds, Combs, Toilet Soaps assorted, with a lot of Old Brown Windsor, Ox Marrow, Perfumed chalk Balls, a very superior article of German Cologne, Extracts assorted, Cologne Bottles very handsome, Teething Rings for children, also a Fresh Supply of Lemons, Oranges, Taffy, Cocoanut Candy, &c. All of which I will sell very low for cash. W. J. **KELLINGER**.

(628) NOTICE. The subscriber having resigned his office as Constable request all persons having claims in his hands for collection, to call and get them or the money. Wm. **NEWBOLD**. April 6th, 1850.

(629) Information to the Public. The undersigned by mutual and undivided consent has removed from the store heretofore occupied by him, and has taken quarters in the one recently vacated by J. M. **WHEDBEE** & Bro, Shoe Dealers. .. The undersigned is also receiving quite a pretty assortment of Staple and Fancy Dry Goods adapted to the spring trade. ... Jas. W. **HINTON**. April 6th, 1850.

6 April 1850

(630) Watch & Clock Repairing. Mr. Adolphus **LOUIS** respectfully informs the Ladies and Gentlemen of Elizabeth City, and the surrounding country, that he is prepared to repair watches and any kind of Jewelry in his line. He may be found in the Office formerly occupied by Doctor **MUSGRAVE**, two doors above the Mansion House. All work warranted to give satisfaction. He solicits a share of your patronage. E. City, April 6th, 1850.

(631) To the Carpenters & Builders of NORTH CAROLINA. The subscriber would earnestly call the attention of the Carpenters and Builders of N. C., adjacent to E. City, Hertford, Edenton and Plymouth, to his Sash Blind and Door Factory. Located on Talbot st. Norfolk Va., where he will receive and execute in the neatest possible manner, all orders that may be sent to him, or to Caleb **SIKES** of E. City, who is agent for the subscriber. ... Jesse H. **SIKES**, Norfolk Va. April 6.

The Old North State.
Vol. 10. "Error is harmless, when truth is left free to combat it." No. 8.
Elizabeth City, N. C. Saturday, April 13, 1850.

(632) Elizabeth-City, April 13, '50. .. IMPROVEMENTS. Nothing so much raises the estimation of a Town as a general system of improvement, and we are proud to say that in the last four or five years our little Village has gone through a general renovation. The old delapidated buildings that once were seen along its streets are to be seen no more. But in their places are to be seen some beautiful dwellings or stores. Among the most conspicious of them is the fine dwelling and store of our enterprising citizen J. M. **WHEDBEE**, Esq., which has recently been erected by James P. **WHEDBEE**, Esq., of Perquimans. The store is occupied by J. M. **WHEDBEE** & Brother as a Shoe Store. It is decidedly the handsomest store in the place. Then there is the beautiful dwelling of our friend, Wm. L. **SHANNON**, Esq., on the site of the late residence of our fellow citizen Samuel **JACKSON**, Esq. Then comes the large and commodious Hotel of our obliging citizen George A. **WILLIAMS**, Esq. A building that would do honor to a much larger town, as a public house. It is not quite finished, but its large and massive columns look out in bold relief. .. There is the neat and substantial dwelling with a store in front, of Leonard **CHAPMAN**, Esq., while on the other side of the street a little below the Bank where one year ago stood an old rickety dwelling and an old Blacksmith Shop, is to be seen a comfortable dwelling, with a bake house near it, where all in want of the "bread of life" can be supplied. They were erected by our townsman John C. **EHRINGHAUS**, Esq. Keep still up the street until you cross the *present* boundary of the City, and you will see the decided improvement to the dwelling of Mrs. Elizabeth **NASH**. Near by the neat and comfortable addition to the dwelling of Jas. S. **LONG**, Esq., meets the eye. You cannot look *long* at that, before your attention is called to the dwelling of Geo. W. **BROOKS**, Esq., on the opposite side now under the carpenters hands, and which when done will be quite an ornament to that part of the town when annexed. We now retrace our steps and all along the street we see improvements going on within doors--painting, papering, &c. Among this class is our friend Jas. W. **HINTON**, Esq., who has recently taken the store vacated by Messrs. **WHEDBEE** & Brother It is painted and grained up in beautiful style. We neglected to state in a proper place a new store lately fitted up by Barney **TISDALE**, Esq., and now occupied by Seth **MORGAN**, Esq., as a Grocery. Also the large addition of Isaiah **FEARING**, Esq., and the elegant portico in front. We have hastily mentioned a few of the many improvements..and shall continue our remarks next week, and mention all we recollect.

(633) Nag's Head Inlet. We lay before our readers to-day some interesting information in regard to the condition of Nag's Head Inlet more than one hundred years ago. We are indebted, for the means of obtaining this information, to Josiah **COLLINS** Esq., who has kindly furnished us with a Chart of the coast from Cape Fear to Currituck Inlet, made by an English navigator by the name of **WIMBLE**, in 1738, one hundred and twelve years ago. Many have supposed, and still entertain the belief that the water in Nag's Head Inlet was never sufficient to enable vessels to enter the Albemarle Sound. But we find by examining this chart which can without doubt be relied on as correct, that in 1738 the time of the survey, there was out side of the Inlet eight feet of water, and in the channel of the Inlet through which vessels passed in the Sound there was four fathoms of water. We find also from the soundings of this navigator that, at the north end of Roanoke Island, there was from six to nine feet of water; while on the west side of the Island where our vessels now pass into the Pamlico Sound there was from nine to ten feet of water. From Collington Island at the east end of the Albemarle Sound, soundings were made as far up as Edenton, the depth varying from two to four fathoms. After entering Perquimans, Little and Pasquotank Rivers the depth given on the chart is three fathoms. Thus it is evident that more than one hundred years ago vessels of a large size could enter with safety and sail any where in the Sound. The question now arises whether by opening Nag's Head Inlet it can be brought into as navigable condition as it was a hundred years ago. ...

(634) WHIG STATE CONVENTION. The chairman of the Whig Central Committee has subscribed the following in reference to a Whig State Convention. .. "It having been referred, by County meetings..to the Central Committee..to designate the day and place for the meeting of the Whig Convention, for the purpose of nominating a Candidate for Governor: Notice is hereby given, that to suit the views and wishes of the largest number, the said Convention will assemble in Raleigh on Monday, the 10th day of June next. At which time and place the Delegates are most respectfully invited to attend. Rich'd **HINES**, Ch'm.

13 April 1850

(635) I. O. O. F. On Friday 3d May at 11 o'clock A. M., Achoree Lodge will turn out in procession to celebrate her third Anniversary; and all transient members of the Order are invited to join in the celebration. The procession will advance to the Methodist Church, where an Address will be delivered by P. G. John **POOL**, Esq., at which place the public is respectfully invited to attend. Jno. B. **FEARING**, P. C. **WILLIANS**, Nathan **MORRIS**.} Committee. E. City, April 13, 1850.

(636) James W. **HINTON**, RETAIL DEALER IN Staple and Fancy Dry Goods. Has just received from the Cities of Baltimore and New York, the *most extensive* and *select* stock of Dry Goods that he has ever shown to the public... His store is on Road street, opposite Barney **TIADALE** Esq, next dooor to Mr. D. **RICHARDSON**. J. W. **HINTON**, April 13th, 1850.

(637) List of Letters Remaining in the Post Office, at Elizabeth City, Quarter ending 31st March, 1850. **ARMOUR** Mrs Mary **ARNOLD** Charles W **ASHBEE** Mrs Maria **BRAY** John **BOONE** Miss Charlotte **BOWEN** Capt M **BELL** Josiah **BARN** Newlis **BERRY** John **BRITE** Jonathan **BALLANCE** Holloway **BAILEY** John **BALLANTREE** Thomas **BRAY** W 2 **BROWN** W H 2 **BRIGHT** Ephriam **BELL** Thos **BROTHERS** Willis **BRADSHAW** Jos R **BURGESS** Mr **BURGESS** Capt W W **COMMANDER** Jas 2 **CAROON** Navel **COMMANDER** Miles **COOKE** Saml T **CARTWRIGHT** Benoni **COLLINS** Jackson **DICKERSON** A T **DILLIN** Silas W **DOWDY** Capt S **DAVIS** Miss Margaret **DELONG** Harvey **DOLPH** Jared **DUNN** Francis **ELLIOTT** Mordeica **EASTON** William **FACEMIRE** George **GRIFFIN** Wm (up co. **GAMBREL** John A **GRAHAM** Dr **GOODMAN** John T **GODFEY** Jos M **GANINGTON** Miss Ann **GAPES** Thos 2 **HOLLOWELL** Ambrose **HERBERT** Mrs Mary **HUBBARD** Charles **HARVEY** Mrs Ann **HADAWAY** Albert **HALSTEAD** Nathan 2 **HARRELL** Mrs Ann L **HUBBARD** Cupt Martin **HARRELL** A & J **HILL** Araph **HALL** Robert (of color) **JENNINGS** Nathan **JORDAN** Prichard **JACKSON** Mrs Mary A **JOHNSON** George **KING** Basset John **KONE** W W **KEATON** Miss Nancy **LAMB** Mrs Sarah E 2 **LABOYTEAUX** Wm 2 **LEWIS** Samuel **LAVITEW** Edward **LORY** Wm **LAMB** S D **LYTLE** Jno S **LOGAN** Peter **MORRIS & STONE** 2 **MC DONALD** Murdock **MYDGETT** Stephen D **MINSTRELS** Aeolian **MULLEN** Miss Mary L **MATHEWS** Richard **MC DANIEL** Flory **MILLER** Jas or Harris E **MEZIC** Capt George **MORGAN** T T **MC COY** Samuel D Mister **SEVERN NICHOLS** J **NEWSOM** Henry **OVERMAN** Mrs Margaret **OLD** Wm **PRITCHARD** George M **PERKINS** Dr J Q **PENDLETON** Robert **PAINE** Wm A **POOLE** Henry (of color) **PENDLETON** Reuben **PETTIGREW** Wm S **PERINE** Thos J **PIKE** John **SPENCE** Kelly **SAWYER** Jerome B **SINCLAIR** J B **SAMPSON** Granville **STONE** George W 2 **SIMMONS** Capt Thos **SEXTON** Wm **STERLING** Capt J 2 **SARN** Wm **TOMS** A C **TOMS** Miss Mary A 4 **TUTTLE** Wm **WESCOTT** John **WALKER** Nathan **WILCOX** George S **WARDELL** Samuel **WAMOUTH** David **WRIGHT** Robert L **WHITE** Miles **WHITLERY** Jas B **WISE** Lieut H A **WILLIS** Ethelbert Persons calling for any of the above letters will please say they are advertised. Wm. E. **MANN**, P. M. March 13

The Old North State.
Vol. 10. "Error is harmless, when truth is left free to combat it." No. 9.
Elizabeth City, N. C. Saturday, April 20, 1850.

(638) *Going it With a rush.*--We find the following in one of our northern exchanges:--Married, In Marcellus, New York, on the 28th ult., Mr. Sylvester **SMITH** to Miss Lidia **DUNCAN**; Mr. Sereno **SMITH** to Miss Cothia **DUNCAN**; and Mr. Charles **DUNCAN** to Miss Emma **SMITH**, all of that place. These marriages were solemnized at the house of Mr. Benjamin Stanton **SMITH**, father of Sereno and Emma, and brother of Sylvester **SMITH**. Charles **DUNCAN** is brother of Lydia and Cothia **DUNCAN**, and Sylvester **SMITH** is uncle to Sereno and Emma **SMITH**. All the parties except Sylvester; are under twenty years of age.

(639) A SINGULAR DISCOVERY. The *Cincinnati Commercial* says there has lately been dug up some 14 feet below the surface of the earth, and more than fifty above high water mark, in the garden of Capt. G. W. **CUTTER**, an elephant's task; which time and the action of the elements have reduced to a substance resembling chalk; it crumbled when taken out of the earth, but a portion of it entire, more than 20 inches long, is in the possession of the proprietor of this place, just above the mouth of Licking, opposite. The whole animal is probably in the bank. If this proves to be a real elephant's tusk..it will prove a singular Zoological fact that elephants did once belong to this country.

(640) Elizabeth-City, April 20, '50. .. NEW GOODS. Our merchants are now receiving their Spring and Summer stock of goods of every description. .. We make it a custom to notice all who may go into any kind of mercantile and mechanical business in our thriving little village, as we think it has a tendency to give importance to the place; therefore, it is with pleasure that we announce that Mr. Thomas **SHANNON** has recently taken the new store lately occupied by Mr. John J. **GRANDY**, opposite Col. **COOK**'s, where he intends keeping a general assortment of every article found in the Dry Goods line, besides a great many other articles usually found in our village stores. .. Mr. Wilson **WILLIAMS** has also taken the store lately occupied by Capt. Thos. **KNIGHT**, near the market, and intends keeping a general assortment Store. ...

20 April 1850

(641) We understand that Mr. Leonidas B. LEMAY, associate editor of the *Raleigh Star*, will be in our town during court week, for the purpose of soliciting subscribers to that sterling Whig journal. The paper has recently been greatly enlarged, and now ranks among the largest of the State. Mr. LEMAY, Sr., has been at considerable expense in getting up such a paper... The terms of the paper are $2 50 in advance, or $3, if payment be delayed three months. ...

(642) The case of Professor **WEBSTER** still occupies the attention of the public. Judging from what we have seen in our exchange papers on the subject, we should say that a very great portion of the people throughout the country entertain the opinion that the evidence given at the trial overthrew the indictment, and that the verdict rendered by the jury was given through prejudice and not according to the testimony. We do not contend for the innocence of Dr. **WEBSTER**, but from the testimony which has been reported, and the verdict given by the jury, we are led to believe that prejudice has had a great influence in the matter. It is said that Gov. **BRIGGS** is not satisfied with the verdict, and will delay for some time to sign a warrant for his execution. The many severe criticisms which have been made in regard to this trial, have evidently had great influence on the public mind. We have seen none however that have endeavored to assert his innocence, but that he has not been proved guilty. We understand that Mr. **CLIFFORD**, the Attorney General, is about to publish a reply to the strictures which have been made, in vindication of the bar and the judiciary of the State.

(643) *North Carolina Gazetteer*. In looking over the proceedings of the Nag's Head Convention, that lately met at Plymouth, we find a resolution approving the publication of a work called the *North Carolina Gazetteer*, now being compiled by Dr. S. J. **WHEELER**. Such a work is greatly needed, to bring before the world, the resources of Carolina. ... *Baptist Messenger*.

(644) A MONTH LATER FROM CALIFORNIA. All the towns of the Sacramento and tributaries, are thriving, particularly the towns of Yubaville, Vernon, Fremont, and a survey recently made on Feather River near its mouth, called Nicolaus. .. A petition has been made to the Legislature, on behalf [sic] Caleb **LYON**, of N. Y. for $1000 for the State Seal, designed and executed by him. ... *N. Y. Evangelist*.

(645) *Correspondence of the Baltimore Patriot*. WASHINGTON, March 15, 1850. Death has been busy in the metropolis this winter. The last distinguished victim is Thomas Jefferson **CAMPBELL**, the Clerk of the House of Representatives.--He died on Saturday last, about 1 o'clock. He had been sick for about a week, and from the first the indications were all unfavorable--so that he gradually sunk into the sleep of death. Mr. **CAMPBELL** was a citizen of Tennessee, and was formerly a member of Congress, from that State. He was elected the Clerk of the House of Representatives in the last Congress, when the Whigs had a majority of the House; and was elected the Clerk of the present House, after a great many ballotings.--He was a man of kind heart, and was greatly esteemed by his personal friends. .. It was his desire that his remains should be removed privately as possible from the city and taken to his former home in Tennessee. They were accordingly yesterday taken in charge by his son, and..conveyed to the depot, and started for his home in Tennessee. The body was deposited in a metallic coffin, similar to that in which Mr. **CALHOUN** was placed. The death of Mr. **CAMPBELL** will revive the difficulty about the organization of the House, and it is feared, retard the public business again. .. Mr. **FORNEY**, the editor of the *Philadelphia Pennsylvanian*..will be presented as a candidate again.--Matthew St. Clair **CLARKE**, who was formerly the clerk, will also be brought forward again. Albert **SMITH** of Maine, is spoken of, and not a few turn their attention to Mr. James C. **WALKER**, the present reading clerk--who would make a first rate officer. Henry Clay **MUDD**, who was formerly connected with the office, may also be brought forward by his friends, who are many. .. Messrs. C. G. **MEMMENGER**, Alfred **HUGER**, and Daniel **RAVENEL**, of Charleston, South Carolina, the committee appointed by the authorities of that city to co-operate with the committee of the United States Senate and others, in making arrangements for conveying home the remains of Mr. **CALHOUN**, have arrived on this city, and taken lodgings at the National Hotel. ...

(646) The trunk of Mr. J. W. **DEMAREST** was recently broken open at Panama, and robbed of specie and valuables to the amount of $10,000. ...

(647) REMOVAL. J. M. **WHEDBEE** & Bro. Have recently taken the large and beautiful store built and finished excusively for them and their trade. The store is situated below their former stand and on the opposite side of the street a few doors below Mr. Barney **TISDALE**s. Their friend Jas. W. **HINTON**, occupying their old stand. He Deals in Dry Goods and will take pleasure in pointing out the store of **WHEDBEE** & Bro. .. Their goods are purchased from the makers and their agents with a small exception, at a very low price. ... Jas. M. **WHEDBEE** & Bro. E. City, April 20th, 1850.

(648) NEW AND FASHIONABLE MILLINERY GOODS, By Mrs. Esther **SIKES**. The subscriber has the pleasure of announcing to the Ladies of this community, that she has received and opened her Spring supply of Millinery Goods, and is fully prepared to furnish them with any thing connected with her line of business. .. She has on hand at present a stock of about $1800, which no

20 April 1850

(648) (Cont.) doubt is the largest ever offered in this market. Feeling desirous to have everything connected with her establishment complete, she has engaged the services of two of the most experienced Milliners that could be found in the city of Norfolk, one of whom is well known to the ladies of this place, Miss Indiana **LINTON**, and Miss Ann **BLACKBURN**.--The ladies..have for several years past been employed in the most fashionable Millinery establishment in Norfolk, to wit, Mrs. **BUTT**'s. ... Elizabeth City, April 20, 1850.

(649) Give heed to what "Caleb" says. The Subscriber has just returned from New York with a large lot of "fixins," for Housekeepers, such as Chairs of all kinds, Sideboards, Divans, Sofas, Book-cases, Wardrobes, Candle stands, Centre Tables, Pier Tables, Bedsteads, Matrimonial Fruit Baskets, &c., &c. ... Caleb **SIKES**. E. City, April 20, 1850.

(650) Carriage and Harness, NEW STOCK JUST RECEIVED. In returning his thanks for the liberal patronage heretofore and continued to be extended to him, the Subscriber with pleasure solicits the attention of his customers and the public generally, to his newly completed stock of *Chariotees, double and single Rockaways, Barouches, Buggies Sulkies,* of the latest and most fashionable styles. His stock of *Harnesses*, also, is complete, new, and of the most recent and approved patterns; yet without reflection upon the elegance and excellence of his assortment of Saddles, Bridles, Martingals, &c. &c. ... Robert **WATKINS**. E. City, April 6, 1850.

The Old North State.
Vol. 10. "Error is harmless, when truth is left free to combat it." No. 10.
Elizabeth City, N. C. Saturday, April 27, 1850.

(651) HORRIBLE REVENGE.--The *Galena Jeffersonian* says, among the overland emigrants for California last Spring, was Mr. **GREEN**, of "**GREEN**s Woollen Factory." Fox River, and two of his sons, the youngest a youth. It is reported that while passing through a tribe of Indians, this young man, naturally full of mischief, killed a squaw. The tribe having become well advised of the fact hastened after the company, and overtook them, and demanded the murderer. At first the demand was resisted; but after the Indians had informed them that they would destroy the company if their request was not granted, the youth was surrendered into their hands. They then stripped him and in the presence of his father and the whole company, they skinned him from his head to his feet. He lived four hours after he was thus flayed.

(652) Elizabeth-City, April 27, '50. .. ARRIVAL OF MR **CALHOUN**'S REMAINS.--The remains of the late Hon. J. C. **CALHOUN** reached here yesterday afternoon, in an extra train of cars, from Acquia Creek, in charge of a joint committee from his native State, and from the two Houses of Congress, and accompanied by the Fredericksburg Guards. .. The corpse of Cadet Henry W. **HILLIARD** (son of the Hon. H. M. **HILLIARD**, of Alabama,) was brought on in the same train of cars... Cadet **HILLIARD** had just received an appointment at the U. S. Military Academy from President **TAYLOR**. It is a singular circumstance that he went on to Washington with Mr. **CALHOUN**, attended his funeral there, and now returns with him in the cold companionship of death.--*Rich. Rep. of Tuesday.*

(653) DIED, In Perquimans County on the 22d inst., Mr. Samuel **NEWBOULD**, in the 67th year of his age. Mr. **NEWBOULD** was one of the oldest citizens of Perquimans, and has left a wife and several children, the most of them though, in a situation every way comfortable.

(654) CONCERT. The "Musical Club," under the direction of J. M. **MATHEWS**, will give an instrumental concert in this place, on Friday evening the 3d of May, at 7 1/2 o'clock P. M. For Programme &c., see small bills. E. City April 27th, 1850.

(655) To all whom it may Concern. The subscriber has taken the new and elegant Store lately occupied by J. J. **GRANDY**, and now offers to the public as complete an assortment of DRY GOODS, As has ever been brought to this market. ... Thos. **SHANNON**. E. City, April 27th, 1850.

(656) St. Mary's school, Raleigh N. C. The 17th Term of this School will commence on the 8th day of June, and continue till the 19th November. For a circular containing full particulars, apply to the subscriber. Albert **SMEDES**, Rector. April 17th, 1850.

The Old North State.
Vol. 10. "Error is harmless, when truth is left free to combat it." No. 11.
Elizabeth City, N. C. Saturday, May 4, 1850.

4 May 1850

(657) Elizabeth-City, May 4, '50. .. There came to our office a day or two since a new paper published in Raleigh, by Mr. Burwell **TEMPLE**, called the "*Southern Advocate.*" The editor announces to the public his intention to support "the *Constitution and Equal Rights:--and keep separate the Church and State.*" We were pleased with the title of the paper, being ourselves strong advocates for Southern rights, but in glancing our eye over its columns we were surprised to see the course the Editor has pursued in his first number. Instead of manifesting that noble, generous, and patriotic spirit, which we look for in every true republican, we think we can trace one of an opposite character. He opposes the proposed plan for constructing the Central Rail Road as being injurious to the commercial interests of the State. In our opinion the construction of this Road on the proposed plan will be the first step towards building up commercial towns in the State. .. We were surprised that a man claiming to be a Minister of the Gospel should attack with such false denunciations and unbecoming language an Order like the Sons of Temperance. He represents the Sons of Temperance assisted by other societies of the day as working under the cloak of benevolence to take away the rights and liberty of the people and establish Catholicism, misrule and disorder in the land. ...

(658) Chowan Association. The 44th Session of this body will commence, in this place on the 16th inst. The Introductory sermon will be preached by Rev. Mr. **FOREY**, Principal of the Chowan Institute. It is expected that this Session, will be of peculiar interest to those, who are the friends and patrons of Missionary and Educational enterprize. Those of our citizens who desire to entertain delegates or other strangers will please send their names to William D. **PRITCHARD** or to Rev. Mr. **HENDRICKSON**.

(659) We received by the last mail the *Albemarle Bulletin*, published at Edenton N. C., and Edited by Mr. T. C. **MANNING**. We are glad to see this Journal appear again in so respectable a form, and hope its new Editor, will meet with..success...

(660) The "oldest inhabitant" is dead. His name was Daniel **HALE**, of Franklin Co., Georgia, and he was 119 years of age!

(661) We learn from the *Washington Union* that Ladislaus **UJHAZY**, late governor of Comorn, with his lady, two daughters, and three sons, Major **BERANYI**, Capt. **GAKAIS**, Capt. **REMENYI**, and Capt. **GENSUTHZ**, left New-York on the 13th instant, for Iowa, to select land for their settlement, and for such of their brave compatriots as may join them.

(662) LETTER FROM MR. CLAY.--The *Ouachita* (Arkansas) *Herald* publishes a letter from this gentleman on a melancholy subject. .. Washington, March 11, 1850. "Dear Sir: I received your obliging letter, communicating the melancholy event of the death of my brother, Porter **CLAY**. Prior to its recept, I had received the proceedings of the Masonic Lodge in your city, testifying its respects to his memory. I am very grateful and thankful for the kindnes extended by you and others to my lamented brother in his last illness, and for the respect paid to his remains in Camden, by the Masonic Order, and other citizens. ... H. **CLAY**. N. L. **FARRIS**, Esq."

(663) Miss **WEBSTER**'s Letter.--The following Card has appeared in relation to Miss **WEBSTER**'s letter recently published: *A Card*.--A letter of Miss Harriet **WEBSTER** has been published, and has gone and is going the rounds of newspapers, contrary to her expectation and consent. The letter to which it was an answer was from a person wholly unknown to her or to her family. The letter contained strong expressions of sympathy and kindness for Dr. **WEBSTER** and his family and requested an answer, of which she and her family regret the publicity. ...

(664) A CARD. The undersigned has recently taken the store lately in the occupancy of Capt. Thos. W. **KNIGHT**, (formerly occupied by Mr. Wm. **MESSENGER**,) and having just received a new stock of Good [sic] selected by himself, respectfully solicits a share of public patronage, which he will endeavor to merit by attention to business, and efforts to please his customers both in the price and the quality of his goods, consisting of an assortment of DRY GOODS, GROCERIES CROCKERY AND HARDWARE, together with a GOOD STOCK OF SHIP CHANDLERY... Wilson W. **WILLIAMS**. E. City, May 4th, 1850.

(665) IN THE CITY. The subscriber has just returned from Baltimore where he purchased a well selected stock of Groceries, and having taken the store on Road street, opposite the store of Jas. W. **HINTON**, has opened the same for the purpose of supplying all, who may be in want of any article in the Grocery line. ... Seth **MORGAN**. E. City May 4th, 1850.

(666) Notice to the Ladies. Mrs. Mary E. **WILLICK**, having just arrived from the North, and having permanently located herself in E. City, offers her services as Mantua Maker to the Ladies of E. City, and vicinity. Having with care selected the latest styles and fashions, she is now prepared to execute in the most faithful manner, and on reasonable terms any work in her line, having been for several years past, connected with one of the most extensive establishment in the City of Baltimore. .. Residence at Mrs. **NASH**'s on Road street above the Bank. May 4th

4 May 1850

(667) John A. **WARROCK**, ATTORNEY AT LAW, *Columbia, Tyrrel County, N. C.* Will attend strictly to the collection, of all claims entrusted to him, in the counties of Tyrrel, Washington, Pasquotank, and Camden. May 4th, 1850.

The Old North State.
Vol. 10. "Error is harmless, when truth is left free to combat it." No. 12.
Elizabeth City, N. C. Saturday, May 11, 1850.

(668) REAL AFFLICTION. A SAD STORY--ELOPEMENT!--HOPE DEFERRED--DEATH. The mysterious disappearance of Mrs. **MILLER**, in November last, at the Falls of Niagara, and the contradictory rumors as to her death, from passing over the cataract, or her more probable elopement, are matters with which our readers are acquainted--Another chapter has been added to this unfortunate affair by the death of the lady's father; harassed by fruitless searches after a lost daughter, and preyed upon by such anxieties as a parent only can appreciate. But recently we were invited to call attention to the fact that both father and husband were in Washington, where they would thankfully receive any information that would guide them in their search. .. The lady..if alive, may be secreted somewhere in Baltimore. She is small in person, in height not more than 4 feet 8 or 10 inches; has black hair and eyes, and somewhat inclined to brunette complexion. .. Mr. **NORVELL** was many years since one of our most valued citizens--a talented editor and an honest man, qualities that ensured him an honorable position in his adopted State, where, after his removal from Philadelphia, he was elected to the U. S. Senate. Our citizens will regret with us the announcement which follows: Detroit, Mich., April 24.--The Hon. J. H. **NORVELL**, U. S. Attorney for this District, died at one o'clock this afternoon, at his residence in this city. Mr. **NORVELL** had arrived from Washington on Sunday morning last, very much indisposed, and he continued to sink, until death relieved him of his pain. ... [*Saturday Courier.*

(669) Mr. Edward **CAREW**, father of the editor of the *Charleston Mercury*, died in that City on Saturday last, of pneumonia. Thirty hours before his death he was engaged in superintending the construction of a plank road near the city. He was a native of Ireland, but came to this country in childhood, and for more than half a century has been a citizen of Charleston.

(670) Elizabeth-City, May 11, '50. .. We find the following Editorial remarks in the *Norfolk Herald* of the 7th inst., in reference to the prevalence of the small pox in that city: "The authorities of Elizabeth City, N. C., have issued a circular, requiring all vessels on which sickness or disease of any kind may exist at the time of their approaching that harbor, to anchor a quarter of a mile from the wharves until they shall be visited by the Health Officer and obtain permission from the Town Commissioners to proceed to take a near position. We find no fault with this wholesome regulation of our worthy neighbor of Elizabeth City; but we do protest against their "Whereas," asserting that "the small pox is now prevalent in Norfolk;" for it is not, nor has it been for more than twelve months; and it is ungenerous on their part to make so unqualified and injurious a declaration. That there has been a few, a very few cases of small pox in the city is not denied; but they were in every instance introduced from abroad, (in one case we are credibly informed the disease was contracted from a cart from Gates county,) and when known immediately sent out to the pest-house, in the rear of the city, before the contagion had time to spread. .. We can assure our country friends that our city is entirely free from small pox or any other contagious disease, and that its general health was never better. We have this assurance not only from the Health Department of the City, but from every member of the faculty we have conversed with upon the subject."

In regard to the above we merely wish to put our friend of the *Herald* right, assuring him that we entertain none but the kindest feelings towards him, and our neighboring city, Norfolk. But we are very confident that he is laboring under a mistake, and not the authorities of Elizabeth City. .. We do not know whether there are at present any cases of small pox in Norfolk, but we can assure the Editor..that there have been five cases in one family of our town, and that it was brought to that family by the Captain of a vessel, coming from Norfolk to this place. We have also been credibly informed that a gentleman residing in Norfolk, was in this place a short time since who said that he had had the small pox at one of the Hotels. Reports have been rife here that there were as many as 200 cases in Norfolk. Therefore the *Herald* must see that our authorities have not been imposed on, or "too hastily given heed to the mendacious rumors" which it thinks have been set afloat by "interested individuals for sinister and sordid purposes." We have been told, (as to the truth of the matter we cannot say,) that the small pox originated in Norfolk which has been raging for several weeks past in Gates county. ...

(671) Elizabeth City Academy. The 4th and last quarter of the scholastic year will commence Monday the 20th inst. A few more pupils would be admitted in each Department. At the close of the year, there will be a Public Examination of the school. S. D. **POOL**. Prin. May 11, 1850.

(672) Office of Literary Board, Raleigh, April 26th, 1850.} The President and Directors of the Literary Fund having resolved to distribute the sum of forty Thousand dollars, in part of the nett income of the Fund the current year, for the support of Common Schools, the same is apportioned among the several Counties on the basis provided by Law, according to the following schedule--

11 May 1850

(672) (Cont.) and will be paid on the application of the persons properly authorized to receive it. The Counties of Alexander, Alamance, Forsythe, Gaston, Union and Watauga, will receive their portions from the Counties, respectively, from which they have been erected. Charles **MANLY**. Ex Officio Pres't of Literary Board.

Counties.	Spring Distribu'n.	Counties.	Spring Distribution	Counties.	Spring Distribution
Alexander	——	Granville	937 "	Rowan	658 "
Alamance	——	Greene	330 "	Rutherford	831 "
Anson	$792 00	Guilford	1107 "	Sampson	635 "
Ashe	444 "	Halifax	800 "	Stanly	288 "
Beaufort	637 "	Haywood	298 "	Stokes	928 "
Bertie	579 "	Henders'n	202 "	Surry	878 "
Bladen	407 "	Hertford	377 "	Tyrrell	251 00
Brunswick	271 "	Hyde	341 "	Union	——
Buncombe	586 "	Iredrell	867 "	Wake	1095 "
Burke	378 "	Johnston	562 "	Warren	589 "
Cabarras	513 "	Jones	233 "	W'shi'gt'n	236 "
Caldwell	306 "	Lenoir	375 "	Watauga	—— "
Camden	306 "	Lincoln	622 50	Wayne	576 "
Catawba	622 50	Macon	289 00	Wilkes	675 "
Cartaret	369 00	Martin	298 "	Yancy	358 "
Caswell	725 "	McDowell	286 "		
Chatham	863 "	Meckl'b'g	962 "		
Cherokee	212 "	Montg'm'y	310 "		
Chowan	319 "	Moore	452 "		
Cleaveland	405 "	Nash	462 "		
Columbus	215 "	N. Hano'r	658 "		
Craven	682 "	North'pt'n	625 "		
Cumberl'd	802 "	Onslow	393 "		
Currituck	358 "	Orange	1,317 "		
Davidson	830 "	Pasquoa'k	453 "		
Davie	416 "	Perqu'imo's	378 "		
Duplin	569 "	Person	493 "		
Edgecom'e	778 "	Pitt	583 "		
Forsythe	——	Randolph	753 "		
Franklin	541 "	Richmond	440 "		
Gaston	——	Robeson	563 "		
Gates	371 "	Roc'i'gh'm	711 "		

May 11th, 1850.

(673) SCHOOLS BOOKS, &C. **OLLENDORFF**'s New method to read French do. Primary Lessons in do. **PARKER**s aid to composition, **OLMSTEAD** Astronomy, **KEIGHTLEY**s Mythology, **PARKER**s Philosophy, **PARLEY**s 1st and 2d Book of History, Spelling Books, Primers, Toy Books, Slates, Slate Pencills, Copy Book &c. All of which are for sale by W. J. **KELLINGER**. May 11.

The Old North State.
Vol. 10. "Error is harmless, when truth is left free to combat it." No. 13.
Elizabeth City, N. C. Saturday, May 18, 1850.

(674) Address of John **POOL**, P. G. at the Celebration of the Anniversary of Achoree Lodge, No. 14, on the 3d inst. Achoree Lodge, No. 14, I. O. O. F. takes unbounded pleasure in returning to Bro. P. G. **POOL**, many thanks for the very able and truly eloquent manner in which he delivered to them this morning, an address on the importance and beauty of our beloved Order, and sincerely hope, if it meet his approbation, he will not refuse to give to us the manuscript for publication. Yours in F. L. & T. John B. **FEARING**, Peter C. **WILLIAMS**, Nathan **MORRIS**,} Com. Friday Evening. [REPLY.] E. City, 4th May, 1850. *Gentlemen*: Your note of the 3rd inst. has been received, and I cannot refuse a compliance with your request. Be pleased to accept my heartfelt thanks for the kind manner in which you have communicated the wish of the Lodge. Yours, in F. L. & T. John **POOL**. Messrs. J. B. **FEARING**, P. C. **WILLIAMS**, Nathan **MORRIS**, Com.

18 May 1850

(675) Elizabeth-City, May 18, '50. .. We would most respectfully inform Mr. Caleb **PEIRCE**, who styles himself a General Advertising Agent in Philadelphia, for Newspapers, that we have already in that City an Agent for our paper, (Mr. V. B. **PALMER**) and that we decline sending him our list of prices, and would impress this upon his mind, that he should always when writing on his *own* business, *pay the postage.*

(676) Cure For Corns.--Mr. W. **BRADSLEY**, of Springfield, Ill., says that salaeratus bound upon these troublesome visiters for a few weeks, with occasional change, will effectually cure them. He has given a fair trial, and would recommend it as an infallible remedy to those afflicted.

(677) WHIG MEETING IN HERTFORD. At a meeting of the Whigs of Perquimans County, held at Hertford on the 13th of May, 1850; the meeting was organized by the appointment of James P. **WHEDBEE**, Esq., Chariman, and Jona. W. **ALBERTSON**, Secretary. The Chairman explained the object of the meeting to be, the appointment of delegates to represent the Whigs of this County in the Convention to be held in Raleigh on the 10th of June next, to nominate a candidate for Governor in the approaching canvass; and also to nominate a candidate, for the House of Commons in the next Legislature, to represent this county--and also to appoint delegates to meet the delegates of Pasquotank County, for the purpose of selecting a candidate to represent the two counties in the next Legislature. .. After the conclusion of the Chairman's remarks, on motion, a committee of five were appointed to retire and prepare resolutions expressive of the sense of the meeting... The committee consisted of the following gentlemen: Nathan **WINSLOW**, Samuel **NIXON**, W. H. **BAGLEY**, Jos. **TOMS**, and E. F. **SMITH**, Esqrs. .. *Resolved*, That in our opinion His Excellency Chas. **MANLY** has discharged the duties incumbent upon him as Chief Magistrate of the State, with abilty, impartiality and patriotism. *Resolved*, That we will give our hearty support to the nominee of the State Convention. *But Resolved*, That we would respectfully recommend the name of the Hon. Wm. B. **SHEPARD** to the Convention... .. On motion, the following gentlemen were appointed delegates to meet delegates from Pasquotank, to nominate a candidate to represent the two counties in the Senate of the next Legislature, viz: Nathan **WINSLOW**, Joseph **WHITE**, Benj. **PRITCHARD**, Jas. **SUMNER**, A. R. **ELLIOTT** and Joseph **TOMS**. .. A committee was appointed to nominate a candidate to represent the County in the Commons of the next Legislature. The committee after deliberation, reported the name of Thomas S. **JACOCKS**, Esq., as the regular nominee. On motion, the Chairman..appointed twenty delegates to the Raleigh Convetion..viz: Thos. F. **JONES**, Dr. C. M. **FORD**, N. **WINSLOW**, Wm. C. **SCOTT**, Col. Elisha **FELTON**, Willis H. **BAGLEY**, Jos. M. **COX**, Jona. **WHITE**, Saml. **SUTTON** Esq., Saml. **NIXON**, Esq., Dr. **JENKINS**, David **WHITE**, Jr., Benj. **MULLEN**, John W. **SUTTON**, James L. **SKINNER**, Thos. E. **SKINNER**, Ed. F. **SMITH**, Jos. **CANNON**, C. W. **HOLLOWELL**, Jona. W. **ALBERTSON**. On motion, the name of the Chairman was added... On motion the meeting adjourned. James P. **WHEDBEE**, Chm'n. Jona. W. **ALBERTSON**, Sec'y.

(678) WHIG MEETING IN CHOWAN. In the proceedings of the Whig Meeting held in the County of Chowan on the 7th inst., the following paragraph appears:--"It was moved by Dr. Wm. C. **WARREN**, and seconded, that a Committee of ten be appointed to attend the Convention in Raleigh to nominate a Candidate for Governor, and that said Committee be and are hereby instructed to vote for Wm. B. **SHEPARD** as our choice for said office; though, should there be a want of concentration on him..to cast their vote for the nominee of said Convention. And, if none of the said Committee shall attend at the said Convention, then, that, John H. **BRYAN**, Esq. be and is requested to cast the vote of said Committee in accordance with the above resolution. The above motions were agreed to unanimously." This is all O. K. let Pasquotank do the same.

(679) For the "Old North State." Mr. Editor:--June Court being the time when the good Whigs will be again called upon to nominate some suitable person to represent Old Pasquotank in the Lower House of the next Legislature; and believing Mr. Editor when we say that Major G. W. **BROOKS** is the man for the times; that he is eminently qualified and fitted to fill the station with credit to himself and honor to the State, that we but speak the sentiments of many *staunch* Whigs. ...

(680) CARRIAGES! CARRIAGES! The subscriber returns thanks for the patronage heretofore bestowed, and respectfully informs the public that he has now on hand direct from the Northern factories, a complete stock of materials, and is prepared to make anything in his line to order. He has also on hand a full assortment of Light Rockaways, Buggies, Sulkies, &c.... Call and examine before purchasing elsewhere at the Factory opposite "Mansion House," on Road street. John **DOES**. May 18th, 1850.

(681) LAND FOR SALE. The subscriber offers for sale, his farm containing 500 acres more or less. The buildings are partly new, but not complete. The range for stock, on, and around this tract of land, is good, and above all, it is a pleasant situation, and is well known to be one of the most healthy places in the upper part of Pasquotank. .. Terms will be made as moderate and accommodating as possible. The subscriber can be found on the premisis at all times. Lewis R. **HINTON**. May 18th, 1850.

(682) SEA BATHING! Old Point Comfort Hotel. This magnificent establishment is now open for the reception of visitors...

18 May 1850

(682) (Cont.) There are very capacious and well arranged Baths Houses with hot Baths and shower Baths and a fine surf and splendid beach for those who prefer the open sea. The hotel situated directly on the bay, and in view of the Atlantic, presents a beautiful prospects, while Fortress Monroe the largest military work in the union, offers to the visitor splendid promenades, daily military Parades and fine music. No place can be more healthy..we had even no cholera here last summer nor have we ever Epidemic diseases of any kind or Fever and Ague and Billious Fever. With drinking water unsurpassed in excellence, we offer the attractions of a fine Band of music and the most beautiful Ball Room in the union. Capt. Marshall **PARKS** will assist in conducting the House this season. TERMS. Board per day $2 00 By the week or the rate of 1 50 per day " " month or the " " 1 00 " " Children under 12 years of age and servants half-price, James S. **FRENCH**. May 1

(683) A CARD. *To Farmers and Merchants in N. C.* The undersinged returns his sincere thanks to his friends in North Carolina for their very liberal patronage during the time he has been engaged in the Forwarding and Commisssion Busines in Norfolk, and respectfully begs a continuance... Commissions on Grain and Cotton one and one quarter per cent, Commissions on Lumber 2 1/2 per cent. J. P. **SHUSTER**. Commerce Street, at the old stand of **SIMMONS & SHUSTER**. Norfolk May 10th, 1850.

(684) *To the Planters Merchants of North Carolina.* The Co-partnership of **SIMMONS & SHUSTER** having dissolved. The undersigned senior partner of the concern, will continue the Commission and forwarding business on his own account. Being thankful for the very liberal patronage heretofore received, hopes by strict attention to business to share a continuance of the same. Commissions on Grain and Cotton 1 1/4 per cent, and on Lumber 2 1/2 per cent. D. D.**SIMMONS**. Norfolk May 10th, 1850.

The Old North State.
Vol. 10. "Error is harmless, when truth is left free to combat it." No. 14.
Elizabeth City, N. C. Saturday, May 25, 1850.

(685) Elizabeth-City, May 25, '50. .. STRUCK BY LIGHTNING. The house of Mr. Wm. L. **SHANNON**, of our town was struck by lightning on Saturday morning last. We have never seen a building more injured, but it gives us pleasure to state that no person was hurt, although there were some 7 or 8 in the house and immediately in the rooms adjoining the part struck. It is supposed that the new tin gutters lately put up had the effect of attracting the lightning from the inside and caused it to do all its damage on the outside of the building. After striking on the north end and carrying away a part of the chimney and end of the building, it passed quite across the gable end to the other corner and escaped by the tin gutter to the ground. ...

(686) A BEAUTIFUL TURN OUT. We saw at the Coach Establishment of Mr. Robert **WATKINS** on Wednesday last, one of the most beautiful Carriages ever built in this section of the State, and in fact, we have never seen it beaten anywhere. ...

(687) ODD FELLOWS. The two State Grand Bodies of this Order--the Grand Lodge and the Grand Encampment of North Carolina--held their annual session in Raleigh during the past week. .. Seven Lodges have been instituted during the past year, and Dispensations granted for two others, which will be Instituted in a few days. Three Encampments have been Constituted, and the prospect is said to be fair for a further increase. The following are the Officers for 1850. GRAND LODGE. Perrin **BUSBEE**, of Raleigh, M. W. Grand Master. Julius **WILCOX**, of Warrenton, R. W. Deputy Grand Master. Wm. D. **COOKE**, of Raleigh, R. W. Grand Sec'y. R. B. **HAYWOOD**, of Raleigh, R. W. Grand Treas'r Dewitt C. **STONE**, of Louisburg, R. W. Grand Warden. Rev. James **DELK**, of Colerain, Bertie county, R. W. Grand Chaplain. John H. **MANLY**, of Raleigh, J. N. **WASHINGTON**, of Newbern,} R. W. G. Reps. Thomas M. **GARDNER**, of Wilmington, W. Grand Conductor. Geo. **LAUDER**, of Fayetteville, W. Grand Guardian. GRAND ENCAMPMENT. Rev. A. Paul **REPITION**, of Wilmington, M. W. Grand Patriarch. O. W. **TELFAIR**, of Washington, M. E. Grand High Priest. Thos. M. **GARDNER**, of Wilmington, R. W. Grand Senior Warden. J. B. **NEWBY**, Fayetteville, R . W. Grand Sribe. Samuel G. **SMITH**, of Fayetteville, R. W. Grand Treasurer. H. G. **TRADER**, of Murfreesborough, R. W. Grand Junior Warden. J. C. B. **EHRINGHAUS**, of Elizabeth City, R. W. Grand Representative. R. B. **HAYWOOD**, of Raleigh, W. Grand Sentinel.

(688) A SENSIBLE NEGRO. **SAM**, a negro man, belonging to Wm. S. **MALLORY**, Esq, who went out in the Barque John G. Colley, to California, about 15 months ago, retured home on Sunday morning, having come by way of the Isthmus, and thence to New York, in which city he remained a week. With every opportunity of retaining his freedom, acquired by visiting so many places where slavery does not exist, he prefered, very sensibly, to return to his master. **SAM** didn't travel through the so called non slaveholding countries for nothing. *American Beacon.*

(689) FOR SALE. A first rate Second hand Washington Press No. 4, that will print a paper whose Columns are 4 or 5 inches longer than the "Old North State," while at the same time they can be made a great deal wider also. Apply immediately at this of-

25 May 1850

(689) (Cont.)fice. Price..less by $20 than one like it can be bought in Philadelphia or New York. Wm. E. **MANN**. May 25th, 1850.

(690) Temperance Bar. I have taken the shop on Road street lately occupied as a "barber shop" where all in want of Rich Lemonade are respectfully requested to call. Families supplied at all times. Give me a call. R. **ELLIOTT** May 25th, 1850.

The Old North State.
Vol. 10. "Error is harmless, when truth is left free to combat it." No. 15.
Elizabeth City, N. C. Saturday, June 1, 1850.

(691) Elizabeth-City, June 1, '50. .. *The Old North State.* We beg leave to call the attention of our readers to a few remarks in reference to the future condition of this Journal. After the present number the paper will be considerably enlarged in size, and S. D. **POOL**, Esq., will take the Editorial chair, and become responsible for what may appear in its editorial columns. It is not necessary for us here to speak of Mr. **POOL**'s political principles, as he is well known, having formerly had the Editorial charge of this paper, to have supported the Whig cause and principles. In resigning our charge of this paper into the hands of our successor, we should feel that we were doing our patrons and readers injustice not to thank them for the very liberal support that they have given us, and the Whig cause. ...

Day of Publication Changed. Our Subscribers who receive their papers by the Southern Mail, are here informed that the day of publication will be changed to Tuesday's, and they will in consequence receive their papers by the Mail on that day instead of Saturday's as heretofore. This arrangement will enable our Subscribers in Washington and Tyrrell Counties, to receive their papers much earlier after the day of publication than they have been doing. For the paper leaving here on Tuesday afternoon reaches Columbia, Tyrrell County, on the following Thursday. So also in regard to Camden and Currituck..will receive them the day after they are published...

(692) AWAKENING OF CONSCIENCE. On the night of the 17th of March, 1850, the store of Mr. William **BUTLER**, in Charleston, S. C., was set on fire, and himself and family had scarcely sufficient time to escape from the rapidly spreading flames. Nothing transpired to indicate the incendiary, or fasten suspicion upon any one. Some days ago, the present Mayor of Charleston received a letter, in an envelope, without a postmark, dated New Orleans, April 25th, in which the writer professes, without making known his name, that he set fire to the premises and received therefor the sum of $200. While coming from New York to Charleston, in 1848, in pursuit of work, he made the acquaintance of two men on board of the steampacket, who urged him to it, saying that Mr. **BUTLER**'s goods were insured; that none but rich men would suffer, &c. After he had fired the building, and escaped from it, he returned, and heard one of Mr. **BUTLER**'s family say the goods were not insured. This awoke regret at once, and the matter has so sorely troubled his conscience since, that he has made the confession of his crime, and enclosed in the letter the sum of $85, which he avers is all he has, with request that it be handed to Mr. **BUTLER**. It has accordingly been paid to that gentleman.

(693) NOTICE. To the Farmers of Pasquotank and the adjoining Counties. I am a Temperance man but not a teetotalist, therefore I need no guardian only to supply me with the good things of life. All those in want of Groceries such as Sugar, Coffee, Flour, Lard, Molasses, French Brandy, Apple do. Holland, or country Gin, &c will please call at the old stand of James S. **LONG**, where you can be supplied with good articles and at fair prices. June 1st, 1850

(694) New Boot & Shoe Establishment. The subscriber having taken the shop, next door to the Post Office on Main st., would most respectfully inform the public that he intends carrying on the BOOT AND SHOE business in all its various branches. Having just received a most splendid stock of materials, and having in his employ a first rate workman, he is prepared to execute all orders for any thing in the above line. ... George **MANNS**. June 1st, 1850.

(695) Pork and Beef. 70 Blls. Newport and Baltimore MESS PORK, 20 Blls. Baltimore Prime and Cargo BEEF For Sale by T. R. **COBB**. June 1st, 1850.

(696) Stray. I have taken up four shoats which have been feeding with the hogs on Mrs. L. S. **POOL**'s farm since January last. Marked 2 upper keels in the right ear and a smothe crop in the left ear, two of them are red and two spotted. There being no ranger in the county, the owner is requested to prove property, pay expenses and take them away. D. H. **KENYON**, June 1st, 1850.

(697) Masonic Notice. The Masonic Fraternity of Perquimans, will celebrate the "Anniversary of St. John the Baptist," at Hertford, on the 24th proxim. An invitation is hereby duly extended to the neighboring Lodges and members of the Fraternity. .. By order of the Perquimans Lodge No. 106. D. **BARCLIFT**, Secretary. June 1st, 1850.

1 June 1850

(698) NOTICE. Was found on the beach in 2d Wrecks District of North Carolina, and sold on the 23d May last by the commissioner of Wrecks for said District, a Yawl Boat 18 feet long, of New Haven built. Any one interested in the same is hereby notified to call on the Subscriber. Samuel JARVIS. Com. Wrecks, District No. 2, N. C. June 1st, 1850.

(699) The illustrated Domestic Bible. BY REV. INGRAM COBBIN M. A. THIS BEAUTIFUL FAMILY BIBLE will be published in twenty-five Numbers, at 25 cents each, and will also be put up in Monthly parts at 50 cents. The distinguished features of this Bible are. 1. Seven hundred Wood Engravings. 2. Many thousand Marginal References. 3. Three finely executed Steel Maps. 4. Numerous Improved Readings. 5. A Corrected Chronological Order. 6. The Poetical Books in metrical form. 7. An Exposition of each Chapter, containing the essence of the best commentators, with much original matter by the editor. .. The regular issue will begin about the first of July, and a number will be published on the first and fifteenth of each month, till the book is complete. Agents are wanted to procure subscribers for this work, and the opportunity is a most favorable one for them to do well. .. Apply, post-paid, to S. HUESTON, 139 Nassau street, New-York. June 1st, 1850.

(700) *THE OLD NORTH STATE.*
"Error is harmless, when Truth is left free to combat it."
Vol. X.] Elizabeth City, N. C. Tuesday June 11, 1850. [No. 16.
Published every Tuesday By MANN & GRIFFIN, Proprietors. Stephen D. POOL, Editor.

(701) Nashville Convention. We would call the attention of our readers to the annexed letter of Messrs. STRANGE & MC REE, appointed in March last by a Convention of the Fayetteville District to represent that District in the Southern Convention, proposed to be held the 1st Monday in June in Nashville, Tennessee. .. This Convention has never had the sympathy of but a very small portion of the people of the good "Old North State," ... Fayetteville, May 11, 1850. Dear Sir: The time for the Nashville Convention is at hand--a meeting pregnant with the most important results to the whole family of man. .. At the New Hanover meeting held in January, one of us felt no hesitation in saying, that by the first Monday in June, it would be plainly seen that southern rights would meet with reasonable consideration from our northern brethren, or that we must prepare to maintain them by dissolution and war. He was mistaken. The mysterious veil of the future still hangs over those events which must decide this question, and no one can safely conjecture in what form they will be revealed. Under these circumstances, what can a convention do? Nothing--nothing at least but mischief. .. We should reserve it for a time of need, when like Samson, wronged by his enemies past all endurance, he might wisely seek their destruction, even though it cost him his life. Sir, we are persuaded that these are the feelings of a large portion of the people of our State in this matter. We should now misrepresent them by participating in any action of a Nashville Convention at this time. .. We shall therefore not take our seats in the convention..unless some change takes place in the aspect of public affairs between now and the first Monday in June. ... Robert STRANGE. G. J. MC REE. Henny I. TOOLE, Esq.

(702) Elizabeth-City, June 11, 1850. .. We are authorized to announce George D. POOL, Esq., as the Whig candidate to represent the County of Pasquotank in the House of Commons of the next Legislature. ... We are authorized to announce Joshua A. POOL, as a candidate for re-election as Sheriff of Pasquotank County.

(703) The schooner Mary, Capt. POINER, will leave E. City, on Tuesday evening the 18th inst., at 7 o'clock P. M. for Washington, N. C. Those persons wishing to avail themselves of this opportunity of attending the dedication of the new Odd Fellows Hall in that place, will please leave their names at this Office or with Mr. Wm. J. KELLINGER as soon as possible, as the number will be limited. It is absolutely necessary that those who intend going should be on board at the appointed time.

(704) The Whig Gubernatorial Convention of Maryland has presented to the voters of that State W. B. CLARKE, as their candidate for Governor. ...

(705) Mr. Thomas WHITE, who lives near our town, will please accept the thanks of one of the publishers for the fine lot of Irish potatoes sent him. He wishes to know if some of his other friends cannot do the same thing.

(706) Whig Meeting. At a meeting of the Whigs of Pasquotank County, held at the Court House in E. City, on the 3d inst. Dr. R. H. RAMSAY was called to the Chair, and Wm. E. MANN appointed Secretary. .. On motion of George D. POOL, Esq., 7 persons, one from each Captain's District, were appointed to meet the delegates of Perquimans for the purpose of selecting some suitable person to represent the two Counties in the next Senate of North Carolina. Under the motion, the Chair appointed the following: District No. 1 Thos. GASKINS, Esq. " " 2 Joseph MULLEN, " " 3 Addison WHEDBEE, " " 4 Geo. D. POOL, Esq. " " 5 Seth MORGAN, " " 6 Job CARVER, " " 7 Joseph B. REED. On motion of Dr. S. D. GRICE, 2 persons from each Captain's

11 June 1850

(706) (Cont.) District were appointed to select a proper person to represent Pasquotank County in the next House of Commons of North Carolina. Under the motion, the Chair appointed from District No. 1 Thos. **GASKINS** Esq., " " John **CARTWRIGHT**. District No. 2 Thos. **HARVEY**, " " Jos. R. **PARKER**. District No. 3 Thomas **BANKS**, " " Wm. **CHARLES**. District No. 4 F. A. **BROTHERS**, Esq. " " Robert **PENDLETON**, District No. 5 Wm. W. **GRIFFIN**, " " James W. **HINTON**, District No. 6 Job **CARVER**, " " Edgar L. **HINTON**, Esq. District No. 7 James E. **WEEKS**, " " Doctrine R. **PERRY**, Esq. The Committee retired for a few moments and returned and presented the name of George D. **POOL**, Esq., which was received by the whole meeting with loud applause. Mr. **POOL** being present wished for time to consult upon the matter of acceptance, and on motion of George W. **CHARLES**, he was granted further time by the meeting. On motion of John **POOL**, a committee of four, consisting of Gilbert **ELLIOTT**, John **POOL**, Dr. S. D. **GRICE**, and Hill **BURGWIN**, was appointed to draft resolutions expressive of the sense of this meeting in reference to the nomination of a Gubernatorial Candidate at the Whig Convention, to be held at Raleigh on the 10th inst. The Committee..reported the substance of the annexed resolutions. 1st. *Resolved*, That His Excellency Charles **MANLY**, in the opinion of this meeting has faithfully performed the duties of his office, and has conducted himself therein with dignity, ability and impartiality. 2d. *Resolved*, That it is also the opinion of this meeting that his re-nomination by the Convention would be highly injudicious, and probably endanger the success of the Whig Party in the approaching campaign--and therefore 3d. *Resolved*, That this meeting recommend to the said Convention the name of the Hon. Wm. B. **SHEPARD**, as the decided choice of the Whig Party not only in this District, but generally throughout the State, and as entitled to the nomination from his high standing and ability, and from his long and hitherto unrewarded services to the State and the Party. .. On motion of George W. **BROOKS**, Esq., the following twenty persons were appointed as delegates to the Raleigh State Convention: Hill **BURGWIN**, Thad F. **BANKS**, Thos. **GASKINS**, Thos. **HARVEY**, Dr. R. H. **RAMSAY**, Jas. E. **WEEKS**, John C. B. **EHRINGHAUS**, Dr. R. K. **SPEED**, George D. **POOL**, Geo. W. **BROOKS**, Jno. L. **HINTON**, Wesley E. **SAWYER**, Gardiner **SAWYER**, Joseph B. **REED**, Wm. E. **MANN**, Geo. W. **CHARLES**, Wm. **CHARLES**, Jno. S. **BURGESS**, Fred. S. **PROCTOR**, and Wm. W. **GRIFFIN**. On motion, Thomas **GASKINS**, Esq., was appointed Chairman of the Pasquotank delegates, and requested to correspond with Albert R. **ELLIOTT**, Esq., Chairman of the Perquimans delegation, for the purpose of finding out the place and time the said delegates would meet. On motion of James W. **HINTON**, the proceedings of this meeting were requested to be published in the "Old North State," *Edenton Bulletin* and the Raleigh Whig papers. On motion the meeting adjourned. R. H. **RAMSAY**, Pres. Wm. E. **MANN**, Sec'y.

(707) METHODIST GENERAL CONFERENCE. The Methodist Episcopal General Conference for the Church South, which assembled at St. Louis on the first of May, adjourned after a session of a few days. The prevalence of the Cholera induced the Conference to make its session much shorter, than it would have been. We noticed last week the election of Dr. **BASCOM** of Kentucky as Bishop, &c. .. The subject of the Boundaries of the North and South Carolina Conference, elicited a zealous and able discussion. .. The discussion was conducted on the part of the North Carolina Conference alone, by Rev. D. F. **DEEMS**, Pastor of the Church of Newbern, against his South Carolina Brethren... We do not see the precise extent of the change that was effected, stated, but learn that the North Carolina Conference will now include Wilmington, Fayetteville &c., hitherto attached to the South Carolina Conference.--[*Newbernian*.

(708) Off for the Frozen Seas. The American Arctic Expedition, consisting of the *Advance* and the *Rescue*, fitted out by Mr. Henry **GRINNELL**, in connection with the United States Government, were towed from the Brooklyn Navy-Yard at noon May 23, and moved slowly down the Bay till they vanished from the sight of our City though the Narrows. ... N. Y. paper?

(709) The Last of the Slaves in New England died at Hanover, New Hampshire, last week, at six score and two. Her name was Jenny **WENTWORTH**. She was in the early part of New England history a slave.

(710) Onderdonkism.--Rev. Sylvester **HOLMES** is on trial at New Bedford, before an ecclesiastical council, for gross and licentious acts towards Miss Emeline **CARVER**, a young orphan girl, an organist in his church. She testifies to the "laying on of hands," &c.

(711) DIED, June 5th, 1850, after a painful illness of 5 weeks, Louisa Jane, daughter of Mrs. Ann **HARRELL**, aged 11 years, 3 mons. and 4 days.

(712) Nag's head Packet. The good Schooner Jno. C. Eringhaus, Capt. **PALIN**, will be put in complete order, and will run the approaching season as a regular Packet from this place to Nag's Head. The days of her running will be Monday, Wednesday and Friday from E. City, and Tuesday, Thursday and Saturday from Nag's Head. Passage as usual $1. ... John **PALIN**. June 11th, 1850.

11 June 1850

(713) Attention R. and R. L. Dragoons. You are hereby ordered to attend a parade of the company at **WEEKS'** Store, on the approaching 4th July, in summer uniform, armed and equipped as the law directs with 10 rounds of blank cartridges. Have your fire arms and accoutrements in good order as they will be inspected on that day. The roll will be called at 11 o'clock, A. M. at which time it is expected that every member will be at his post. By order of the Capt. Jas. W. **HINTON**. June 11th, 1850. The object of the parade being ordered to **WEEK**'s [sic] Store, is for the purpose of joining in with the Woodville Guards in appropriately celebrating our National Anniversary and partaking with them (by invitation) of a public dinner. G. W. **B**. Capt.

(714) Going! Going!! Gone!!! The undersigned, having been appointed County and State Auctioneer, is ready at all times to discharge his duties faithfully and to the satisfaction of those who may entrust business in his hands. Jas. S. **LONG**, Auc. June 11th, 1850.

(715) NOTICE. Pursuant to an order of the County Court of Pasquotank, I shall proceed to sell at the late residence of Benjamin N. **OVERMAN**, on Wednesday the 10th, of July next, three tracts of land--terms made know on the day of sale. Philip A. R. C. **CAHOON**, Adm'r. June 11, 1850.

(716) NOTICE. There will be a regular meeting of Pasquonaux Lodge of Free and accepted Masons, on the evening of the first Wednesday of each and every month. W. W. **GRIFFIN**, Sec'y. June 11th, 1850.

(717) Pork and Beef. 70 Bbls. of New York and Baltimore Mess Pork. 20 Bbls. of cargo and Prime Beef. 4000 lbs of of [sic] Ham, Shoulder, and Side Bacon, for sale by T. R. **COBB**. June 11th, 1850.

THE OLD NORTH STATE.
"Error is harmless, when Truth is left free to combat it."
Vol. X.] Elizabeth City, N. C. Tuesday June 18, 1850. [No. 17.

(718) [From the *Southern Cultivator*.] Horma, Oglethorpe Co., Ga., March 16, 1850. *Mr. Editor*--I have seen some accounts given in your paper of turnip raising. I have, for the last ten or fifteen years, raised the largest that have been raised in this section-- turnips weighing from eight to twelve pounds. I had two drawn from my patch, the 15th of this month, one weighing fifteen pounds and the other sixteen and a half, which are the largest I have ever raised. If doubts should arise in the minds of any of your subscribers, my young man or overseers, who attend to my business, can testify to the correctnees of their weight, as he weighed them in my pressence, as well as that of others. .. Large turnips will not grow on poor land. .. I am in the habit of sowing from four to eight acres in turnip seed; and it will require from twelve to twenty loads of such manure as I use to make one acre rich--fifty bushels to the load or eight hundred bushels scattered broadcast. .. Your friend, &c., George **LUMPKIN**.

(719) Launch.--The steamer New York, 700 tons burthen, was launched on Saturday at New York, from the yard of Wm. **BROWN**, with steam on, and proceeded at noon on her trial trip down the bay.

(720) The Little Precocities, Kate and Ellen **BATEMAN**, who have been played [sic] tragedy, comedy, &c. in the principal cities, are about to be taken from the stage.

(721) Drowned.--A man, named Henry **GLATFELTER**, of York county, Pa., was drowned in the river, below Columbia, on Thursday morning last, by being drawn into the sluice in a boat. A boy on the boat escaped.

(722) Another mysterious Woman has attempted to poison herself at Buffalo. She was found on Monday in one of the rooms of the Western Hotel, suffering from the effects of poison. She gave her name as Mrs. Alonzo **ALLEN**.

(723) A New Church, for the English portion of the congregation of the First Lutheran Church, is to be built at York, Pa., making the third one..in that place. The architect is Jacob **GOTWAIT**.

(724) Singular Relationship.--Josiah **POMEROY** and Phebee G. **FARNUM** intermarried the other day in Massachusetts. In this marriage, it is said by the papers that a singular relationship takes place. The bridgroom becomes a brother to a neice of his, and that neice becomes sister to an uncle, the bride becomes aunt to one of her own brothers, and a sister to that brother's mother-in-law. The bride is aunt to a farther and his children.

(725) Elizabeth-City. June 18, 1850. .. DISTRESSING EVENTS. Nash **HOSKINS**, second son of Charles **HOSKINS**, Esq., committed suicide on last Saturday at the plantation of his father, about ten miles from this place. He rose on that day early, as was

18 June 1850

(725) (Cont.) his custom, and rode out to attend to feeding the stock. This being done he mounted his horse, remarking to a negro woman close by, that he intended to kill himself. This assertion was not regarded by the old servant, as she had of late frequently heard the same words fall from his lips, and apparently with quite as resolute a determination to execute the threat as was evinced on this occasion. This time however he gave her the little money he had in his pocket, saying he should have no further use for it, and then taking a little boy behind him, golloped off towards the dwelling house. Dismounting on his arrival at the house, he walked in and taking up a gun, and ammunition, was about to leave, when a younger brother and the overseer said to him that breakfast was then ready, and pressed him to eat before he started on his hunting excursion. He declined doing so, saying that he would be there again in a few minutes, and immediately went out to a bridge on the road, accompanied by the little boy, and commenced loading his gun, when he discovered that he had left the caps. He returned to the house, got a box of caps, and completed the preparations for his destruction. Placing the gun on his shoulder he asked the boy if he would like to have a Squirrel or Rabbit, to which an affirmative answer being given, he directed him to wait at the edge of the woods, and when he heard the report of the gun to come in and he should find one. The directions were complied with, the unfortunate young man entered the woods, the gun was fired, and the boy ran in to find his master a corpse. He had placed the breech of the gun against a tree, and muzzle to his breast, and it is supposed moved the trigger by a stick. The load passed obliquely in the breast, and out at the side, producing instantaneous death. A misunderstanding or disagreement with his father is thought to have been the cause of this sad catastrophe. The deceased was about 30 years old, and was unmarried.

On Wednesday the 5th inst., Joseph **BENBURY**, son of William **BENBURY**, Esq. of this County, met with an untimely end. He was standing on a small platform about ten feet from the ground, and was coming out of the door of the second story of a Barn, before which this platform was placed. In stepping out to make way for some one to pass, he missed his foothold, and fell backwards on his head, fracturing his skull in several places. He survived five or six hours. The deceased had just attained his majority, and was a young gentleman of very exemplary character. *Albemarle Bulletin.*

(726) Convention of the Protestant Episcopal Church in the Diocese of North Carolina. This body assembled at Elizabeth City on the 29th ult, and was organized by the Rt Rev. L. S. **IVES**, President *Ex officio*, taking the Chair, and Edward L. **WINSLOW**, Esq, being appointed Secretary. .. On Thursday the Bishop read his Journal and address to the Convention, from which we make the following extract in relation to the doctrines which have given rise to so much diversity and perplexity of opinion in the Diocese, viz: "It remains to notice one of my official acts during the present year, which has been the occasion of a good deal of misapprehension and which requires of me a few words by way of safeguard. I refer to the issuing of a Pastoral letter relating to the action of the last Convention of this Diocese. Without going into a defence of the grounds which seemed to me to make the publication of that letter necessary, I would express my deep regret, that any of the statements should in any degree have admitted the idea of an intention on my part to question the motives, the truthfulnes, or faith of my Clergy. .. Finally, I do not teach nor hold, that our branch of the Catholic Church is from any cause either in heresy or schism, or that she is destitute of the true Sacramental system. .." R. S. **MASON**, *Chairman.* The Convention proceeded to ballot for President of the Convention to preside in the absence &c of the Bishop as required by the Constitution, which ballotting resulted in the election of the Rev. Dr. **MASON**. It being desirable that the difficulties which for some time has disquieted the Doicese, should be settled..the Bishop..read to the Convention the following memorial and address, viz:--*Brethren of the Convention:* Aware that the difficulties in the Diocese, which I have alluded in my address, still threaten the peace of the same; and being anxious to..restore harmony and good will, I hereby ask of you a committee of Clergymen and Laymen, to investigate all the circumstances connected therewith, and to report to a future meeting of this body. L. Silliman **IVES**, Bishop of N. Carolina. May 31, A. D. 1850. On motion it was resolved, that this memorial be referred to a committee, consisting of four Clergymen and four Laymen, and that said committee be chosen by ballot.--The Convention then proceeded to ballot..which resulted in the election of the following gentlemen:--*Clergyman* Rev. Mr. **BUXTON** Rev. Dr. **DRANE**, Rev. Dr. **MASON**, Rev. Mr. **JOHNSTON**, *Laymen*, Messrs. Josiah **COLLINS**, Augustus **MOORE**, George W. **MORDECAI**, James W. **BRYAN**. .. On Saturday of the Convention, the following gentlemen were elected Delegates to represent this Diocese in the General Convention to be held in the city of Cincinnatti in September next.-- *Clergymen*, Rev. Dr. **DRANE**, Rev. Dr. **MASON**, Rev. Mr. **BUXTON**, Rev. Mr. **JOHNSON**. *Laymen*, Messrs. Josiah **COLLINS**, John S. **EATON**, John W. **WRIGHT**, Edward L. **WINSLOW**. *Alternates.*--Clergy, Rev. Mr. **WATSON**, Rev. Mr. **FORBES**, Rev. Mr. **CHESHIRE**, Rev. Mr. **SNOWDEN**. Laity, Messrs, R. **PIEMONT**, James W. **BRYAN**, Fred. J. **HILL**, John H. **BRYAN**. ... *Newbernian.*

(727) Married. On Thursday last, by the Rev. Wm. **GRANT** Mr. Richard G. **NEWMANS**, to Miss Elizabeth **GILBERT**.

(728) R. & R. L. DRAGOONS. You are hereby ordered to attend a meeting of the company, to be held in the Court House in E. City on Saturday, 29th July, at 3 o'clock P. M. A full meeting of the company is desired, as business of importance may come before the meeting. Attend without uniform. By order of the Capt. J. W. **HINTON**, O. S. June 18th, 1850.

18 June 1850

(729) NAG'S HEAD. The subscriber respectfully announces to the public, and especially to the Citizens of this Section of North Carolina, that he has recently become the Proprietor of the Hotel at this delightful and fashionable Watering place, and in making this announcement, he begs to assure them that the Establishment will undergo not only a change of managers; but also an entire alteration in the mode in which it will be conducted. He is now preparing to add a Piazza to the Sea-side of the building which will materially enhance its comfort, and he also designs to make such change and alterations in the internal arrangement of the House, the furniture of the Chambers, &c. as will not fail to meet with the approbation of his Visitors. .. The domestic and culinary Department will be under the supervision of Thomas L. MILLER, Esq., whose well earned reputation in this matter will be fully sustained by the Table which will be spread at the Hotel this season. .. The House will be open for the Reception of Boarders on the first of July. The rates of board will be Per month, $20 Room furnished by the boarders, $18 By the Week, $7 By the Day, $1,50. Children under twleve years, and servants half price. A. J. BATEMAN. Edenton June 18th, 1850.

THE OLD NORTH STATE.
"Error is harmless, when Truth is left free to combat it."
Vol. X.] Elizabeth City, N. C. Tuesday June 25, 1850. [No. 18.

(730) Elizabeth-City, June 25, 1850. .. ICE! ICE! ICE! The thanks of the citizens are due to our townsman, Dr. R. PIEMONT for supplying us with this great Summer luxury. The ice is of fine quality, and will be on hand during the entire Summer. ...

(731) DROWNED. We learn that a son of Jesse RHODES Esqr, who lives near Eliz. City, was drowned while swimming in the River near this place, Sunday evening last. The body we learn has been found. We hope this accident will prove a warning to our young friends.

(732) Tuesday Morning, 9 o'clock. Convention met pursuant to adjournment. The minutes being read, additional Delegates from Catham, Caldwell, Granville, and Lenoir, appeared and took seats in the Convention. .. Mr. MENDENHALL moved that the Body proceed at once..to the great business for which the Convention had assembled--a nomination for Governor, and would take the liberty of nominating for that station the present able, and enlightened Chief Magistrat--Charles MANLY, of Wake. Mr. TROY of Robeson, begged leave to add to the nomination the name of that sterling Whig Patriot--Andrew JOYNER, of Halifax. Mr. SIMMONS, of Halifax, begged the Gentleman to withdraw the name of Col. JOYNER, as it was the earnest wish of the latter, that his name should not be brought before the Convention--and especially in opposition to that of the present able incumbent. After some further conversation, the nomination was withdrawn; and the Convention proceeded to vote... [When the County of Chowan was called, Hon. Jno. H. BRYAN stated that he had been appointed an alternate Delegate for each of the Counties of Chowan, Washington and Pasquotank, and in conjunction with another gentleman, for the County of Carteret. The first three Counties had expressed their preference for the Hon. W. B. SHEPARD..and he..felt it his duty to make their sentiments known. He had learned, from Mr. SHEPARD himself, that that gentleman neither contemplated nor wished that he should be in the way of the nomination of our present chief Magistrate. ...] The Secretaries proclaimed the result to be--74 votes cast, of which Charles MANLY had received the whole... .. Gov. MANLY accepted the nomination... Gov. IREDELL introduced the following Resolution... *Resolved*, As the opinion of the members of this Convention, that the practice which has prevailed on the part of the candidates for Governor of travelling through the States and making political addresses to the people, is unnecessary, unjust and not in accordance with true republican principles... *Resolved, therefore*, that the Candidate nominated..by this Convention be not required to canvass the State in person; provided, the Democratic Convention about to assemble in this city shall not require their candidate, so to do. A communication was received from the Governor, tendering the hospitalities of the Executive Mansion to the Convention, on that evening. The Convention..adjourned to half past 3 o'clock.
    3 1/2 o'clock, P. M. Hill BURGWYN, Esq., of Pasquotank, presented his credentials as a Delegate and took a seat in the Convention. .. Mr. J. F. SIMMONS, of Halifax, moved that the Whig Executive Committee, or its Chairman, be clothed with power to designate the time for holding the next Whig Convention. Agreed to. .. The Chairman..declared the Convention, adjourned, *sine die*. James T. MOREHEAD, President. Seaton GALES, W. H. MAYHEW, P. W. WOOLEY,} Secretaries
    EXECUTIVE COMMITTEE, *Appointed at the Whig State Convention for 1850.* 1st Dist. N. W. WOODFIN, of Buncombe, Col. B, S. GAITHER, of Burke, Gen. S. F. PATTERSON, of Caldwell, 2nd do Col. H. L. ROBARDS, of Rowan, N. L. WILLIAMS, of Surry, C. A, PARKS, of Wilkes, 3rd do H. W. GUION, of Lincoln, Absalom MYERS, of Anson, Alexis KELLY, of Moore, 4th do [blank] 5th do W, A. GRAHAM, of Orange, R, B. GILLIAM, of Granville, Isaac CLEGG, of Chatham, 6th do Richard HINES of Wake, Andrew JOYNER, of Halifax, Nathan WILLIAMS, Johnston, 7th do George DAVIS, of New Hanover, Dr. H. A. BIZZEL, of Sampson, Jno. A. ROWLAND, of Robeson, 8th do Chas, EDWARDS, of Greene, W. H. WASHINGTON, of Craven, Josiah HALSEY, of Tyrrell, 9th do D. A. BARNES, of Northampton, Lewis THOMPSON, of Bertie, W. B. SHEPARD of Pasquotank.

25 June 1850

(733) SONS OF TEMPERANCE. The annual election for officers of the National Division of the North American Sons of Temperance, took place at Boston on the 14th inst. The following is the result:--M. W. P., John W. **OLIVER**, of New York; M. W. A., J. **LINTON**, of Tennessee; M. W. Scribe, F. A. **FICKHARDT**, of Pennsylvania; M. W. Treasurer, J. B. **WOOD**, of Pennsylvania; M. W. Conductor, S. L. **TALLY**, of New Burnswick, British Provinces; M. W. Sentinel, W. **ENNIS**, N. C.; M. W. Chaplain, A. L. **STONE**.

(734) ITEMS. .. J. T. **HEADLY**, the author, is erecting a residence on the Hudson. .. The Census--Jos. C. G. **KENNEDY**, of Pennsylvania, was on Friday appointed by the U. S. Senate as Superintendent of the Census. ... Arlington **BENNET**, acquitted at New York of the $9,000 forgery, is said to be the victim of a foul conspiracy. .. A mulatto, named **BOB**, emancipated by Hon. James **HARLIN**, of Kentucky, has made $12,000 in California in three months keeping a tavern! Mr. Jacob **SNYDER** of Deerfield, N. Y., aged about 35, was struck by lightning on the 17th, instantly killed, with his horse. .. Death from Eating Pie-Plant.--A little daughter of Isaiah **STRYKER** residing near Williamsport, Lycoming county, Pa., died last week from eating a quantity of the garden vegetable called rhubarb, or pie-plant. Railroad accident.--On Friday last, Mr. Henry **HAGER**, of York, Pa., had his left arm horribly crushed by falling between two cars, on the Baltimore and Susquehanna railroad, in Shrewsbury township, about 19 miles below York.

(735) Married. At the residence of Mr. Wm. **GLOVER**, by the Rev. Mr. **CROSS**, John **POOL**, Esq. to Miss Narcissa D. daughter of Capt. Spencer **SAWYER**, all of this place. At Sunsbury, Gates County, Thursday 20th inst., by the Rev. Mr. **SANDERS**, George W. **BROOKS**, Esqr., to Miss Margaret A., eldest daughter of James **COSTIN**, decd.

(736) DIED, On the 13th of June 1850, at the residence of Col. James **LEIGH**, **DURANT**s Neck, Perquimans County, Margaret Stevenson **LEIGH**, wife of Edward A. **LEIGH**, Esqr, and daughter of the late Gen'l. Jonathan H. **JACOCKS**. Mrs. **LEIGH** was born 13th Dec. 1825, and hence it is seen that she was called away from this world when it was first opening upon her in all its delights and interest. Not yet twenty-five years of age, with a husband devotedly attached to her, and an infant daughter endowed with health and promise, she had much in life to love and the power to love in its greatest energy. Nature had give [sic] her a peculiar energy of character. All her affections were active and vigorous, she was sanguine and hopeful. Her natural appreciation of life and its enjoyments was keen and intense. Her position in life opened before her the prospect of unstinted ability to do whatever she might desire. But from all this God in his wise Providence, called her. A long and painful illness was his merciful preparation for her. He weaned her, by suffering, from a world which he had given her peculiar power to enjoy; only in order to direct her thoughts and affections to another and better, which shall not pass away. .. Mrs. **LEIGH** has left behind her the remembrance of a kind and excellent character. She was much and justly beloved, by those who knew her. ...

(737) Cholera.--Two deaths from cholera occurred in the Choctaw school under the Rev. Mr. **MC ALLISTER**, at Fort Coffee, during the week previous to the 3d instant.--One was a son of Mr. **MC ALLISTER**, and the other a negro boy.

(738) Mule Strayed. On Monday the 17th inst., a likely young Mule jumped into my field and had been in my enclosure ever since. He is very black and sleek, and is in good order. He looked as if he has strayed from some drove. The owner is requested to call and on proving property and paying charges he can take him. After the usual notice, if no owner calls, he will be sold according to law. Dempsey **CARTWRIGHT**. June 25, 1850.

(739) Pure No. 1 White and Black Lead, Linseed Oil, Putty, Window Glass, 8 by 10 and 10 by 12, and Spinning Wheels for sale by T. R. **COBB**. June 25th, 1850.

THE OLD NORTH STATE.
"Error is harmless, when Truth is left free to combat it."
Vol. X.] Elizabeth City, N. C. Tuesday July 2, 1850. [No. 19.

(740) Elizabeth-City, July 2, 1850. .. DEMOCRATIC MEETING. At a meeting of the Democratic party of Pasquotank, held at the Court House in Elizabeth City, June 29th 1850, Col. Jas. C. **SCOTT** was appointed chairman, and Wm. D. **PRITCHARD**, Secretary. The object of the meeting was explained by the chair, when on motion it was agreed that the chair appoint a committee of three to report the name of some suitable person to represent this county in the House of Commons in the ensuing Legislature. The chair appointed..Willet **HERRINGTON**, E. L. **STEPHENS**, and Keeling **WHITEHURST**, Esqrs., who after retiring a few minutes, returned and reported the name of Caleb L. **WHITEHURST**, Esq., as a fit person to represent this County in the House of Commons in the next Legislature, which nomination was unanimously concurred in by the meeting, and Wm. **FORBES**, Wm. D. **PRITCHARD**, and Edmund T. **SAWYER**, were appointed to wait on Mr. **WHITEHURST** and inform him of his nomination and request him to accept of the same. On motion, the chair appointed the following delegates to confer with delegates from Perquimans to select a suitable person to represent the first Senatorial district of North Carolina in the next session of the State

2 July 1850

(740) (Cont.) Legislature, viz: Willet **HERRINGTON**, Wm. **FORBES**, and Davis **WHITEHURST**, to which delegation, on motion, the Chairman was added. The following resolutions were offered and adopted unanimously. *Resolved*, That this meeting heartily approve the nomination of David S. **REED**, the Democratic nominee for Governor of the State of North Carolina, and that we will use all honorable means to secure his election, *Resolved*, That the proceedings of this meeting be published in the *Old North State*, with a request that the *N. C. Standard*, and *Southern Argus* copy the same. On motion the meeting adjourned. Jas. C. **SCOTT**, Ch'n. Wm. D. **PRITCHARD**, Sec'y.

(741) THE METHODIST CHURCH CASE IN ALEXANDRIA.--We have noticed that a suit was pending in the Supreme Court, at Alexandria, to determine the right to the property of the Methodist Church in that town. A petition was filed on the part of the "Church," praying that the Court would appoint other trustees of the property, as those holding it had refused to allow either party to use the church. The trustees..say that they supposed that they were appointed to hold the property till the conflicting claims to it should be determined--that the church had remained closed because the two parties had refused their offer to occupy the church alternately. Pending the suit, a petition was presented on the part of certain members of the "Church South," praying to be made parties. This prayer was denied by Judge **TYLER**, who on Monday, delivered his opinion that the trustees had failed to perform their duty, which failure was tantamount to a refusal to act. The Court then appointed the following gentlemen as trustess: Benoni **WHEAT**, John **WOOD**, Wm. **VEITCH**, Wm. N. **BERKLEY**, Henry L. **SIMPSON**, John **SHACKLEFORD**, and John T. **CREIGHTON**. This decision is virtually in favor of the "Church North."

(742) A STRIKING RELIC. Mr. E. B. **THOMPSON**, of this city, and now a compositor in the office of this paper, has in his possession a very interesting historical relic, a small embroidered cambric pocket-handkerchief, which was used by Charles I. upon the scaffold, and is stained with his blood. It came originally from John **FENWICKE**, who was Major of Calvary [sic] in **CROMWELL**'s army, and in that capacity was required to be present at the execution of the unhappy monarch. The relic passed from his family to that of Jacob **LYELL**, whose wife emigrated at New Jersey near the close of the 17th century, and was connected with the **FENWICKE** family. She gave it to her daughters, who kept it with the greatest care and at their death it passed into another branch of the family, and has finally come into possession of Mr. **THOMPSON**. Its authenticity seems to be clearly traced and proved beyond doubt. The handkerchief is of small size--and the figure of the Scottish thistle is embroidered around the edges. Upon one corner is a very small figure of a crown. It is thickly stained with dark spots, some of which are as large as a dollar--the others smaller. The linen is considerably discolored by time. It seems to have been ironed but not washed.--*Courier*

(743) THE CASE OF Dr. JOHN W. **WEBSTER**.--Boston, June 18.--In the Supreme Judicial Court this morning, Chief Justice **SHAW** pronounced the decision of the court on the petition of Professor **WEBSTER** for a writ of error. The court refused to grant the petition, and the case remains as before. There is little probability of the prisoner's escaping..his awful sentence.

(744) ITEMS. .. The residence of Dr. W. C. **NOEL**, Eddyville, Ky., was destroyed by fire on Saturday week. No insurance. A monument is about to be erected at Boonsborough, Ky., to the memory of Daniel **BOONE**, the pioneer of Kentucky. .. A young lawyer, named John A. **COLLINS**, a native of Maysville, Ky., but who had recently settled in the neighborhood of New Orleans, died in the latter city on the 9th inst. He is said to have been a man of brilliant talents and unusual eloquence. ...

(745) HANNAH MORE ACADEMY, (Situated one mile from Reisterstown.) BALTIMORE COUNTY, MD. FIFTEEN MILES FROM BALTIMORE, ON THE BALTIMORE & REISTERSTOWN TURNPIKE ROAD. This Institution will be reopened for the Board and Education of Young Ladies, on the First Monday in November, the winter session, and the First Monday in May, the summer, under the supervision of MRS. **LYON**, whose constant aim will be to make it worthy the patronage of all who may wish to commit their daughters to her care. The course of instruction will embrace all the higher and lower English studies, together with the French and Latin Languages. The situation combines all that could render a Boarding School pleasant, being one of the most healthy in the country, and at a convenient distance from the City of Baltimore, stages and omnibusses passing every day. Charge from the time of entrance. TERMS: Board, English Branches, Fuel, Lights, Washing and Bedding, per session of 5 months, $75 00 Music, including use of Piano, per quarter, 10 00 Drawing and Painting, per quarter 5 00 French or Latin, per quarter, 5 00 Stationery will be charged at Booksellers prices. .. Board, Tuition, &c one half in advance. .. TRUSTEES: RIGHT REV. BISHOP **WHITTINGHAM**, Baltimore, Md. James M. **CAMPBELL**, Esq Balto., Md. Franklin **ANDERSON**, Esq, Reistertown Md. Rev. Dr. Thos. **ATKINSON**, Balto., Md. Dr. Chew **VAN BIBBER**, REFERENCES: Hon. Henry **CLAY**, Ashland, Ky. Right Rev. Bishop **KEMPER**, Indiana. Henry T. **DUNCAN**, Esq., Lexington, Ky. John W. **HUNT**, Esq. Rev. Dr. Andrew **WYLIE**, President of Indiana University, Bloomington, Ind. Rev. W. H. **M'GUFFY**, Virginia. Rev. Willian **ARMSTRONG**, Wheeling, Va. Rev. J. Avery **SHEPHERD**, Cool Spring, N. C. James **DUNLOP**, Esq., Pittburg, Pa. John **FROST**, A. M. Philadelphia. F. F. **FAGAN**, Plymouth, N. C. July 2d 1850.

(746) MEDICAL DEPARTMENT OF HAMPDEN SIDNEY COLLEGE, RICHMOND, VA.--The thirteenth Annual Course of

2 July 1850

(746) (Cont.) Lectures will commence on Monday, the 14th of October, 1850, and continue until the 1st of the ensuing March. The commencement for conferring degrees will be held about the middle of March. R. L. **BOHANNAN**, M.D., Prof. of Obstetrics and Diseases of Women and Children. L. W. **CHAMBERLAYNE**, M. D., Prof. of Materia Medica and Therapeutics. S. **MAUPIN**, M. D., Prof. of Chemistry and Pharmacy. Chas. Bell **GIBSON**, M. D., Prof. of Surgery and Surgical Anatomy. Carter P. **JOHNSON**, M. D., Prof. of Anatomy and Physiology. David H. **TUCKER**, M. D., Prof. of Theory and Practice of Medicine. Arthur E. **PETICOLAS**, M. D., Demonstrator of Anatomy. The study of Practical Anatomy may be prosecuted with the most ample facilities, and at very trifling expense. Clinical Lectures are regularly given at the College Infirmary and Richmond Almshouse. The Infirmary, under the same roof with the College and subject to the entire control of the Faculty, is at all times well filled with medical and surgical cases, and furnishes peculiar facilities for clinical instruction. Many surgical operations are performed in presence of the class; and the students being freely admitted to the wards, enjoy, under the guidance of the Professors, unusual opportunities for becoming familiar with the symptoms, diagnosis and treatment of disease. Expenses--Matriculation fee, $5. Professors' fees, $105. Demonstrator's fee, $10. Graduation fee, $25. The price of board, including fuel, lights and servants' attendance, is usually 3 or $3 1/2 per week. The catalogue, &c. containing fuller information concerning the institution will be forwarded to those applying for it, or specific inquiries will be answered by letter. Address, S. **MAUPIN**, M. D., Dean of the Faculty. July 2d, 1850.

(747) NOTICE. The Subscriber offers for sale his House and Lot at Nag's Head. Apply to Peter W. **HINTON**, No. 10, Roanoke Square, Norfolk, Va.

(748) Drugs, Medicines, &c. The Subscriber would respectfully inform his friends and public generally that having purchased the stock of Dr. Lewis **WARROCK**, and taken the stand occupied by him, he is now prepared to fill all orders in his line which may be entrusted to him, with *neatness, punctuality* and *dispatch*. ... L. K. **SAUNDERS**. July 2, 1850.

(749) For Sale or Rent. The property at Nag's Head, formerly belonging to Doct. Samuel **MATHEWS**, late of Elizabeth City, N. C. and now owned by S. D. **LAMB** Esqr. and know [sic] as Social Hall. Any persons wishing to purchase or rent a desirable place at Nag's Head, either as a private residence, or for the purpose of opening a public house, will do well to secure the above. Terms easy. For particulars apply to John **BLACK** Esqr., Elizabeth City, N. C. July 2d, 1850.

THE OLD NORTH STATE.
"Error is harmless, when Truth is left free to combat it."
Vol. X.] Elizabeth City, N. C. Tuesday July 9, 1850. [No. 20

(750) Elizabeth-City, July 9, 1850. .. We are requested to announce the name of C. L. **WHITEHURST**, Esqr., as the Democratic Candidate to represent the County of Pasquotank in the House of Commons in the next Legislature North Carolina.

(751) Keep it before the people that DAVID S. **REED**, the Deomcratic Candidate for Governor, did (notwithstanding his letter of denial in the last *Raleigh Standard,*) vote for the "**WILMOT** Proviso" as contained in the Oregon Bill.
Keep it before the people that this same David S. **REED**, while a member of the N. C. Legislature in 1840--'41, voted against the repeal of the odious law, then on our Statute Books giving the power to the County Courts to hire out "free white men."

(752) Celebration of the 4th at Woodville, According to previous notice the Woodville Guards assembled at their usual parade ground, when after a short delay they took up the line of march for the residence of Dr. R. B. **BAKER**, for the purpose of receiving Col. **SKINNER** and Staff. Captain **JORDAN** in behalf of the Guards, extended to the Colonel and his brother officers a hearty reception. This ceremony being over, they countermarched and took up their position opposite the residence of the Rev. Mr. **GRANT**, for the purpose of receiving the Rough and Ready Light Dragoons from Pasqnotank, who soon made their appearance, and were welcomed by Captain **JORDAN** in the same manner... .. The line being formed, marched to the grove selected for the occasion, where after one of the most beautiful and appropriate prayers by the Rev. Mr. **GRANT**, Adjt. Wm. E. **MANN** arose and after delivering a brief historical sketch of the origin and adoption of the Declaration of Independence, read that National document in a clear and forcible manner. He was followed by Capt. Geo. W. **BROOKS**, who delivered one of the best orations that it has ever been the privilege of the writer..to listen to. .. Great credit is due to Mr. Cason **GREGORY** and the committee of arrangements for the ample table set for so large a crowd--every thing *in the greatest plenty was to be had,* and but for the rain all would have enjoyed themselves much. I cannot close these proceedings without noticing the many courtesies extended to strangers by the citizens of Woodville, generally, and by Messrs. **FORD** and **PERRY** in particular. ... Z.

(753) List of Letters Remaining in the Post Office, at Elizabeth City, Quarter ending 30th June 1850. Any Dag'n Artist **ASHCROFT** Mrs. Luvinia **BROTHERS** Charles **BROOKS** Wm. **BURGESS** Jno. **BANKS** Wm. C. **BRUCKS** Miss

9 July 1850

(753) (Cont.) Catharine BURGESS Capt. Wm. 2 BROZIER Jos. L. BANKS Jas. W. BARRENTON Annes BARBIER L. BANKS Jno. & Wm. F. BURGESS Major BAILEY Wilson BENTON Thos. BUTCHER Geo. H. BRITT Elias CROSS Washington 2 CHESSIRE David CARVER Job CRICKMORE Benj. CAIN Wm. B. CORTELL Malichi COTTEN Isaac CLARK Capt. Rich'd H. DEVER Jno. DUGAN Wm. H. 2 DAVIS Fanny of Color DELLON Miss Penny DOWDY Capt. Saml EASTON Wm. FORBES Mrs. Sarah Ann GODFREY Mary GRIFFIN Mrs. Margaret GILFORTE Leidey HAUGHTON T. S. HARREL B. & J. HOGAN Wm. HOLLOWELL Alfred of color JACKSON Mrs. Levinia JONES Rev. C. P. KYLE Wm. P. KNOWLS Thomas KNIGHT T. W. 2 KEATON Jim (of color) KEATON Wm. KEATON Miss Winnefred KERBY Rodgers 2 LOUIS Adolphus LINDSAY Cader MORRIS Thomas O. MOORE Alfred W. MOORE Britton MAISON Rev. C. A. MILLS Wm. H. MARKEUS E. MC COY S. D. MITCHELL Saml. MONCHEN Mrs. Sophia MASON Wm. MARSHALL A. C. MARSH Bennett MOORE Alfred W. [sic] MILLER Capt. B. T. MULLEN Jas. & Jos. NASH Rev. J. ONEAL Mrs. Mary OWENS Wm. OVERMAN Mrs. Elizabeth OVERMAN Mrs. Sarah PARKS Marshall 2 PENDLETON Robert 2 PEARSON Gilbert of color PENDLETON Reubin RINALDI W. S. RIED Miss Elizabeth RUSSELL Jos. REDICK Bearl SAWYER Mrs. Ann B. SAWYER Master Jno. W. SAWYER Mrs. Nancy SANDERLAND R. A. SMALL Hannah A. SANDERLIN Trimigan SPENCE Abel STONE Milicent SHELDON Rev. Anson SIKES Capt. A. STERLING Capt. Jno. SAWYER Griffin TONIS A. C. TUTTLE John M. 2 TART Wm. TAYLOR Miss Eunice WHITE J. WHITING Alex. WHITING Henry WARMOTH David WHITE James WALSH Martin WALKER Seth WILSON John G. WISE John J. YOUNG O. whole number 115. Persons calling for any of the above letters will please say they are advertised. Wm. E. MANN, P. M. July 9

(754) BAUM'S HOTEL. The Subscriber having put his House in complete order will open it on the 6th July for the accommodation of all who may favor him with their patronage. .. His table will be at all times furnished with the best that can be procured and the Bar will be supplied with the best of Liquors, Cigars, &c., and a plenty of that great luxury--ICE. .. Mr. L. WOODHOUSE will upon application take any passengers across from his dwelling to the Hotel--Passage 37 1/2 cts. Horses taken care of until the return of their owners. A. BAUM. July 9, 1850.

(755) Opposite the Banking Depot. The Subscriber has for sale Fifty Gallons Copal Varnish, No. 2, in Canisters, holding from 3 to 5 gallons, warranted good. Also, about 50 lbs. Curled Hair. Varnish at $1 75 per gallon. Hair at 25 cts. per lb. .. C. SIKES. July 8th 1850.

(756) DISMAL SWAMP CANAL COMPANY, Norfolk, July 6th 1850.} The Directors of this Company give notice, that on or about the 25th of August, it is intended to draw the water off from the Canal, for the purpose of cutting some new recesses, widening others, &c. By order of the Board of Directors. James CORNICK. President of the Dismal Swamp Canal Company. July 9th, 1850.

THE OLD NORTH STATE.
"Error is harmless, when Truth is left free to combat it."
Vol. X.] Elizabeth City, N. C. Tuesday July 16, 1850. [No. 21.

(757) The nomination of George LITTLE Esq., as U. S. Marshal for the District of North Carolina, has been confirmed by the Senate.

(758) THRILLING TALE. Mr. Archy STANHOPE--a groggery sentimentalist, residing in Buckley street, Philadelphia-- conceived the harrowing suspicion that his wife was not as passionately fond of him as a lady of good taste should be; and to put the matter to a fair trial, he hit on a little stratagem, which he put in practice the other day, with the result hereafter to be detailed. He took a suit of clothes and made an effigy of himself, by stuffing the garment with a quantity of straw, which had lately been discharged from an old bed. Having suspended the figure to a rafter in the garret by means of a piece of clothes line, he ensconced himself behind a pile of rubbish, in the same garret to watch the effect. After a while a little daughter came up after a jumping rope, and caught a glimpse of the suspending figure. She ran down the stairs screaming, "Oh mother, daddy's hung himself." "Now for it," thought Archibald, in ambuscade; "we shall have a touching scene presently. "Hung himself!" he heard Mrs. STANHOPE repeat as she walked leisurely up stairs; "he hasn't got spunk enough for such a thing, or he would have done it long ago. Well, I do believe he has done it, however," she continued, as she came in view of the straw representative. "Molly, (to the little girl,) I think he ought to be cut down. You had better go down into the kitchen and get a knife, my dear, but don't go too fast, or you might fall and hurt yourself. Stay--I forget; there's no knife in the kitchen sharp enough. You can go round to Mr. HOLMES, the shoemaker, in Sixth he's only two squares off, and ask him to lend us his paring knife; tell him to whet it a little before he sends it. And, Molly, while you are in the neighborhood, you can call at your aunt Sukey's and ask how the baby is. And, Molly, you can stop at

16 July 1850

(758) (Cont.) the grocery store as you come back and get me a pound of seven cent sugar. "Poor Archy," sighed Mrs. **S.**, when her daughter had departed, "I think I ought to have let him had his own way for once in his life; he used to say that I was always crossing him. I wish he hadn't spoiled that new clothes line, though--an old rope might have answered his purpose." Here a voice, which sounded like that of the supposed suicide, broke in on Mrs. **STANHOPE**'s soliloquy, with--"you confounded old Jezebel--I'll be the death of you." Mrs. **S.** thinking this must, of course, be a ghostly exclamation, uttered a wild scream, and attempted to escape down a narrow staircase. Archibald, starting from his place of concealment, gave chase. Mr. **S.** stumbled midway on the flight of steps--and Mr. **S.** having just reached her and made a grasp at her disheveled hair as it streamed backward, the amiable partners were precipitated to the bottom together. Both were badly bruised, and the cries of the lady raised the neighborhood.--Archibald was arrested for making a disturbance and practising on the tender sensibilities of his wife. He was recognised in the sum of $200, and jocularly proposed his suspended effigy as security--but "straw bail," as he found to his sorrow, is not acceptable under the administration of Mayor **JONES**.--*Pennsylvanian.*

(759) Elizabeth-City, July 16, 1850. .. DEATH OF THE PRESIDENT. A great man has indeed fallen! The Patriot, the Hero and Statesman lies still in the cold embrace of death. The memory of his *great deeds* and the influence of his *bright example* are all that remain to a mourning country of Gen. ZACHARY **TAYLOR**! .. The illness of President **TAYLOR** was sudden and most violent, in a few short days prostrating his almost iron constitution and bringing him rapidly to the verge of the grave. On the 4th he participated with his fellow citizens in the celebration of our National Jubilee--his exposure to a sun of unusal [sic] intensity it is thought, brought on the malady which terminated fatally at 10 1/2 o'clock P. M. the 9th inst. Gen'l **TAYLOR** retained the entire possession of his faculties up to the time of his death. His last words were: "I have always done my duty; I am ready to die; my only regret is for the friends I leave behind me."

(760) The citizens of Elizabeth City, are requested to meet at the Court House, on to-morrow evening at 8 o'clock, to adopt such measures as to them may seem proper, in order to manifest their respect for the memory of Gen. ZACHARY **TAYLOR**, late President of the United States. Jos. H. **POOL**, Intendant of Police. July 16, 1850.

(761) From the *Republic*. DEATH OF PRESIDENT TAYLOR. We are called upon to discharge the inexpressibly painful duty of announcing the death of President **TAYLOR**, which took place last night at half-past 10 o'clock. He was in the enjoyment of his usual health on Thursday last, the 4th instant, and participated in the celebration of the day. Early the next morning, he was attacked with cholera morbus, and remittent fever supervening, the best medical attendance failed to arrest the progress of the disease. We are requested to say that the Executive Departments of the Government will be closed in consequence of the death of the President.

(762) CUBA EXPEDITION.--The New Orleans papers publish the following names of persons against whom indictments have been found by the Grand Jury of the U. S. District Court, for violation of the Act of Congress of 1818, by setting on foot an expedition against the island of Cuba, viz: John A. **QUITMAN**, (Governor of Mississippi.) Judge Cotesworth Pinckney **SMITH**, (of the Supreme Court of Mississippi,) John **HENDERSON**, (late Senator from that State,) J. L. **O'SULLIVAN**, (late Editor of the *Democratic Review*, and son of a former Minister to Spain,) John F. **PICKETT**, (late Consul at Turks Island,) Theodore **O'HARA**, (late Major in the United States Army,) C. R. **WHEATE**, Peter **SMITH**, A. **GONZALEZ**, Thomas Theodore **HAWKINS**, W. H. **BELL**, N. J. **BUNCH**, L. J. **SIGUR**, (State Senator,) Donatien **AUGUSTIN**, Brigadier, General, and commander of the Legion, and General Narciso **LOPEZ**, making in all sixteen [sic] persons.

(763) Married. On July 11th, by Rev. C. R. **HENDRICKSON**, Mr. Amos **TRUEBLOOD** to Mrs. Abi **DOZIER**, all of this place.

(764) STATE OF NORTH CAROLINA, Currituck County. Court of Pleas and Qr., Sessions May Term 1850 Caleb J. **ETHEREDGE**, Admimstratot [sic] of Caleb **ETHEREDGE**, Sr., deceased.} Petition. vs. Andrew **ETHEREDGE**, Jasper **ETHEREDGE**, James **WHITE** and wife Maria, John **GILMAN** and wife Caroline, Lovey **ETHEREDGE**, Tully **WILLIAMS**, Guardian to Catharine **ETHEREDGE** and Adolphus **ETHEREDGE**, heirs at law of Caleb **ETHEREDGE**, dec'd. It appearing to the Court that Andrew **ETHEREDGE** one of the defendants is an inhabitant of another State. It is ordered by the Court that Publication be made for six successive weeks in the "Old North State," for the said Andrew **ETHEREDGE**, to appear at the next Term of this Court of Pleas and Quarter Sessions, to be held for the County of Currituck, at the Court House in Currituck, on the last Monday in August next, and answer Plead or demur or Judgment Pro confessor, will be taken against him. Attest. B. T. **SIMMONS**, C. C. C. July 16th.

(765) EQUITY LAND SALE. Will be sold on the 14th, day of October next, (being Monday of October Superior Court for Perquimans County) before the Court House door in the town of Hertford, the lands belonging to the Estate of Edmund B. **SKINNER**

16 July 1850

(765) (Cont.) dec'd., lying on the south west side of Perquimans river between that river and Menzis creek in the part of the County known as **HARVEY**'s Neck. The tract known as the Home Place contains three hundred and sixty acres more or less--208 of which are cleared and in a fine state of cultivation, the fences around and on the plantation are good and in good order. The buildings are many of them new, and all are in good order. The dwelling House, nearly new, is large and commodious, there are two good cisterns, built of brick and cement with filters. One other tract known as the **LANSTON** and **PARSONS** land adjoining the above described tract, contains 687 acres, of which 270 acres are cleared and in a fine state of cultivation, both said tracts are situated on the river; any one wishing further information can be accommodated by calling on Mr. John **SKINNER** who will take pleasure in showing the land. ... E. F. **SMITH**, C. M. E. Hertford, July 16th, 1850.

(766) To Invalids. The subscriber having been appointed agent in this County, for the sale of Doct. **AYER**'s "Cherry Pectoral," respectfully informs all persons suffering with Coughs, Colds, Consumption, &c., that he has a few dozen bottles in store. W. J. **KELLINGER**. July 16th, 1850.

THE OLD NORTH STATE.
"Error is harmless, when Truth is left free to combat it."
Vol. X.] Elizabeth City, N. C. Tuesday July 23, 1850. [No. 22.

(767) Elizabeth-City, July 23, 1850. .. *From the Zanesville* (Ohio) *Courier*. MILLARD **FILLMORE**, Called by a dispensation of Providence to the Presidency of the United States, is eminently qualified to properly perform the duties of that important station; and an alleviation of the sorrow which the people feel for the loss of President **TAYLOR** is only to be found in the fact that so competent, and judging from his past history, so true a man is to succeed him. We have not space at present to say much of Mr. **FILLMORE**'s character and career. He is in his fiftieth year; has long enjoyed the confidence of his native State; did valuable service to the country when he was a member of Congress; has recently presided over the deliberations of the Senate with ability and impartiality; and we have no doubt will perform the duties of the Executive office, in a manner creditable to himself and beneficial to his country.

(768) PROSPECTUS OF THE *DEMOCRATIC PIONEER*. The subscriber proposes to publish, in the town of Elizabeth City, N. C., a WEEKLY DEMOCRATIC PAPER under the above title. As its title indicates, the "PIONEER" will be devoted to the dissemination and advocacy of the great cardinal principles of the Democratic party... Upon the great question of the day--the Slavery question--being thoroughly imbued with Southern feeling, and having no particle of sympathy with the fanatical and hypocritical agitators of the North, who would reduce us to a state of vassalage too humiliating to be borne, the "PIONEER" will resist, to the utmost, the reckless spirit of aggression, which, if not repelled, will desolate our homes and subject us to the yoke of Northern dictation. .. The size of the "PIONEER" will be as large as the "Old North State," printed with entirely new materials. The first Number will be issued about the 1st of August, and regularly, thereafter, upon the following terms. Single copy, per annum, $2 5 Five copies, do. 11 00 Ten copies, 20 00 L. D. **STARKE**, Elizabeth City, N. C., July 23d, 1850.

(769) The New York Life Insurance Company would respectfully notify the people of the Eastern portion of North Carolina, that it has been in successfull operations for upwards of five years... .. The advantages of life insurance are inestimable. It is not only the duty of all men to provide for their families while living, but to see they are not left on the cold charities of an unfeeling world at their death. .. For further information and insurance apply to the Agent, John **BLACK**, Esq., Elizabeth City N. C.

(770) Perquimans Academy. The final examination of the pupils of this institution will take place on the 29th and 30th, days of this month. The friends of the pupils, and the public generally are invited to attend, and participate in the exercises. On the last day of the examination, an address will be delivered by Thos. F. **JONES**, Esq. Hertford, July 23d, 1850.

(771) NOTICE. Will be sold on Monday, August the 6th, 1850, at ten o'clock A. M. the Schooner Fanny and materials and Cargo, consisting of about 550 Bales of Cotton, 70 Bales of Cotton yarn. Now lying on the Beach, three miles south of Chickamicomico. By order of the Captain. Cyrus **HOOPER** Com. Wrecks. July 23d.

(772) Silver Ware. Just received per **ADAMS** & Co's Express, a large lot of Silver Ware, consisting of Silver Table Forks, do. desert do. Do. do. Spoons, do. Tea do. dessert do. Ladles, Sugar Tongs, Salt and Mustard Spoons, Cups, Napkin Rings, &c. ... J. M. **FREEMAN**, Norfolk, Va. July 23d.

(773) Nag's Head Packet. The good Schooner EMPIRE, Capt. **SIMMONS**, having been put in complete order, will run the balance of the season as a regular Packet from this place to Nag's Head. ... Josiah **SIMMONS**. July 23d, 1850.

30 July 1850

THE OLD NORTH STATE.
"Error is harmless, when Truth is left free to combat it."
Vol. X.] Elizabeth City, N. C. Tuesday, July 30, 1850. [No. 23.

(774) Swarming Bees--*An Easy Method if Feasible.*--Moses **WINDSOW**, of Westbrook, Ct., some time since communicated the following method of hiving bees, which, if it succeeds, will save a great part of the difficulty, danger and loss that often occurs. .. Drive down two stakes about three feet apart, fifteen feet in front of the bee-house; tie a cross piece across the stakes, three feet from the ground. Take a board about one foot wide and twenty feet long--one end on the ground at the foot of the hives, and the other end at the cross-piece between the stakes. Put up the board at the commencement of the swarming season; rub the under side with some sweet herbs, and sprinkle it every day with salt water. The bees will then pitch on the under side of the board; when settled, lift up the other end, and set a barrel under it, to raise it to a level; turn the board over, and set the hive over the swarm. Secure it against being blown over, and the work is done. ... [*Rural New Yorker.*

(775) Elizabeth-City, July 30, 1850. .. "AS YOU WERE." Our paper will in future be issued as formerly on Saturday, (commencing on the 3d Aug.) Many of our country subscribers have informed us that as they are in the habit of calling at the Post Office only on Saturday, they would greatly prefer it, upon that day. Our town subscribers it will suit as well: and the compositors of the Office and the "Printers Devil" are unanimous for the change. Our patrons may rest assured that after the next we shall change no more.

(776) Will our friends, Mark **HATHAWAY**, Esq. of Hertford, and A. A. **PERRY**, Esq., of Woodville, forward us the Election returns from Perquimans? ... We return our thanks to Arthur **JONES**, Esq, for the present of delightful new honey sent us.--Can't some one else serve us in the same manner? Mr. James M. **WHEDBEE**, will please accept the thanks of one of the proprietors, for the present sent him in the shape of 7 mammoth Irish potatoes. It is no use to say what they weighed or measured, but suffice it to say, they were amply sufficient to supply the usual dish of potatoes for a dinner of a family of 8 persons. ...

(777) Whigs of Pasquotank. We appeal to you to come forward Thursday next and cast your votes for GEORGE D. **POOL**, Esq., for the Commons. He is known to you all, as a man of sound common sense, and business habits. He has been reared from boyhood among you, and all his interests are identical with yours, will you not yield him a cordial support? .. And so not forget to deposit at the same time, a vote for CHARLES **MANLY**, the Whig candidate for Governor.

(778) Senatorial Voters of Pasquotank and Perquimans, we are sure that no word of exhortation are [sic] necessary from us to induce to come to the Polls next Thursday, and cast your votes for the Hon'l Wm. B. **SHEPARD**. ...

(779) At a meeting of the citizens of Elizabeth City, held in the Court House pursuant to notice of the Mayor on Friday evening 19th July, for the purpose of making preliminary arrangements for the proper manifestation of regard for the memory of the lamented and distinguished late President of the United States. On motion of Gilbert **ELLIOTT**, Esq., Jos. H. **POOL**, Mayor of Elizabeth City, was called to the chair, and G. W. **BROOKS** appointed Secretary. The chairman briefly..explained the object of the meeting. G. **ELLIOTT** then addressed the meeting in his usually appropriate manner, and at the conclusion of his remarks suggested the appointing of a committee to draft resolutions expressive of the sense of this meeting, and to make all nesssary arrangements for a public manifestation of our regard for the memory of the illustrious and lamented President. On motion of G. W. **CHARLES**, it was resolved that the chair appoint said committee and that it consist of twelve. Whereupon the chairman appointed the following gentlemen...: Gilbert **ELLIOTT**, G. W. **CHARLES**, James **BARBER**, Wm. E. **MANN**, Capt. Wm. **SIMMONS**, Dr. S. D. **GRICE**, Geo. A. **WILLIAMS**, S. D. **POOL**, Wm. W. **GRIFFIN**, John **POOL**, Wm. H. **CLARK** and G. W. **BROOKS**. ... On motion, *Resolved*, That the proceedings of this meeting be published in the "Old North State."

(780) From the *Republic*. THE NEW CABINET. On Saturday last, the President transmitted a message to the Senate containing the nominations of the following named gentlemen as the members of the new Cabinet, all of whom were confirmed: Daniel **WEBSTER**, (of Massachusetts,) Secretary of State. Thomas **CORWIN**, (of Ohio,) Secretary of the Treasury. J. A. **PEARCE**, (of Maryland,) Secretary of the Interior. W. A. **GRAHAM**, (of North Carolina,) Secretary of the Navy. Edward **BATES**, (of Missouri,) Secretary of War. N. K. **HALL**, (of New York,) Postmaster General. John J. **CRITTENDEN**, (of Kentucky,) Attorney General. ...

(781) DIED... Died at her residence near E. City, on the 24 inst. Mrs. Margaret A. **SCOTT**, wife of Capt. Jas. C. **SCOTT**, aged 37 years, leaving four daughters, one son, an aged father, and a devoted brother. .. Her illness was of short duration having been sick a little more than one week... On Saturday the 19 inst., Mary Virginia, infant daughter of Robert and Cornelia F. **WATKINS**, aged 4 months.

30 July 1850

(782) Old Port Wine, The Pure Juice. I have on hand 25 gallons of Superior Port Wine, an article that has been highly recommended to be of a very Superior quality, for *medicinal use*. .. Also a Fresh Lot of Medicines, Paints, Oils, Dye Stuff, Perfumery, Fancy articles, Etherial Oil, Lamps, &c. The above are for sale cheap for cash, at the Drug Store of J. E. **DEFORD**. Road Street Elizabeth City. July 30th.

THE OLD NORTH STATE.
"Error is harmless, when Truth is left free to combat it."
Vol. X.] Elizabeth City, N. C. Tuesday, August 3, 1850. [No. 24.

(783) Elizabeth-City, August 3, 1850. .. ELECTION RETURNS. No news--Telegraph wires out of order--expect something by our next issue. N. B. **MANLY**'s majority in Pasquotank is 173. In Perquimans 36. Chowan 39. .. The aggregate vote of this county (Pasquotank) is very small, falling even below that of 1848. The falling off has been all on the Whig side. The following is the vote for Governor and Commons for this County.

	MANLY.	**REID.**	**POOL.**	**WHI'ST**
E. City,	238	174	235	165
Bridgefield,	64	12	70	9
Nixonton,	64	3	64	2
Newland,	24	28	20	28

SHEPARD re-elected to the Senate--no opposition--Joshua A. **POOL**, Sheriff of Pasquotank. Willis H. **BAGLEY**, re-elected Sheriff of Perquimans. Thos. S. **HOSKINS** is also re-elected Sheriff of Chowan. The Whig Telegraphic wires between us and Camden have commenced to work since the above was written, as the annexed returns will show. ..

	MANLY w.	**REID** d.	**BARNARD** w.	**PERKINS** d.
Cam. C. H.	133	43	46	14
Old Trap,	246	13	119	10
Canal Bridge	118	29	61	17

MANLY's maj. 412--**RARNARD** 185. Caleb **BARCO**, (Whig) elected to the Commons--no opposition. **DAILY** re-elected Sheriff.

(784) Hon. R. C. **WINTHROP** has been appointed by the Governor of Massachsetts to fill the vacancy occasioned by the resignation of the Hon'l Daniel **WEBSTER**. Hon'l Thomas **EWING** late Sect'y of the Interior has also received the appointment as Senator from Ohio. Mr. **PEARCE** declines the Secretaryship tendered him. **CONRAD** of Louisiana or **GENTRY** of Tenn. will in all probability obtain the appointment.

The *Republic* states that during the protracted and dangerous illness of the Hon. John C. **CLARK**, B. F. **PLEASANTS**, Esq., has been appointed by the Secretary of the Treasury Acting Solicitor. We are gratified to hear that Mr. **CLARK** is recovering.

(785) The Lynching of **GRAYSON**, the negro man accused of murder, at Culpeper, was attended by several incidents worthy of note. The *Richmond Times* thus relates two: "We hear that Mr. William **GREEN**, one of the most prominent citizens of Culpeper, appeared before the mob, and used every effort of eloquence and persuasion to induce them to desist from their illegal purpose. They thanked him for his advice, but declared that they would have the life of the negro. Another gentleman is said to have displayed the most remarkable bravery, in endeavoring to save the negro at the jail. Taking his position at the door, he is represented to have invited any nine men in the crowd to come forward and make with him a band of ten, to resist with their lives the assault upon the jail. The proposition not being responded to, he deliberately took paper, and, before the faces of the mob, wrote down the names of all the persons he recognized, avowing his purpose to report them to the legal authorities. Such conduct deserves the unmeasured applause and support of the community."

(786) The venerable relict of Judge Simeon **BALDWIN** died in New Haven, Tuesday, at the advanced age of eighty-five. She was the last surviving child of the Hon. Roger **SHERMAN**, the signer of the Declaration of Independence.

(787) Presidents of the United States. We copy from the *Boston Almanac* for 1850, the following brief and comprehensive sketches of the twelve Presidents of the United States. These were prepared by Lemuel **SEATTUCK**, Esq., well known for his accurate statistical works: George **WASHINGTON**, first President of the U. S., for the first and second terms, 1789-1797, was born in Westmoreland Co., Va., Feb. 22, 1732, and died at Mount Vernon, Dec. 14, 1799, aged 67 years, 9 months, 21 days. He was the son of Augustine **WASHINGTON**, by Mary **BALL**, his second wife. A planter, commander of American Army during the Revolution, and was twice unanimously elected President of the U. S. He married, Jan. 6, 1759, Martha, daughter of John **DANBRIDGE**, and widow of Daniel P. **CUSTIS**, of New Kent Co., Va. She died May 22, 1802, aged 70. **WASHINGTON** died without issue.

3 August 1850

(787) (Cont.) John **ADAMS**, second President of the U. S., for the third term, 1797-1701 [sic,] was born in Quincy, Oct. 30, 1735, and died in his native town, July 4, 1826, aged 90 years, 8 months, 4 days. He was the son of John **ADAMS** and Susanna **BOYLSTON**, graduated H. C. 1755; a lawyer and distinguished leader in the American Revolution. Vice President, 1789-1797.--He married, Feb. 24, 1764, Abigail, daughter of Rev. Wm. **SMITH**, of Weymouth.--She died Oct. 28, 1818, aged 74. Their Children were: 1, Abigail, born July 14, 1765; 2, John Quincy, born July 11, 1767; 3, Susanna, born Dec. 28, 1768; 4, Charles; 5, Thomas Boylston, born Sept. 15, 1771;

Thomas **JEFFERSON**, third President of the U. S., for the fourth and fifth terms, 1801-1809, was born in Shadwell, Albemarle Co., Va., April 2, 1743, and died at Monticello, Orange Co., Va., July 4, 1826, aged 83 years, 3 months, 2 days. He was the son of Peter **JEFFERSON** and Jane **RANDOLPH**, was educated a lawyer, and was the author of the Declaration of Independence. He married, Jan. 1, 1772, Martha **SKELTON**, widow of Bathurst **SKELTON**, and daughter of John **WAYLES**. She died in 1782, leaving two daughters, one of whom died unmarried, the other married Mr. **RANDOLPH**, whose son, Thomas Jefferson **RANDOLPH**, complied his memoir writings.

James **MADISON**, Fourth President of the U. S., for the sixth and seventh terms, 1809-1817, was born near Port Royal, Va., March 16, 1751, and died at Montpelier, Orange county, Va., June 28, 1836, aged 85 years, 3 months, 12 days. He was the son of James **MADISON**, by his wife Nelly **CONWAY**, of Orange county, graduated at Princeton College, N. J., 1771, and held many important offices beside President. He married in 1791, Dolly **PAYNE**, the widow of Mr. **TOOD**, a lawyer of Philadelphia. She was born May 20, 1767, and died in Washington, July 12, 1840, aged 82 years, 1 month, 22 days. She left a son, Mr. Payne **TOOD**, by her first husband, but had no issue by Mr. **MADISON**.

James **MONROE**, Fifth President of the U. S., for the eighth and ninth terms, 1817-1825, was born on the paternal estate in Wstmoreland county, Va., April 2, 1759, and died in the city of New York, July 4, 1831, aged 72 years, 3 months, 2 days.--He was the son of Spence **MONROE** and Elizabeth **JONES**. He graduated at William and Mary College, in 1776, and was by profession a lawyer. At his 2d election, as President, he received every electoral vote, excepting one from New Hampshire, given for J. Quincy **ADAMS**. He married in 1786, Miss **KORTRIGHT**, of N. York, by whom he had two daughters, one of whom married Mr. **HALE**, of Va., the other L. S. **GROSVENEUR**, Esq., of New York.

John Quincy **ADAMS**, Sixth President of the U. S., for the tenth term, 1825-1829, was born in Quincy, Mass., July 11, 1767, and died at the Capital in Washington, Fed. 23, 1818, aged 80 years, 7 months, 12 days. He was the son of John **ADAMS** and Abigail **SMITH**, graduated at Harvard College, 1787, stuided law, but devoted most of his life to public affairs. He married July 26, 1797, Louisa Catherine **JOHNSON**, daughter of Joshua **JOHNSON**, a citizen of Maryland, though at the time of her birth, Feb. 12, 1775, a resident of London. By her, who still survives, he had three children; George Washington died unmarried; John died Oct. 23, 1834, and Charles Francis.

Andrew **JACKSON**, Seventh President of the United States, for the eleventh and twelfth terms, 1829-1837, was born in Waxsaw, South Carolina, March 15, 1767; and died at the Hermitage, near Nashville, Tenn., June 8, 1845, aged 78 years, 2 months and 23 days. He was the son of Andrew **JACKSON** and Elizabeth **HUTCHINSON**, natives of Ireland, and of Scotch descent. He was educated a lawyer, and admitted to practice in North Carolina, 1786; removed to Nashville, 1788; was a representative and senator in Congress; spent a considerable portion of his life in the military profession, and gained great celebrity at the battle of New Orleans, January 8, 1815. He married, but died without issue.

Martin **VAN BUREN**, Eighth President of the United States, for the thirteenth term, 1837-1841, was born in Kinderhook, Columbia county, N. Y., December 5, 1782, and is still living. He was the son of Abraham **VAN BUREN** and Maria **GOES**, both of respectable families of Dutch descent, living on the Hudson. He was educated a lawyer, without having graduated at any college. He has held many public offices in the gift of his native State and Nation, besides those of President and Vice President of the United States. He married in 1806, Hannah **GOES**, of Columbia county, who died in 1818. By her..had four sons.

William Henry **HARRISON**, Ninth President of the United States, elected for the fourteenth term, 1841-1845, was born in Berkley, Charles county, Virginia, February 9, 1773; and died in Washington, while in office, April 4, 1841, aged 68 years, 1 month and 23 days. He was the son of Benjamin **HARRISON**, one of the signers of the Declaration of Independence and Miss **BASSET**. He was a military General, Governor, Representative and Senator in Congress. He was a planter at North Bend, Ohio. He married in 1795, a daughter of John Cleaves **SYMMS**, founder of the Miami Settlement, by whom he had five sons and four daughters. Four sons and one daughter died before their father.

John **TYLER**, Tenth President of the U. States, for fourteenth term, 1841-1845, elected Vice President, but served as President, the same term, after the 4th April, 1841, in place of **HARRISON**, who had died. He was born in Charles City county, Va., March 29, 1790, and still living near Williamsburg, Va. He was the second son of Judge John **TYLER**, graduated at William and Mary College, and was educated a lawyer. He married first, in 1813, Letitia **CHRISTIAN**, of New Kent county, Va., who died at Washington, September 10, 1842, leaving three sons and three daughters; and secondly, June 26, 1844, Julia **GARDNER**, daughter of David **GARDNER** of New York.

James Knox **POLK**, Eleventh President of the United States, for the fifteenth term, 1845-1849, was born in Mecklenburg, North Carolina, Nov. 2, 1795, and died at Nashville, Tenn., June 15th, 1849, aged 53 years, 7 months and 13 days. He was

3 August 1850

(787) (Cont.) the oldest of 10 children, and graduated at the University of North Carolina in 1818; studied law, and settled in Nashville. He was elected, 1823, member of the State Legislature, and, in 1825, a member of Congress, in which office he continued many years. He was speaker of the House of Representatives, 1835-1840, nad [sic] afterwards two years Governor of Tennessee. He married a lady of Tennessee, but died without issue.

Zachary **TAYLOR**, Twelfth President of the United States, for the sixteenth term, 1849-1854, was born in Virginia, Nov. 24, 1781, and is now in office at the age of 65. His parents removed to Kentucky, where many of their connections now reside. He has spent a large portion of his life in the military profession. He married a lady of Virginia, and has had five children, one of whom died in early life. His oldest daughter married Dr. **WOOD**, surgeon in the army; Sarah Knox, his 2d daughter, married Jefferson **DAVIS**, Mississippi, and died soon after; Elizabeth married Mr. **BLISS**, his private secretary; Richard, his only son, lives on his father's plantation in Baton Rouge, La.

Millard **FILLMORE**, who, by the death of the [sic] President **TAYLOR**, becomes acting President of the United States, is the second Vice President who has been raised to the Chief Magistracy by the death of the President. He was born at what is now called Summer Hill, Cayuga county, New York, January 7, 1800, and is now, consequently, in the 51st year of his age. His father moved from Bennington, Vt., and is a plain, independent farmer. Millard enjoyed in youth, only the common advantages of a farmer's son, but by his natural talent and love of books, has gradually raised himself to the high post which he now occupies as the Chief Magistrate of the United States. -- Though Mrs. **TAYLOR** may have belonged to Virginia, at the time of her marriage, she was a native of Calvert county, Md. Her family name was **SMITH**.

(788) PROFESSOR WEBSTER. .. The *Boston Journal* gives the following account of an interview between Ephraim **LITTLEFIELD**, janitor of the Medical College, and Prof. **WEBSTER**, which took place at Leverett jail on Wednesday afternoon: At the solicitation of Professor **WEBSTER** Mr. **LITTLEFIELD**, the janitor of the Medical College, and principal witness for the government on the trial of Prof. **WEBSTER**, visited the jail, and had an interview with the condemned man in the presence of Mr. **ANDREWS**, the jailor. As he went in the cell, Prof. **WEBSTER** greeted him with great cordiality, taking him by the hand, and told him he had long been desirous of seeing him, in order to make his acknowledements to him. Professor **WEBSTER** said he had done him, **LITTLEFIELD**, great injustice, and asked his forgiveness. ... **LITTLEFIELD**..has purchased a farm in Sharon, Vt., with the reward paid him for discovering the murderer of Dr. **PARKMAN**.

(789) Married. Near Williamston, N. C. on the 23d. inst, by the Rev. C. B. **HASSELL**, Dr. J. H. **BURNETT**, to Miss S. A. **FOLK**.

THE OLD NORTH STATE.
"Error is harmless, when Truth is left free to combat it."
Vol. X.] Elizabeth City, N. C. Saturday, August 10, 1850. [No. 25.

(790) Elizabeth-City, August 10, 1850. .. The celebration of the Obsequies in honor of General Zachary **TAYLOR**, late President of the United States was observed in this place Thursday last. The day was fine and pleasant..and a large concourse of people from this, and adjoining counties, was in attendance. The procession formed at the Academy ground at 11 o'clock under the direction of the Chief Marshal, W. E. **MANN** Esq. and his Aids, and preceded by the Musical Club of E. City, marched to the Baptist Church... The Masonic Fraternity, Independent Order of Odd Fellows, Pasquotank Division No. 21, Sons of Temperance, Marion Section Cadets of Temperance, many of the children of the Schools and citizens joined in the procession. .. The Eulogy delivered by Gilbert **ELLIOTT** Esq. was an eloquent and chaste production, doing justice to the occasion and the theme.

(791) KILLED BY LIGHTNING. Joseph **HARRISON**, a sailor on board the packet Empire, plying between this place and Nag's Head, was struck by lightning, the afternoon of the 6th inst., and instantly killed. He was being hoisted to the masthead for the purpose of repairing some trifling damage, when the lightning struck the mast, killing him and stunning the negroes who were hoisting him. .. We learn that the lightning entirely stripped the unfortunate young man, and that in that situation he was precipitated overboard by a lurch of the vessel, while his clothing fell to the deck. Although the vessel was immediately anchored, and search made for the body, no trace of it could be found. We understand that his mother resides in Portsmouth, and we are requested by the Captain to state that his clothes and other things, belonging to him, can be had by sending for them.

(792) BARN BURNT. The Barn of a free negro, named Benj. **PERRY**, living at the head of Little River in this County, was struck by lightning last Friday, and entirely consumed.

(793) Hon. Henry A. **WISE**. This gentleman is a candidate in Accomac county, for the Reform Convention of Virginia, and according to the *Snow Hill Shield*, is..opposed by some of the leading democrats of the county. At a meeting at Temperanceville, on Saturday last, an altercation occurred between him and Mr. David **WALLOP**, an influential democrat. The *Shield* says:

10 August 1850

(793) (Cont.) After some angry words, between them, Mr. WISE is said to have made some reckless declaration..to Mr. WALLOP, and the motives which prompted his course, which Mr. WALLOP, pronounced "d----d lie," upon which Mr. WISE, though the aggressor, dealt him a blow, which would probably have cost WISE his life, but for the interference of bystanders who prevented further difficulty,--WALLOP is still unredressed--and as both are men of high mettle "the end is not yet."

(794) Religious Notices. The Episcopal Church at Nags Head will be consecrated by the Bishop of the Diocese on Sunday 18th of August. Rev. George W. CARRAWAY, will preach at the Primitive Bethlehem Church, near E. City on the 21 and 22 inst.

(795) Albemarle Institute, An English and Classical Boarding and Day School, for Boys, ELIZABETH CITY, NORTH CAROLINA, George M. WILDER, *Principal*. The subscriber will open on the last Monday in September next, an Institution of the above description, designed to be permanently located at this place, affording an extensive and thorough course of instruction for boys in all the various branches of an English and Classical Education. .. The large and commodious building which has been lately repaired and put in complete order, and which has been occupied as a Hotel by Maxey SANDERLIN, Esq., has been engaged, and ample arrangements made for the accomodation of pupils from abroad to board in the family with the Principal, who has had many years' experience in the business of teaching, and having conducted an Institution of a similar character at the North, assures those who may patronize this Institution that the most watchful care will be exercised over the pupils committed to his charge. The building is located in a retired part of the Town, sufficiently removed from public view to ensure freedom from all local influences that are calculated to defeat the ends of a course of mental training. Mr. SANDERLIN and lady, who are well known in this community for their piety and moral worth, will have the charge of the Boarding department, and who will spare no pains in rendering the boarders comfortable and happy, and in furnishing as good a table as the market can afford.
    COURSE OF STUDY. First Class. Reading, Spelling, Defining, Geography, History, Arithmetic, Grammar, Penmanship, and Composition of sentences. MIDDLE CLASS. Grammar, Arithmetic, Geography, Philosophy, Ancient and Modern History, Ancient Geography, Use of Globes, Geometry, Latin, Greek, French, Algebra, Penmanship, Composition and Declamation. SENIOR CLASS. Latin, Greek, French, Algebra, Geometry, Trigonometry, Mensuration of heights and distances, Surveying, Bookkeeping, Natural, Moral, and Intellectual Philosophy, Chemistry, Geology, Astronomy, Uranography, Botany, Rhetoric, Logic, Political Economy, Composition and Declamation. .. The Principal deems it unnecessary that anything should be said here in reference to himself, having been engaged in the business of teaching for a number of years past in this place; but for the benefit of those who are unacquainted with him, he would beg leave to refer to the following gentlemen residents of E. City: Rev. W. W. KENNEDY, Rev. C. R. HENDRICKSON, R. K. SPEED, M. D., G. J. MUSGRAVE, M. D., C. C. GREEN, Col. W. G. COOK, I. FEARING, J. M. WHEDBEE, J. W. HINTON, J. C. SCOTT, John POOL, Attorney at Law, G. W. BROOKS, Attorney at Law, Hon. Wm. B. SHEPARD. Application may be made by letter to the Principal, or to any of the above Gentlemen, from whom Circulars may be obtained. George M. WILDER. Elizabeth City, August 6th, 1850.

(796) Private Residence for Sale. The subscriber will sell at public auction at the Court House door in Eliz. City, on Monday of the Superior Court in Pasquotank (the 21st of Oct.) the property upon which he now resides. This property consists of several distinct lots, which will be offered separately, viz: the lot purchased of John J. GRANDY, (upon which the dwelling house, kitchen &c. are situated, fronting on the road 219 feet and running back 160 feet, containing a very large garden and yard) will be sold by itself; likewise the brick house lot, where Ambrose KNOX formerly resided, fronting on the river 120 feet, and running back to a lane. At the same time a vacant front lot and wharf will be sold. The above property will be sold at one, two, and three years credit, for notes with approved security, interest from date. Possession to be given on the first of January next. The furniture will be disposed of afterwards either at private or public sale. Wm. B. SHEPARD. Eliz. City, August 10, 1850.

(797) NOTICE. Will be sold or leased out at Camden Court House on Tuesday of September county court, the Tavern belonging to the County. If not sold it will be leased out for three years. Terms made known on the day of sale. Miles LAMB. County Trustee. aug. 10

(798) Medical Notice. Dr. C. A. RIDDICK having located himself at the residence of Mr. Thomas HARVEY, Pasquotank County, would respectfully tender his professional services to the vicinity and public generally. He would state, that circumstances demanding his absence for the ensuing two or three weeks, he may be found at the aforementioned residence, at all times after the 1st of September next. Pasquotank, August 10, 1850.

(799) Daguerreotypes. To the Ladies and Gentleman of Elizabeth City and surrounding Country. A Daguerreotype if a good one, is a memento of all others the most appreciated. The subscriber has promised to visit Elizabeth City, and will do so about the 20th of the present month and will remain a few weeks, during which time he will be happy to accommodate all who may wish to *"Secure the shadow ere the substance fade."* ... G. W. MINNIS. Eliz. City, August 10, 1850.

10 August 1850

(800) The College of St. James, Washington Co., Maryland. The Diocesan College of the Prot. Episcopul Church. The ninth annual session will open on Monday, Oct. 7th, 1850, and continue till the next "commencement day" the last Thursday in July 1851. New students are recommended to enter at the opening of the session, but are received at any time they apply and the charge is estimated from the date of their entrance. .. In the Mercantile Classes, the study of the Greek language is omitted and its place supplied by additional studies in modern languages, Book-keeping, Statistics, &c. The location of the College is entirely healthful, and, by its distance from towns and villages, very favorable to good morals and order. The whole annual charge, the same in the College and Grammar School for the session of ten months is two hundred and twenty-five dollars, payable semi-annually in advance. Applications to be made to John B. **KERFOOT**, Rector. College of St. James, P. O. M'd. aug 10

THE OLD NORTH STATE.
"Error is harmless, when Truth is left free to combat it."
Vol. X.] Elizabeth City, N. C. Saturday, August 17, 1850. [No. 26.

(801) Elizabeth-City, August 17, 1850. .. LOST. A promissory note, drawn by Benjamin **MULLEN**, for $150, payable to the Subscriber, three months after date, interest from date, and dated between the 1st and 15th of August inst. All persons are hereby forewarned trading for said note, as the payment thereof will be stopped. Robert **WATKINS**. aug. 17

(802) TRUST SALE. By virtue of a Deed of Trust from Wm. **LABOYTEAUX** to me made, will be sold on the first Saturday in October next, before the Court House door in Elizabeth City, the Houses and lots now occupied by the said Wm. **LABOYTEAUX** at the corner of Market and Road streets, for the purposes specified in said Deed of Trust.--Terms cash. W. W. **GRIFFIN**, Trustee. August 17th, 1850.

(803) Valuable and Real Estate FOR SALE, By virtue of a Decree of the Court of Pleas and Quarter Sessions, of Chowan County, the undersigned will offer for sale before the Court House door in the town of Edenton, On the 5th day of November next, the following Real Estate of which Elizabeth L. **LITTLEJOHN** died seised: An undivided Half of that valuable Tract of Land, lying and being in the County aforesaid, known as the HOLLY GROVE TRACT, consisting of 896 acres, of which about 100 are cleared, and in a good state of cultivation. The Land is well adapted to the growing of Corn, Cotton, Peas and wheat--has a small Dwelling House on it, and all other houses that are necessary. The quality of the Land is equal to any in the County. The same estate of the said Elizabeth L. **LITTLEJOHN** in a TRACT OF LAND in Pitt County, containing about 500 Acres, lying on Swift Creek Swamp, and adjoining the lands formerly belonging to Henry **CANNON**, Dennis **CANNON** and others. The same estate of the said Elizabeth L. **LITTLEJOHN** in the following Lots or parcels of Land, in the town of Edenton, to wit: Lots Nos. 31, 32, 33, part of Lot No. 30, and one half of Lots Nos. 52, 53, 54, 55, upon which Lots Elizabeth L. **LITTLEJOHN** lived at her death. They are situated in a pleasant part of the town--have on them a large and comfortable, double two storied Dwelling House, and every other building necessary for the comfort and convenience of a family. Also, the following Lots or parcels of Land: The Tract known as the "TAN-YARD," and the Lots known in the old plan of the town by letters F and G. Of these Tracts or Lots last mentioned the said Elizabeth L. **LITTLEJOHN** died solely seised.

In all the other Tracts or parcels of Land above mentioned the undersigned is a tenant in common of one half; and she will sell her estate at the same time she disposes of the late Elizabeth L. **LITTLEJOHN** in the same--thereby conveying to the purchasers an absolute estate in all the above mentioned property. If the sale shall not be completed on the 5th day of November, it will be continued from day to day until the Lands above described shall be sold. ... Ann C. **BLOUNT**, Adm'x Edenton, Aug. 17, 1850.

THE OLD NORTH STATE.
"Error is harmless, when Truth is left free to combat it."
Vol. X.] Elizabeth City, N. C. Saturday, August 24, 1850. [No. 27.

(804) Elizabeth-City, August 24, 1850. .. (OFFICIAL.) *Report of the Superintendent of the United States Coast Survey to the Secretary of the Treasury, in relation to changes in Hatteras Inlet, North Carolina.* Coast Survey Station, July 27, 1850.} Sir--I have the honor to transmit a report by Lieut. Com'dg. R. **WAINRIGHT**, U. S. N., assistant in the Coast Survey, on the changes at the inlet South of Cape Hatteras, re-examined by my direction, and would respectfully request authority to publish the report for the benefit of navigators. The chart of the new reconnoissance will be engraved and published as soon as practicable. Very respectfully, yours, Signed, A. D. **BACHE**. *Superintendent U. S. Coast Survey.* Hon. Thomas **CORWIN**, *Secretary of the Treasury.* (COPY.) U. S. Coast Survey Office, Washington, July 26th, 1850.} Sir--I have the honor to report, that in obedience to your instructions, I made a re-examination of Hatteras Inlet in June last, and found many changes from the reconnoissance of the previous year. The entrance between the outer breakers has shifted more to the northward and eastward, and nearer the beach. The east point has washed away, and made more to the northward and eastward in Pamlico Sound. The west point has made more out

24 August 1850

(804) (Cont.) into the inlet towards the northward and eastward. There is between the outer breaker, from ten to twenty feet at mean low water, and twelve feet can be carried up to a good anchorage inside the sand spits. Six feet can be carried over bulk-head into Pamlico Sound. A sluice has opened to the northward of the east point of the inlet, which makes a good harbor for small vessels. I would not recommend buoys to be placed in the inlet, as it is not in a permanent condition, and they might therefore mislead if any change should occur. For this reason, as well as that the tide runs so strong that vessels are in danger of being swept upon the numerous sand spits or shoals, I would advise all vessels unacquainted with the inlet, to take a pilot, who may be obtained by hoisting their flag at the fore. I would recommend a buoy to be placed on Long Shoal in Pamlico Sound, to prevent vessels touching on it, and as a..guide in making for the bulk-head from the Sound side. A sketch of the reconnoissance is in progress. ..Signed, R. **WAINWRIGHT**, *Assistant Coast Survey*. Prof. A. D. **BACHE**, *Superintendent U. S. Coast Survey*.

(805) NOTICE. All who are in want of Spring and Summer Dry Goods, will do well to give the subscriber a call before purchasing elsewhere. Although his stock is much reduced, still he has on hand some desirable goods; such as brown and bleached Shirtings and Sheetings; Northern Homespuns, Sacking, Calicoes, Lawns, Gloves, Hosiery, &c. ... Jas. W. **HINTON**. E. City, August 24, 1850.

(806) Harness and Saddlery. The subscriber having taken the shop recently fitted up by Mr. Thos. B. **STUMPH** and adjoining his Livery Stables, is prepared to make or repair Harness or Saddles--to newly cover or mend Barouche or Gig Tops, and in fine to do every thing in his line with neatness and despatch. ... Robert A. **SAWYER**. Elizabeth City, August 24, 1850.

(807) BOND'S HOTEL AND STAGE OFFICE, Edenton, N. C. The undersigned takes this method of informing the public, that this well known House, has lately undergone a thorough repair, having had eleven new and comfortable rooms added to it, which in addition to the former number, makes it decidedly the most spacious and comfortable House in this section of the State,..having now thirty-seven bed rooms, mostly new, and also a good and comfortable reading room connected with the establishment. This Hotel fronts the South with a double piazza of one hundred and thirty-five feet. .. But before we conclude, we would tender our thanks to our friends for the liberal support they have extended to us for nearly seven years past. Samuel T. **BOND**, Proprietor. August 24, 1850.

(808) HOTEL NOTICE. The undersigned respectfully informs his friends and patrons, that at the solicitations of the Proprietors of the National Hotel, he will continue its management in their behalf, and endeavor to merit the liberal share of patronage which the Hotel has heretofore enjoyed and which he still solicits for it. David F. **KEELING**. Norfolk, August 24, 1850.

(809) Perquimans Male and Female Academy, HERTFORD, N. C. The exercises of this Institution will be resumed on the 1st of October under the following Board of Instruction: John **KIMBERLY**, M. A. Principal. Benj. S. **BRONSON**, B. A. Miss Caroline **SMITH**. No trouble, nor expense has been spared to secure assistance of the highest respectably. Young men may be prepared for any class in college, or they may complete the entire collegiate course at the institution. For the standing and scholarship of the students prepared for college by the Principal of this institution, reference may be had to the President and Faculty of the University of N. Carolina. The female department will be under the charge of Miss Caroline **SMITH** aided by competent assistance. In this department will be taught all the branches usually taught in Seminaries of the first class. The male and female departments are entirely disconnected, excepting, that they are under the same superintendence. The institution is furnished with every educational facility. It has a library, a very superior cabinet of minerals and an excellent chemical and philosophical apparatus, to which the pupils have free access. The academic year is divided into two sessions, of twenty weeks each. .. TERMS. FOR THE MALE DEPARTMENT. For the Primary Studies, per session, $10 For the English and Mathematical, do. 15 For the Classical with the above, do. 20 FEMALE DEPARTMENT. For the Elementary course, per session, $8 For the higher English Branches do. 12 For the Fr. and ancient Languages, each do. 5 For Music on Piano and Guitar, do. 15 For the use of Instrument, do. 2 For Drawing, Painting, needlework, do. 5 One half of the tuition fees will be required in advance, the balance at the close of the session. Interest will be charged on every account not closed at the end of a term. Circulars will be forwarded on application to Jos. M. **COX**, Hertford, N. C. .. Hertford, August 20th, 1850.

(810) University of Maryland. THE NEXT SESSION will begin on MONDAY, the 14th of October, 1850, and close 1st March, 1851. Nathan R. **SMITH**, M. D., Surgery. Wm. E. A. **AIKEN**, M. D., Chemistry and Pharmacy. Samuel **CHEW**, M. D., Therapeutics, Materia Medica and Hygiene. Joseph **ROBY**, M. D., Anatomy and Physiology. Wm. **POWER**, M. D., Theory and Practice of Medicine. Richard H. **THOMAS**, M. D., Midwifery and Diseases of Women and Children. George W. **MILTENBERGER**, M. D., Pathological Anatomy. .. Clinical Lectures four times a week, by Professors **SMITH** and **POWER**, in the Baltimore Infirmary with the privilege of daily visits to its wards without charge to the students... Fees for the Lectures $90 to $95; Practical Anatomy $10; Matriculation $5; Graduation $20. William E. A. **AIKEN**, Dean. Baltimore, August 10, 1850.

31 August 1850

THE OLD NORTH STATE.
"Error is harmless, when Truth is left free to combat it."
Vol. X.] Elizabeth City, N. C. Saturday, August 31, 1850. [No. 28.

(811) Elizabeth-City, August 31, 1850. .. The *National Intelligencer* mentions the singular fact that George Washington Parke **CURTIS**, esq., of Arlington, near this city, had just paid his respects to Mr. **FILLMORE**, the thirteenth President of the United States, and that he had shaken hands with every man who had worn that honor. ... *Union.*

(812) Young Ladies' Seminary. This Institution, under the management of Mrs. **HENDRICKSON**, will commence its Fifth session of five months in October 1, 1850. TERMS: Payable half in advance. Common English Branches, $10 00 Higher English Branches, 15 00 Latin & French, (each) 10 00 Drawing & Painting, (each) 7 00 Music on the Piano, 25 00 Embroidery included in the above. Young Ladies can be accommodated with good Board by Maxey **SANDERLIN**, Esq., for $6 00 per month.

THE OLD NORTH STATE.
"Error is harmless, when Truth is left free to combat it."
Vol. X.] Elizabeth City, N. C. Saturday, September 7, 1850. [No. 29.

(813) Neutral Ink.--Experiments have often been made with the view of producing an ink which will not be affected by acids, and which will not corrode metalic pens. Dr. W. B. **FAHNESTOCK**, of Lancaster, has succeded, after four years' experiments, in producing a neutral ink of a very fine color, which contains no acids and which acids will not erase. For manuscripts or records to be preserved, and for official papers, it is just the thing desired. We remember reading a few years ago a pamphlet by Dr. J. R. **COXE** of this city printed with an ink which he obtained by the deliquescence of a fungus which he found in Washington Square. This ink was also proof against acids, and seemed to be preserved, but probably the difficulty of obtaining the material prevented its manufacture except as an experiment. Dr. **FAHNESTOCK** seems to have hit upon something which is not liable to this objection. The proprietors of the ink are Mr. Wm. **MEESER** and Mr. Henry **GIBBS**.

(814) Elizabeth-City, September 7, 1850. .. We return our thanks to the Hon. Geo. E. **BADGER**, U. S. Sen'r, for a copy of the Report on the Finances of 1849 and 1850, as also to the Hon. Geo. **ASHMUN** of Mass., for a copy of his speech on the President's Message. Will some friend send us a copy of the speech of the Hon. Pierre **SOULE**, on the Compromise? We are pleased to see that the appointment of our friend, Geo. W. **CHARLES**, Esq., as Collector of the District of Camden, has been confirmed by the Senate, we were also pleased to notice the confirmation of Mr. Nixon **WHITE**, as purser in the Navy.

(815) An Honest Debtor.--Mr. W. T. **BUSH** combmaker, of Northboro', seven years ago failed, and was obliged to settle with his creditors for 25 cents on a dollar, promising, if ever able, to pay the balance. Yesterday he sent to each creditor the balance of his dues, with the interest due for the whole seven years. Mr. **BUSH** has been during that time doing a fair business, though he met with somewhat of a loss by fire about two years since. [*Boston Traveller.*

(816) Henry A. **SCHOOLCRAFT**, of Sacramento, California, is now on a visit to his relatives in Albany. He is about 25 years of age, and went out to California as a private soldier in Col. **STEVENSON**'s Regiment. After his discharge from the United States service, he obtained employment as bookkeeper for Capt. **SUTTER**, and has since accumulated an estate valued at $350,000. While in Captain **SUTTER**'s employ, he had at one time the paying off of 600 clerks and surveyors, not one of whom received less than $13 per day. He states that during his stay with Capt. **SUTTER**, $15,000,000 of that gentleman's money passed through his hands.

(817) DIED. Departed this life in Currituck Co., of typhus fever, on the 21st, August last, Mr. Wm. **GREGORY**, in the 22d year of his age; leaving a devoted companion to mourn her loss. He was a devoted and affectionate husband, a kind and charitable neighbor, and was generally beloved by all who knew him. **L**.

(818) JOHN J. **GRANDY**, WHOLESALE GROCER, AND COMMISSION MERCHANT, No. 10, **CAMPBELL**'s Wharf, NORFOLK, VA. Sept. 7, 1850.

(819) STATE OF NORTH CAROLINA, Currituck County. Whereas at Spring Term, of the Superior Court of Equity, for the County of Currituck, Eleanor **FISK**, wife of Martin **FISK**, filed her bill of complaint against the said Martin **FISK**, her husband; therein praying for alimony and a divorce "*a mensa et thoro*" and it appearing to the satsfaction of the Court, that the said Martin **FISK**, is not a resident of the State, it was therefore ordered, adjudged and decreed, that publicttion be made in the "Old North

7 September 1850

(819) (Cont.) State," for six weeks, for the said **FISK** to appear at the next Court of Equity, for said County, on the 6th Monday after the 4th Monday in September next, there an [sic] then to answer said bill of complaint; otherwise judgment will be rendered pro confesso. At office, Currituck Court House, Sept. 4th, 1850. Witness my hand and seal B. M. **BAXTER**, C. M. E. Sept. 7

(820) A Store for Rent at **SAWYER**s Creek. The subscriber will rent his Store out on moderate terms if application be made soon. It is not necessary to say that the stand is as good a one, as can be found in the County. For further application, apply to James M. **FEREBEE**. Currituck Co. Sept. 7

(821) NOTICE. The subscriber being desious of closing up his business, offers the Farm on which he resides, containing 336 acres, about 425 thousand of which is cleared and in a good state of cultivation. The lands is in the lower part of **DURANT**s Neck adjoining the lands of Miles **ELLIOTT**, Richard **BARCLIFT** and others. He wishes to sell at private sale but if not before the first of January he expects to sell at public sale. Terms will be accommodating. Joseph **LAYDEN**. Sept. 7th, 1850.

(822) Principe and Havanna Cigars. 2000 Star Brand Principe, 2000 Puerto " do. 1000 La norma Havanna, 5000 Half Spanish &c. All of which are for sale cheap by W. J. **KELLINGER**.

THE OLD NORTH STATE.
"Error is harmless, when Truth is left free to combat it."
Vol. X.] Elizabeth City, N. C. Saturday, September 14, 1850. [No. 30.

(823) Mass Meeting at Macon. On Thursday morning, August 22, the citizens of Georgia convened at the large and extensive warehouse of Messrs. **FIELD** and **ADAMS**, and proceeded to organize their meeting. The meeting was opened with prayer by Rev. Mr. **MARTIN**. Ex-Governor **MC DONALD** and Judge C. B. **STRONG** were appointed Presidents: Vice Presidents. H. G. **LAMAR**, of Clark; John H. **MC MATH**, of Meriwether; Gen. H. H. **TARVER**, of Twiggs; John H. **TUCKER**, of Stewart; Washington **CLEVELAND**, of Murray; Joseph L. **HELLAND**, of Jones; Dr. Wm. C. **DANIEL**, of Chatham; Allen **COCHRAN**, of Monroe; Maj. S. H. **HOWARD**, of Muscogee. Secretaries: C. A. L. **LAMAR**, of Chatham: Thomas **HARDEMAN**, Jr., of Bibb. On motion, the following gentlemen were appointed a committee to draft resolutions expressive of the sense of the meeting on the subject of the Missouri Compromise, and the Southern Question, as it now exists with Congress and the people: Col. Henry G. **LAMAR**, Chairman; S. J. **RAY**, of Bibb; Col. **HOWARD**, of Crawford; Mr. **RAMSEY**, of Harris; and Mr. **MOULTRIE**, of Bibb.
During the absence of the Committee, the meeting was addressed by Hon. R. B. **RHETT**, of South Carolina, in an eloquent and patriotic speech, insisting on Southern rights, the Missouri Compromise to the 36 deg. 30 min., as the ultimatum; rallying the people to stand up to their principles and to defend their rights as attempted to be invaded by Congress, the Administration, and the North, to the last extremity. The speech was loudly applauded throughout; three hearty cheers were given at the conclusion by the meeting. The following are the resolutions reported by the Committee: *Resolved*, That we approve the Resolutions and Address of the Nashville Convention, and recommend them to the cordial support of the people of Georgia. *Resolved*, That in recommending the people of Georgia to acquiesce in the application of the Missouri Compromise line of 36 deg. 30 min. to the Territories of the United States, with the recognition of slavery south of that line, we propose the acquiescence for the sake of the peace of the country, and the preservation of the Union. *Resolved*, That it is the Constitutional right of the citizen to be protected in the enjoyment, in the public territory, of any property which, by the laws of the State of which he is an inhabitant, he is authorized to own; and to withold from him this protection, is to debar him of a constitutional right. *Resolved*, That the admission of California into the Union, with her pretended organization, will be the sanction of the most unjustifiable aggressions of intruders upon the public Treasury, on the rights of fifteen sovereign States of this Union. *Resolved*, That the Territorial policy of a majority of the two Houses of Congress, is to prevent, forever, the admission of another slave State into the Union, subvert the rights of the South in the public territories, and eventually to abolish slavery in the States; thus converting a Government which was established for the protection of all, into an engine of attack and spoliation of a portion of its members. *Resolved*, That we invite those who meditate these aggressions, to pause before they perpetrate a wrong which they cannot remedy, and to which a people having the spirit of freemen will never submit. *Resolved*, That should the event occur in which it shall become the duty of the Governor, under the direction of the last Legislature, to call a convention of the people of Georgia, to consider of the necessary measures of safety to the State, it is the opinion of the meeting that our Senators and Representatives in Congress should immediately return to their States, and unite with their constituents in consultation and action on such measures... *Resolved*, That the message of President **FILLMORE** to Congress, strongly intimating his determination, by force of arms, to prevent a sovereign member of the confederacy from enforcing its laws in territory which it *bona fide* claims to be within its boundary, is without warrant in the Constitution or laws, and if he attempts to carry his purpose into effect, the public liberty and the safety of the Constitution demand that his conduct should be investigated at the instance of the branch of this government holding the power of impeachment... After

14 September 1850

(823) (Cont.) reading of the resolution, Hon. Mr. **YANCY** of Alabama, was called to the stand, and attracted the attention of the meeting in an eloquent speech of an hour and a half in length. .. Mr. **COCHRAN**, of Alabama, next took stand, and followed in the strain of the former speaker. The meeting then adjourned for dinner. At three o'clock the meeting convened, and Hon. W. T. **COLQUITT** took the stand. He enlisted the attention of the audience for some time in his usual interesting manner. The resolution [sic] were adopted by acclamation, and the meeting adjourned at six o'clock. ...

(824) Elizabeth-City, September 17 [sic,] 1850. .. GREAT NEWS. The glorious news from Washington City of the passage on Friday last, of the Texas Boundary Bill, conjointly with that providing a Territorial Government for New Mexico, followed up as this action was on Saturday by the passage of the Bill, admitting California as a State, and that establishing a government for Utah, has put us in too good a humor to exult over a defeated foe. ...

(825) The *Washington Republic* of this morning has the following announcement: The circumstances which led lo the change in the editorial department of the *Republic* in May last, no longer existing, the undersigned cheefully surrenders to John O. **SARGENT** Esq., one of its able founders, the future control of its columns. Allen A. **HALL**.

(826) A. C. **BULLITT**, Esq., one of the editors of the *Picayune*, and recently of the *Washington Republic*, and who is now on a visit to Europe, is spoken of in the New Orleans papers as a candidate to fill the vacancy in the House of Representatives occasioned by the resignation of Mr. **CONRAD**.

(827) Religious Notice. Mr. Editor:--Please insert the following appoinments for the 4th Quarterly Meetings on the Norfolk District. Hertford, at Evans Sept. 21 and 22; Edenton Sept. 28 and 29; Pasquotank at New Hope Oct 4 and 5; Eastville at Johnsonton Oct. 11 and 12; Gates at **FLETCHER**'s Chapel Oct. 18 and 19; Elizabeth City Oct. 26 and 27; Camden at MC BRIDEs Nov. 2 and 3. Jas. D. **COULLING** P. E.

(828) $20 reward. A black Mare belonging to the subscriber, was stolen from the pasture of Wm. H. **DAVIS**, Esq., in the lower part of this county, in the latter part of July last. The hind hoofs of the mare are turned considerably in, and she had a white spot on her neck just below her left ear--she was suckling a colt about 3 months old at the time she was taken. The mare is the same driven by me, for the last three years, previous to last fall. I will pay a reward of $20 for her delivery to me in E. City, and $10 additional for the apprehension of the thief. G. W. **BROOKS**. Sept. 14, 1850.

THE OLD NORTH STATE.
"Error is harmless, when Truth is left free to combat it."
Vol. X.] Elizabeth City, N. C. Saturday, September 21, 1850. [No. 31.

(829) Elizabeth-City, September 21, 1850. .. DEDICATION. The new church edifice lately built at South Mills, Camden county, by the Church at **SPENCE**'s, will be opened for the worship of God, on the 4th Lord's day in September. The Dedication sermon will be preached at 11 o'clock, A. M., by C. R. **HENDRICKSON**, Pastor of the E. City Baptist Church. The meeting will continue several days.

(830) The freshet in North Carolina.--*Scarcity of Breadstuffs*.--Our Southern exchanges generally, from Virginia to Florida, teem with the destruction to bridges, roads and crops by the late freshets. The farmers in North Carolina, however, on the Roanoke especially, appear to be the greatest sufferers, and a very short supply of breadstuffs is anticipated. The *Weldon Herald*, of the 5th, says: "We think two hundred thousand barrels of corn besides cotton, wheat, hogs, &c., a very moderate calculation of the loss occasioned by the freshet, which is the greatest that has been known in our day, at least." .. The freshet, so far as we have been able to learn was universal on the Roanoke, from beginning to end, and the loss sustained by farmers and others beyond conception. In short, we may say, that the rich Roanoke low grounds have been swept completely, from the mountains to the seaboard, with the single exception of Mr. James C. **JOHNSTON**'s lands, whose low grounds were *efficiently* protected by well-built dams. The loss in Halifax will not fall short of 150,000 bushels of corn, while that of Northampton must exceed that amount, as there has been no exception like that of Mr. **JOHNSTON** in that county. ..

We give below, says the *Halifax* (N. C.) *Republican*, the names of the most important Farmers in our immediate neighborhood and vicinity, who have suffered by the Freshet. N. M. **LONG**, 3 or 4000 Barrels. D. W. L. **LONG**, 1 or 2000. Estate A. A. **AUSTIN**, 2000. Col. A. **JOYNER**, 1 or 2000. Mrs. **EPPS**, 1 or 2000. John **PONTON**, 500. J. J. **LONG**, 2 or 3000. W. A. **DANIEL**, 1000, or 1500. W. H. **GRAY**, 1000 or 1500. John H. **FENNER**, 1000 or 1500. Gen'l. **PERSONS**, 1 or 2000. J. J. **BELL**, 1 or 2000. T. P. **BURGWYN**, 2000 to 2500. H. K. **BURGWYN**, 2000 to 2500. W. H. **DAY**, 1000. D. **CLANTON**, 500. P. S.--We regret to learn that in addition to loss of Crop, Mr. T. P. **DEVEREUX**, lost a considerable quantity of live stock.

21 September 1850

(831) Appointment by the President. *By and with the advice and consent of the Senate.* Alexander H. **STUART**, of Va., to be Secretary of the Interior, vice Thomas M. T. **MC KENNAN**, resigned. .. Mr. **STUART** is one of the most prominent and efficient members of the Whig party in this State. He was on the **HARRISON** and **TAYLOR** Whig Electoral ticket of Virginia, and proved himself, in the discussion between the orators of the two parties, one of the ablest, best-informed, and most eloquent of the champions of Whig principles. When a member of the Virginia Legislature, he occupied a high station as a statesman and as a debater. He was elected a member of the House of Representatives from the Augusta district in 1841, and soon acquired a national reputation in that body, by his services in effecting an organization of the House, after weeks of confusion, and by a uniform ability, tact, eloquence, and dignified and courteous bearing. ...

(832) A LUMP OF GOLD. The wife of Mr. Solomon **GEER**, residing a few miles from this place, found a lump of gold on the day of the big rain, or the day after, which weighed *sixty pennyweights*! It was lying in the edge of the spring branch when she discovered it, the rain having washed the dirt off it, and left its tempting beauty bare. *Mountain Banner*.

(833) Fugitive Arrested.--In April last a jewelry store at Wilmington, N. C., was entered and robbed, and two men named James, alias Edward **COLE**, and ---- **WALTON**, were arrested on the charge of committing the burglary. The stolen goods were found on them, and they were committed to jail, but on the 13th of the same month, together with a colored man, succeeded in breaking out. Officer Thos. **GORMAN**, of this city, having ascertained the retreat of **COLE**, proceeded to Philadelphia last week and arrested him. On Saturday last he was brought on to Baltimore and committed by Justice **GRAY** to await the requisition of the Governor of North Carolina.--*Balt. Sun*.

(834) NOTICE. Absconded from my employment, my indented apprentice Quinton **UPTON**, who left my employment without the least provacation.--He was raised in Camden County, N. C., whither I supposed he has gone. I forewarn any person or persons from employment or harboring him.--I will give the sum of five dollars to any person who may detect the one who may so offend the law, so that I may bring the offender to justice. Thomas S. **MAYER**. Sept. 21.

(835) ALBEMARLE INSTITUTE. Pupils will be received into the Primary Department of the Institute at $3 per quarter. It is desirable that students designing to connect themsleves with the school should be present, if possible, at the opening of the Primary, English and Classical Departments on the 30th of September, in order that the classes may be formed to the best advantage. Books can be obtained in town at reasonable prices. G. M. **WILDER**, Principal. E. City, Sept. 21, 1850.

THE OLD NORTH STATE.
"Error is harmless, when Truth is left free to combat it."
Vol. X.] Elizabeth City, N. C. Saturday, September 28, 1850. [No. 32.

(836) Elizabeth-City, September 28, 1850. .. DEATH OF THE KENTUCKY FAT BOY.--Andrew **BRAND**, the Kentucky Fat Boy, died in this city this morning after an illness of about four weeks. He was a native of the town of Calhoun, Davis county, Ky., and was in the sixteenth year of his age. He probably was the largest human being in existence, weighing no less than 537 pounds. He came to this city for the purpose of attending the State Fair, but was immediately attacked with his last illness. He was accompanied by a brother and other friends, and everything that human wisdom could suggest was done to prolong his existence and alleviate his sufferings.--*Albany Altas*, Wednesday.

(837) THE FIRST DRAYMAN.--The first person who ever drove a dray in Cincinnati, is now living in Newport Ky. There were no wagon makers among us in early day when he opened in the business, and the vehicle was of his own construction.--The shafts were made of saplings, the axle-tree of a hickory log, and the wheels were made of the rounds of a sycamore stump sawed to the thickness of about 4 inches, and tired. Instead of a horse he drove an ox, harnessed up with a raw bull hide. What a sight that old dray would be now, and, if it existed, its primitive rudeness would command veneration.--The name of the pioneer drayman is Elijah **PIERCE**.--*Cincinnati Commercial*.

(838) The Dead of 1850.--The list of persons of note who have deceased during the first half of the present year embraces many distinguished names. We notice some of them: John C. **CALHOUN**, Franklin E. **ELMORE**, Sargeant S. **PRENTISS**, Daniel P. **KING**, Zachary **TAYLOR**, Brig. General **MASON**, Commodore **JONES**, J. Newland **MAFFIT**, Adam **RAMAGE**, S. Margaret **FULLER**, Emperor of China, Sir Robert **PEEL**, Duke of Chambridge, and President **BOYNER**. *Albany Register*.

(839) DIED. "Blessed are the dead who die in the Lord." Of a painful and lingering illness, which he bore with christian fortitude, Samuel M. **LEWIS** departed this life on the 13th inst., in the 29th year of his age, leaving an affectionate mother and sister to

28 September 1850

(839) (Cont.) mourn their loss in the death of an exemplary member of the Protestant Episcopal Church.

(840) CHAIRS, FURNITURE, &c., ALWAWS ON HAND, CHEAP. By an arrangement with Manufacturers, we are enabled to furnish almost any article that may be called for in the CHAIR AND FURNITURE LINE, at the very lowest prices... The following are some of the leading articles, viz: Wood, Cane and Hair Seat Chairs, various patterns and style of finish, and Rocking Chairs to suit, Children's Chairs, Bureaus, Sideboards, Tables, Sofas, Wash Stands, Cots, Bedsteads, Looking Glasses, Mattresses, Beds, Wood and Cane Seat Stools, Feathers, Office Chairs, Safes, Cribs, Cushions, Clocks, Hat Racks, Secretaries and Book Cases. Orders from Town or Country promptly attended to. J. H. & Jos. **NASH**. Near the Ferry Wharf. Norfolk, Sept. 28th

THE OLD NORTH STATE.
"Error is harmless, when Truth is left free to combat it."
Vol. X.] Elizabeth City, N. C. Saturday, October 5, 1850. [No. 33.

(841) Elizabeth-City, October 5, 1850. .. By the Census recently taken by Wm. **NEWBOLD**, Esq., Assistant Marshal we find the total population of the County of Pasquotank to be 8,918. Of which 5,834 are free inhabitants, and 3,103 are slaves. The exact number of free negroes we have not learned. The population of E. City and surburbs numbers nearly two thousand.

(842) P, M. W. P. Philip S. **WHITE**. Having been requested to make some appointments for Brother **WHITE**, after the adjournment of the Grand Division, after consultation with some of the brethren in the East, we have determined upon making the following: Edenton, Monday 28th at night. Hertford, Perq. Wednesday 30th Woodville, Thursday 31st. Elizabeth City Nov. 1st at night. Camden C. Ho. do. 2d and at night in E. City. Plymouth on the 4th of November. Bro. **WHITE** is travelling for the good of the Order, and visits this State by invitation; and as he is under no salary, it is expected that wherever he may lecture, there will be contributions raised to pay his expenses and remunerate him for his services. *Spirit of the Age.*

(843) Wm. M. **BURWELL**, Esq. This gentleman has entered upon active duties as one of the Editors of the *Washington Republic*. Mr. **B**. is a racy as well as a ready writer.--*Rich. Republican.*

(844) THE FIRST ARREST UNDER THE FUGITIVE SLAVE BILL, &c. New York, Sept. 28. The first arrest under the Fugitive Slave Bill, recently passed by Congress, was made in this city to-day. It appears that a lady of Baltimore, Md, named Mary **BROWN**, owned a number of slaves, among whom was one named Jas. **HAMLET**, who took it into his head to flee to New York two years ago, since which time he has been living in this city. Mrs. **BROWN** gave up all hopes of reclaiming him but as soon as possible after the passage of the act referred to, she instituted measures to secure him. She sent on proofs of ownership, and a warrant was issued for the arrest of the slave yesterday. Mr. **BROWN**, the deputy marshal, took the matter, in hand, and took him into custody in Water street. He was immediately conveyed before Mr. **GARDNER**, the United States Commisioner, and his identity proven by Mrs. **BROWN**'s son and son-in-law. An order was immediately issued for his return, and in all probability he is now on his way to Baltimore. When **HAMLET** was arrested, he gave a signal to a number of colored persons in the neighborhood, and but for the presence of a number of officers, he would have been taken from the Deputy Marshal by force. There is a very great excitement among our colored population on the subject, and several hundred are now around the Tombs, imagining that **HAMLET** is confined there. ...

(845) Married. On Thursday night 3d inst., by S. Davis **GRICE**, Esq., Mr. Norris **LOVETT** to Miss Mary **RIGGS**, all of this County.

(846) DIED. Thomas, youngest son of Mr. Barnard **BERRY**, died at his father's residence on the 27th of September, after an illness of six days--aged 3 years 8 months and 27 days. He was a most lovely child...

(847) Emporium of Elegance and FASHION! The season has again arrived when the Subscriber is enabled to show to the public a NEW, RICH and SELECT stock of Staple and Fancy Dry Goods! ... Jas. W. **HINTON**. Oct. 5, 1850.

(848) NOTICE. My wife Mary Jane having left my house and taken with her my children--all persons are hereby forwarned against rendering her aid, and protection under the penalty of the law or giving her any credit upon my account, as no bills contracted by her will be pad. Jas. M. **FEREBEE**. Currituck, Oct. 5.

(849) Sundries received..today. 67 boxes Soap, 25 do. Mould Candles, 35 doz. Brooms, 48 nests Covered Buckets, 30 Cases Boots and Shoes, 5 do. highly polished Rubbers, also Mustard, Extract Lemon, Brick Dust, Chocolate, Wrapping Twine, Shoe

5 October 1850

(849) (Cont.) Brushes, &c. E. GURNEY, CHERRY & FERRALL's warehouse, Commerce Street. Norfolk, Oct. 2.

(850) The subscriber has taken the second floor of Messrs. CHERRY & FERRALL's warehouse, on Commerce Street, and offers for sale a well selected stock of Boots, Shoes, Sole Leather, Shovels Spades, Cut Nails, Covered Buckets, Painted Pails and Tubs... E. GURNEY. Norfolk, Oct. 5.

THE OLD NORTH STATE.
"Error is harmless, when Truth is left free to combat it."
Vol. X.] Elizabeth City, N. C. Saturday, October 12, 1850. [No. 34.

(851) Elizabeth-City, October 12, 1850. .. NOTICE. The Members of the Nag's Head Convention are expected to meet, pursuant to adjournment at Edenton on Thursday the 7th of next month. ... A. JOYNER, President.

(852) JULIA AND JENNY [sic.] Julia DEAN, a charming actress, has got the enthusiasm of the West in her favor, and at St. Louis, on the 22d ult, there was so much competition for seats at her benefit that the auctioneer's hammer had to settle the matter. As high as nine dollars premium was paid.

(853) The *Raleigh Standard* is mourning over the removal of a Democrat from the "petty" Collectorship of Windsor, and the substitution of a Whig in his place, hear him: "We learn that Mr. John S. SHEPARD, Democrat, has been removed from his post as Collector at Windsor, in this State, and Mr. G. W. MCLAUGHON, Whig, put in his place. ...

(854) TERRIBLE COLLISION AT SEA. We published, on Saturday, a telegraphic report of the terrible collision between the U. S. steamship Southerner and the bark Isaac Meade, which resulted in the loss of that vessel, with fourteen of her passengers and eight of her crew. The accident occurred on Friday at 2 o'clock, A. M., in latitude 38° 39', according to the log, when the wind was blowing a gale to the north, and the sea was high. A sail was described on the larboard bow of the steamer, when her helm was put hard a-port and the engine backed, but unfortunately the bark, supposing the steamer to be a ship standing in to the shore, put her helm to the starboard to cross the steamer's bows, when she was struck and sunk in less than five minutes. .. The bark was struck by the Southerner full in the bowsprit, which was driven in like a wedge, and split the vessel open in front. On board the steamer the shock was scarcely felt, while the bark was sent under almost instantaneously. .. Mr. STANTON, one of the passengers, who was on deck when the contact took place, immediately ascended one of the masts, but was washed loose before he could reach the top. Another person, Mrs. BRADLEY, who occupied a cabin on deck was seized by her husband, who happened to be awake, and hurried out a back entrance of the cabin, but before they could gain the deck, they were washed away by the sea. Mr. BRADLEY was afterwards saved. As the steamer was making shallow water, Captain BERRY had been fortunately called, and was on deck at the time of the accident. .. Cap. BERRY gives great credit to Capt. J. C. BERRY, Capt. LEUBECH, Thomas VAIL, and his crew generally, for their efforts to save life. .. The Isaac Mead was built by Jabez WILLIAMS, in Williamsburgh, in 1841, was of three hundred and eighty-four tons burthen, and was insured for $19,500. The freight was insured for $1,000.--*Balt. Pat.*

(855) SHOOTING IRONS. The subscriber has on hand a few fine double barrel Guns, which he will sell low. R. WHITE. E. City, Oct. 12, 1850.

(856) MRS. ANN BELL, Has just returned from the North with a new stock of Millinery goods which she will take pleasure in accommodating the public with, at her old stand. E. City, Oct. 12.

(857) List of Letters Remaining in the Post Office, at Elizabeth City, Quarter ending 30th Sept. 1850. ARMOUR Capt Benj. Artist Daguerotypes BALLANCE Capt. H. BALL, J. J. BARBEE E. BRYANT Wm. T. BENBURY Miss Penny BANKS Miss Mary E. BANKS Wm. F. BENBURY Richard BULLOCK Benj. K. BUNDY Elizabeth Ann BAITMAN Joseph BENTLY James BANKS Andrew BAKER Andrew COPES Capt. Peter 3 CARVER Elias CASEY Caroline V. CARTWRIGHT Langstor DOLL Rev. Penfield DELONG Harvey DOWSON Mrs. Kesiah DILLARD Miss E. M. GODFREY Mary GLASS Jos. Wirt GRANT Rev. W. HINTON Wm. S. HARVEY Miss Margaret HASKET Henry HOLT Samuel HARRIS Grandy JENNINGS Nathan JOHNSTON Lucius JOHNSTON Cornelia 2 JACKSON Hezekiah JONES Wm. KONE Rev. W. 2 MULLEN Miss Mary L. MULLEN Dr. MUNDEN Thos. R. MOORE Mrs. Susan J. MORRIS & STONE MILLER Thos. J. MOSELY Tully LEE Capt. Doxey 2 LUTTS Mrs Charlotte LONG Wm. LAMB Alfred LEE Nancy OVERMAN Nathan PIKE Kesiah PERKINS Mrs. M. C. REID Edwin 2 REED Mrs. Nancy RUDDOCK Nicy RULON John H. RUSSELL Jos. D. REED Margaret REID Miss M. A. 2 TUTTLE John M. TROTMAN Rev. Q. H. TAYLOR Miss Mahaly TILLETT Thomas Esq. TURNER Andrew TOMS Lemuel THOMAS Charles STANTON Isaac

12 October 1850

(857) (Cont.) SMITH John SHANNONHOUSE B. J. STONE Dr. G. W. SAWYER Mrs. Lydia SMITHSON David SPENCER J. S. SIMONS Frank SPRUILL Benjamin WILLIAMS Enoch WHITE Henry H. Persons calling for any of the above letters will please say they are advertised. Wm. E. MANN, P. M. Oct. 12

(858) MESS PORK. Just received, and for sale 50 barrels of New York City inspected Mess Pork, by Robinson WHITE. E. City, Oct. 12.

THE OLD NORTH STATE.
"Error is harmless, when Truth is left free to combat it."
Vol. X.] Elizabeth City, N. C. Saturday, October 19, 1850. [No. 35.

(859) Elizabeth-City, October 19, 1850. .. DELEGATES TO THE NAG'S HEAD CONVENTION. As we promised in our last paper, we give to-day the names of the Delegates from this County to the Nag's Head Convention. .. Hon. Wm. B. SHEPARD, Dr. SPEED, Gen. EHRINGHAUS, Jos. H. POOL, John POOL, Capt. Wm. SIMMONS, Wm. F. MARTIN, Dr. GRICE, Wm. SHANNON, Addison WHEDBEE, Dr. R. H. RAMSAY, Seth MORGAN, Geo. D. POOL, Mark S. SAWYER, John A. WARROCK, John C. EHRINGHAUS, Wm. H. DAVIS, Jr., Jos. R. PARKER, Thos. GASKINS, Gilbert ELLIOT, Joshua A. POOL, G. W. BROOKS, Thomas HARVEY, Jos. MULLEN, Thos. D. KNOX, John BLACK, Wm. E. MANN, Job CARVER, Wm. S. HINTON, Geo: W. HINTON, Jos. PRITCHARD, Elias CARVER; Edgar L. HINTON, Jos. B. REED, John F. BUTT, John SMALL, Jas. E. WEEKS, Francis A. BROTHERS, Dr. O. F. BAXTER, Daniel SAWYER, Caleb L. WHITEHURST, Stephen D. POOL, Willet HERRINGTON, Thaddeus F. BANKS, Robt. PENDLETON, James BANKS, Doctrine R. PERRY, F. S. PROCTOR, Geo. A. WILLIAMS, Shadrach D. CARTWRIGHT, Jas. L. MULLEN, W. W. GRIFFIN, John L. HINTON, John J. GRANDY, Arthur JONES, and John THOMPSON.

(860) OLD POINT HOTEL.--The *Portsmouth* (Va.) *Pilot* says The Old Point Hotel has changed hands! Our old friend Colonel J. S. FRENCH has sold out his magnificent Hotel establishment (at a high figure) to Mr. MEHAFFY, of Gosport Irons Works, Joseph P. REYNOLDS, late of California, and Mr. J. C. WESTON, of this county. ...

(861) Picture of General WASHINGTON.--Miss STUART, a daughter of the distinguished artist, Gilbert STUART, has, at the request of a number of Californians, copied her father's celebrated likeness of WASHINGTON for the Senate of California.

(862) Mr. HARRIS, the editor of the *Brattleboro' Eagle*, has been sued for a libel by Obadiah H. PRATT, who lays his damages at $3,000. The affair has grown out of the MINER and LYMAN quarrel in the Congressional District. *N. Y. Cour. & Enq.*, 10th.

(863) NOTICE Is hereby given to all whom it may concern that the subscriber will petition the next Legislature for an extention of his Charter of the Parkville road, granted last session, from the head of Little River, near Parksvill [sic,] to John SPEIGHT's in Perquimans County, down the road cut by Aaron ALBERSTON. W. R. ABBOTT. Oct. 19, 1850.

(864) OLD THINGS PASS AWAY. .. The subscriber..hereby tenders a goodly quantity of heartfelt gratitude to the public for past patronage, and..promising to sell the goods enumerated in the annexed catalogue at the VERY LOWEST PRICES. The following.. may be found in the subscriber's warehouse, to wit: Chairs of all kinds from $7 to $40 per doxen, Rocking do; High Post Bed Steads..Bureaus; Side Boards; Divans; Sofas..Portable Wash Stands; Work Stands; Candle do; Book Cases, &c. &c. ... Caleb SIKES. Oct. 19, 1850.

(865) Desirable Property for Sale. The subscriber offers for sale his house and lots situated in the town of Hertfod N. C. The property is located in the central [sic] of the town, and comprises three half acre lots, bounded on two sides by the most public streets running through the town, and on the back by the river which is easy of access and affords a beautiful view from the dwelling. The house is a large commodious and elegant building two stories high with a well finished garret, and convenient closets--disposed in various parts of the house. It is built of the finest and best materials, entirely new, having been occupied but little over two years--and is one of the most desirable residence [sic] in the section of the country--no village in the state offers superior advantages and respect to locality, society and facilities for education. The situation holds out flattering inducements to a skilful physician to locate, and any person desirous of a pleasant and handsome residence and a home in an intelligent moral and refined community--can in this opportunity find a consumation of his wishes. The terms will be made to suit the convenience of the purchaser. The furniture and other house-keeping articles (perfectly new) will be disposed of with the house if desired. If not disposed of before that time by private contract, the property will be sold at public sale on the 11th day of November next. Enquire of Dr. N. C. SKINNER at Hertford. N. C. SKINNER. Oct. 19.

19 October 1850

(866) Night School. Having been solicited to do so, I intend to open next Monday evening, at the Academy, a night School for the benefit of the young men and apprentices of the place, whose business pursuits prevents them from attending a day school. Reading, Writing, Arithmetic, Grammar and Geography will be taught. Terms, 11 weeks, $5. S. D. **POOL**. Oct. 19.

(867) NEW GOODS! The Subscriber having recently returned from the North now offers..a RARE, CHOICE, and SELECT assortment of GOODS. His Stock of Dry Goods is large and varied, while his other assortment of READY MADE CLOTHING, BOOTS & SHOES, HARDWARE, GROCERIES, Paints, Oils, &c, is of the most ample kind. ... T. R. **COBB**. oct 19

(868) PUBLIC ATTENTION SOLICITED! READY MADE CLOTHING! The subscriber has in store an excellent assortment of Ready Made Clothing of the latest and most approved styles. .. Through this medium the subscriber returns his thanks to the public for the liberal encouragement he has hitherto received in the Tailoring business, and begs leave to solicit a continuance of the same. All are invited to call at the store nearly opposite Messrs. Jas. M. **WHEDBEE** & Bro. and a few doors below Jas. W. **HINTON**'s Dry Good Store, which place they will find the subscriber all attention. Leonard **CHAPMAN**. E. City, Oct. 19.

THE OLD NORTH STATE.
"Error is harmless, when Truth is left free to combat it."
Vol. X.] Elizabeth City, N. C. Saturday, October 26, 1850. [No. 36.

(869) Elizabeth-City, October 26, 1850. .. OUR SUPERIOR COURT. The Fall Term of our Superior Court, Judge **CALDWELL** presiding, is now in session. Yesterday, George **FOX** was tried before his Honor on a charge of murdering, about 10 months ago, Jackson **PUGH**--the Jury has returned a verdict of manslaughter, against him. John **EVANS**, a white man, convicted of stealing a *goose*, was on Thursday last, sentenced by Judge **CALDWELL**, to receive thirty-nine lashes. He underwent the sentence of the law, yesterday. ...

(870) DOMESTIC MANUFACTURES. The *Charleston Mercury* says: "We have received from Mr. John H. **STEIMEYER** a sample of Broom Corn, raised on his farm in St. Andrew's Parish, and also a sweeping Broom manufactured at the same place, which in appearance and durability will contrast most favorably with any imported from the North. .. We also learn that Henry S. **TEW** of Mount Pleasant, Christ Church Parish, has engaged in the cultivation of Broom Corn, and has established a Broom Factory, from which he has already forwarded specimens of his manufacture to this City. He also contemplates the establishment of a Bucket Factory. ..."--[*Rich. Rep.*

(871) TEMPERANCE LECTURE. On Friday last, Philip S. **WHITM**, esq., late head of the Order of the Sons of Temperance in the United States, delivered two lectures to the citizens of Hillsborough and its vicinity, which surpassed, perhaps, any thing of the kind ever heard by our citizens. ... --*Hillsborough Recorder*.

(872) DIED. At Portsmouth, N. C., Capt. Samuel **WALLACE** aged about 38. Capt. W. left this place in good health on board his vessel for a voyage to New York. On reaching Portsmouth he was taken down with bilious fever and died in eight days. He was much respected while living, and his death is greatly deplored. He left a wife and children.--*N. State Whig*. He was buried by the Sons of Temperance and Odd Fellows.

(873) LARGE SALE OF LAND, NEGROES, STOCK, &C. On Thursday, the 28th day of November next, I shall offer for sale all of my LAND, lying in Currituck County, together with all of my NEGROES, STOCK, Farming Utensils and a large and commodious Store at **SAWYER**'s Creek. Also a Lighter that will carry about 100 barrels. The land is of good quality, and among the Negroes are some excellent farm hands. Terms of sale and further particulars will be made known on the day of sale. The sale will take place at my residence. James M. **FEREBEE**. Currituck County, Oct. 26th, 1850.

(874) WRECK SALE. Will be sold, on Monday 28th inst., on the sea beach, near Old Currituck Inlet, the hull of the ship Louisa, and materials. Said ship is coppered and copper fastened. Also as much of her cargo as may be saved consisting of Dry Goods, Hard and Glass ware, and sundry other articles, &c. &. Said ship (**LOHMANN** master) was wrecked on a voyage from Bremen for Baltimore. Sale will commence at 12, o'clock M. Sold for benefit of owners or underwriters. By Jno. M. **JONES**, Comme'r. of Wrecks. Currituck County, Oct. 26.

(875) MANTUA MAKING. Miss Laura **WHITING** of Norfolk respectfully informs the Ladies of Elizabeth City, and vicinity that she is now prepared to execute Mantua Making in all its branches and in the most fashionable manner, she can be found at the residence of George W. **KELLINGER**. Oct. 26, 1850.

26 October 1850

(876) SONS OF TEMPERANCE. There will be a public meeting of Pasquotank Division No. 21 Sons of Temperance, at the Baptist Church, on the first and second nights of November next. Past Most Worthy Patriarch, Philip S. **WHITE**, is expected to address the Division and the public generally on the subject of Temperance. Mr. **WHITE** is at head of the order in America, and we have been informed that he is a lawyer of eminence in Philadelphia, and a very interesting speaker... Exercises to commence at 7 o'clock. L. C. **SCOTT**, J. W. **HINTON**, G. M. **WILDER**,} Committee of Arrangements.

(877) **MURRAY & CLARK**, MILLWRIGHTS & MACHINISTS, Elizabeth City, N. C. We are pleased to observe that a gradual increase of the spirit of domestic patronage is manifesting itself in our community. Among others we can boast of its beneficial effects, and would here tender thanks to our patrons, soliciting a continuance of their favors so long as we continue to merit them.

(878) STATE OF NORTH CAROLINA. Pasquotank County. Court of Pleas and Qr. Sessions--Sept. Term, 1850. Legatees & Devisees of John **BAILEY** Senior vs. The heirs at Law of John **BAILEY**.} Issue Deviravet vel non. It appearing to the satisfaction of the Court, that John **HODGES** and Artimesia, formerly Artimesia **BAILEY**, defendants in this case are not inhabitants or residents of this State, it is ordered by the Court that publication be made for six weeks in the "Old North State" newspaper, published in the town of Elizabeth City, that the said John **HODGES** and wife may appear at the next term of this Court, to be held on the first Monday in December next, then and there to plead, answer or demur, or judgment pro confesso will be entered as to them. Witness, William W. **GRIFFIN**, Clerk of the said Court, at Elizabeth City, the first Monday in Sept. 1850. Wm. W. **GRIFFIN**, Cl'k. oct 22

THE OLD NORTH STATE.
"Error is harmless, when Truth is left free to combat it."
Vol. X.] Elizabeth City, N. C. Saturday, November 2, 1850. [No. 37.

(879) Elizabeth-City, November 2, 1850. .. A TURNIP--BEAT IT IF YOU CAN. We were presented on Tuesday last, by James M. **FEREBEE**, Esq., with a turnip that was a turnip. It weighed five pounds and measured 2 feet one and a half inches round. It was first rate--can't some one else do so? If you have no large ones, send in the small, we can judge of the quality just as well.

(880) NAG'S HEAD CONVENTION. This body meets in Edenton on Thursday next. We hope all the delegates from this and the other counties will be in attendance. We see by the last Edenton paper that ample arrangements will be made to accommodate all who may be present. T. S. **HOSKINS**, Esq. who lives near Edenton after giving us an invitation to stop at his house, said "please state in your paper that my house is open to all who may call, that the latch string will be found on the out side."

(881) "HOME GUARDS." We are pleased to learn that a volunteer corps of Infantry has been organized in our town with the above title. The company numbers, at the present, 28 members, which number is daily on the increase. At an election of Officers last Wednesday night week, the following were chosen for one year: J. C. B. **EHRINGHAUS**, Capt. Wm. F. **MARTIN**, 1st Lieutenant, Wm. E. **MANN**, 2d Lieutenant, John M. **MATHEWS**, 3d Lieutenant, Wm. J. **KELLINGER**, 4th Lieutenant, Wm. R. **CARSON**, 1st Sergeant, Jas. W. **HINTON**, 2d Sergeant. .. Some of our citizens, too old themselves to enlist, but recollecting the military ardor of their youth, have kindly offered to equip others, who are unable to purchase their own uniforms. ...

(882) MESSRS. **CABELL** AND **BEARD**. We find the following "pair of declarations" in several of our exchanges: "In the *Florida Republican*, of the 15th inst., (August) I am charged with the Declaration *that I would prefer a* Dissolution of the Union *to the passage of the late bill, now no more, which was misnamed the Compromise Bill.* I acknowledge the declaration, and shall plead justification. John **BEARD**." "Major **BEARD** is for '*dissolution of the Union*' because of the passage of the Texas Boundary, California and Territorial Bills, which together make up the 'Omnibus' or Compromise Bill. I am not.--*The issues are* Union or Dinunion--I am for Union. E. C. **CABELL**." The opinion of these two men are directly antagonistical. The people of Florida at whose hands they were seeking the gift of a seat in the House of Representatives, having demanded of them an expression of their views of the measures of the late Congress, each declares them in the above manner. ... --*Wilmington Aurora.*

(883) President **FILLMORE** was expected to have been present at the Fair yesterday, and his appearance on the ground was anxiously looked for by those present. The following letter received by the committee of invitation yesterday, explains the reason of his non-attendance:--*Balt. Pat.* Washington, Oct. 22, 1850. Gentlemen:--I have received your invitation to attend the Exhibition of the Maryland State Adgricultural Society, to be held in Baltimore, on the 23d, 24th and 25th inst., and have to assure you that it would afford me great pleasure to have it in my power to be present on that occasion, as I feel a deep interest in everything calculated to promote the agricultural prosperity of the country. My official duties, however, are such, I regret to say, that I cannot with propriety allow myself that high gratification. I am, gentlemen, truly yours, Millard **FILLMORE**. Messrs.

2 November 1850

(883) (Cont.) Chas. B. **CALVERT**, John **GLENN**, W. M. **CAREY**, G. W. **DOBBIN** and J. C. **WALSH**, Committee of Invitation.

(884) $10 REWARD. Ranaway from the farm of the subscriber on 22nd ult., a negro man named **BILL**. He is about five feet eight inches high, stout built, and quite black. The above reward will be paid if he is taken and delivered to me, or placed in jail so that I can get him. L. S. **POOL**. E. City, Nov. 2, 1850.

(885) A farm in Texas for Rent, On Buffalo river between Houston and Galveston city. The above farm, belonging to Charles W. **SUMNER**, now in California, will be rented to a good tenant for the ensuing year 1851, at a reasonable rate. It presents many advantages to farmers intending to remove from this part of the country, who have never been in Texas, as they can remove their families, servants, furniture &c., all the way by water and be landed by steamboat at the door. The tract contains between 3 and 400 acres mostly prairie with about 40 acres in excellent cultivation. The building [sic] consist of two new cottages, not large but comfortable with dairy, smoke-house, barn &c., and the yard shaded by evergreen water oaks, there is a level green 7 or 8 feet high above the river. It is a good place for a ferry, and is only 8 miles from Houston, 7 miles from Lynchburg, and 5 miles from Harrisburg where a railroad is commencing to run to the Rio Grande and thence to California. There is a young peach orchard and 20 or 30 fig bushes. Sugar, cotton, corn, irish and sweet potatoes, melons, and all kinds of vegetables grow finely. The neighborhood abounds in wild game, such as deer, turkeys, wild ducks, geees, prairie hens &c., and across the river are large droves of wild hogs, while 11 miles below on Galveston bay, the finest oysters and fish are caught. The situation is healthy, and very pleasant in summer as the sea breeze blows direct from the sea across the prairie. The agent, Hon. J. W. **BRASHEAR**, resides in Houston. Charles W. **SUMNER**. Nov. 2, 1850.

(886) HERTFORD ACADEMY. John **KIMBERLEY**, M. A. Principal. Benj. S. **BRONSON**, B. A. Miss Caroline **SMITH**, " Martha B. **NEWELL**. Pupils are received at any time during the term, and charged only from the time of their admission. The institution, in the number and character of the teachers engaged, and its educational facilities, now offers to pupils opportunities, rarely to be met with, of pursuing a thorough course of instruction. ... Hertford, Nov. 2, 1850.

THE OLD NORTH STATE.
"Error is harmless, when Truth is left free to combat it."
Vol. X.] Elizabeth City, N. C. Saturday, November 9, 1850. [No. 38.

(887) Elizabeth-City, November 9, 1850. .. Mrs. General **GAINES**' friends deny that she has applied to the State Legislature for a pension. She has petitioned Congress for one, and the suits which she has brought relative to the property of Daniel **CLARKE**, whose daughter she claims to be, are still undecided.

(888) Married. On Thursday evening 7th inst, by the Rev. Jos. A. **TURNER**, Mr. Wm. R. **CARSON**, to Miss Sarah Ann **PALMER**. We return them our thanks for the cake sent us, and wish them a long and a happy life.

(889) Ho! every one that Hungers, Just call at the NEW and CHEAP GROCERY establishment recently commenced on Road street by the undersigned. The subscriber has just received from the city of Baltimore a select stock of Family Groceries..Rio Coffee, Java do; Molasses, brown Sugar, Steam refined do; Loaf do; Good Mess Pork; Bacon; Lard; Candles; Soap; Rice; Mace; Copperas; Saltpetre; Butter Crackers, Soda do; &c., &c., &c. .. The public are particularly invited to call one door below Barney **TISDALE**'s Esq., at the store formerly occupied by Seth **MORGAN**... Wilson W. **WILLIAMS**. Nov. 9.

(890) 1200 LBS OF CHOICE COTTON Yarn from No. 4 to N. [sic] 16. Just received and for sale by T. R. **COBB**. Nov. 9.

(891) STATE OF NORTH CAROLINA, Pasquotank County, Fall Term, 1850.} Ordered by the Court that a special Superior Court be held for this County, on the second Monday in December next, for the trial of civil and equity business. It is also ordered that the Clerk make publication thereof &c. Teste: Daniel **RICHARDSON**, Clerk. Nov. 9.

(892) "HOME GUARDS!" Yoy are commanded to attend a Drill of the Company, at the Court House, on Tuesday evening 12th inst., at 7 o'clock. By order of the Captain. Wm. R. **CARSON**, 1st Serg't. Nov. 9.

THE OLD NORTH STATE.
"Error is harmless, when Truth is left free to combat it."
Vol. X.] Elizabeth City, N. C. Saturday, November 16, 1850. [No. 39.

16 November 1850

(893) *Superior Pianos.*--Mr. J. E. BOSWELL, of this city, has, within a few days past, deposited in the grand saloon, an elegant piano of his own manufacture, enclosed in a rosewood case of much beauty, and is provided with an iron frame and all those improvements which give strength and value to the instrument. Its tone has been pronounced superior by all who have heard it, being full, rich, and sweet; grand piano in this respect. It is a harp attachment, enabling the performer to agreeably vary its tone. ...-- *Balt. American.*

(894) Elizabeth-City, November 16, 1850. .. NAG'S HEAD. Pursuant to appointment, a meeting of delegates was held in Edenton the 7th and 8th inst., over which J. H. LEARY, Esqr. of Chowan presided. .. Col. OUTLAW, our Representative gave his views of the practicability of the work and of the probability of succeeding in obtaining an appropriation from the General Government, in furtherance of the scheme. .. On motion of Henry BURGWIN of Halifax, it was resolved that a memorial be drawn up and presented to the next Legislature, praying that body to instruct our Senators to use all their influence in carrying forward this great work. ...

(895) Internal Improvement Meeting. A meeting of the citszens of Princess Anne County was held on Thursday, the 7th November, at Kempsville; when, on motion, Wm. ROBERTS was called to the Chair, and James S. GARRISON, Jr. appointed Secretary. The object of the meeting made known by the Chairman, was to be for the purpose of establishing a connection of the waters of Elizabeth river, via the Eastern Branch and Currituck Sound with the City of Norfolk, by the construction of a canal, granted by the Virginia Legislature last session. It was on motion resolved, that the Chairman appoint a Committee of five to draw up resolutions expressive of the sense of this meeting. Whereupon the Chairman appointed John PETTY, James S. GARRISON, Sr., John C. WISE, Dr. Wm. MORGAN, and James S. GARRISON, Jr., and reported the following resolutions through James S. GARRISON, Jr., which were unanimously adopted. 1. Resolved, That the Chairman appoint a Committee of twelve to attend the Engineer while he is engaged in making the survey. The following gentlemen, viz: Thos. WARD, Caleb BATTEN, Willis FENTRESS, Major LAND, Charles WHITEHURST, G. WILLIAMS, Wm. GRIGGS, James HUBBARD, Chas. WILLIAMS, and David M. WALKE, Jr., were appointed. 2. Resolved, That the Chairman appoint a Committee of five to take care of the Engineer and procure quarters for his accommodation while engaged in making the Survey, viz: Wm. ROBERTS, John PETTY, Wm. C. BURROUGHS, James FENTRESS, and Wilson H. C. LOVETT. 3. Resolved, That the Chairman appoint a Committee of three to set forth the advantages of this route, and recommend it to those interested, and in the section through which it is located. The following gentlemen, viz: John C. WISE, John PETTY, and James S. GARRISON, Sr. Whereupon, on motion, the Chairman was added to the Committee. ... On motion the meeting adjourned. Wm. ROBERTS, Chairman. Jas. S. GARRISON, Jr. Secretary.

(896) J. B. GODWIN, DENTIST, Continues to operate in all the branches of his profession, at his office, corner of Road and Market streets, Elizabeth City. REFERENCES: S. D. GRICE, M. D., G. J. MUSGRAVE, M. D., R. K. SPEED, M. D., Gen. J. C. B. EHRINGHAUS, Rev. E. M. FORBES, H. BURGWN, Esq., G. ELLIOTT, Esq. J. W. HINTON, Esq. J. BLACK, Esq., Wm. E. MANN, Esq.

(897) NOTICE. Persons who take the *Baltimore Patriot* at this office, and wish to settle for the same, are respectfully informed that I have a list giving me the date of there several subscriptions.--Persons who wish to subscribe for the *Patriot* can do so by applying to me. Wm. E. MANN, Agent. Nov. 16, 1850.

(898) TO THE SICK & AFFLICTED. DR. SWAYNE'S Celebrated Family Medicines. .. We think Dr. SWAYNE's Family Medicines are giving more satisfaction than any preparations of the present day.--The Compound Syrup of Wild Cherry, a pure and delightful bitters, extracted from the best quality of wild cherry bark, combined with valuable roots, has never been equalled in its curative powers, for coughs, colds, spitting of blood, and all lung and breast complaints. .. The above are prepared only by Dr. SWAYNE, N. W. corner of Eight and Race streets, Philadelphia, and for sale wholesale & retail by J. E. DEFORD. Sole agent for Pasquotank County. Nov. 16, 1850.

THE OLD NORTH STATE.
"Error is harmless, when Truth is left free to combat it."
Vol. X.] Elizabeth City, N. C. Saturday, November 23, 1850. [No. 40.

(899) Elizabeth-City, November 23, 1850. .. ALARM OF FIRE. Last Wednesday morning at 3 1/2 o'clock our citizens were startled from their slumbers by that most alarming of all sounds, the "Fire Bell." The alarm proceeded from the upper part of the shop, occupied as a jewelry store, by Col. W. G. COOK. The room in which the fire originated was used as a bed room by Mr. W. A. BASSET. Fortunately but little damage was done.--.. We will not enquire where was the newly organized fire company...

23 November 1850

(900) MORE TURNIPS. No one coming forward to beat the Turnip presented to us not long since, by Jas. M. **FEREBEE**, Esq., of Currituck county, he has again presented us with more of the same sort. On this occasion he brought from his farm 18 Turnips, which weighed in the aggregate 77 pounds 2 ounces. Our friend Jno. B. **SKINNER**, Esq., of this county, not wishing to be outdone in the vegetable line, and having no turnips of the "large breed" on hand, sent us a Radish, that beat any thing ever seen by us in that line. It measured, in length 18, and in circumference 14 inches--and weighed 2 1/2 lbs. **M**.

(901) Private Boarding House. The Subscriber having fitted up the large and commodious House, opposite the store of M. O. **JORDAN**, Esq., is prepared to accommodate Boarders. Young gentlemen would be preferred. Terms made known on application. Elizabeth **NASH**. nov. 23

(902) NOTICE. The Subscriber will sell his wood Land, commonly known by the name of the Rocky Hock woods, containing about 40 acres. On the land is some very good Pine timber for rails, together with fire wood of all kinds. The land adjoins the lands of Addison **WHEDBEE**, Esq., and Lydia **PALIN**, and lies near Newbegin Creek. For further particulars apply to the Subscriber or Jas. W. **MULLEN**, Esq. Wm. A. **MULLEN**. nov 23

(903) Notice. There was found on the sea beach in wreck District no. 2, about 2000 feet of white pine Scantling, without any marks or numbers. The same was sold on the 30th September last Wm. **WOODHOUSE**, Com. of Wr'ks. nov 23

THE OLD NORTH STATE.
"Error is harmless, when Truth is left free to combat it."
Vol. X.] Elizabeth City, N. C. Saturday, November 30, 1850. [No. 41.

(904) Miscellaneous. The Volunteer Counsel. A TALE OF JOHN **TAYLOR**. We copy the following, says the *Evening Bulletin*, from the New York Sunday *Times*. The subject of it, John **TAYLOR**, was licensed, when a youth of twenty-one, to practice at the bar of Philadelphia. He was poor, but well educated, and possessed extraordinary genius. The graces of his person, combined with the superiority of his intellect, enabled him to win the hand of a fashionable beauty. Twelve months afterwards the husband was employed by a wealthy firm of the city, to go on a mission as land-agent to the West. As a heavy salary was offered, **TAYLOR** bade farewell to his wife and infant son. He wrote back every week, but received not a line in answer. Six months elapsed, when the husband received a letter from his employers that explained all. Shortly after his departure for the west, the wife and her father removed to Mississippi.--There she immediately obtained a divorce by an act of the Legislature, married again forthwith, and to complete the climax of cruelty and wrong, had the name of **TAYLOR**'s son changed to **MARKS**--that of her second matrimonial partner! This perfidy nearly drove **TAYLOR** insane. His career, from that period, became eccentric in the last degree; sometimes he preached, sometimes he plead at the bar; until, at last, a fever carried him off at a comparatively early age.

At an early hour on the 9th of April, 1840, the court house in Clarkesville, Texas, was crowded to overflowing. Save in war-times past, there had never been witnessed such a gathering in Red river county... .. About the close of 1839, George **HOPKINS** one of the wealthiest planters and most influential men of Northern Texas, offered a gross insult to Mary **ELLISTON**, the young and beautiful wife of his chief overseer. The husband threatened to chastise him for the outrage, whereupon **HOPKINS** loaded his gun, went to **ELLISTON**'s house, and shot him in his own door. The murderer was arrested, and bailed to answer the charge. The occurrence produced intense excitement; and **HOPKINS**, in order to turn the tide of popular opinion, or at least to mitigate the general wrath, which at first was violent against him, circulated reports infamously prejudicial to the character of the woman who had already suffered such cruel wrong at his hands. She brought her suit for slander. And thus two causes, one criminal, and the other civil, and both out of the same tragedy, were pending in the April Circuit Court for 1840. The interest naturally felt by the community..became far deeper when it was known that **ASHLY** and **PIKE** of Arkansas; and the celebrated S. S. **PRENTISS** of New Orleans, each with enormous fees, had been retained by **HOPKINS** for his defence: The trial, on the indictment for murder, ended on the 8th of April, with the acquittal of **HOPKINS**. ..

The slander suit was set for the 9th , and the throng of spectators grew, in numbers as well as excitement; and what may seem strange, the current of public sentiment now ran decidedly for **HOPKINS**.--His money had procured pointed witnesses, who served most efficiently his powerful advocates. Indeed, so triumphant had been the success of the previous day, that when the slander case was called Mary **ELLISTON** was left without an attorney; they had all withdrawn. .. "Have you no counsel?" Inquired Judge **MILLS**, looking kindly at the plaintiff. "No sir; they have all deserted me, and I am too poor to employ any more," replied the beautiful Mary; bursting into tears. "In such a case, will not some chivalrous member of the profession volunteer?" asked the judge, glancing around the bar. The thirty lawyers were silent as death. Judge **MILLS** repeated the question. "I will, your honor," said a voice from the thickest part of the crowd situated behind the bar. At the tones of that voice many started half way from their seats and perhaps there was not a heart in the immense throng which did not beat something quicker, it was so unearthly sweet, clear, ringing, and mournful. The first sensation, however, was changed into general laughter, when a tall, gaunt,

30 November 1850

(904) (Cont.) spectral figure, that nobody present remembered ever to have seen before, elbowed his way through the crowd, and placed himself within the bar. His appearance was a problem to puzzle the sphinx herself. His high, pale brow, and small, nervously-twitching face seemed alive with the concentrated essence and cream of genius; but then his infantine blue eyes, hardly visible beneath their massive arches, looked dim, dreamy, almost unconscious; and his clothing was so exceedingly shabby that the court hesitated to let the cause proceed under his management. "Has your name been entered on the rolls of the State?" demanded the judge suspiciously. "It is immaterial about my name's being on *your* rolls," answered the stranger, his thin, bloodless lips curling up into a fiendish sneer. "I may be allowed to appear once, by the courtesy of the court and bar. Here is my license from the highest tribunal in America," and he handed Judge **MILLS** a broad parchment. The trial immediately went on.

In the examination of witnesses the stranger evinced but little ingenuity, as was commonly thought. He suffered each one to tell his own story, without interruption, though he contrived to make each one tell it over two or three times. .. The examination being ended, as counsel for the plaintiff he had a right to the opening speech, as well as the close; but to the astonishment of every one he declined the former, and allowed the defence to lead off. Then a shadow might have been observed to flit across the fine features of **PIKE**, and to darken even the bright eyes of **PRENTISS**. They saw that they had *caught a Tartar!* but who it was, or how it happened, was impossible to guess. Col. **ASHLEY** spoke first. He dealt the jury a dish of that close, dry logic, which years afterwards, rendered him famous in the Senate of the Union. The poet, Albert **PIKE**, followed, with a rich rain of wit, and a hail-torrent of caustic ridicule, in which you may be sure neither the plaintiff nor the plaintiff's ragged attorney was either forgotten or spared. .. It was then the stranger's turn. .. But now at last he rises--before the bar railing, not behind it--and so near the wondering jury that he might touch the foreman with his long bony finger. With eyes still half shut, and standing, rigid as a pillar of iron, his thin lips curl as if in measureless scorn, slightly part, and the voice comes forth. At first, it is low and sweet..while the speaker proceeds without a gesture or the least sign of excitement to tear in pieces the argument of **ASHLY**... Anon, he came to the dazzling wit of the poet-lawyer, **PIKE**. .. In five minutes **PIKE**'s wit seemed the foam of folly, and his finest satire horrible profanity, when contrasted with the inimitable sallies and exterminating sarcasms of the stranger, interspersed with jest and anecdote that filled the *forum* with roars of laughter. Then, without so much as bestowing an allusion on **PRENTISS**, he turned short on the perjured witnesses of **HOPKINS**, tore their testimony into atoms, and hurled in their faces such terrible invective that all trembled as with an ague, and two of them actually fled dismayed from the court house. .. His eye began to glare furtively at the assassin, **HOPKINS**, as his lean, taper finger slowly assumed the same direction. He hemmed the wretch around with a circumvallation of strong evidence and impregnable argument, cutting off all hope of escape. He piled up huge bastions of insurmountable facts. .. He drew a picture of murder in such appalling colors, that in comparison hell itself might be considered beautiful. .. He closed by a strange exhortation to the jury, and through them to the bystanders. He entreated the panel, after they should bring in their verdict for the plaintiff not to offer violence to the defendant, however richly he might deserve it; in other words, "not to lynch the villian, **HOPKINS**, but leave his punishment to God." This was the most artful trick of all, and the best calculated to ensure vengeance.

The jury rendered a verdict for fifty thousand dollars; and the night afterwards **HOPKINS** was taken out of his bed by lynchers, and beaten almost to death. As the Court adjourned, the stranger made known his name, and called the attention of the people, with the announcement--"John **TAYLOR** will preach here this evening at early candle light." ...

(905) Elizabeth-City, November 03 [sic,] 1850. .. FIRE! PROTECTION!! Mr. Editor: A new Fire Company has recently been organized in the town of Elizabeth City. All are interested in its success--I, therefore..appeal to every one to come forward and give countenance and support to the company. A set of Hose, Fire Buckets, Ladders and Axes &e., are needed to fully equip the Company and render it efficient. Will not those of our citizens, who are mostly deeply interested come forward and subscribe their means liberally for the purchase of these adjuncts of a good Company? .. Property-holders, the Company is for your benefit and interest, will you sustain it, if you, will give to the committee (Messrs. A. E. **JACOBS**, J. M. **MATHEWS** and L. K. **SAUNDERS**) who may wait upon you enough to complete and fully equip the organization. A Friend of the Company.

(906) STATE OF NORTH CAROLINA, Pasquotank County. Court of Pleas and Qr. Sessions--Sept. Term, 1850 Wardens of the Poor of Pasq'k. Co. vs. John B. **MANSARD**'s Heirs.} Attachm't. Whereas an Attachment against the property of the heirs of John **MANSARD** has been served at the instance of the Wardens of the Poor for the county of Pasquotank, and it appearing to the satisfaction of the Court that the said heirs are non residents of this State, it is therefore ordered that publication be made for six weeks in the "Old North State," published in the town of Elizabeth City, that the said Heirs may appear at March term 1851 of Pasquotank county Court of Pleas and Quarter Sessions, then and there to answer or demur, or judgment pro confesso will be entered as to them. Witness, Wm. W. **GRIFFIN**, Clerk of the said Court, at Elizabeth City, the first Monday in Sept. 1850. Wm. W. **GRIFFIN**, Cl'k. nov. 30

(907) The Subscriber has removed from Messrs. **CHERRY** & **FERRALL**s warehouse to the new House on the lower end of **CAMPBELL**s wharf where he designs to keep a well selected stock of New England Manufactures. Such as Boots, Shoes, Brogans, Nails, Spades, Shovels, Pails, Brooms, Buckets, Soap, Candles &c., which will be sold on favorable terms for cash or ap-

30 November 1850

(**907**) (Cont.) proved city acceptances. E. **GURNEY**. Norfolk, Nov. 25th 1850.

THE OLD NORTH STATE.
"Error is harmless, when Truth is left free to combat it."
Vol. X.] Elizabeth City, N. C. Saturday, December 7, 1850. [No. 42.

(**908**) Elizabeth-City, December 7, 1850. .. PASQUOTANK vs CURRITUCK CO. (Turnips the Issue.) We were presented on Thursday last, by Mr. Wesley E. **SAWYER**, of our county, with four turnips, which weighed in the aggregate 25 pounds and 12 ounces. The largest one weighed 8 pounds 2 ounces and measured *around* 30 *inches*. Our friend **FEREBEE** will have to *pull up* again to be even with old Pasquotank. We should like to know which one of our subscribers raises the best *turkeys*. Suppose some of them send in and let us judge.--Christmas is coming and a good fat turkey from a *paying* subscriber would go first rate. Those who dont pay of course have no turkeys to send. **M.**

(**909**) SUICIDE.--Mr. Geo. P. **MARTIN**, of Edgefield District, S. C., committed suicide while on a visit to Autauga county, Alabama, on the 19th last, by shooting himself with a rifle.

(**910**) DIED. In this place on Sunday last, Salvadora, daughter of William and Sarah **LABOYTEAUX**, aged five years one month and 23 days. .. This dear little creature was the pride of her affectionate parents and well she might be, for the writer of these lines can bear ample testimony that she was possessed of qualities that woudl have done honor to one of much older years. ...

(**911**) NOTICE. A public address, on the subject of Temperance, will be delivered by Bro. George W. **BROOKS** before the Pasquotank Division No. 21 S. of T., and the public generally, in the Methodist Church at Elizabeth City on the last Thursday in December. All transient brethren are invited to participate on the occasion. Exercises will commence at 7 o'clock, P. M. G. M. **WILDER**, Wm. J. **KELLINGER**, J. T. **SALTER**.} Committee of Arrangement. Dec. 7th, 1850.

(**912**) Notice. The subscriber having administered upon the Estate of Jonathan **BANKS**, deceased, hereby notifies all persons indebted to the same, to come forward and settle up, and those having claims will present them duly authenticated for payment, or this notice will be plead in bar of their recovery. Benoni **CARTWRIGHT**, Adm'r. Dec. 7th, 1850.

(**913**) THE OYSTER HOUSE. I would most respectfully inform the citizens of Elizabeth City and the surrounding country that I have taken part of the lower floor of the brick store opposite the Mansion House, where I intend keeping a general EATING RSTABLISHMENT. Oysters prepared in any way to suit the customer. Hot Coffee, Buck-wheat-cakes, Pork and Beef Steaks, and Eggs served up various styles will also be furnished at a moments notice. Persons can gain admittance at any time of the night by knocking at the door. James B. **RUSSELL**. Dec. 7th.

THE OLD NORTH STATE.
"Error is harmless, when Truth is left free to combat it."
Vol. X.] Elizabeth City, N. C. Saturday, December 14, 1850. [No. 43.

(**914**) Elizabeth-City, December 14, 1850. .. APPOINTMENTS OF THE VIRGINIA AND N. C. CONFERENCE. Norfolk District--J. D. **COWLING** P. E. Norfolk--Cumberland St., R. **MICHAELS**, Bute street--F. S. **MITCHELL**. Granby street--J. E. **EDWARDS**. Portsmouth--J. **MANNING**. African Mission, to be supplied. Gosport--Jos. J. **EDWARDS**. Eastville--H. H. **GRAY**. Gates--J. M. **SAUNDERS**. Edenton, to be supplied. Hertford--W. **REED**, W. W. **KENNEDAY** sup. Pasquotank--W. M. **WARD**. Elizabeth City--J. A. **DOLL**. Camden--H. **BILLUPS**. Princess Anne--G. N. **WINFREE**. Currituck Mission, to be supplied. **DURANT**s Neck and Pasquotank Mission.--A. **CARNER**. Next session of the Conference to be held in Alexandria.

(**915**) NORTH CAROLINA LEGISLATURE. HOUSE OF COMMONS. .. Mr. **JONES** also reported back the memorials of Burwell **TEMPLE**, and others, against the incorporation of the Sons of Temperance, with a recommendation that they be referred to the Committee on Private Bills. Concurred in. ...

(**916**) NOTICE. Being determined to leave the County, I request all persons having work at my Shop, to call immediately and get it. Jos. N. **BELL**. Dec. 14, 1850.

THE OLD NORTH STATE.
"Error is harmless, when Truth is left free to combat it."
Vol. X.] Elizabeth City, N. C. Saturday, December 21, 1850. [No. 44.

21 December 1850

(917) Elizabeth-City, December 21, 1850. ... CHRISTMAS. In accordance with the long established usage there will be no paper issued from this office next Saturday. This is done that those connected with the office may have an opportunity of enjoying the festivities of the occasion. The editor, publishers and compositors of the *Old North State* extend to all its readers (paying ones particularly) the compliments of the season--wishing each and all a "merry Charistmas and a happy New Year." Wont some one send us, the *Editor* a turkey.

(918) *From the Democratic Pioneer*. PUBLIC MEETING. At a meeting of a portion of the citizens of Elizabeth City and Pasquotank county, without distinction of party, held at the Court-House on Saturday afternoon, 14th inst., "for the purpose of considering the many and continued aggressions of the North upon the rights and honor of the South, and of giving expression to their feelings in relation to the policy the South ought to pursue in this emergency,"--on motion of Dr. G. J. **MUSGRAVE**, Gen. J. C. B. **EHRINGHAUS** was called to the Chair and on motion of L. D **STARKE**, Esq., Mark S. **SAWYER**, was elected Secretary. On motion of L. D. **STARKE**, Esq., a committee of five was appointed to prepare and report business for the action of the meeting, whereupon the chair appointed the following..: L. D. **STARKE**, Dr. G. J.**MUSGRAVE**, Wm. **CHARLES**, Thomas D. **KNOX**, and Jno. **POOL**, who after retiring for a short time, returned and submitted the following report, (John **POOL**, Esq. dissenting.)

    Whereas, for a series of years, a fanatical agitation has been systematically kept up by the Northern people, upon the subject of slavery, alike ruinous to the South and threatening to the Union, and whereas, at the last session of Congress, a series of measures was adopted for the purpose of allaying excitement, restoring harmony, and averting the dangers to which the Union itself was exposed; and whereas, the people of the South, in a spirit of conciliation and devotion to the Union, conceded everything to the North, and received only in return a law guaranteeing the recovery of their slaves who might escape into non-slaveholding States, commonly called the Fugitive-slave-law, which was but the re-enactment of a pre-existing constitutional provision; and whereas, said law has been virtually annulled and rendered inoperative by the fanatical obolitionists of the non-slaveholding States, who, in disregard of the hallowed associations of a common ancestry, and in contempt of the law and the guarantied rights of the South, still persist in waging an unholy crusade against our institutions--insulting--threatening, and imprisoning our citizens who may seek to recover their property according to law and under the provisions of the Constitution; and whereas, the Legislature of Vermont has, unanimously, with the exception of a single vote, substantially abrogated and set at defiance the fugitive slave law; and whereas, a crisis has arrived in our history, which requires prompt and decisive action on the part of the South against the outrages and aggressions of the North, which seem to "grow by what they feed on." Therefore, in consideration of these things, be it. 1. *Resolved*, That we regard with the profoundest veneration and deepest affection the Union established by our forefathers, and would seek, by all the means within our power, its preservation and perpetuity. 2. *Resolved*, That the repeal or modification of the fugitive-slave law by Congress will be regarded by us, and we believe by the South generally, as a sufficient cause for, and will inevitably result in a dissolution of this Union. 3. *Resolved*, That as the abolitionists of the non-slaveholding States have been faithless to the solemn obligations of the national compact--have asserted the supremacy of a "higher law" than the Constitution of our Country, and are ceaseless in their attacks upon Southern Institutions and Southern honor, it is the right, it is the bounden duty of the aggrieved party to adopt such measures as are best calculated to protect themselves and restore their aggressors to a sense of propriety and justice. 4. *Resolved*, That we regard the measure of *commercial retaliation* as entirely constitutional and proper; and that the Legislature of North Carolina should adopt this policy, and pass a law imposing a tax upon all Northern manufactured or imported goods sold in this State... 5. *Resolved*, That the citizens throughout the State, and especially the Merchants and Farmers be urged to co-operate with us in our efforts to throw off our dependence on the North, by giving preference to Southern bottoms in all cases of shipping, by encouraging the direct importation of foreign goods into Southern ports, and by giving their aid and support to Southern industry and manufacturers. 6. *Resolved*, That the firm, manly and patriotic stand assumed by the Senator from this District, the Hon. Wm. B. **SHEPARD**, on the slavery question, deserves and receives our most cordial and enthusiastic approbation. 7. *Resolved*, That copies of these resolutions be transmitted to our Senator and Representative in the Legislature, with the request that they urge the necessity of levying a discriminating tax on Northern goods before their respective bodies.

    Mr. **STARKE** sustained the report in a brief address. A spirited discussion then ensued between Messrs. **POOL** and **SPEED** in opposition to, and W. F. **MARTIN**, Esq. in favor of the report. The hour growing late and the attendance thin, after various propositions..the meeting finally agreed to have the proceedings published, and adjourn to Saturday, 4th January, 1851, in order that there might be a more general turnout of the people. J. C. B. **EHRINGHAUS**, Ch'n. Mark S. **SAWYER**, Sec'y.

(919) Married. At the Merchant's Hotel in Gatesville, N. C., on Thursday evening, the 5th inst., by Wm L. **BOOTHE**, Esq., Mr. Henry L. **EURE**, of Nansemond county, Va., to Miss Martha Jane **LOVETT**, of the former place.

(920) New Drugs, Medicines, &c., The Subscriber returns his sincere thanks to his friends and the public..for their kind patronage, and respectfully informs them that he has just received from the North a full and complete assortment of every thing in his line... L. K. **SAUNDERS**. Dec. 21.

21 December 1850

(921) ST. JOHN'S DAY. There will be a public address before the Pasquonaux Lodge of Free and Accepted Masons, at the Baptist Church, at 12 o'clock M., on Friday 27th inst. All transient brethren and adjoining Lodges are requested to join the procession. Wm. W. **GRIFFIN**, Wm. H. **CLARK**, M. O. **JORDAN**.} Committee. (*Pioneer* copy.) Dec. 21.

(922) STATE OF NORTH CAROLINA, Pasquotank County. *Superior Court of Equity--Fall Term*, 1850. Ann M. **DAILEY** vs. Josiah **DAILEY**.} Petition for Divorce. In this case it appearing that a copy of the petition and subpeona, were issued to the defendant in manner as by the statute in such cases is required, and the return thereon being that the defendant is not to be found. Proclamation being publicly made at the Court House door by the Sheriff for the said defendant to appear and answer as commanded by the subpoena, and the said defendant failing to appear; it is ordered by the Court, that publication be made in the "Old North State" for three months, for the said Josiah **DAILY** to appear at the next term of this Court to be held at Elizabeth City, the 4th Monday after the 4th Monday in March next, and answer the plaintiffs' petition. Witness, John D. **EHRINGHAUS**, Clerk and Master for the County of Pasquotank, this 16th day of December, in the year 1850. John C. **EHRINGHAUS**, C. & M. E. Dec. 21.

(923) FLOUR & PORK. Just received from Baltimore 65 Bbls. of Family & Superfine Flour of excellent quality and brands. ALSO, 15 Bbls. of Baltimore Hard Mess Pork. T. R. **COBB**. Dec. 21.

(924) ST. MARY'S SC_OOL, RALEIGH, N. C. The 18th Term of this School will commence on the Fourth day of January 1851, and continue till the 7th of June. For a Circular containing full particulars, apply to the Subscriber. Albert **SMEDES**, Rector. December 21st, 1850.

END

INDEX

A

ABBOTT
W. R. 863
Wm. R. 358,543,609
ABERT
J. J. 222
ADAM
____ 69
ADAMS
____ 772,823
Abigail (SMITH) 787
Allen 585
Charles 787
Charles Francis 787
George Washington 787
J. Quincy 787
John 787
John Quincy 204,787
Louisa Catherine (JOHNSON) 787
Susanna 787
Susanna BOYLSTON 787
Thomas Boylston 787
ADDINGTON
Charles C. 247
W. H. 16,85,119,137
ADKINSON
____ 444
ADRIANCE
D. G. 371
AGERY
____ 444
AIKEN
William E. A. 810
Wm. E. A. 810
AINSLEY
____ 559
AINSWORTH
____ 570
ALBERSTON
Aaron 863
ALBERTSON
Aaron 863
Jona. W. 224,677
William 240
ALDEN
James 381
ALEXANDER
Angeline E. 96

ALEXANDER
Benj. 271
Joseph 49,87
Wm. J. 220
ALISON
R. Taylor 299
ALLEN
____ 514,722
Alonzo 722
Benj. 271
John 581
John, Sr. 118
T. 29
Thomas 9,73,88
Thos. 423
W. B. 483,580
William B. 244
Wm. 381
Wm. B. 71,74,131, 271,605
ALLISON
____ 340
Robert 465
ALVIADO
Martin 381
AMIS
J. S. 224
AMPUDIA
____ 320
ANDERSON
Franklin 745
John A. 601,609
W. 330
W. G. 190
Wm. G. 186
ANDREWS
____ 488,788
Jno. N. 443
John L. 488
ANTHONY
____ 578
Whitmel H. 545
APPLETON
____ 327
APPRENTICES
UPTON
Quinton 834
ARAM
____ 441
ARMOR
John 146
ARMOUR
Benj. 857
Mary 512,637

ARMSTEAD
Clarissa (BURNUM) 417
John 417
Thomas S. 609
Wm. 609
ARMSTRONG
J. D. 609
Willian 745
ARNOLD
Charles W. 637
Wm. L. 609
ARONHOUSE (See also EHRINGHAUS)
Brooks 512
ASHBEE
Maria 637
Samuel M. 381
ASHCROFT
Luvinia 753
ASHE
W. S. 300
Wm. S. 264
ASHLEY
____ 904
ASHLY
____ 904
ASHMUN
Geo. 814
ASHTON
Oscar 381
ASSOCIATION
Chowan 658
ASTOR
____ 371
ATKINSON
Thos. 745
AUGUST
P. F. 236,246,395
AUGUSTIN
Donatien 762
AUSTIN
A. A. 830
Bateman 381
AYDLETT
Thomas 82
AYDLOTT
Wm. D. 512
AYER
____ 766
AYERS
Cassindra 512

B

B.
G. W. 112,713
T. 517
BABB
James B. 495
John E. 495
Sarah 495
William 495
BACHE
A. D. 234,804
BACON
Edward 271
Geo. W. 381
Joseph 118
BADGER
____ 138
Geo. E. 158,814
BADHAM
John 609
William 190
BAGBY
____ 574
BAGLEY
D. W. 609
James 44
W. H. 677
Willis H. 677,783
BAILEY (See also BALEY)
____ 404
Artimesia 878
John 637,878
John D. 381
John, Jr. 381
John, Sr. 878
S. 381
Wilson 753
BAILY
____ 428
BAIN
Alexander 445
BAITMAN (See also BATEMAN)
Joseph 857
BAKER
____ 584
Andrew 857
Blake 495
Nannie T. (JOHNSTON) 479
R. B. 752
Richard B. 479
W. J. 551
William J. 551

BAKER
Wm. J. 562,609
BALANCE
____ 512
Holaway 512
BALDWIN
____ 786
Simeon 786
BALEY (See also BAILEY)
John, Sr. 55
BALL
J. J. 857
BALLANCE
____ 381
H. 857
Hol. 271
Holloway 637
BALLANTREE
Thomas 637
BALLARD
C. W. 389
Charles E. 609
Chas. E. 562
Rob't. H. 562
BALTIMORE
____ 497
BANKS
Adam G. 585
Andrew 857
Benj. F. 381
Geo. W. 512
James 553,859
Jas. W. 753
Jno. 381,753
John 381,512
Jonathan 555,912
Mary E. 857
Parthnea 271
Thad. F. 609,706
Thaddeus F. 225, 358,553,859
Thomas 706
Thos. F. 358
Wm. 753
Wm. C. 271,512
Wm. F. 753,857
BARBEE
E. 857
BARBER
Cornelius 281
James 398,779
Luke White 281
Margaret 281

129

BARBER
  Margaret Adlum 281
  Mary Virginia 281
  Susan Roles 281
BARBIER
  L. 753
BARCLIFT
  D. 697
  Richard 821
BARCO
  C. 609
  Caleb 783
BARKER
  Jacob 208
BARN
  Newlis 637
BARNARD
  ___ 783
  John 609
BARNES
  C. W. 609
  D. A. 609,732
  Jas. 405
  Jno. C. 19
  John C. 228
BARNITZ
  ___ 299
BARNUM
  ___ 299,625
BARRANGER
  D. M. 406
BARRENTON
  Annes 753
BARRINGER
  D. M. 264,318
  Daniel M. 220
BARRINGTON
  Joe 444
BARRON
  ___ 554
BASCOM
  ___ 707
BASNIGHT
  Benj. L. 271
  Benjamin S. 118
BASSET
  ___ 787
  W. A. 899
BASSETT
  William 118
  Wm. A. 272
BATCHELOR
  ___ 581
BATEMAN (See also BAITMAN)
  A. J. 54,190,729

BATEMAN
  Ellen 720
  Kate 720
BATES
  Edward 780
BATTEN
  Caleb 895
BATTLE
  C. C. 585
  J. A. 271
BATTY
  ___ 581
BAUGHMAN
  George 28
BAUM
  A. 250,754
BAXTER
  ___ 443
  B. M. 324,819
  O. F. 443,553,859
BAYARD
  Charles Carroll 621
  Richard 442
BAYLOR
  B. 443
BEAL
  ___ 380
BEALE
  ___ 125,393
BEAMSLEY
  Dick 593
  Grace 593
  Mercy 593
BEARD
  John 882
BEASLEY
  Jessee 160
  John B. 609
BECK
  Deliverance 593
  Strange 593
BECKER
  Peter 467
BECKWITH
  Thomas 609
BEEL
  Affee 118
BELL
  ___ 363,512
  Affey 512
  Ann 626,856
  C. 263
  Chloe 165
  J. J. 830
  J. M. 271
  James M. 381

BELL
  Jane 165
  John 165,611
  Jos. N. 916
  Joseph C. 165
  Joseph N. 20,135, 362,533
  Josiah 637
  Mary 165
  Thos. 637
  W. H. 762
  Wm. C. 563
BENBON
  J. 163
BENBURY
  Joseph 725
  Penny 857
  Richard 857
  William 725
BENDALL
  Free Grace 593
  Hopefor 593
  Reform 593
BENJAMIN
  S. C. 609
BENNET
  Arlington 734
BENNETT
  B. 609
  J. N. 163
  R. O. 163
  Thomas 371
BENTLY
  James 857
BENTON
  ___ 138,451,465
  Thomas H. 283
  Thos. 753
BERANYI
  ___ 661
BERKLEY
  Wm. N. 741
BERNEY
  ___ 69
BERRITT
  Jas. G. 380
BERRY
  ___ 854
  A. 609
  Abner 82
  Barnard 846
  Benjamin 525
  J. C. 854
  John 637
  John G. 11
  Thomas 846

BERY
  A. 590
BETHELL
  Wm. D. 68
BETHUNE
  Alex. 180
  George W. 343
BETTS
  Royston 28
  Wm. M. 381
BEWSTER
  Osmyn 488
BIDWELL
  J. 441
BILLUPS
  H. 914
  J. W. 190
BIZZEL
  H. A. 732
BLACK
  J. 896
  John 459,553,749, 769,859
BLACKBURN
  Ann 648
BLAKE
  Bennet T. 185
BLAKEMER
  Henry 468
BLANCHARD
  John L. 118
BLANKET
  Thomas 614
BLISS
  ___ 787
  Elizabeth (TAYLOR) 787
BLOODGOOD
  ___ 60
BLOUNT
  Ann C. 803
  Edmund C. 609
BOARD
  Literary 672
BOCOCK
  Thos. H. 152
BOGARDUS
  C. S. 132
BOGGS
  ___ 160
  L. W. 441
BOHANNAN
  R. L. 746
BOND
  Alexander 536
  J. C. 609

BOND
  James C. 609
  Jas. C. 609
  Sam'l. T. 170
  Samuel T. 807
  T. E., Jr. 389
BOON
  John E. 54
BOONE
  Charlotte 637
  Daniel 744
BOOTHE
  William L. 562
  Wm. L. 919
BOREN
  Louis 444
  Mosey 444
BOSTICKS
  ___ 444
BOSWELL
  J. E. 377,893
BOTTETOURT
  ___ 460
BOTTS
  C. T. 441
BOURKE
  Louisa 254
BOW
  Timothy 381
BOWEN
  M. 637
BOWIE
  ___ 219
BOWLEY
  ___ 418
BOWLY
  ___ 36,105
BOYD
  ___ 308
BOYDEN
  Nathaniel 264
BOYLE
  J. McC. 609
BOYLSTON
  Susanna 787
BOYNER
  ___ 838
BRABBLE
  J. D. 609
BRADLEY
  ___ 854
BRADSHAW
  Jos. R. 637
  Joseph R. 452
BRADSLEY
  W. 676

130

BRAGG
Braxton 257
Elizabeth B. (ELLIS) 257
BRAND
Andrew 836
BRANT
John N. 271
BRASHEAR
J. W. 885
BRAY
Ambrose W. 512
John 637
W. 637
Wallis 271
BRENEMAN
A. 110
BREWSTER
Osmyn 488
BRIGG
___ 456
BRIGGS
___ 642
BRIGHT
Ephraim, Big 271
Ephriam 637
BRITE
Jonathan 637
BRITT
Elias 753
BROADFIELD
R. H. 48, 145
Robert H. 67
BROCKETT
Mary A. 271
BRONSON
Benj. S. 809, 886
BROOK
Henry L. 140
BROOKE
___ 413
BROOKFIELD
John 381
BROOKS
G. W. 196, 482, 553, 679, 779, 795, 828, 859
Geo. W. 197, 632, 706, 752
George W. 553, 706, 735, 911
James 451
Margaret A. (COSTIN) 735
Wm. 753
BROSIER
Martha 118

BROTHER
___ 65, 507
BROTHERS
___ 61, 65
Burwell 298
Charles 753
Charles B. 196
F. A. 706
Francis 479
Francis A. 553, 859
Miles 381
Willis 637
BROUGHTON
T. G. 181, 210
BROWN
___ 581, 844
Benjamin 496
E. 441
Laura M. 391
Mary 844
Neil S. 173, 574
Sam'l 496
Thomas B. 127, 381
Thompson S. 430
W. H. 637
William J. 451
Wm. 719
BROZIER
Jos. L. 753
Thomas 381
BRUCKS
Catharine 753
BRUER
George W. 609
BRUFF
James M. 26
Jas. M. 26
BRYAN
___ 163
James W. 726
Jno. H. 732
John H. 585, 678, 726
Sidney 512
BRYANT
___ 160
Benj. T. 248
William T. 421
Wm. T. 857
BRYDEN
Seth 311
BUCHANAN
___ 309
David 512
BUCKHART
George 194
BUCKINGHAM

BUCKINGHAM
J. T. 426
Jos. T. 352
BUGBEE
C. M. 202
BULL
Reuben C. 27
BULLITT
A. C. 826
Alex. C. 139
BULLOCK
Benj. K. 857
BUNCH
James L. 609
Micajah 524
N. J. 762
BUNDY
Elizabeth Ann 512, 857
William 118
BUNTLINE
Ned 371
BURCHER
Casann (SCOTT) 164
John 164, 271, 521
BURDEN
Wm. 179
BURFOOT
J. W. 590
BURGESS
___ 58, 414, 637, 753
Jno. 753
Jno. S. 706
John 11, 146, 381
John S. 75
W. W. 637
William 216
Wm. 21, 753
Wm. B. 296, 306
Wm. W. 226, 236, 552
BURGWIN
H. 461
Henry 894
Hill 459, 706
Mary (PHILLIPS) 461
BURGWN
H. 896
BURGWYN
H. K. 601, 609, 830
Hill 732
T. P. 830
T. Pollock 203

BURGWYNN
H. K. 545
T. P. 545
BURKE
___ 342
Edmund 91
Samuel 271
BURNAP
Job 334
BURNETT
J. H. 601, 609, 789
Peter H. 522
S. A. (FOLK) 789
BURNS
Ann 277
Catherine 277
BURNUM
Clarissa 417
BURR
David J. 51
BURROUGHS
J. J. 401
Wm. C. 895
BURT
___ 581
BURTON
J. W. 163
BURWELL
___ 528
Wm. M. 843
BUSBEE
Johnson 585
Perrien 180
Perrin 687
BUSH
W. T. 815
BUSK
James 563
BUTCHER
Geo. H. 753
BUTLER
James 512
Jane 271
Susan 485, 512
Thos. Wilson 485
William 692
Wm. 110
BUTT
___ 50, 648
Jane G. 512
John 381
John F. 553, 859
BUXTON
___ 726

C

CABELL
E. C. 882
CADWORTH
J. H. 381
CAHOON
___ 40
Philip A. R. C. 715
CAIN
Wm. B. 753
CALDWELL
___ 869
Greene W. 264
Jos. P. 300
Joseph P. 264
CALHOUE
John C. 368
CALHOUN
___ 327, 645
Andrew 327
Cornelia 327
J. C. 652
James 327
John 327
John C. 623, 838
Patrick 327
Willie 327
CALVERT
Chas. B. 883
Samuel 609
CAMERAN
John A. 271
CAMPBELL
___ 818, 907
James M. 745
Thomas Jefferson 645
CANNON
___ 450
Dennis 803
Henry 803
Jas. J. 609
Jos. 677
CANTERS
___ 188
CAPRON
L. 110
CAREW
Edward 669
CAREY
W. M. 883
CARILLO
J. A. 441
CARL
Henry 584
CARMEAN
___ 444

CARMOTH
Mary 381
CARNATHAN
Davis 271
CARNER
A. 914
CAROON
Navel 637
CAROTHERS
___ 444
CARR
P. 465
CARRAWAY
George W. 794
Joseph G. 224
CARRINGTON
___ 444
N. 561
CARROLL
___ 143
CARSON
Sarah Ann (PALMER) 888
Wm. R. 881, 888, 892
CARSTARPHEN
W. D. 609
CARTER
David 49
James 562
Wm. F. 224
CARTWRIGHT
Benoni 637, 912
Caleb 154
Dempsey 738
Isabella 551
Isaiah 551
John 706
Langstor 857
M. 512
Mahaly 551
Marmaduke 381
Penina 551
Reuhamy 551
Samuel 492
Shadrach D. 553, 859
Sophia 551
CARVER
Elias 553, 857, 859
Emeline 710
Job 553, 706, 753, 859
CASEY
___ 381
Caroline V. 857
Dempsey 212, 381
Patsey 239

CASS
Lewis 155
CATHCART
___ 125
CAUX
___ 202
CHALK
Margret 269
CHAMBERLAYNE
L. W. 746
CHAPMAN
Eliza 489
Leonard 74, 244, 483, 632, 868
Leonard M. 580
CHARLES
G. W. 75, 387, 567, 779
Geo. W. 706, 814
George W. 504, 706
Wm. 77, 130, 228, 706, 918
CHERRY
___ 849, 850, 907
A. 417, 489
G. J. 609
Jos. B. 609
CHESHIRE
___ 726
CHESSIRE
David 753
CHESSON
J. B. 609
John B. 609
CHEW
___ 309
Samuel 810
CHILDS
Henry 160
Thomas 369
CHIPMAN
Walter 441
CHOWAN
David Stone 248
CHRISTIAN
Letitia 787
CHURCH
James C. 376
CINTEELY
John 494
CIRCUS
Great Western 576, 581
CLANTON
D. 830
CLARK

CLARK
___ 19, 358, 877
Colin M. 545
D. A. 167
Daniel 276
John C. 434, 784
Myra 276
Rich'd H. 753
Sallie (JACKSON) 395
W. J. 264
Wm. H. 395, 779, 921
CLARKE
Daniel 887
Matthew St. Clair 645
Samuel 271
W. B. 704
CLARKSON
J. 381
CLARY
W. G. 609
CLAY
___ 138, 256, 537, 539, 564
C. M. 320
Cassius M. 219, 500
H. 662
Henry 442, 745
Porter 662
CLAYTON
___ 138, 369
J. M. 393
T. G. 512
Thos. 609
CLEGG
Isaac 732
CLEMENS
Edward 561
CLEMENTS
P. P. 609
CLEMMONS
E. 602
Edward 602
CLEVELAND
___ 444
Washington 823
CLIFFORD
___ 642
CLINGMAN
T. 264
T. L. 264, 300
CLUB
Musical 654
CLUFF
___ 19

CLUFF
Mathew 421
COBARRUVIA
J. M. 441
COBB
T. R. 306, 695, 717, 379, 867, 890, 923
Thomas R. 88
Thos. R. 502
COBBIN
Ingram 699
COCHRAN
___ 823
Allen 823
COCKEY
___ 24, 299
COHEN
P. M. 87
COLE
Edward 833
James 833
COLEMAN
___ 431
Chapman 431
COLLINS
___ 609
Jackson 637
Jane R. 495
John A. 744
Josiah 601, 609, 633, 726
Miles 495
Patrick 284
COLQUITT
W. T. 823
COLT
___ 202
COMANN
Wm. H. 271
COMMANDER
James 118
Jas. 637
Jos. 348, 384
Miles 512, 637
COMMANN
Robert S. 118
Wm. H. 118
COMPANIES
Baltimore and Su-queanna Rail Road 299
Broadbrook Manufacturing 412
Central Railroad Banking 591
Dismal Swamp Canal

COMPANIES
Dismal Swamp Canal 230, 756
New York Life Insurance 769
Norfolk & Roanoke Steam Boat Line 588
Panama Railroad 407
CONE
C. O. 389
CONRAD
___ 784, 826
CONSTABLES
NEWBOLD Wm. 628
CONWAY
Nelly 787
COOK
___ 640
Thomas 392, 447
W. G. 795, 899
William G. 149
COOKE
Saml T. 637
W. D. 180
Wm. D. 261, 687
COOPER
___ 309
Arthur 189
Enos 444
George D. 309
COPES
Peter 857
CORCORAN
___ 318
CORNELIUS
___ 581
CORNICK
James 230, 756
CORNWALLIS
___ 573
CORPREW
Wilson 50
CORTELL
Malichi 753
CORWIN
Thomas 780, 804
CORY
Nelson 47
COSTELLOW
___ 602
COSTEN
James K. 562
COSTIN
James 735

COSTIN
Margaret A. 735
COSTLEE
Thomas 561
COTTEN
Isaac 753
COTTER
W. T. 263
COTTON
Seaborne 593
COULLING
Jas. D. 827
COURTS
D. W. 68
COVINGTON
___ 193
COWLES
Wesley 299
COWLING
J. D. 914
COWPER
R. G. 609
COX
James 444
John 609
Jos. M. 344, 372, 677, 809
Jos. M. 475
R. H. 609
Wm. S. 401
COXE
J. R. 813
CRANK
Caleb T. 512
CRAWFORD
Geo. W. 369
George W. 209
CRAYTON
Philip 141
CREIGHTON
John T. 741
CREMER
H. 6
CRICKMORE
Benj. 753
CRITTENDEN
___ 431
John J. 780
T. L. 201
CROMWELL
___ 742
CROOK
James 444
CROSBY
___ 615
CROSS

CROSS
___ 735
Joseph 286
Washington 753
Wm. H. 562
CROWNOVES
___ 444
CRUMP
Wm. W. 140
CUGLER
R. R. 591
CULPEPPER
Henry 481
J. 211
Z. 23, 626
Zion 39, 135, 296, 306, 362, 363, 462, 482
CURRAN
A. 609
CURTIS
George Washington Parke 811
P. 616
CUSHMAN
Charlotte 442
CUSTIS
Jack 460
CUTTER
G. W. 639
CUYLER
R. M. 381

D

DAIL
Harvey 279
Richard 381
DAILEY
Ann M. 922
John 512
Josiah 922
DAILY
___ 783
Josiah 922
DALRYMPLE
Robert 608
DANBRIDGE
John 787
Martha 787
DANIEL (See also DANNIEL)
J. R. J. 264, 300
John 140
Raleigh T. 140
W. A. 830
W. L. 609

DANIEL
Wm. C. 823
DANNEL
___ 49
DANNIEL
M. J. 511
DARBY
William 429
DARRICUTT
___ 330
DASHIELL
G. W. F. 214
Geo. W. F. 131, 483
George W. F. 35
DAUGHTERY
William G. 562
Wm. G. 562
DAUGHTRY
William G. 551
DAUGHTY
Wm. G. 511
DAVENPORT
Doctrine P. 609
George W. 609
H. W. 609
J. B. 609
J. F. 609
James F. 609
R. 609
Silas 609
Wm. D. 609
DAVES
John 248
DAVIS
___ 381
Elizabeth 282
Garrett 575
George 732
Isaac 512
J. B. 381
James M. 118
Jefferson 539, 787
John W., Jr. 280
Lowry 282
M. 290
Margaret 637
Miles 381
R. B. 609
Sarah Knox (TAYLOR) 787
Wm. C. 609
Wm. H. 19, 61, 358, 828
Wm. H., Jr. 553, 859
DAY
W. H. 830

DE PEDRORENA
Miguel 441
DE ROSSETT
William L. 248
DEAN
Julia 852
DEBERRY
Edmund 264, 300
DEBRERY
Edmund 267
DECATUR
___ 554
DECORMIS
Edward 241
DEDMAN
T. R. 585
DEEMS
D. F. 707
DEFORD
J. E. 526, 568, 617, 782, 898
John E. 502
DELACOUR
James A. 564
DELK
___ 519
James 687
DELLON
Penny 753
DELONG
Harvey 512, 637, 857
DEMAREST
J. W. 646
DEMBY
Nathaniel 284
DENBY
Nathaniel 284
DENT
L. S. 441
DESSANER
A. W. 610
DEVER
Jno. 753
DEVERAU
John 609
DEVERAUX
Thos. P. 19, 358
DEVEREUX
James F. 609
John 546
T. P. 609, 830
Thomas P. 545, 601, 609
DEXTER
Franklin 488
DICKENS

DICKENS
___ 380
DICKERSON
A. T. 637
DICKSON
___ 519
DILLARD
E. M. 857
DILLIN
Silas W. 637
DIMMICK
K.. H. 441
DINLEY
Fathergone 593
DIXON
___ 497
Ebenezer 160
DOBBIN
G. W. 883
J. C. 68
DODGE
C. 110
DOENICH
___ 187
DOES
John 322, 680
DOLL
___ 540
J. A. 914
Penfield 857
DOLPH
Jared 381, 637
DOMINGUEZ
M. 441
DONALDSON
___ 98
DONIPHAN
___ 141
DONNELL
R. S. 264
Richard S. 292
DORCY
A. 118
DOUGHERTY
___ 202
DOUGLASS
George 371
DOW
Jesse E. 380
DOWDY
S. 637
Saml 753
DOWNING
Henry 609
Joseph 609
DOWSON

DOWSON
 Kesiah 857
DOZIER
 A. L. 601, 609
 Abi 763
 Abner L. 609
 E. L. 82, 609
 Ed L. 82
 Tully 609
 Tully L. 609
DRANE
 ___ 726
 Henry Martyn 248
DRAPER
 Lorenzo 201
DREW
 Henry 381
DRUMMOND
 R. Q. 604
DUER
 ___ 451
DUFFY
 ___ 342
DUGAN
 Wm. H. 753
DUNCAN
 Charles 638
 Cothia 638
 Emma (SMITH) 638
 Henry T. 745
 Lidia 638
DUNHAM
 Chas. 143
DUNLOP
 James 745
DUNN
 Francis 637
 Michael 161
DUNSTON
 Wm. 381
DURANT
 ___ 399, 525, 736, 821, 914
D'WOLF
 Henry 124
DYER
 James B. 325
DYOTT
 ___ 87

E

EARICKSON
 Rederick 54
EASTON
 William 637

EASTON
 Wm. 753
EATON
 G. L. 581
 John S. 726
EBORN
 Wm. 109
EDDY
 Oliver T. 175
 Wm. H. 110
EDGAR
 ___ 581
EDNEY
 Cartwright 606
 Edward 606
 Newton 606
EDWARDS
 Chas. 732
 J. E. 914
 Jos. J. 914
EHRINGHAUS
 (See also
 ARONHOUSE)
 ___ 553, 859
 J. C. 61, 282, 443
 J. C. B. 180, 459, 590, 601, 609, 687, 881, 896, 918
 John C. 94, 438, 553, 632, 859
 John C. B. 207, 706
 John D. 922
EIDSON
 Mormon H. 465
ELKINS
 ___ 444
ELLIOT
 Gilbert 859
ELLIOTT
 A. R. 677
 Aaron 381, 512
 Albert R. 706
 G. 896
 Gilbert 197, 272, 459, 553, 706, 779, 790
 Miles 821
 Mordeica 637
 R. 690
 Thomas, Sr. 438
ELLIS
 ___ 271
 A. J. 441
 Elizabeth B. 257
ELLISON
 Francis H. 321
 William J. 321

ELLISON
 Wm. J. 601, 609
ELLISTON
 ___ 904
 Mary 904
ELMORE
 Franklin E. 838
EMERSON
 ___ 578
ENGLISH
 William H. 80
ENNIS
 W. 733
EPPS
 ___ 830
ESTILL
 ___ 444
ETHEREDGE
 Adolphus 764
 Andrew 764
 Caleb J. 764
 Caleb, Sr. 764
 Catharine 764
 Jasper 764
 John B. 609
 Josiah 512
 Lovey 764
 Tart 238
 Thomas 82
ETHERIDGE
 Wm. B. 609
ETHRIDGE
 J. H. 609
 Wm. D. 609
EURE
 Henry L. 919
 Martha Jane
  (LOVETT) 919
 Mills H. 562
 Nathaniel 562
EVANS
 George 79, 134, 451
 Humphery 353
 John 869
EWELL
 John 401
EWING
 Butcher 546
 Thomas 784

F

FACEMIRE
 George 637
FAGAN
 F. F. 609, 745

FAGAN
 N. B. 609
FAHNESTOCK
 W. B. 813
FAIR
 Bourbon (Ky.)
  Agricultural 431
FAIRBANKS
 ___ 340
FALLUN
 M. 441
FARGO
 Thomas B. 187
FARNHAM
 ___ 592
FARNUM
 Phebee G. 724
FARRALLY
 John W. 451
FARRANGE
 ___ 46
FARRIS
 N. L. 662
FAUNTLEROY
 Thos. T. 328
FAUQUIER
 J. W. 473
FEARING
 I. 577, 795
 Isaiah 632
 J. B. 674
 J. Bartlett 196
 Jno. B. 635
 John B. 674
 Oliver 54, 75
 Virginia 577
FELTON
 Elisha 677
 Mary 381
 R. R. 609
 Richard 525
FENDALL
 ___ 299
FENNER
 John H. 545, 830
FENTRESS
 James 895
 Willis 895
FENWICKE
 John 742
FEREBEE
 ___ 381, 908
 D. 590
 D. D. 590, 609
 Ed 82
 Edwin 82

FEREBEE
 James 82
 James M. 373, 410, 820, 873, 879
 Jas. M. 848, 900
 Mary Jane 848
 S. R. 381
 Wilson 82
 Wm. E. 274
FERGUSON
 ___ 105
FERRALL
 ___ 849, 850, 907
 M. 609
FERRELL
 ___ 444
FESSENDEN
 B. F. 609
FHIEN
 John H. 24
FICKHARDT
 F. A. 733
FIELD
 ___ 823
 J. B. 441
FILLMORE
 ___ 811, 823
 ___ (SMITH) 787
 Millard 155, 767, 787, 883
FINNELL
 W. H. 229
FISHER
 ___ 581
 Geo. F. 229
 Wm. D. 271
FISK
 Eleanor 819
 Martin 819
FITZGERALD
 H. 259
FLETCHER
 ___ 827
 Francis 308, 512
FLOURNEY
 ___ 152
FLOYD
 James N. 609
FOLAND
 Peter 110
FOLGER
 J. W. 125
FOLK
 S. A. 789
FONTAINE
 Charles 301

FONTAINE
Chas. 301
Madison R. 301
William 301
FOOTE
Thomas M. 201,611
FORBES
____ 726
E. M. 408,489,896
Edward M. 177
Elizabeth 381
Evan 82
Sarah Ann 753
Stephen 166,177
Wm. 740
FORD
---- 512,609,752
C. M. 19,358,609, 677
Chas. M. 609
John 444
FOREY
____ 658
FORNEY
____ 645
FORSYTH
____ 309
FOSTER
S. C. 441
FOWLER
J. S. 441
FOX
George 508,869
FRANKENSTEIN
John 391
FRANKLIN
John 571
FREDERICKS
____ 327
FREEMAN
E. B. 585
J. M. 45,147,339, 411,772
John B. 609
FREMAN
J. M. 315
FREMONT
____ 125
J. C. 393
FRENCH
____ 319
B. B. 380
Emely 118
J. S. 860
James S. 682
FRESHWATER

FRESHWATER
Elizabeth 225
FRIEND
John S. 454
FROST
John 550,745
FULERTON
Robert 465
FULLER
S. Margaret 838
Willis H. 585
FURGERSON
W. A. 609

G

GAINES
____ 887
Edmund Pendleton 209,276
Edmund Pendleton, Jr. 276
Francis Henry Toulman 276
Francis Young 276
Henry T. 276
Myra (CLARK) 276
GAINS
____ 320
GAITHER
B. S. 732
GAKAIS
____ 661
GALES
Seaton 585,732
GALLAGHER
John S. 380
GALLAHER
John S. 416
GALLATIN
Albert 302
GALLOP
B. 512
Hodges 83
GALT
Dickie 7
GAMBREL
John A. 61,637
GAMBRIL
John A. 41
GAMBRILL
____ 24
GANINGTON
Ann 637
GAPES
Thos. 637

GARDNER
____ 844
David 787
Julia 787
Thomas M. 687
Thos. M. 687
GARRETT
A. F. 609
GARRISON
David 179
James S., Sr. 895
Jas. S., Jr. 895
Wm. Loyd 597
GASKINS
Elizabeth (FRESHWATER) 225
Thomas 225,706
Thos. 553,706,859
GATLING
Geo. 248
John 562
Reddick 609
Riddick 562
GAUL
____ 581
GAYLORD
J. F. 609
GEER
Solomon 832
GENSUTHZ
____ 661
GENTRY
____ 784
GHISELIN
J. D. 60
GIBBS
Henry 813
GIBSON
Chas. Bell 746
Nathan 512
GIDDINGS (See also GITTINGS)
Joshua R. 380
GILBERT
E. 441
Edward 522
Elizabeth 727
Timothy 118,256, 532
GILFORTE
Leidey 753
GILL
James 609
GILLETT
R. H. 434

GILLIAM
H. A. 609
J. R. 601,609
John R. 609
R. B. 732
GILLICHEN
Sam'l 563
GILMAN
Caroline 764
John 764
GITTINGS (See also GIDDINGS)
John S. 24
GIVENS
Mathew 465
GLASS
J. W. 609
Jos. Wirt 857
GLATFELTER
Henry 721
GLENN
John 883
R. Henry 66
GLOVER
J. 197
William 19,56,248
Wm. 77,358,735
GODFEY
Jos. M. 637
GODFREY
Mary 512,753,857
GODWIN
J. B. 329,336,402, 459,609,896
GOES
Hannah 787
Maria 787
GOLDSMITH
M. 548
GONZALEZ
A. 762
GOODMAN
____ 277
Barney 562
John T. 637
GOOK
Wm. G. 34
GORDAN
Joseph P. 165
GORDON
Francis 381
Geo. B. 562
George B. 609
John C. 253,298,562
Joseph P. 350
Stephen 381

GORMAN
Thos. 833
GOTWAIT
Jacob 723
GOURLEY
Adam G. 465
GRAEFENBURG
____ 374
GRAHAM
____ 201,497,637
Edward 248
W. A. 732,780
William A. 220
GRAIN
Peter, Sr. 333
GRANBERRY
Josiah T. 122
Willism G. 248
GRANDY
____ 190
C. W. 33,260
J. 215
J. J. 364,531,655
John J. 37,455,553, 583,640,796,818,859
Sarah 381
Thos. F. 609
Thos. S. 609
W. S. 82
Willis 609
Willis S. 609
GRANT
____ 752
Deacon 179
W. 857
Wm. 727
GRAY
____ 162,833
Eliza (CHAPMAN) 489
H. H. 914
Thaddeus S. 271
W. H. 830
Wesley 512
Wm. B. 489
GREELEY
Horace 92
GREEN
____ 651
C. C. 8,101,117,227, 252,795
Noah 609
Thomas 371
Thomas J. 320
William 785
GREENE

135

GREENE
Robert Cochran 248
GREER
Nathaniel 444
GREGORY
____ 358
Cason 752
George 93
Thomas 437
Wm. 817
Wm. N. 271,358
GRESHAM
Thos. B. 50
GREY
Job 381
GRICE
____ 508,553,609, 859
S. D. 197,239,269, 288,336,443,459,609, 706,779,896
S. Davis 845
GRIDELY
Return 593
GRIDLEY
Believe 593
GRIFFIN
____ 700
Margaret 753
W. W. 157,241,323, 553,716,802,859
William W. 878
Wm. 637
Wm. W. 88,282,606, 706,779,878,906,921
GRIFFITH
S. M. 110
GRIGG
A. J. 444
GRIGGS
Joseph 271
Wm. 895
GRINNEL
Moses H. 571
GRINNELL
____ 299
Henry 708
GROSVENEUR
L. S. 787
GUION
H. W. 732
J. A. 616
GUNNISON
J. W. 222
GURLEY
W. P. 609

GURNEY
E. 849,850,907
GUTHRIE
Elijah 271
GUYTHER
D. C. 609
GWIN
W. M. 441

H

HADAWAY
Albert 637
HAGER
Henry 734
HAGNER
Peter 380,416
HAIGH
Wm. H. 287
HALE
____ 787
Daniel 660
HALEY
____ 444
John 512
S. 441
HALL
Allen A. 825
J. Prescott 132
N. K. 780
HALLECK
H. W. 441
HALSEY
Jos. 609
Joseph 601,609
Josiah 732
R. S. 609
W. 388
Wm. 29,129,148, 206,251,346,347,605
HALSTEAD
Nathan 637
HAMDEN
James 271
HAMILTON
Alexander 451
Zera 381
HANCE
S. S. 87
HAND
Jacob 142
HANDY
W. R. 389
HANES
William 609
HARDEMAN

HARDEMAN
Thomas, Jr. 823
HARDENBURG
T. H. 180
HARDIN
Ben 554
HARDING
Jesper 124
HARDISON
H. 609
HARDY
____ 61,65,519
H. B. 609
H. C. 33,260,282
T. B. 609
HARLIN
James 734
James M. 160
HARNEY
Sarah E. 303
Thomas 381
Wm. A. 548
HARPER
Samuel 54
HARREL
Abner 609
B. 753
J. 753
HARRELL
A. 271,637
Abner 609
Ann 711
Ann L. 637
Isaac H. 562
Isaac L. 253
Isaac S. 298
Isacc S. 298
J. 271,637
Louisa Jane 711
Sally ;271
Starky 609
Wm. H. 562
HARRIS
____ 862
C. A. 389
Grandy 857
John 389
Martin 196
R. 163
Wiley P. 284
HARRISON
____ 831
____ (BASSET) 787
Benjamin 787
Joseph 791
William Henry 787

HARRISON
Wm. S. 381
HARTMAN
J. P. 365
HARTNELL
W. E. P. 441
HARTWELL
W. B. 448
HARVEY
____ 163,474,765
Ann 637
H. J. 609
James 412
Margaret 857
Thomas 553,798, 859
Thos. 609,706
HARWOOD
Eliza Fisk 7
J. R. 7
Joseph C. 118
HASKET
Henry 857
HASKETT
Henry 271
HASSELL
C. B. 789
Solomon 609
T. L. 609
HASTINGS
L. W. 411
HATHAWAY
____ 71
B. 601
B. W. 609
James W. 169
Mark 776
T. 71
HATSEL
Wm. F. 563
HAUGHTON
T. S. 224,753
Tippoo S. 381
HAWK
____ 444
HAWKINS
Elizabeth 598
Harmon 465
Hope 593
Littlebury 284
Thomas Theodore 762
HAYES
____ 592
HAYS
Jack 98

HAYWOOD
Edward Graham 248
G. W. 585
R. B. 585,687
R. W. 585
HEADLY
J. T. 734
HEAGY
H. D. 110
HEATH
R. R. 609
Thos. C. 512
HEENEY
John 561
HEINRICH
Carl 61
HELLAND
Joseph L. 823
HELLEN
Wm. Penn 563
HENDERIXON
Andrew 271
HENDERSON
Jas. 619
John 762
John B. 465
HENDRICKSON
____ 658,812
C. R. 303,367,408, 443,523,565,763,795, 829
HENLEE
N. W. 512
HENRICKSON
C. R. 164
HENRIE
Dan Drake 320
HENRIQUEZ
H. 441
HENRY
B. 381
John 609
Joseph 424
Louis 248
Patric 342
HERBERT
Mary 637
HERR
____ 299
HERRINGTON
Willet 553,740,859
HICKS
Charles F. 221
Mary E. 598
HILL
____ 444

HILL
Araph 637
Fred. J. 726
Henry 441
Isaac 394
Mercer 444
W. J. 609
Whitmel H. 545
HILLIARD
H. M. 652
Henry W. 199,652
HINES
____ 585
E. C. 224,609
Rich'd 634
Richard 585,732
HINTON
____ 585
C. L. 183
Edgar L. 553,706, 859
Geo. W. 553,859
J. W. 115,245,565, 636,728,795,876,896
James W. 72,76,126, 236,459,636,706
Jas. W. 246,535,596, 607,629,632,647,665, 713,805,847,868,881
Jno. L. 543,706
John L. 75,419,553, 859
John W. 270
Lewis R. 681
Martha 270
P. W. 313,419,512
Peter W. 312,400, 747
Wm. S. 553,857,859
HITER (See also HYTER)
Henry 512
HOBBS
George 381
HOBSON
J. 441
HODGDON
John 354
HODGES
Artimesia 878
Artimesia (BAILEY) 878
John 878
William 443
HOGAN
Wm. 753

HOLLAND
J. W. 506
James W. 512
HOLLINGSROTH
J. McH. 441
HOLLOWELL
Ambrose 637
C. W. 677
HOLMES
____ 758
John Lyon 224
John Wright 248
Sylvester 710
HOLSOM
Josephine C. B. 489
HOLT
Samuel 857
HONE
Philip 132
HOOD
Sarah 462
Wm. H. 585
HOOKER
William 87
HOOPER
Cyrus 771
Wm. E. 36,418
HOPE
J. B. 151
HOPKINS
Chas. C. 501
George 904
Mary F. (PALMER) 501
HOPPE
J. D. 441
HORN
Charles E. 428
HOSKINS
Charles 725
Nash 725
T. S. 880
Thos. S. 783
HOUSTON (See also HUESTON)
____ 320
Alex. 510
J. S. 441
HOWARD
____ 823
S. H. 823
W. D. M. 441
HOWELL
J. 271
HOYT
Edmund S. 248

HUBBARD
Charles 637
James 895
Martin 637
HUDGINGS
Thos. W. 609
HUESTON (See also HOUSTON)
S. 699
HUFFORD
James H. 465
HUGER
Alfred 645
HUGHES
____ 320,407
HULL
____ 613
Elizabeth 200
HUMPHREYS
F. 110
HUMPHRIES
David 324
Sarah 324
HUNT
John W. 745
HUNTER
____ 64
E. R. 64
T. 75,392,414
Timothy 255
William I. 89
HURDLE
Hiram 551
Joseph T. 551
HUTCHINSON
Elizabeth 787
HYDE
Will E. 118
HYNCK
J. S. 110
HYTER (See also HITER)
Henry 381

I

INDIAN TRIBES
Camanche 413
Cherokee 439
Choctaw 737
Seminole 477
Wyandot 232
INDIANS
BILLY BOW LEGS 293,477
BUFFALO HUMP

INDIANS
BUFFALO HUMP 413
James KELL 439
John ROSS 439
SIX KILLER 439
William P. POWELL 309
WA-KAN-YE-KE-WING 425
INVENTIONS
Typewriter 175
IREDELL
____ 585,732
IRVIN
Thomas 444
IRVINE
John 110
ISRAEL
B. 386
IVES
L. S. 168,726
L. Silliman 726
Martha H. 518

J

JACKSON
____ 444
Andrew 787
Barney 381
C. C. 153
Charles T. 615
Chlotilden 484
Elizabeth HUTCHINSON 787
George 288
Hezekiah 857
J. A. 609
James S. 190
John 381
Levinia 753
Mary A. 637
Phebe (SCOTT) 288
Sallie 395
Samuel 271,632
William 381
JACOBS
A. E. 386,530,552, 905
E. 609
JACOCKS
Grizell P. 525
Jas. G. 381
Jonathan H. 736

JACOCKS
Margaret Stevenson 736
Thomas S. 677
Thos. S. 61,358,609
JAMES
Francis 271
JARVES
James J. 427
JARVIS
Samuel 698
Thomas C. 118
JAYNE
D. 214
JEAN
____ 581
JEFFERSON
Jane RANDOLPH 787
Peter 787
Thomas 787
JELSAW
____ 444
JENINGS
____ 612
JENKINS
____ 677
JENNINGS
Jos. 196
Joseph 381
Nathan 637,857
William 341,612
JEWELL
____ 202
JINKINS
Joseph 381
JINNINGS
Fred 239
Patsey CASEY 239
JOHNSON
____ 12,726
C. E. 585
Carter P. 746
Cave 283
G. B. 581
George 637
Joshua 787
Louisa Catherine 787
Reverdy 378
JOHNSTON
____ 299,726
Asa 609
Charles E. 479
Cornelia 857
James C. 609,830
Jas. C. 19,358

JOHNSTON
Lucius 857
Nannie T. 479
Samuel I. 479
Thomas S. 609
JONES
____ 444,758,838, 915
A. 609
A. L. 197
Alfred 585
Andrew Mc. 118
Ann (REY) 417
Arthur 473,553,586, 776,859
C. P. 753
E. W. 609
Elizabeth 787
H. C. 68
J. B. 381
J. P. 151
Jno. M. 874
John M. 190,609
Jos. S. 190
Lewis 488
Marthana 381
Matilda 381
R. 209
T. F. 609
Thomas F. 61,601, 609
Thos. F. 344,372, 609,677,770
W. D. 585
Wm. 515,857
Wm. R. 417
JORDAN
____ 65,752
A. S. 562
Elenor E. 118
John P. 590,601,609
Louisa 271
M. O. 901,921
Matthew O. 475
Prichard 637
JOYNER
A. 545,609,830,851
Andrew 601,609, 732
JUDSON
E. Z. C. 371

K

KANE
____ 299

KEATON
Nancy 637
KEATON
Winnefred 753
Wm. 753
KEE
Jesse R. 562
KEELING
David F. 808
KEEP
____ 615
KEIGHTLEY
____ 673
KELLENGER (See also KILLINGER)
Geo. W. 37
KELLER
John J. 99
KELLINGER
George W. 875
W. J. 556,627,673, 766,822
Wm. J. 531,609,703, 881,911
KELLY
____ 456
Alexis 732
KEMPER
____ 745
KENDALL
____ 202,445
Amos 232,445
KENDING
____ 299
KENNEDAY
W. W. 914
KENNEDY
Jos. C. G. 734
W. W. 75,795
KENNERLY
Augustine 361
KENT
____ 201
KENYON
D. H. 696
KERBY (See also KIRBY)
Rodgers 753
KERFOOT
John B. 800
KILLINGER (See also KELLINGER)
Wm. J. 541
KIMBALL
____ 189
KIMBERLEY

KIMBERLEY
John 886
KIMBERLY
John 372,809
KING
____ 125,404
Basset John 637
Daniel P. 838
Solomon 12
Thomas Butler 440, 624
Thos. Butler 451
KINGSLOW
Russell 421
KINNE
____ 611
KIRBY (See also KERBY)
Rodgers 512
KISSAM
Saml. 609
KITE
Joseph 350
Joseph Eamin 350
Malachi 350
Susan 350
KNELLER
George 381
KNIGHT
R. B. 609
T. W. 753
Thos. 640
Thos. W. 423,664
KNOWLS
Thomas 753
KNOX
Ambrose 796
Thomas 609
Thomas D. 918
Thos. D. 553,859
KONE
W. 857
W. W. 637
KORTRIGHT
____ 787
KRAUSS
Henry 21
KYLE
Wm. P. 753

L

L.
____ 817
LA GUERRA
P. 441

LABOYTAUX
Wm. 402,459
LABOYTEAUX
John 271
Salvadora 910
Sarah 910
William 910
Wm. 637,802
LADD
____ 179
LAFAYETTE
____ 529
George Washington 529
LAIB
____ 271
LAMAR
C. A. L. 823
H. G. 823
Henry G. 823
LAMB
____ 58,414
Alfred 857
C. G. 242,512,609
Cornelius G. 609
John 410
Miles 82,797
S. D. 81,637,749
Sarah E. 637
William 118
LAND
Edward 401
Major 895
LANE
Wm. K. 264
LANG
____ 271
E. H. 233
LANGDON
Samuel Walter 248
LANSTON
____ 765
LARAMMINE
Lewis 425
LARKIN
T. O. 441
LASSITER
Timothy H. 253,562
LASTER
Ann 271
LATHAM
C. 609
Charles 609
LAUDER
Geo. 687
LAVERTY

LAVERTY
C. M. 392,414
Charles M. 82
John 178
LAVITEW
Edward 637
LAWG
Wm. 585
LAWRANCE
Abbott 366
LAWRENCE
Abbott 201,318,366
LAYDEN
Joseph 821
LE BARBIER
F. 569
LE FORREST
____ 247
LEARNED
S. J. 457
LEARY
J. H. 601,609,894
John H. 609
Thos. H. 51
Thos. H., Jr. 609
LEE
____ 12,562
Doxey 857
Lewis 229
Nancy 857
LEIGH
____ 271
Edward A. 736
James 736
Jas. 358
John P. 43,61
Margaret Stevenson (JACOCKS) 736
LEMAY
J. B. 585
Leonidas B. 641
Leonidas B., Sr. 641
T. J. 585
LEMMETT
J. R. 190
LEMY
Leonidas B. 585
LENNOX
James 572
LESTER
R. S. 381
LEUBECH
____ 854
LEWIS (See also LOUIS)

138

LEWIS
  Durham 118
  E. 110
  James R. 512
  Mary G. 408
  Samuel 637
  Samuel M. 839
  Watson, Jr. 609
LIDDEN
  ___ 271
LIGON
  John 585
LINCOLN
  Levi 352
LIND
  Jenny 625
LINDSAY
  Cader 753
  David 271
LINDSEY
  E. C. 609
  Ed. C. 102
  J. B. 609
  J. J. 609
LINTON
  A. J. 733
  Indiana 648
LIPMAN
  ___ 581
LIPPARD
  George 223
LIPPINCOTT
  B. S. 441
LIPPITT
  F. J. 441
LISTER
  Sarah 381
  Wm. 512
LITTLE (See also LYTLE)
  George 757
  James 63
LITTLEFIELD
  ___ 470
  Ephraim 788
LITTLEJOHN
  Elizabeth L. 803
LODGES
  Achoree, No. 14 115, 166, 674
  Grand, of NC 115
  United States, of the 180
  I. O. O. F. 635, 674
  Grand 180
  Independent Order

LODGES
  Independent Order of Odd Fellows 790
  Masonic 662, 697
  Odd Fellows 565, 596, 687, 872
  Pasquonaux 716, 921
  Widow's Son 493
LOGAN
  Peter 637
LOHMANN
  ___ 874
LONG
  ___ 444
  D. W. L. 830
  J. J. 830
  James 620
  James S. 693
  Jas. S. 632, 714
  Martha S. 512
  N. M. 830
  W. L. 609
  Wm. 381, 857
LOPEZ
  Narciso 762
LORY
  Wm. 512, 637
LOUDON
  H. F. 62, 325
LOUIS (See also LEWIS)
  Adolphus 630, 753
LOUTHER
  Sam'l J. 562
LOVETT
  M. J. 512
  Martha Jane 919
  Mary (RIGGS) 845
  Norris 845
  Wilson H. C. 895
LOWRY
  Ann 381
LOWTHER
  Wm. D., Jr. 609
LUCE
  William 465
LUMPKIN
  George 718
LUTON
  David 512
LUTTS
  Charlotte 857
LYELL
  Jacob 742
LYMAN

LYMAN
  ___ 862
LYON
  ___ 745
  Barbray Ann (WINDLEY) 93
  Caleb 644
  Francis S. 276
  William H. 93
LYONS
  C. 441
LYTLE (See also LITTLE)
  Jno. S. 637

M

M.
  ___ 900, 908
MABANE
  H. N. 358
MC ALISTER
  J. 118
MC ALLISTER
  ___ 737
MC BOYLE
  J. 601
  John 609
MC BRIDE
  ___ 827
MC CANDLESS
  John 162
MC CARTY
  ___ 554
MC CARVER
  M. M. 441
MC CLEES
  Charles 609
  Jessee 49
  Jno. 609
  Jos. 609
MC CLEESE
  ___ 501
MC CLELLAN
  T. 160
MC CLUNG
  ___ 201
MC COLLUM
  ___ 576, 581
  T. 581
MC CONNELL
  G. W. 110
MC CORKLE
  Joseph W. 99
MC CORMICK
  ___ 299

MC COY
  ___ 509
  James 190
  Joshua 509
  S. D. 753
  Samuel D. 637
MC CUBBIN
  ___ 299
MC CULLERS
  John 585
MC CULLOCH
  ___ 201
MC CULLOH
  George W. 99
MC CULLOUGH
  ___ 232
MC DANIEL
  Flory 637
MC DEAL
  Fanny 381
MC DONALD
  ___ 823
  Murdock 637
MC DONNELL
  Wm. H. 589
MC DOUGAL
  G. 512
  John 522
MC DOUGALD
  J. G. 224
MC ELDOWNEY
  R. 412
MC ELWEE
  James D. 465
MC INTOSH
  ___ 16
MC KAIN
  J. R. 613
MC KAY
  James J. 264
MC KEARY
  Henry 271
MC KENNAN
  Thomas M. T. 831
MC KENNEY
  W. M. 443
MC KREE
  J. J. 381
MC LANE
  ___ 309
MC LAUGHLIN
  James 444
MC LAUGHON
  G. W. 85
MC LEAN
  John 69

MC MAHON
  ___ 276
MC MATH
  John H. 823
MC MILLIAN
  D. 180
MC MORINE
  ___ 458
  John 603
  Martha 603
MC MULLEN
  John 36, 418
MC NIDER
  Wm. 169
MC PETERS
  ___ 444
MC PHAILS
  Authur 563
MC REE
  G. J. 701
MC REY
  S. H. 609
M'GUFFY
  W. H. 745
MACINTOSH
  William 18
MACKEY
  James A. 465
MADDOX
  ___ 299
MADISON
  Dolly PAYNE TOOD 787
  James 155, 787
  Nelly CONWAY 787
MADIYETT (See also MIDYETT)
  Edward 381
MAFFIT
  J. N. 234
  J. Newland 838
MAGNIN
  H. 349
MAISON
  C. A. 753
MALLORY
  ___ 519
  Wm. S. 688
MANDER
  John 188
MANING (See also MANNING)
  Charles G. 609
MANLY
  ___ 783

MANLY
Charles 379,672, 706,732,777
Chas. 677
J. H. 585
John H. 180,687
Langdon C. 379

MANN
___ 700
W. E. 256
William E. 459
Wm. E. 1,195,196, 236,271,326,381,397, 512,553,587,609,637, 689,706,752,753,779, 790,857,859,881,896, 897

MANNEY
J. 563
James L. 563

MANNING (See also MANING)
___ 40
J. 914
T. C. 659

MANNS
George 694

MANSARD
John 906
John B. 906

MANSFIELD
H. 550

MARCH
John B. 495
S. 549

MARCHANT
G. C. 512

MARCUM
John 512

MARCY
William G. 441

MARDRE
Joseph 524

MARKEUS
E. 753

MARKS
___ 904

MARSH
Bennett 271,512, 753
Geo. P. 201

MARSHALS
BROWN
___ (Dep.) 844
LITTLE
George (U.S.) 757

MARSHALS
NEWBOLD
Wm. (Asst.) 841

MARSHALL
___ 442
A. C. 753
J. G. 335
John 444

MARTIN
___ 823
C. F. 443
Enoch 465
G. T. 54
Geo. P. 909
Geo. T. 54
James G. 557
Pearl 488
Robert B. 248
Samuel 233
W. F. 197,918
Wm. F. 166,553, 859,881

MASON
___ 554,569,838
Charles 497
John Y. 283
R. S. 726
Wm. 753

MATHEWS
J. M. 197,595,654, 905
John 235,881
Richard 637
Samuel 409,749
Sarah G. 409
T. R. 61
William P. 409

MATTHEWS
John M. 166,562
Thomas R. 105

MAUPIN
S. 746

MAYER
Thomas S. 834

MAYHEW
W. H. 732

MAYORS
JONES
___ 758
POOL
Jos. H. 779
Joseph H. 521

MEADE
R. K. 152

MEADS
Alfred 512

MEADS
Robert 271
Stanton 381

MEARES
Walker 248

MEDILL
___ 141

MEEDS
Samuel T. 381

MEESER
Wm. 813

MEHAFFY
___ 860

MEHAN
Andrew 98

MEISCHEAU
Sophia 82

MELLVANE
A. Murray 176

MELSON
___ 171
William 171

MEMMENGER
C. G. 645

MENDENHALL
___ 732
Nerus 360

MERCER
___ 559

MEREDITH
___ 141
W. M. 234

MERRILL
Harum 488

MERSER
James B. 118

MESSENGER
Wm. 88,420,664

MEZIC
George 637

MICHAELS
R. 914

MIDGETT (See also MYDGETT)
E. B. 517

MIDYET
Louis 49

MIDYETT (See also MADIYETT)
E. B. 231

MIER
___ 320

MIFFLIN
___ 460

MILHADO
___ 105

MILLER
___ 376,468,585, 668
B. T. 753
Charles 271
H. W. 585
Harris E. 637
Henry 609
J. G. 468
James 444
Jas. 637
M. W. 585
Samuel 444
Thomas L. 729
Thos. J. 609,857
W. L. 233

MILLS
___ 904
Ann 573
Wm. H. 753

MILLSON
John S. 152

MILNA
Constance 593

MILTENBERGER
George W. 810

MINER
___ 862

MINIGIRODE
Chas. 7

MINNIS
G. W. 799

MINSTRELS
Aeolian 513,637

MISKELL
Thos. J. 190,542

MITCHEL
___ 271
Wm. J. 609

MITCHELL
F. S. 914
James 14
Jas. 95
Saml. 753
Sarah 118
William 385

MIZELL
A. J. 609
W. W. 609

MONCHEN
Sophia 753

MONROE

(KORTRIGHT)
787
Elizabeth JONES

MONROE
Elizabeth JONES 787
James 787
Spence 787

MONTAGUE
H. W. 585

MOORE
___ 444
A. W. 163
Alfred W. 753
Aug. 358,601
Augustus 358,609, 726
B. 163
B. F. 183,441
Britton 753
Clayton 609
Frederic S. 248
G. C. 609
G. L. 609
Robert 189,444
Susan J. 381,857
Wm. 443

MORDECAI
George W. 726
Jacob 585

MORE
Moss 444

MOREHEAD
James T. 732

MORGAN
James M. 547
Nancy 547
Seth 553,632,665, 706,859,889
T. T. 637
Wm. 895

MORRIS
___ 207,299,637, 857
Eason A. 271
J. B. 24
Mordecai 196,358
Nathan 635,674
Rose 277
Thomas O. 512,753

MORRISETT
W. M. 493

MORRISON
Daniel S. 381

MORSE
___ 445
S. F. B. 445

MORTON
Jeremiah 152

140

MOSELY
___ 293
Tully 857
MOSHIEM
___ 570
MOULTRIE
___ 823
MUDD
Henry Clay 645
J. H. Clay 299
MULATTOES
BOB 734
MULING
Mointha 381
MULLEN
___ 39,857
Benj. 677
Benjamin 358,801
F. N. 358
Francis N. 512
James 381
James W. 381
Jas. 753
Jas. L. 358,553,859
Jas. W. 902
Jos. 553,609,753, 859
Joseph 271,706
Mary L. 637,857
Wm. A. 902
MULLER
L. 271
MUNDEN
Simon 172
Thos. R. 857
MURDEN
Benj. 381,512
Sophia 512
MURPHEY
E. F. 516
Wm. H. 516
MURPHY
William 381
MURRAY
___ 19,358,877
MURRY
Eli 163
MUSGRAVE
___ 533,534,630
G. J. 443,795,896, 918
George J. 459
MYDGETT (See also MIDGETT)
Stephen D. 637
MYERS

MYERS
Absalom 732

N

NAGLE
S. S. 110
NAINHOUSE
S. T. 381
NANTZE
Richard 381
NASH
___ 455,666
Elisha 620
Elizabeth 632,901
H. K. 264
J. 259,753
J. H. 259,840
James 164,381,478
Jos. 840
Sebra WILLIAMS 164
NEALE
Abner P. 229
NEGROES
Alfred HOLLOWELL (of color) 753
ANNE 401
ANNY 401
ANTHONY 401
Benj. PERRY 792
BETSEY 401
BILL 884
BOB 463
BRIDGEY 460
CHARLES 401
DANIEL 401
DENBY 401
DINEY 401
Fanny DAVIS (of color) 753
FRANK 401
GEORGE 384
Gilbert PEARSON (of color) 753
GRAYSON 785
HANNAH 401
HENRY 437
Henry POOLE (of color) 637
Isaac WHITE (of color) 381
JACK 401
Jas. HAMLET 844
Jenny

NEGROES
Jenny WENTWORTH 709
Jim KEATON (of color 753
JOE 404,444,460
John JENKINS (of color) 404
JOSH 444
Marian RICHARDSON 356
Martan GLADDED 356
MARY 55
Menemin CALHOUN 327
MILES 404
MOSES 525
NAPOLEON 401
NED 401
NOAH 404
PETER 458
PHILIP 401
Polydore CALHOUN 327
Robert HALL (of color) 637
SAM 401,444,688
SAREY 401
SOLOMON 279
THADDEUS 401
VENUS 401
VINCENT 573
Wade HAMP'ON 353
WASHINGTON 384
NEIMYER (See also NIEMYER)
John H. 105
NELSON
Hugh 460
John 54
NESBIT
___ 299
NEVILLE
T. 581
NEWBERRY
Abram 609
NEWBOLD
Wm. 628,841
NEWBOULD
Samuel 653
NEWBY
___ 65,385

NEWBY
J. B. 180,687
Mary 381
Thomas 358
NEWELL
Martha B. 886
NEWMAN
A. 152
NEWMANS
Elizabeth (GILBERT) 727
Richard G. 727
NEWSOM
Henry 637
NICHOLLS
Jehu 609
T. B. 609
NICHOLS
J. 637
NIEMEYER (See also NEIMYER)
Henry V. 582
NIXON
Francis 19,344,358, 372
Samuel 677
NOBLE
___ 179
NOE
Wm. D. 563
NOEL
W. C. 744
NOLAND
___ 273
NORCOM
Jos. C. 609
NORCUM
J. C. 601,609
NORFLEET
James E. 90
NORRIS
Sam'l. P. 585
NORTON
___ 444
M. 441
NORVELL
J. H. 668
John 468
NOTTINGHAM
___ 160
W. J. 42

O

OAKLEY
Allen 273

O'BAR
Alford 444
O'BAR
Alfred 444
ODEN
Hezekiah 465
O'HARA
Theodore 762
OLD
William 419
Wm. 359,400,512, 637
OLDHAM
___ 160
OLIVER
John W. 733
OLLENDORFF
___ 673
OLMSTEAD
___ 673
ONEAL
Mary 753
O'NEILL
James 371
ORD
P. 441
OREM
John M. 412
OSBORN
James W. 220
O'SULLIVAN
J. L. 762
OUTLAW
___ 292,894
David 108,256,264, 300
OVERMAN
Benjamin N. 715
Elizabeth 753
Margaret 637
Nathan 381,857
Sarah 753
OVERTON
Elizabeth 381,512
OWENS
Daniel D. 243
James 381
Wm. 753
OXLY
Elizabeth 512

P

P.
B. R. 232
PAGE

PAGE
  Anderson 585
PAINE (See also PAYNE)
  ___ 439,451
  R. T. 134
  Robert T. 79
  Thomas I. 118
  Wm. A. 637
PALIN
  John 241,712
  Lydia 902
PALMER
  ___ 433
  James 381
  Mary F. 501
  Sarah Ann 888
  Susanna 118
  V. B. 675
  W. R. 49,381
  William R. 49
  Wm. R. 49
PARKER
  ___ 673
  Alexander 266
  David 562
  Foxhall A. 70
  Jos. R. 553,706,859
  Richard 152
  Robt. S. 163
PARKMAN
  ___ 510,544,615, 622,788
  George 470,488
PARKS
  C. A. 732
  Loyd 450
  Marshalk 588
  Marshall 682,753
PARLEY
  ___ 673
PARSONS
  ___ 765
PATRICK
  Selby 87
PATTERSON
  ___ 51
  Billy 174
  S. F. 732
PAUL
  F. M. 560
PAXTON
  Richard 51
PAYNE (See also PAINE)
  Dolly 787

PEARCE (See also PIERCE)
  ___ 784
  J. A. 780
  Samuel 565
PEARSON (See also PIERSON)
  ___ 444
  H. D. 133
PECK
  C. L. 441
PEEL
  Robert 838
PENDER
  Thos. E. 609
PENDLETON
  Burgess 381
  John F. 271
  Reuben 381,637
  Reubin 753
  Robert 358,381, 637,706,753
  Robt. 553,859
  Timothy D. 196
PENN
  ___ 497
PERINE
  Thos. J. 637
PERKINS
  ___ 39,783,857
  Erastus 600
  J. Q. 381,512,637
  James H. 600
  M. C. 857
  Martin C. S. 381
PERRY
  ___ 512,752
  A. A. 776
  Cader 381
  Doctrine R. 553, 706,859
  Priston 609
PERSON
  ___ 292
  Thos. J. 264
PERSONS
  ___ 830
PETICOLAS
  Arthur E. 746
PETTIGREW
  C. L. 601,609
  Charles L. 609
  Wm. S. 637
PETTY
  John 895
PEYTON

PEYTON
  Bailie 201
  Balie 370
PHELPS
  Henderson B. 609
PHILIPS
  William H. 110
PHILLIPS
  A. 461
  Mary 461
PHINNEY
  E. 352
PICKETT
  John F. 762
PICO
  A. M. 441
PIEMONT
  R. 726,730
PIERCE (See also PEARCE)
  Caleb 675
  Charles 310
  Elijah 837
  John 512
PIERSON (See also PEARSON)
  Gilbert 381
PIKE
  ___ 904
  Albert 904
  John 271,637
  Kesiah 857
PINER
  George 381
PIPKIN
  John D. 562
PIVER
  Leroy 563
PLEASANTS
  B. F. 784
  John H. 6
POINER
  ___ 703
POLK
  ___ 283,328
  James K. 80,218
  James Knox 787
POMEROY
  Josiah 724
  Phebec G. (FARNUM) 724
PONS
  ___ 293
PONTON
  John 830
POOL

POOL
  ___ 503,566,696, 783
  Beverly 444
  C. S. 503
  Geo. D. 154,553, 706,859
  George D. 225,358, 702,706,777
  J. J. 490,507
  Jno. 918
  John 197,236,246, 553,635,674,706,735, 779,795,859,918
  Jos. H. 100,553, 760,779,859
  Joseph H. 19,75, 358,521
  Joshua A. 292,553, 702,783,859
  L. S. 696,884
  Narcissa D. (SAWYER) 735
  S. D. 3,15,323,566, 671,691,779,866
  Stephen D. 503, 553,700,859
POOOL
  Geo. D. 553
POPE
  A. 554
  Fountain 554
  Henry 554
PORT
  ___ 369
PORTER
  Augustus 468
POSTMASTERS
  BENBON
  J. 163
  BENNETT
  J. N. 163
  R. O. 163
  BRENEMAN
  A. 110
  BRYAN
  ___ 163
  BURTON
  J. W. 163
  BUTLER
  Wm. 110
  CAPRON
  L. 110
  DODGE
  C. 110
  EDDY

POSTMASTERS
  EDDY
  Wm. H. 110
  FEREBEE
  Wm. E. 274
  FOLAND
  Peter 110
  GILBERT
  Timothy 118
  GRIFFITH
  S. M. 110
  HALL
  N. K. (Gen.) 780
  HARRIS
  R. 163
  HARVEY
  ___ 163
  HEAGY
  H. D. 110
  HUMPHREYS
  F. 110
  HYNCK
  J. S. 110
  IRVINE
  John 110
  KELLER
  John J. 99
  LEWIS
  E. 110
  MANN
  Wm. E. 271,381, 512,637,753,857
  MC CONNELL
  G. W. 110
  MC CORKLE
  Joseph W. 99
  MC CULLOH
  George W. 99
  MOORE
  A. W. 163
  B. 163
  MURRY
  Eli 163
  NAGLE
  S. S. 110
  PARKER
  Robt. S. 163
  PHILIPS
  William H. 110
  RODGERS
  D. G. 110
  SANDERS
  John H. 163
  SCHECK
  John D. 163
  SCOTT

142

POSTMASTERS
SCOTT
  J. 110
SEDWICK
  J. J. 110
SEXTON
  Wm. 110
SKINNER
  John 91
SPEICE
  Adam 99
STAFFORD
  Wm. 110
STEVENSON
  D. R. 110
SWOPE
  Emanuel 110
WARLEY
  J. D. 110
WEST
  J. W. S. 163
WHEELER
  Samuel J. 163
WHITFIELD
  W. T. 163
WILCOX
  Owin 110
WILL
  Elizabeth 110
POTTER
  ___ 289
POUDER
  ___ 299
POULE
  Wm. 512
POUSSIN
  ___ 369
POWELL
  ___ 279
  Paulus 152
POWER
  Wm. 810
POWL
  ___ 110
POYNER
  Jas. 381
PRATT
  ___ 488
  Jabez 488
  Obadiah H. 862
PRENTISS
  S. S. 904
  Sargeant S. 838
PRESTON
  Wm. 461
PREUSS

PREUSS
  ___ 125
PRICE
  Augustus M. 17
  Nathan 271
  Needham 585
PRIMROSE
  ___ 585
PRITCHARD
  ___ 455
  Benj. 677
  George M. 637
  Jos. 553,859
  William D. 235,658
  Wm. D. 256,740
PROCTOR
  F. S. 553,570,859
  Fred. S. 706
  Isaac 180
  John W. 352
PROFFIT
  George H. 451
PUGH
  ___ 508
  Jackson 869
  Jos. 465
PULLEN
  Henry 592
PURDY
  Mary 512
PURVIS
  Robert 309

Q

QUITMAN
  ___ 550
  John A. 762

R

RABOTEAU
  Ch. C. 585
RAILING
  Joseph 381
RAILROAD
  Baltimore and
    Susquehanna 734
  Central 657
  Erie 407,430
  Panama 407
  Seaboard and
    Roanoke 405
RAMAGE
  Adam 838
RAMIREZ

RAMIREZ
  ___ 441
RAMSAY
  A. 202
  R. H. 553,706,859
RAMSEY
  ___ 823
  J. 54
  R. H. 61
RANDALL
  ___ 289,424
RANDOLPH
  ___ 787
  John 609
  Thomas Jefferson
    787
RANGERS
  Texas 320
RAPER
  D. D. 53
  Elizabeth N.
    (TRUEBLOOD)
    523
  Robert 523
RAPP
  A. W. 375,473
RARNARD
  ___ 783
RASCOE
  H. E. 458
  Henry E. 562
RAVENEL
  Daniel 645
RAY (See also REY)
  S. J. 823
RAYMOND
  Lyman 498
RAYNER
  ___ 138
  K. 68
  Keneth 609
  Kenneth 538
REDDAL
  ___ 309
REDDING
  ___ 87
REDICK (See also
  RIDDICK)
  Bearl 753
REED (See also
  RIED) 573
  David S. 740,751
  Elizabeth 271
  Jos. B. 553,859
  Joseph B. 381,706
  Marenda

REED
  Marenda
    (TRUEBLOOD)
    479
  Margaret 857
  Nancy 857
  Thomas 561,602
  Thos. 479
  W. 914
REID
  ___ 783
  David 264
  Edwin 857
  Lemuel S. 157
  M. A. 857
  William F. 480
  Wm. 512
REIMEN
  Henry 24
RELFE
  Stephen 579
REMENYI
  ___ 661
REPITION
  A. Paul 687
RESTIEUX
  Thomas 488
REY (See also RAY)
  Ann 417
REYNOLDS
  ___ 581
  Joseph P. 860
RHETT
  R. B. 823
RHODES
  ___ 561,731
  Elisha H. 285
  James 285
  Jesse 731
  Liddy 512
  Wm. L. 609
RICE
  Dan 576,581
  William H. 444
RICH
  John 444
RICHARDSON
  ___ 161
  D. 636
  Daniel 35,265,891
RIDDICK (See also
  REDICK)
  C. A. 798
  Henry 457,562
  John 495,496,562
  Jos. 562

RIDDICK
  Willis F. 562,601,
    609
RIED (See also
  REED, REID)
  Elizabeth 753
RIGGS
  ___ 561,602
  Mary 845
  Solomon S. 561
RILEY
  ___ 349,439,441
RINALDI
  W. S. 753
RIVES
  W. 460
  Wm. C. 201,318
ROBARDS
  H. L. 732
ROBERTS
  Elizabeth 271
  James L. 609
  Mills 171,562
  Wm. 895
  Wm. D., Jr. 38
ROBINSON
  ___ 444
  Charles E. 540
  E. C. 329,337
  Edward Mott 111
  Elizabeth 118
  Martha A. SWAIN
    540
ROBY
  Joseph 810
RODGERS
  ___ 351
  D. G. 110
  Stephen 278,297
ROGERS
  Peleg 585
  Sion 585
  Sion H. 585
  Sion, Sr. 585
  Wm. 512
ROOT
  ___ 585
  C. G. 585
ROUTLE
  Wm. R. 271,381
ROWLAND
  Jno. A. 732
ROYSTER
  J. D. 180
RUDDOCK
  Nicy 857

143

RULON
John H. 857
RUMLEY
Brian H. 563
James, Jr. 563
RUSSELL
Dempsey 495
James B. 913
Jessee 118
Jos. 753
Jos. D. 857
M. 24
RUTTER
Lucinda 620
William 512

S

ST. VRAIN
____ 125
SALMON
John 98
SALTER
____ 533
J. T. 398,534,911
SAMPLE
S. H. 609
SAMPSON
Granville 637
SANDERLAND
R. A. 753
SANDERLIN (See also SAUNDERLIN)
____ 2,213
Caleb 213,235
Maxcy 88
Maxey 795,812
Trimigan 753
Wm. W. 82
SANDERS
____ 735
John 381
John H. 163
Wm. 512
SANGSTON
G. E. 104
J. A. 104
L. 104
SANSTON
____ 104
SANSUM
____ 444
SAP
Orlando 444
SARGENT
John O. 825

SARGENT
John S. 139
SARN
Wm. 637
SAUNDERLIN (See also SANDERLIN)
Maxcy 547
SAUNDERS
Agustus C. 487
Benjamin 562
J. M. 914
L. K. 10,23,87,116, 128,272,453,471,473, 491,502,748,905,920
R. J. 54
Romulus M. 220
SAWIN
____ 510
SAWYER
____ 373,509,820, 873
Ann B. 753
Daniel 553,859
Edmund T. 740
Gardiner 706
Griffin 753
Isaac 144
Jerome B. 637
Jno. W. 753
Joseph 509
Lydia 857
M. 271
M. S. 609
Mark D. 358
Mark S. 553,609, 859,918
Nancy 753
Narcissa D. 735
Newton 408
Robert A. 37,118, 806
Robt. A. 532
S. T. 473
Spencer 735
Susan (SPENCE) 144
Susan (TRUEBLOOD) 408
Wesley E. 706,908
SCANTLAND
James M. 294
SCHECK
John D. 163
SCHOOLCRAFT
Henry A. 816

SCOTT
____ 550
Casann 164
J. 110
J. C. 115,795
Jas. C. 256,740,781
John 193,512
L. C. 876
Margaret A. 781
Phebe 288
Wm. C. 677
SCULL
Joseph J. 609
SEATTUCK
Lemuel 787
SEDDON
James A. 152
SEDWICK
J. J. 110
SEELY
Wm. A. 537
SEMPLE
R. 441
Robert 441
SEVERN
____ 637
SEWARD
____ 611
SEWER
Jonathan 271
SEXTON
Wm. 110,637
SHACKLEFORD
John 741
SHANNON
John 512
Thomas 640
Thos. 655
W. E. 441
W. L. 115
Wm. 308,542,553, 859
Wm. L. 632,685
SHANNONHOUSE
B. J. 857
SHARBER
Miles 381
Miles M. 271
SHARBORO
David 282
John 282
Miles 282
Thomas 282
SHARP
Stark 601
Starkey 609

SHARP
Starky 609
SHAVER
____ 110
SHAW
____ 743
R. G. 544
Robert G. 470
SHELDON
Anson 753
SHEPARD
____ 783
John S. 853
W. B. 732
Will B. 30,138
Wm. B. 538,553, 601,609,677,678,706, 778,795,796,859,918
SHEPHARD
S. S. 609
SHEPHERD
A. H. 264
J. Avery 745
Robert 118
SHEPPARD
Augustine 300
Augustus L. 6
Lorenzo B. 132
SHERIFFS
BAGLEY
Willis H. 783
DAILY
____ 783
HOSKINS
Thos S. 783
POOL
Joshua A. 702,783
SHERMAN
Roger 786
SHERWOOD
W. S. 441
SHIELD
Charles H. 65
R. H. 609
SHIELDS
____ 319
SHIRDREN
Thomas 381
SHOOK
Nathan 444
SHORT
H. B. 609
Taomas 444
William 444
Wm. 444
SHUSTER

SHUSTER
____ 684
J. P. 683
Jacob 142
Jacob P. 81
SIDELL
William H. 407
SIGUR
L. J. 762
SIKES (See also SYKES)
A. 753
B. J. 609
C. 755
Caleb 136,205,422, 578,631,649,864
Esther 192,382,648
Jesse H. 631
Thomas 271
SIMMONS
____ 683,684,732
B. T. 304,609,764
D. D. 684
Daniel D. 81
J. F. 732
James 609
Josiah 512,773
Martha 304
S. S. 24
Thos. 637
William 49,602
Wm. 521,553,561, 779,859
SIMONS
____ 188
Frank 857
SIMPSON
Benjamin 121
Henry L. 741
Jessee 381
SIMRIL
M. G. 118
SINCLAIR
J. B. 637
SINCLARE
____ 410
SISCO
A. 86,596
Ann 32
SKINNER
____ 458,752
Ann 271
Benjamin 358
Caroline 258
Edmund 358
Edmund B. 474,765

SKINNER
Eliza Fisk (HARWOOD) 7
J. B. 618
J. S. 352
James L. 677
Jno. B. 900
Jno. W. 609
John 91, 248, 765
John B. 436
John Creecy 248
John M. 308
Jos. H. 458
Joshua 19, 51, 358, 609
Mary Catharine 258
N. C. 865
N. Chapman 258
T. L. 7
Thos. E. 677
Wm. R. 190, 609

SLOAN
WilliaM 368

SMALL
Hannah A. 753
John 553, 609, 859
Wilson 444

SMALLWOOD
M. 609

SMEDES
Albert 656, 924
Aldert 168

SMITH
___ 330, 787
Abigail 787
Albert 645
Aristides S. 349
Benjamin Stanton 638
Bird 444
C. H. 513
Caleb B. 79, 134
Caroline 809, 886
Chamness T. 465
Cotesworth Pinckney 762
Cothia (DUNCAN) 638
Daniel 602
Daniel S. 561
E. F. 609, 677, 765
E. M. 513
Ed F. 677
Edward F. 609
Emma 638
Isaac 857

SMITH
J. H. 512, 609
J. W. 513
James N. 545, 601, 609
James R. 609
James T. 399
John 581, 857
Josephine C. B. (HOLSOM) 489
Josiah T. 489
Leondias L. 349
Levi 179
Lidia (DUNCAN) 638
Marcellus 271
Murdoc 381
Nathan R. 810
P. F. 592
Peter 762
R. H. 25, 609
Richard 69, 609
Richard H. 545, 609
S. G. 180
Samuel G. 687
Sereno 638
Sylvester 638
Thos. L. 434
Truman 611
W. N. H. 609
Walter 69
William 444
William N. H. 404
Wm. 787
Wm. N. H. 68
Wm. R. 545, 609

SMITHSON
Cally 381
David 857

SNELL
Franklin 609

SNOWDEN
___ 726

SNYDER
___ 161
Henry 299
J. R. 441
Jacob 734

SOCIETIES
Agricultural 203
AmericanBible 194
Cadets of Temperance 246, 577, 790
Essex County Agricultural 352
Ethnological 432

SOCIETIES
Maryland State Agricultural 883
Massachusetts, for Promoting Agriculture 352
Middlesex, of Husbandmen and Manufacturing 352
Norfolk Agricultural 352
Perquimans Friends 5
S. of T. 911
Sons of Temperance 236, 246, 353, 367, 390, 565, 596, 657, 733, 790, 871, 872, 876, 915
Virginia Historical 460
Worcester County Agricultural 352

SOHIER
Edward D. 488

SOMERVILLE
___ 320

SOULE
Pierre 814

SOUTH
John 465

SPALDING
H. C. 403

SPEDD
Rufus K. 116

SPEED
___ 135, 553, 859, 918
R. K. 459, 601, 609, 706, 795, 896
Rufus K. 39, 128, 471, 491

SPEICE
Adam 99

SPEIGHT
John 863

SPENCE
___ 829
Abel 753
Daniel 144
James 82
Kelly 637
Susan 144
Wilson 144

SPENCER
J. S. 857

SPENCER
John C. 451

SPOONER
Alden 106

SPRINGER
Wm. P. 271

SPRUILL
B. A. 609
B. J. 609
Benjamin 857
H. G. 601, 609
John T. 609
S. B. 609
Samuel B. 609
Sophia 381

SQUIER
E. G. 432

SQUIRES
E. G. 611

STAFFORD
Wm. 110

STALLINGS
W. 562
Whitmel 562, 609

STANFORD
Thomas 465

STANHOPE
___ 758
Archibald 758
Archy 758
Molly 758

STANLEY
Edward 292

STANLY
E. R. 616
Edw. 68
Edward 138, 237, 264, 300, 499, 538

STANSBURY
___ 299
Howard 222

STANTON
___ 854
Isaac 857

STAPLES
___ 65, 105

STARKE
L. D. 768, 918

STEARNS
A. 441

STEELE
___ 413
J. Nevitt 469

STEIMEYER
John H. 870

STEPHENS

STEPHENS
E. L. 740

STEPHENSON
Stephen 585

STERLING
J. 637
Jno. 753
John 271

STEUART
W. M. 441

STEVENS
Charles H. 512
Thaddeus 299

STEVENSON
___ 816
D. R. 110

STEWARD
Charles 332

STEWART (See also STUART)
___ 466
Lispenard 466

STILES
___ 451

STONE
___ 207, 576, 581, 637, 857
A. L. 733
Alicent 512
D. W. 581
Dewitt C. 687
G. W. 857
Geo. W. 512
George W. 637
J. W. 401
Milicent 753

STOUGH
Alfred 512

STOWE
Wm. 229

STRANGE
Robert 701

STRONG
C. B. 823

STRYKER
Isaiah 734

STUART (See also STEWART)
___ 861
Alexander H. 831
Gilbert 861

STUBBS
J. R. 609

STUMP
Thomas B. 150

STUMPH

STUMPH
  Mary G. (LEWIS) 408
  Thomas B. 404,408
  Thos. B. 806
SUBWAY
  446
SULLIVAN
  Cornelius 441
SUMMER
  James M. 609
SUMNER
  Charles W. 885
  James M. 358,381
  Jas. 677
  Wm. 609
SUTTER
  ___ 160,592,816
  J. A. 441
SUTTON
  John W. 677
  Saml. 677
SWAIN
  Martha A. 540
  Thomas 609
SWARTWOUT
  ___ 284
SWAYNE
  ___ 898
SWEETZER
  ___ 451
SWIFT
  ___ 442
SWOPE
  Emanuel 110
SYKES (See also SIKES)
  Caleb 59,113
  Esther 114
SYME
  ___ 528
SYMMS
  ___ 787
  John Cleaves 787
SYMONS
  Jacob 512
  Synthia A. 381

T

TABB
  E. P. 84,120,314, 338,351,476,514
  Thomas C. 305
TABER
  Job 44

TALLY
  S. L. 733
TAPPAN
  William B. 249
TART
  Wm. 753
TARVER
  H. H. 823
TATEM
  F. W. 609
  Geo. W. 215
  Samuel 381
TAYLOR
  ___ 4,69,80,90, 140,223,299,320,378, 444,550,585,652,761, 767,831
  A. 305
  Angus 118
  Argus 271
  Arthur 305
  Bayard 522
  Elizabeth 787
  Eunice 753
  John 904
  Mahaly 857
  Richard 787
  Sarah Knox 787
  Zachary 256,759, 760,787,790,838
TEALL
  ___ 221
TEFFT
  Henry A. 441
TELFAIR
  D. W. 180
  O. W. 687
TEMPLE
  Burwell 657,915
TEMPLETON
  ___ 208
  James L. 465
TEW
  Henry S. 870
THATCH
  Benj. W. 271
  Benjamin W. 118
THOMAS
  Charles 330,857
  Richard H. 810
  Wilson 6
THOMASON
  Richard W. 451
THOMPSON
  ___ 595
  E. B. 742

THOMPSON
  John 106,381,553, 859
  Lewis 609,732
  Wm. B. 513
THORN
  ___ 497
THORNTON
  David 269
  Margret (CHALK) 269
THURSTON
  L. F. 125
  Phineas 22
TIADALE (See also TISDALE)
  Barney 636
TILLETT
  Isaac 316
  Thomas 857
TILLITT
  Durant A. 248
TILLOU
  F. R. 289
TISDALE (See also TIADALE)
  ___ 127
  Barney 279,325, 632,647,889
TOBIAS
  M. J. 149
TOLER
  John 271
  Lydia 271
TOMS
  A. C. 43,61,637
  Jos. 677
  Joseph 19,677
  Lemuel 857
  Mary A. 637
TONIS
  A. C. 753
TOOD
  Dolly 787
  Payne 787
TOOLE
  Henny I. 701
  Henry I. 449
TORKSEY
  John W. 165
TOTTEN
  ___ 407
TOWNER
  R. A. 381
TOWNSEND
  S. P. 87

TRADER
  H. G. 687
TRAUTWINE
  ___ 407
TRAVIS
  William 118,271
TRIGG
  Lilburn H. 140
TRIPPE
  ___ 588
TROTMAN
  Q. H. 857
TROY
  ___ 732
TRUEBLOOD
  Abi DOZIER 763
  Amos 763
  Elizabeth N. 523
  Joshua 505
  Marenda 479
  Morris 271,464
  Susan 408
TUCKER
  David H. 746
  John H. 823
  W. H. H. 585
TURNER
  Alfred A. 153
  Andrew 857
  Cyrus 500
  Elsbury W. 184
  James 465
  Jos. A. 888
  Joseph 219
  Margaret 153
  Nathan 184
TUTTLE
  ___ 179
  John M. 753,857
  Wm. 637
TWIGGS
  ___ 477,550
TWINE
  Wm. H. 172
TYLER
  ___ 451,741
  John 787
  Julia (GARDNER) 787
  Letitia CHRISTIAN 787

U

UJHAZY
  Ladislaus 661

UMPHREY
  Willis 271
  Wilson 381
UNDERWOOD
  ___ 138
UNION
  Western Art 391
UPTON
  Quinton 834
USQUHART
  James B. 65

V

VAIL
  Thomas 854
VALENTINE
  William D. 601,609
  Wm. D. 609
VALLEJO
  M. G. 441
VALLOUX
  ___ 187
VAN BIBBER
  Chew 745
VAN BUREN
  ___ 477
  Abraham 787
  Hannah GOES 787
  Maria GOES 787
  Martin 787
VAN WINKLE
  Henry 275
VANDENBERG
  ___ 330
VANEY
  Nathan 465
VATTEMARE
  Alexander 68
VAUGHAN
  ___ 613
  T. G. 57
  Thomas G. 103
  Thomas R. 465
VEITCH
  Wm. 741
VENABLE
  A. W. 264
  Abraham W. 300
VERMUILE
  T. L. 441
VERNUM
  George M. 340
VINTON
  ___ 451
VOHESS

VOHESS
Geo. W. 381

W

W.
G. 460
WADE
___ 387,504,559
Abigal 512
WAINRIGHT
R. 804
WAINWRIGHT
R. 804
WALBRIDGE
Hiram 380
WALKE
___ 259
David M., Jr. 895
WALKER
___ 6,189,381,
512,602
C. 118
Caleb 381
Hugh 271
J. 441
James C. 645
Joshua C. 248
Nathan 637
Robert J. 283
Seth 753
WALLACE
Samuel 872
WALLOP
David 793
WALSH
J. C. 883
Martin 753
WALSTON
Tim. 562
WALTERS
___ 16,85,137
Simon 562
WALTON
___ 833
WAMOUTH (See also WARMOTH)
David 637
WARBLE
David 156
WARCH
Solomon 381
WARD
Thos. 895
W. M. 914
WARDELL

WARDELL
Samuel 637
WARE
Elias 299
WARLEY
J. D. 110
WARMOTH
David 753
WARREN
T. D. 609
Thos. D. 51,358
Wm. C. 51,678
WARROCK
John A. 553,667,
859
L. 374,375
Lewis 15,748
WASHINGTON
___ 89,155,460,
529,572,600,861
Augustine 787
George 787
J. N. 687
Lund 460
Martha
(DANBRIDGE)
CUSTIS 787
Mary BALL 787
W. H. 68,732
WASHINTGON
___ 573
WATCHEL
John 271
WATERS
H. H. 609
WATKINS
Cornelia 240
Cornelia F. 781
Mary Virginia 781
Robert 31,240,357,
650,686,781,801
WATSON
___ 726
WATTERS
Samuel P. 248
WATTS
___ 64
WAUGH
John S. 303,390
Sarah E.
(HARNEY) 303
WAYLES
John 787
Martha 787
WEBB
___ 451,611

WEBB
Benjamin L. S. 609
L. H. 609
L. S. 609
M. W. 190
WEBSTER
___ 470,510,544,
615,622,642,663,788
Daniel 327,780,784
Edward 327
Fletcher 327
Harriet 663
John W. 488,743
WEEK
___ 713
WEEKS
___ 713
J. E. 609
James E. 196,609,
706
Jas. E. 553,706,859
WEIRMAN
___ 299
WELLS
T. A. 271
WESCOTT
John 118,637
WESKETT
James 118
WEST
J. W. S. 163
WESTON
Harriet 25
J. C. 860
Richard 25
WHEAT
Benoni 741
WHEATE
C. R. 762
WHEDBEE
Addison 553,706,
859,902
J. M. 295,396,565,
629,632,647,795
J. P. 609
James M. 776
James P. 632,677
Jamms P. 61
Jas. M. 647,868
Jas. P. 358
Joshua S. 112
Louisa 112
WHEELER
S. J. 609,643
S. T. 609
Samuel J. 163

WHIDBEE
T. C. 169
WHILLON
John 381
WHI'ST (See also WHITEHURST)
___ 783
WHISTLER
___ 331
WHITE (See also WHITM)
___ 301,444,468
A. 233
Albert 82,364
David, Jr. 385,677
Emelia 271
Francis 105
H. W. 118
Henry H. 857
J. 233,753
James 753,764
James C. 582
Jara 271
Jeptha 5,464,609
Jona. 677
Joseph 609,677
Joshua 123
Josiah 609
Maria 764
Miles 61,65,78,
105,381,637
Nixon 448,814
Osborne 512
Philip S. 842,876
R. 855
Robinson 858
Thomas 191,217,
512,705
Wm. 271
WHITEAKER
John B. 609
WHITEHEAD
D. W. 511
M. J. (DANNIEL)
511
WHITEHURST
(See also WHI'ST)
___ 381
C. L. 750
Caleb L. 553,740,
859
Charles 563,895
Davis 196,512,740
Keeling 740
WHITELEY
___ 54

WHITELY
Sap 444
WHITFIELD
W. T. 163
WHITING
Alex. 753
Henry 753
Laura 875
WHITINGTON
W. R. 54
WHITLERY
Jas. B. 637
WHITLEY
___ 171
E. S. 171
WHITM (See also WHITE)
Philip S. 871
WHITNEY
Charles 342
Vigil 276
William Wallace 276
WHITSON
James 271
WHITTINGHAM
___ 745
WHITTLESEY
Elisha 201
WIER
___ 444
WILCOX
___ 512
George S. 637
Julius 687
Juslius M. 180
Owin 110
WILDER
G. M. 197,326,345,
390,472,520,594,835,
876,911
Geo. M. 197,236,
246
George M. 291,
317,795
Marsaall P. 352
Wm. H. 190
WILEY
S. H. 441
WILKINS
Mary 118
WILL
Elizabeth 110
WILLARD
E. D. 435
WILLEY

147

WILLEY (See also WILLIE)
  Henry 562
  John 562
WILLIAMS
  ____ 65, 105, 271, 309, 384
  A. C. 609
  Abner 2
  Allen 496
  Archibald 319
  Barton 381
  Benjamin 496
  Betsy 496
  Bill 125
  Chas. 895
  Enoch 857
  G. 895
  Geo. A. 521, 553, 779, 859
  George A. 76, 632
  Henry 171
  Jabez 854
  John G. 229
  Jordan 496
  Louisa 496
  Martha 496
  N. L. 732
  Nancy 496
  Nathan 732
  P. C. 674
  Peter C. 674
  Robert 496
  S. 417, 489
  Sarah 496
  Sebastian 46
  Sebra 164
  Sophia 496
  Tully 764
  W. W. 463
  Wilson 640
  Wilson W. 196, 664, 889
  Wm. K. 609
WILLIAMSON
  Jessee A. 190
WILLIANS
  P. C. 635
WILLICK
  Mary E. 666
WILLIE (See also WILLEY)
  H. 609
WILLIS
  Ethelbert 637
WILLS

WILLS
  Josiah 51
WILMOT
  ____ 283, 465, 528, 751
  Davy 597
WILSON
  ____ 444
  Geo. A. 383
  John G. 753
  Nathaniel 456
  Wm. 443
  Wm. G. 609
WIMBLE
  ____ 609, 633
WINANS
  William I. 331
WINDLEY
  Barbray Ann 93
WINDSOR
  John 271
WINDSOW
  Moses 774
WINFREE
  G. N. 914
WINSLOW
  Edward L. 726
  John R. 5, 385
  N. 677
  Nathan 61, 65, 677
WINSOR
  ____ 592
WINSTON
  James 65
  P. H. 609
WINTHROP
  ____ 380
  R. C. 155, 784
WISE
  ____ 125
  H. A. 637
  Henry A. 793
  John C. 895
  John J. 753
WOMBLE
  John 52, 519
WOOD
  ____ 299, 507, 512, 787
  J. B. 733
  James 271
  John 279, 741
  Mary M. 279
WOODBURY
  ____ 284
WOODFIN

WOODFIN
  N. W. 732
WOODHOUSE
  L. 754
  Wm. 250, 903
WOODWARD
  Thomas G. 302
  Wm. 198
WOODY
  Wm. 290
WOOL
  ____ 550
WOOLEY
  P. W. 732
WOOLS
  ____ 69
WOOTEN
  J. C. 381, 512
WORF
  Wm. 271
WORTH
  ____ 182, 444, 550
WRIGHT
  ____ 87, 276
  Adam E. 248
  D. M. 307
  George W. 522
  J. J. 208
  James A. 248
  John W. 726
  Robert L. 637
WYLIE
  Andrew 745
WYMAN
  ____ 615
  Elbridge 271
  Lucy A. 271
WYNNE
  Richard I. 49

X

None

Y

YANCY
  ____ 823
  A. P. 609
YARBROUGH
  Edw. 180
YARREL
  P. W. 609
YEATMAN
  Griffin 107
YELLOTT

YELLOTT
  ____ 299
  Coleman 299
YOUNG
  O. 753
  O. B. 506

Z

Z.
  ____ 752
ZANE
  Elizabeth 232

INCOMPLETE NAMES

  ____
  Albert 598
  Charles I 742
  James 552
  Jenny 852
  Joshua 76
  Julia 276
  Junius 368
  Rhoda 276
  Samson 701
  Sukey 758

FEMALE GIVEN NAME INDEX

____ (BASSET) HARRISON 787
____ (KORTRIGHT) MONROE 787
____ (SMITH) FILLMORE 787
____ BALDWIN 786
____ BASSET 787
____ KORTRIGHT 787
____ SMITH 787
____ STANHOPE 758
____ SYMMS 787
____ SYMMS HARRISON 787
A. SISCO 86,596
Abi DOZIER 763
Abi DOZIER TRUEBLOOD 763
Abigail (SMITH) ADAMS 787
Abigail SMITH 787
Abigal WADE 512
Affee BEEL 118
Affey BELL 512
Alicent STONE 512
Angeline E. ALEXANDER 96
Ann (REY) JONES 417
Ann B. SAWYER 753
Ann BELL 626,856
Ann BLACKBURN 648
Ann BURNS 277
Ann C. BLOUNT 803
Ann GANINGTON 637
Ann HARRELL 711
Ann HARVEY 637
Ann L. HARRELL 637
Ann LASTER 271
Ann LOWRY 381
Ann M. DAILEY 922
Ann MILLS 573
Ann REY 417
Ann SISCO 32
Ann SKINNER 271
Annes BARRENTON 753
Artimesia (BAILEY) HODGES 878
Artimesia BAILEY 878
B. GALLOP 512
Barbray Ann (WINDLEY) LYON 93
Barbray Ann WINDLEY 93
Betsy WILLIAMS 496
Cally SMITHSON 381
Caroline GILMAN 764
Caroline SKINNER 258
Caroline SMITH 809,886
Caroline V. CASEY 857
Casann (SCOTT) BURCHER 164
Casann SCOTT 164
Cassindra AYERS 512
Catharine BRUCKS 753
Catharine ETHEREDGE 764
Catherine BURNS 277
Charlotte BOONE 637
Charlotte CUSHMAN 442
Charlotte LUTTS 857
Chloe BELL 165
Chlotilden JACKSON 484
Clarissa (BURNUM) ARMSTEAD 417
Clarissa BURNUM 417
Constance MILNA 593
Cornelia F. WATKINS 781
Cornelia JOHNSTON 857
Cornelia WATKINS 240
Cothia (DUNCAN) SMITH 638
Cothia DUNCAN 638
Dolly PAYNE 787
Dolly PAYNE TOOD 787
Dolly PAYNE TOOD MADISON 787
E. M. DILLARD 857
E. M. SMITH 513
Eleanor FISK 819
Elenor E. JORDAN 118
Eliza (CHAPMAN) GRAY 489
Eliza Chapman 489
Eliza Fisk (HARWOOD) SKINNER 7
Eliza Fisk HARWOOD 7
Elizabeth (FRESHWATER) GASKINS 225
Elizabeth (GILBERT) NEWMANS 727
Elizabeth (TAYLOR) BLISS 787
Elizabeth Ann BUNDY 512, 857
Elizabeth B. (ELLIS) BRAGG 257
Elizabeth B. ELLIS 257
Elizabeth DAVIS 282
Elizabeth FORBES 381
Elizabeth FRESHWATER 225
Elizabeth GILBERT 727
Elizabeth HAWKINS 598
Elizabeth HULL 200
Elizabeth HUTCHINSON 787
Elizabeth HUTCHINSON JACKSON 787
Elizabeth JONES 787
Elizabeth JONES MONROE 787
Elizabeth L. LITTLEJOHN 803
Elizabeth N. (TRUEBLOOD) RAPER 523
Elizabeth N. TRUEBLOOD 523
Elizabeth NASH 632,901
Elizabeth OVERMAN 753
Elizabeth OVERTON 381, 512
Elizabeth OXLY 512
Elizabeth REED 271
Elizabeth RIED 753
Elizabeth ROBERTS 271
Elizabeth ROBINSON 118
Elizabeth TAYLOR 787
Elizabeth WILL 110
Elizabeth ZANE 232
Ellen BATEMAN 720
Emelia WHITE 271
Emeline CARVER 710
Emely FRENCH 118
Emma (SMITH) DUNCAN 638
Emma SMITH 638
Esther SIKES 192,382,648
Esther SYKES 114
Eunice TAYLOR 753
Fanny MC DEAL 381
Flory MC DANIEL 637
Francis H. ELLISON 321
Free Grace BENDALL 593
Grace BEAMSLEY 593
Grizell P. JACOCKS 525
Hannah A. SMALL 753
Hannah GOES 787
Hannah GOES VAN BUREN 787
Harriet WEBSTER 663
Harriet WESTON 25
Hope HAWKINS 593
Hopefor BENDALL 593
Indiana LINTON 648
Isabella CARTWRIGHT 551
Jane BELL 165
Jane BUTLER 271
Jane G. BUTT 512
Jane R. COLLINS 495
Jane RANDOLPH 787
Jane RANDOLPH JEFFERSON 787
Jenny ____ 852
Jenny LIND 625
Josephine C. B. (HOLSOM) SMITH 489
Josephine C. B. HOLSOM 489
Julia (GARDNER) TYLER 787
Julia ____ 276
Julia DEAN 852
Julia GARDNER 787
Kate BATEMAN 720
Kesiah DOWSON 857
Kesiah PIKE 857
Laura M. BROWN 391
Laura WHITING 875
Leidey GILFORTE 753
Letitia CHRISTIAN 787
Letitia CHRISTIAN TYLER 787
Levinia JACKSON 753
Liddy RHODES 512
Lidia (DUNCAN) SMITH 638
Lidia DUNCAN 638
Louisa BOURKE 254
Louisa Catherine (JOHNSON) ADAMS 787
Louisa Catherine JOHNSON 787
Louisa Jane HARRELL 711
Louisa JORDAN 271
Louisa WHEDBEE 112
Louisa WILLIAMS 496
Lovey ETHEREDGE 764
Lucinda RUTTER 620
Lucy A. WYMAN 271
Luvinia ASHCROFT 753

FEMALE GIVEN NAME INDEX

Lydia PALIN 902
Lydia SAWYER 857
Lydia TOLER 271
M. A. REID 857
M. J. (DANNIEL) WHITEHEAD 511
M. J. DANNIEL 511
M. J. LOVETT 512
Mahaly CARTWRIGHT 551
Mahaly TAYLOR 857
Marenda (TRUEBLOOD) REED 479
Marenda TRUEBLOOD 479
Margaret A. (COSTIN) BROOKS 735
Margaret A. COSTIN 735
Margaret A. SCOTT 781
Margaret Adlum BARBER 281
Margaret BARBER 281
Margaret DAVIS 637
Margaret GRIFFIN 753
Margaret HARVEY 857
Margaret OVERMAN 637
Margaret REED 857
Margaret Stevenson (JACOCKS) LEIGH 736
Margaret Stevenson JACOCKS 736
Margaret TURNER 153
Margret (CHALK) THORNTON 269
Margret CHALK 269
Maria ASHBEE 637
Maria GOES 787
Maria GOES VAN BUREN 787
Maria WHITE 764
Martha (DANBRIDGE) CUSTIS 787
Martha (DANBRIDGE) CUSTIS WASHINGTON 787
Martha (WAYLES) SKELTON 787
Martha (WAYLES) SKELTON JEFFERSON 787
Martha A. SWAIN 540
Martha A. SWAIN ROBINSON 540
Martha B. NEWELL 886
Martha BROSIER 118

Martha DANBRIDGE 787
Martha H. IVES 518
Martha HINTON 270
Martha Jane (LOVETT) EURE 919
Martha Jane LOVETT 919
Martha MC MORINE 603
Martha S. LONG 512
Martha SIMMONS 304
Martha WAYLES 787
Martha WILLIAMS 496
Marthana JONES 381
Mary (PHILLIPS) BURGWIN 461
Mary (RIGGS) LOVETT 845
Mary A. BROCKETT 271
Mary A. JACKSON 637
Mary A. TOMS 637
Mary ARMOUR 512,637
Mary BALL 787
Mary BALL WASHINGTON 787
Mary BELL 165
Mary BROWN 844
Mary CARMOTH 381
Mary Catharine SKINNER 258
Mary E. BANKS 857
Mary E. HICKS 598
Mary E. WILLICK 666
Mary ELLISTON 904
Mary F. (PALMER) HOPKINS 501
Mary F. PALMER 501
Mary FELTON 381
Mary G. (LEWIS) STUMPH 408
Mary G. LEWIS 408
Mary GODFREY 512,753, 857
Mary HERBERT 637
Mary Jane FEREBEE 848
Mary L. MULLEN 637,857
Mary M. WOOD 279
Mary NEWBY 381
Mary ONEAL 753
Mary PHILLIPS 461
Mary PURDY 512
Mary RIGGS 845
Mary Virginia BARBER 281
Mary Virginia WATKINS 781

Mary WILKINS 118
Matilda JONES 381
Mercy BEAMSLEY 593
Milicent STONE 753
Mointha MULING 381
Molly STANHOPE 758
Myra (CLARK) GAINES 276
Myra CLARK 276
Nancy KEATON 637
Nancy LEE 857
Nancy MORGAN 547
Nancy REED 857
Nancy SAWYER 753
Nancy WILLIAMS 496
Nannie T. (JOHNSTON) BAKER 479
Nannie T. JOHNSTON 479
Narcissa D. (SAWYER) POOL 735
Narcissa D. SAWYER 735
Nelly CONWAY 787
Nelly CONWAY MADISON 787
Nicy RUDDOCK 857
Parthnea BANKS 271
Patsey CASEY 239
Patsey CASEY JINNINGS 239
Penina CARTWRIGHT 551
Penny BENBURY 857
Penny DELLON 753
Phebe (SCOTT) JACKSON 288
Phebe SCOTT 288
Phebee G. (FARNUM) POMEROY 724
Phebee G. FARNUM 724
Reuhamy CARTWRIGHT 551
Rhoda ____ 276
Rose MORRIS 277
S. A. (FOLK) BURNETT 789
S. A. FOLK 789
S. Margaret FULLER 838
Sallie (JACKSON) CLARK 395
Sallie JACKSON 395
Sally HARRELL 271
Salvadora LABOYTEAUX 910
Sarah Ann (PALMER)

Sarah ANN (PALMER) CARSON 888
Sarah Ann FORBES 753
Sarah Ann PALMER 888
Sarah BABB 495
Sarah E. (HARNEY) WAUGH 303
Sarah E. HARNEY 303
Sarah E. LAMB 637
Sarah G. MATHEWS 409
Sarah GRANDY 381
Sarah HOOD 462
Sarah HUMPHRIES 324
Sarah Knox (TAYLOR) DAVIS 787
Sarah Knox TAYLOR 787
Sarah LABOYTEAUX 910
Sarah LISTER 381
Sarah MITCHELL 118
Sarah OVERMAN 753
Sarah WILLIAMS 496
Sebra WILLIAMS 164
Sebra WILLIAMS NASH 164
Sidney BRYAN 512
Sophia CARTWRIGHT 551
Sophia MEISCHEAU 82
Sophia MONCHEN 753
Sophia MURDEN 512
Sophia SPRUILL 381
Sophia WILLIAMS 496
Susan (SPENCE) SAWYER 144
Susan (TRUEBLOOD) SAWYER 408
Susan BUTLER 485,512
Susan J. MOORE 381,857
Susan KITE 350
Susan Roles BARBER 281
Susan SPENCE 144
Susan TRUEBLOOD 408
Susanna ADAMS 787
Susanna BOYLSTON 787
Susanna BOYLSTON ADAMS 787
Susanna PALMER 118
Synthia A. SYMONS 381
Virginia FEARING 577
WA-KAN-YE-KE-WING 425
Winnefred KEATON 753
Zera HAMILTON 381

150

PUBLICATIONS INDEX

Advocate 281
Albany Atlas 836
Albany Register 838
Albemarle Bulletin 659,725
American 342
American Beacon 688
American Railroad Journal 331
Atlas 488
Balt. American 412,536,893
Balt. Pat. 572,854,883
Balt. Patriot 161,222,413, 442
Balt. Sun 189,833
Baltimore American 522
Baltimore Clipper 331,377
Baltimore Patriot 78,132, 182,218,234,299,318,370, 380,451,539,561,611,645, 897
Baltimore Potriat 378
Baltimore Sun 529
Baptist Messenger 256,643
Batesville (Ark.) Eagle 273
Beacon 305
Belfast Journal 354
Bible Society Record 194
Binghamton Rep. 334
Boston Advertiser 615
Boston Almanac 787
Boston Atlas 139,366,499
Boston Courier 426
Boston Cultivator 310
Boston Herald 510
Boston Journal 355,788
Boston Mail 133
Boston Transcript 111
Boston Traveller 815
Brattleboro' Eagle 424,862
Buffalo Commercial 611
Buffalo Commercial Advertiser 468
Buffalo Courier 468
Buffalo Republican 468
Cadet of Temperance 560
Charleston Courier 353,599
Charleston Mercury 669,870
Cincinnati Commercial 639, 837
Cincinnati Gazette 391
Cincinnati Gazettt 327
Common School Advocate 360

Courier 742
Courier and Enquirer 275
Danville Register 301
Democratic Banner 465
Democratic Pioneer 768,918
Democratic Review 762
E. City Star 240
Edenton Bulletin 706
Edenton Sentinel 270,562
Evening Bulletin 904
Florida Republican 882
Franklin (Tenn.) Review 597
Galena Jeffersonian 651
Gazette 6
Gladiator 109,358
Greensboro Patriot 301
Halifax (N. C.) Republican 830
Hartford Times 428
Highland Messenger 290
Hillsborough Recorder 871
Independence (Mo.) Expositor 160
Indianapolis Journal 391
Intelligencer 140
Lexington (Va.) Gazette 200
Louisville Courier 335,445
Louisville Journal 223,546
Missouri Repub. 465
Missouri Republican 319
Mountain Banner 832
N. C. Standard 740
N. Orleans Picayune 276
N. S. Whig 292
N. State Whig 872
N. Y. Com. 247
N. Y. Cour. & Enq. 862
N. Y. Courier 394
N. Y. Enquirer 448
N. Y. Evangelist 644
N. Y. Express 415,445
N. Y. Her. 70
N. Y. Journal of Commerce 141,624
N. Y. Sun 202,427
N. Y. Tribune 600
Nashville Union 294
National Intelligencer 69, 134,369,413,811
New Haven Courier 302
New Jersey State Gazette 232
New Orleans Bee and

New Orleans Bee and Picayune 139
New York Commercial 467, 615
New York Courier and Enquirer 139,451,611
New York Evening Post 179, 466
New York Express 451
New York Herald 544
New York Journal of Commerce 332,407
New York Mirror 430
New York Sun 277
New York Tibune 522
New York Tribune 289,574
Newark Advertiser 311
Newbernian 616,707,726
Norfolk Beacon 189
Norfolk Herald 151,268,670
North Carolina Gazetteer 643
North State Whig 563
Ouachita (Arkansas) Herald 662
Patriot 208
Pendleton (S. C.) Messenger 368
Pennsylvanian 758
Pennsylvanian Inquirer 124
Phil. N. American 497
Phil. North American 162
Philadelphia Inquirer 621
Philadelphia North American 571
Philadelphia Pennsylvanian 412,645
Picayune 826
Pittsburg Advocate 461
Plow, the Loom and the Anvil, The 91,352
Port Tobacco Times 573
Portsmouth (Va.) Pilot 405, 860
Post 488
R. Times 343
Raleigh Register 25,224
Raleigh Standard 256,751, 853
Raleigh Star 641
Raleigh Times 180,183
Register 138

Republic 139,309,393,761, Republic 780,784
Rich. Rep. 652,870
Rich Republican 843
Richmond (Ky.) Chronicle 500
Richmond Times 356,785
Roanoke Republican 358
Rockingham (Va.) Register 612
Rural New Yorker 774
Rutherford Telegraph 193
San Augustine Union 444
Saturday Courier 668
Savannah Georgian 293
Scientific American 233
Snow Hill Shield 793
Southern Advocate 657
Southern Argus 740
Southern Cultivator 718
Southern Democrat 546
Spirit of the Age 842
St. Louis Republican 598
St. Louis Union 188
Star (of Syracuse) 221
Talequah Advocate 439
Telegraph 283
Times 904
Transcript 593
Union 309,811
Washington Republic 825, 826,843
Washington Union 80,159, 256,661
Weldon Herald 203,830
Wheeling Gazette 6
Wilmington Aurora 449,882
Winchester Virginian 328
Zanesville (Ohio) Courier 767

151

LOCATION INDEX

ACADEMY
Elizabeth City 295,323, 503,566,671
Hannah More 745
Hertford 886
Hickory Ground 383
Perquimans 344,770
Male and Female 372,494, 809
U. S. Military 652
West Point 407

ALMSHOUSE
Richmond 746

BACK
Hog's 247

BARRACKS
Jefferson (MO) 6

BAY
Bull's 234
Chesapeake 305
Kittyhawk 316
Tampa 293

BEACH
Bodys Island 517
Currituck 102
Great 102
Hatteras 454

BOARDINGHOUSE
ROBINSON's 444

BOTTOMS
Colorado 444

BRANCH
spring 832

BRIDGE
Canal 783
Cayuga 468
Great 557
London 401
NEWBY's 65,385
River 400

CANAL
Dismal Swamp 230,251, 268,609,756
Orapeake, and Turnpike 253,298

CAPE
Fear 633
Hatteras 234,340,447,804

CHAPEL
FLETCHER's 827
RILEY's 439

CHURCH
Baptist 211,547,565,790, 876,921

CHURCH
E. City Baptist 829
Episcopal 794
Evans 827
?Johnsonton 827
Lutheran, First 723
M. E. 71,153
MC BRIDE's 827
Methodist 741,911
Methodist Episcopal 71, 166,236,540
Southern 439
New Hope 827
Primitive Bethlehem 794
Prot. Episcopul 800
Protestant Episcopal 726, 839
Maryland, of 54
St. Andrew's 461

CITIES
Balt. 161,189,222,412,413, 442,536,572,854,883,893
Baltimore 12,17,22,24,26, 28,32,34,36,54,61,69,78,86, 87,103-105,126,132,175, 182,218,234,299,318,331, 365,370,377,378,380,392, 418,450,451,456,522,529, 531,539,558,559,561,564, 596,611,627,636,645,665, 666,668,717,745,810,833, 844,874,883,889,897,923
Balto. 745
Boston 44,87,98,111,121, 133,139,202,229,249,310, 327,355,366,426,427,428, 470,488,499,510,544,554, 561,593,615,733,743,787, 788,815
Charleston 87,234,302, 327,353,561,599,645,669, 692,870
Cincinnati 107,284,327
Cincinnatti 320,726
Galveston 885
Morfolk 60
N. Orleans 276
N. Y. 70,87,141,202,233, 247,394,415,427,445,448, 624,644,708,862
N. York 29,318,346,446, 787
New Orleans 98,139,182, 208,209,257,327,444,445,

CITIES
New Orleans 692,744,762,787,826,904
New York 27,41,44,61,98, 113,114,126,136,139,156, 179,254,275,277,286,289, 302,309,332,370,371,380, 382,407,430,432,451,466, 467,522,537,544,561,571, 572,574,600,611,615,617, 636,649,661,688,689,692, 699,717,719,734,769,787, 844,858,872,904
Norfolk 7,11,14,16,26,33, 42,43,47,51,61-63,65,81,84, 85,95,103,105,119,120,137, 147,151,181,189,198,210, 259,262,268,305,312-315, 337,338,339,349,351,352, 401,417,419,443,447,473, 476,514,516,519,549,561, 583,588,604,608,619,631, 648,670,683,684,747,772, 808,818,827,840,849,850, 875,895,907,914
Phil. 162,333,497
Philadelphia 16,18,44,87, 119,142,214,223,352,356, 378,412,442,460,468,536, 571,572,617,621,645,668, 675,689,745,758,787,833, 876,898,904
R. 343
Raleigh 25,68,180,183, 185,224,248,256,379,585, 634,641,656,657,672,677, 678,687,706,751,853,924
Rich. 652,843,870
Richmond 43,51,52,65, 284,356,519,746,785
St. Louis 187,188,202,222
San Francisco 440,441
Washingt'n 209
Washington 4,14,80,95, 98,132,139,141,142,159, 189,201,299,318,320,369, 370,378,380,394,403,434, 435,451,499,564,571,598, 609,623,624,645,652,661, 662,668,787,804,824-826, 843,883

COLLEGE
Baltimore, of Dental Surgery 389

COLLEGE
Greensboro' Female 13
Hampden Sidney 746
Harvard 787
Massachusetts Medical 488
Medical 470,788
Princeton 787
St. James, of 248,800
South Carolina 327
William and Mary 787

COUNTIES
Accomac (VA) 793
Adams (PA) 110
Alamance 672
Albany (NY) 110
Albemarle (VA) 787
Alexander 163,672
Alleghany (MD) 99
Anson 264,672,732
Appromattox (VA) 301
Armstrong (PA) 110
Ashe 264,672
Augusta (VA) 831
Austin (TX) 444
Autauga (AL) 909
Baltimore (MD) 745
Beaufort 264,672
Bertie 25,108,109,264, 417,601,609,672,687,732
Bibb (GA) 823
Bladen 264,672
Bradford (PA) 110
Brunswick 264,672
Buncombe 264,672,732
Burke 264,672,732
Burleston (TX) 444
Butler (PA) 110
Cabarras 672
Cabarrus 264
Caldwell 264,672,732
Calvert (MD) 69,787
Camden 82,87,165,242, 248,264,337,350,358,359, 397,400,493,506,543,578, 587,590,609,667,672,691, 783,797,827,829,834,842, 914
Caroline (MD) 54
Cartaret 672
Carteret 264,732
Caswell 264,672
Catawba 264,672
Catham 732

153

COUNTIES
Cattaraugus (NY) 110
Cayuga (NY) 787
Charles (VA) 787
Charles City (VA) 787
Chatham 264,672,732
Chatham (GA) 823
Chautauque (NY) 110
Cherokee 264,672
Chowan 264,358,437,
458,479,601,609,658,672,
678,732,783,803,894
Clark (GA) 823
Cleaveland 264,672
Columbia (GA) 353
Columbia (NY) 787
Columbus 264,672
Craven 264,672,732
Cumberl'd 672
Cumberland 264
Currituck 94,263,264,
304,324,373,397,410,578,
601,609,672,691,764,817,
819,820,848,873,874,900,
908,914
Currituk 274
Dauphin (PA) 110
Davidson 264,672
Davie 264,672
Davis (KY) 836
Duplin 264,672
Edgecom'e 672
Edgecomb 368
Edgecombe 264
Edgefield (SC) 909
Elizabeth City (VA) 151
Essex (MD) 352
Fayette (TX) 444
Forsythe 672
Franklin 264,672
Franklin (GA) 660
Fulton (NY) 110
Gaston 264,672
Gates 57,89,253,264,270,
298,404,457,458,495,496,
551,562,609,670,672,735,
827,914
Gonzales (TX) 444
Granville 224,264,672,
732
Greene 264,672,732
Guilford 13,163,264,360,
672
Halifax 163,264,601,609,

COUNTIES
Halifax 672,732,830,894
Harlan (KY) 194
Haywood 264,672
Henders'n 672
Henderson 264
Hertford 163,224,264,
601,609,672,914
Huntingdon (PA) 110
Hyde 49,264,454,672
Iredell 264
Iredrell 672
Jackson (MO) 160
Johnston 264,672,732
Jones 264,672
Jones (GA) 823
Lancaster (PA) 110
Lenoir 264,672,732
Lincoln 264,672,732
Lycoming (PA) 734
Macon 264,672
Madison (KY) 219,500
Madison (NY) 110
Martin 224,264,609,672
Mathews (VA) 417
McDowell 264,672
Meckl'b'g 672
Mecklenburg 264,787
Meriwether (GA) 823
Middlesex (MA) 488
Mifflin (PA) 110
Monroe (GA) 823
Montgm'y 672
Montgomery 264
Montgomery (OH) 99
Moore 264,672,732
Murray (GA) 823
Muscogee (GA) 823
N. Hano'r 672
Nansemond (VA) 511,919
Nash 264,672
New Hanover 264,701,732
New Kent (VA) 787
Norfolk (VA) 383,456,557
North'pt'n 672
Northampton 163,203,
264,609,732,830
Oglethorpe (GA) 718
Onedia (NY) 110
Onslow 264,672
Orange 264,672,732
Orange (VA) 787
Pasqnotank 752
Pasquoa'k 672

COUNTIES
Pasquotank 19,40,155,
172,241,264,282,288,322,
337,358,384,390,397,400,
419,421,438,480,482,485,
550,553,565,578,587,589,
606,609,667,677-679,681,
693,702,706,715,732,740,
750,777,778,783,796,798,
827,841,876,878,891,898,
906,908,911,914,918,922
Perq. 842
Perqu'imo's 672
Perquimans 5,11,19,122,
123,184,264,337,344,358,
372,397,399,448,464,474,
489,524,525,578,601,609,
632,653,677,697,706,736,
740,776,778,783,863
Perquimons 248
Person 264,672
Pickens (SC) 327
Pike (MO) 465
Pitt 264,672,803
Posquotank 55
Princess Anne (VA) 50,
305,401,895,914
Randolph 264,672
Red river (TX) 904
Richmond 264,672
Robeson 264,672,732
Roc'i'gh'm 672
Rockingham 264
Rowan 163,264,672,732
Rutherford 193,264,672
Sampson 264,672,732
Schoharie (NY) 467
Smith (TN) 294
Southampton (VA) 65
St. Lawrence (NY) 110
St. Louis (MO) 125
Stanly 264,672
Stewart (GA) 823
Stokes 264,672
Suffolk (MA) 488
Surry 264,672,732
Tishemingo (MS) 285
Tompkins (NY) 110
Twiggs (GA) 823
Tyrell 264,433,509
Tyrrel 87,97,609,667
Tyrrell 49,501,672,691,
732
Union 264,672

COUNTIES
W'shi'gt'n 672
Wake 264,585,672,732
Warren 264,672
Washington 264,601,609,
667,691,732
Washington (MD) 248,
800
Washington (PA) 110
Watauga 672
Wayne 163,264,672
Westmoreland (VA) 787
Wilkes 264,672,732
Worcester (MA) 352
Wstmoreland (VA) 787
Yancy 264,672
York (PA) 721
York (VA) 489
COURT HOUSE
Cam. 783
Camden 82,242,797,842
Currituck 304,819
COVE
Hatteras 234
CREEK
Acquia 652
Acquin 229
Buffalo 200
hunting, Upper 54
Menzis 765
Neshaminy 176
Newbegin 100,589,902
St. Leonard's 69
SAWYER's 373,820,873
Spring 290
Swift 803
Wheeling 232
DEPOT
Banking 755
DISTRICT
Columbia, of 125
D. C. 281,403
FACTORY
GREENs Woolen 651
FALLS
Niagara 247,468
of 668
FARM
Hickory 475
Hook 592
KELLY's 456
FERRY
GRAY's 162
FIELD

FIELD
POTTER's 289
FISHERY
North Bend 307
FOREIGN LOCATIONS
Africa 327
America, Central 432,611
Austria 451,611
Barbadoes 392,447
Belfast 342
Belgium 327
Berlin 201
Bogora 201
Bogota 611
Bremen 874
Bristol 614
Buena Vista 257
Canada 87,513,598
Canstantinople 201
Chagres 370
Chargres 407
Chili 201,370
China 280,838
Comorn 661
Cuba 569,762
Demarara 561
Dublin 342
England 201,280,318, 341,342,351,427,497,612, 614
Europe 309,445,826
France 201,284,318,369, 427
Germany 70
Great Britain 342
Halifax 340,415
Havana 592
Havre 201
Holland 537
Irapuato 143
Ireland 277,342,669,787
Jalapa 202
Japan 280
Lagrange 529
Laguayra 602
Leon 432
Limon 407
Liverpool 120,201
London 581,787
Madrid 406
Magdalene river 407
Marseilles 284
Mexico 6,79,134,143, 202,320,393,444,451,539

FOREIGN LOCATIONS
Monahan County, Ireland 277
Naples 621
New Burnswick 733
New Granada 407
New Grenada 201
Palenque 432
Panama 522,592,646
 bay of 407
Paris 406,529
Perote 320
Plan del Rio 202
Provinces, British 733
Prussia 70
Rio Janeiio 392
Rio Janeiro 201
Russia 331,430
Saint Thomas 561
St. Petersburg 574
St. Thomas 561,602
Sandwich Islands 427
Sheffield 351
Spain 201,220,762
Spaine 318
Suffolk 341,612
Toronto 598
Trinidad 561,602
Turks Island 762
Valparaiso 592
Venezuela 201,469
Vera Cruz 202
Vesuvius 621
Vienna 451
West Indies 87
FORT
Coffee 737
Hamilton 376
Henry 232
Hill 327
Independence 286
McHenry 369
Monroe 682
SUTTER's 160
GULF
the 444
HALL
Colton 441
Congress 330
Odd Fellow's 565,600,703
HARBOR
Beaufort 563
Boston 98,121
Charlott's 293

HEAD
Nag's 83,94,191,217,242,
Nag's 243,278,295,297, 313,553,588,609,633,643, 712,729,747,749,773,791, 794,851,859,880,894
Nagg's 590,601
HILL
Bunker 98
Wheeling 232
HOSPITAL
Cholera 277
Massachusetts General 470
Sisters of Charity 320
HOTEL
American 44
BAUM's 250,754
BOND's 807
Eagle 468
Edenton 170
Exchange 468
Farmers Inn 37
Fountain 22
KENDING's 299
MC NIDER's 169
Merchant's 57,103,511, 919
Nag's Head 83,191,217, 295
National 435,645,808
Old Point 860
Old Point Comfort 682
SANDERLIN's 213
Star 444
U. S. 169
Union 619
United States 169
WALTERS' City 16,85, 137
Western 722
WILLIAMS, S., of 417
HOUSE
ASTOR 371
Custom 47,504
Eutaw 78
Mansion 15,145,150,167, 322,336,386,630,680,913
 MASON's 569
Market 548
Revre 327
RILEY's Gardens 349
Round Top 444
INDIAN NATION

INDIAN NATION
Camanche 413
Cherokee 439
 Delaware District 439
 Going Snake District 439
INFIRMARY
Baltimore 810
INLET
Currituck 633
Old 874
Hatteras 234,804
Nag's Head 633
Nagg's Head 590
Roanoke 609
INSTITUTE
Albemarle 795,835
Chowan 658
Concord Male and Female Classical 506
English & Classical 295, 345,472,520,594
Female 359
Female Classical 185
Franklin 412
Maryland 377
Mechanics' 412
Norfolk Female 349
INSTITUTION
Deaf and Dumb, for the 261
IRON WORKS
Gosport 860
ISLAND
Chickamicomico 771
Collington 633
Goat 468
Kent 54
RANDALL's 289
Roanoke 238,504,633
LAKE
Lepin 98
Salt, Great 222
Utah 222
LANDING
Fort 49,501
LIBRARY
Hall of the Apprentices' 353
LIGHT
Hatteras 234
LINE
MASON and DIXON's 497
Pennsylvania 299

155

MONUMENT
National 429
WASHINGTON National 89,155
MUSEUM
Chinese 333
NAVY YARD
Brooklyn 708
NECK
BOYD's 308
DURANT's 399,525,736, 821,914
HARVEY's 474,765
OCEAN
Atlantic 682
the 545
PARISH
Brandon 7
Christ Church 870
St. Andrew's 870
PLANTATION
?Baudon 479
Hermitage 787
Land of Promise 50
Monticello 787
Montpelier 787
?Mount Pleasant 557
Mount Vernon 787
POINT
BRIGG's 456
Comfort, Old 151,682
Pleasant 58
Stumpy 49
Union 616
WADE's 387,504,559
RAILROAD
Central 563,657
Erie 407,430
Panama 407
Seaboard and Roanoke 405
RIDGE
Dry 384
Indian 263
RIVER
Alligator 49
Little 87
Beedi 444
Buffalo 885
Colorado 444
Elizabeth 456,895
Eastern Branch 895
Feather 592,644
Fox 651

RIVER
Guadaloupe 444
Hudson 333,734,787
James 333
Licking 639
Little 278,297,308,464, 618,633,792,863
Lynnhaven 401
Mississippi 444
Missouri 160
North 179
Ohio 444,460
Pasquotank 543,633
Patuxent 69
Perquimans 633,765
Red 444
Rio Grande 320,444,885
Roanoke 830
Susquehanna 299
Trinity 444
Yeopim 307
ROAD
Baltimore & Reisterstown Turnpike 745
BUTT's 50
Parkville 863
Toll 543
ROCK
Plymouth 327
SCHOOL (See also ACADEMY,COLLEGE, INSTITUTE,SEMINARY, UNIVERSITY)
Choctaw 737
St. Mary's 168,656,924
Singing 595
Trinity 168
SEMINARY
Riddicksville 457
Young Ladies's 812
SETTLEMENT
Miami 787
SHOAL
Long 804
WADE's Point 559
SHORE
Narrow 250
SOUND
Albemarle 130,307,545, 562,609,633
Croaton 609
Croetan 171
Currituck 895
Pamlico 633,804

SPRINGS
Nanticoke 334
Red Sulphur 294
STATES
Ala. 613
Alabama 199,276,293, 327,444,480,652,823,909
Ark. 273
Arkansas 554,662,904
California 125,143,160, 286,311,440,441,451,522, 563,592,624,644,651,688, 734,816,823,824,860,861, 882,885
Upper 222
Conn. 600
Connecticut 143,302,412, 550,598,611
Ct. 179,774
Delaware 497
Florida 6,293,468,477, 830,882
Ga. 613,718
Georgia 141,451,591,660, 823
Ill. 676
Illinois 98,319
Ind. 745
Indiana 79,80,341,391, 451,745
Iowa 661
Kentucky 138,194,219, 445,554,575,707,734,744, 780,787,836
Ky. 125,194,201,431,500, 745,837
La. 201,787
Louisiana 380,784
Maine 79,121,134,354, 451,645
Maryland 54,69,99,161, 234,377,380,497,704,780, 787,800,810,883
Mass. 201,229,343,498, 787,814
Massachsetts 784
Massachusetts 133,327, 352,366,724,780
Md. 12,28,32,36,61,86, 175,248,369,418,596,745, 787,844
Me. 201,561
Mich. 668
Michigan 468

STATES
Minesota 425
Miss. 201,444
Mississippi 240,285,341, 380,762,787,904
Missouri 141,160,283, 319,444,451,465,610,780, 823
Mo. 6,160,202
N. J. 286,787
N. Y. 201,330,376,734, 787
N. York 561
New England 149,352, 499,709
New Hampshire 327,394, 709,787
New Jersey 232,742
New Mexico 125,824
New York 92,110,132, 276,638,733,780,787
Ohio 99,141,380,391,444, 451,611,767,780,784,787
Oregon 138,283,335,751
Pa. 176,194,721,723,734, 745
Pennsylvania 110,299,497, 733,734
R. I. 592
Rhode Island 124
S. C. 211,302,368,561, 613,692,909
South Carolina 234,597, 623,645,707,787,823
Tenn. 294,341,784,787
Tennessee 173,276,341, 574,597,611,645,701,733, 787
Texas 98,182,320,413, 444,824,882,885,904
Utah 222,824
Va. 16,26,33,42,43,47,50, 51,52,61,62-66,81,84,85, 119,120,137,147,151,200, 201,259,262,279,301,312, 313-315,333,338,339,351, 370,383,384,417,419,434, 473,476,489,511,514,516, 519,549,557,582,608,612, 619,631,745-747,772,787, 818,831,860,919
Vermont 424,528,918
Virginia 140,152,341,356, 380,460,468,528,604,745,

STATES
Virginia 787,793,830,831, 895,914
  Eastern 50
  Vt. 201,787,788

STORE
WEEKS' 713

SWAMP
Dismal 230,251,268,279, 384,609,756
Swift Creek 803

TAVERN
WHITE's 444

TERRITORY
Minesota 425

THEATRE
Walnut Street 442

TOWNS
Akron 391
Albany 87,179,816,836, 838
Alexandria 370,741,914
Andover 133
Annapolis 234
Annopolis 161
Arlington 811
Arostook 354
Ashland 745
Augusta 353,613
? Ballahack 525
Bastrop 444
Batesville 273
Baton Rouge 787
Bealleville 110
Beaufort 563
Bedford 528
Belfast 354
Bennington 787
Berkley 787
Binghampton 276
Binghamton 334
Bloomington 745
Boonsborough 744
Bourbon 431
Bowling Green 465
Brattleboro' 424,862
Brenham 444
Bridgefield 783
Bridgeport 613
Bristol 176
Broadalbin 110
Brooklyn 708
Brownsville 444
Buena Vista 320

TOWNS
Buffalo 247,468,611,722
Butler 110
Caldwell 444
Calhoun 836
Cambridge 343,460,488
Camden 613,662,814
Cannonsby 110
Carlisle 467
Cazenovia 110
Cerro Gordo 294
Charlotte 180,220
Charlottesville 612
Chesapeake 24
Chillicothe 611
Cincinnati 391,639,837
Clarkesville 904
Colerain 687
Columbia 24,299,509,667, 691,721
Columbus 284,451
Concord 394
Cool Spring 745
Cooperville 110
Croatan 77,130
Crockett 444
Culpeper 785
Danville 301
Dayton 99
Deep Creek 384
Deerfield 734
Demopolis 276
Detroit 468,668
Dudley 163
Dunnsville 110
Eastville 827,914
Eddyville 744
Eden 424
Edenton 7,19,51,54,71,90, 123,169-171,190,224,248, 270,307,389,507,509,540, 545,562,581,588,609,631, 633,659,706,803,807,827, 842,851,880,894,914
El Paso del Norte 444
Elizabethtown 110,224
Embarcados 160
Encarnation 320
Everettsville 163
Fairfield 110
Fayetteville 180,687,701, 707
Foxtown 500
Franklin 597

TOWNS
Fredericksburg 652
Fredicksburg 413
Fremont 644
Frostburg 99
Galena 651
Galveston 444
Gatesville 57,65,103,248, 404,495,496,511,551,562, 919
Gennaros 444
Georgetown 189,281
Germantown 194,301
Gosport 860
Goveneur 110
Green Plains 163
Greensboro' 13,301,360
Groton 428
Halifax 19,424,545,830
Hanover 709
Harrisburg 885
Hartford 428,611
Heleha 284
Hertfod 865
Hertford 11,54,61,258, 278,297,344,372,385,389, 475,487,494,524,581,631, 677,697,765,770,776,809, 827,842,865,886
Hickory 110
Hickory Ground 383
Hickory Grove 475
Hillsborough 871
Horma 718
Houston 444,885
Hudson 561
Independence 160
Indianapolis 391
Jackson 203
Jacksonville 293,444
Kempsville 305,895
Kinderhook 787
Kittaining 110
La Grange 444
Lagrange 444
Lancaster 299,813
Leacock 110
Leverett 788
Lewistown 110
Lexington 200,283,745
Lincolnville 354
Linden 616
Los Angeles 441
Louisburg 687

TOWNS
Louisville 125,223,335, 445,546,554,575
Lowell 498
Luthersville 163
Lynchburg 885
Macon 823
Madison 335
Mansfield 110
Marcellus 638
Marietta 110
Marshfield 327
Maysville 744
McSherrytown 110
Memphis 276
Middlesex 352
Milton 310
Mobile 276,613
Monterey 294,441
Montgomery 613
Mount Pleasant 870
Mt. Pisgah 163
Murfreesboro' 609
Murfreesborough 687
Murfresboro' 163
Nanticoke 334
Nashville 98,218,294,341, 597,701,787,823
Natchez 444
New Bedford 111,710
New Haven 302,550,698,786
Newark 311
Newbern 163,229,248, 499,616,687,707
Newburgh 179
Newland 783
Newport 837
Nicolaus 644
Nixonton 40,278,395,618, 783
North Bend 787
North Huton 110
North View 281
Northboro' 815
Norwich 600
Norwick 600
Oak Ridge 163
Old Trap 783
Orwell 110
Ouachita 662
Oxford 421
Parksville 543
Parkville 863

TOWNS
Patterson 286
Pendleton 327,368
Petersburg 528
Pilatka 293
Pittburg 745
Pittsburg 461
Pittsburgh 232
Platsburg 561
Plymouth 49,54,229,545, 553,559,562,588,590,601, 609,631,643,745,842
Pool Town 505
Port Royal 787
Port Tobacco 573
Portland 561
Portsmouth 42,64,279, 405,582,791,860,872,914
Providence 211,592
Quincy 787
Reisterstown 745
Rensselaerville 110
Richmond 500
Roanoke 238,358
Rochester 330
Rockingham 612
Saco 121
Sacramento 441,644,816
Sag Harbor 106
St. Louis 320,361,598, 610,707,852
Salisbury 327
San Antonio de Bexar 182
San Augustine 444
San Diego 441,592
San Francisco 522,563, 592
San Joaquin 441
San Jose 393,441
San Juan 202
San Luis Obispo 441
Sanannah 293
Santa Barbara 441
Santa Fee 125,202
Savannah 591
Shadwell 787
Sharon 788
SHAVER's Creek 110
Snow Hill 793
Sonoma 440,441
South Mills 359,400,506, 829
Springfield 676
Stonington 179,428

TOWNS
Suffolk 66
Summer Hill 787
Sunsbury 253,457,735
Syracuse 221
Tahlequah 439
Taos 125
Tarborough 9,72,73
Temperanceville 793
Tonawanda 468
Travis 444
Troy 179
Tuscumbia 480
Vernon 644
Wadesborough 560
Warrenton 180,687
Washington 93,229,248, 256,687,703
Waterville 110
Waxsaw 787
Weldon 163,203,830
West Chester 162
Westbrook 774
Westfield 110
Weston 610
Weymouth 787
Wheeling 6,232,745
Williamsburg 7,787
Williamsburgh 179,854
Williamsport 734
Williamston 93,171,224, 321,789
Wilmington 133,180,224, 248,449,687,707,833,882
Winchester 328,468
Windsor 25,109,853
Woodville 19,61,399,475, 713,752,776,842
Wrightsville 299
Yarmouth, North 316
York 299,723,734
York Sulphur Springs 110
Yorktown 573
Yubaville 644
Zanesville 767
TOWNSHIP
Shrewsbury 734
TRACT
Campbel Ridge 410
Holly Grove 803
Juniper Ridge 410
Social Hall 749
Tan-Yard 803
UNIVERSITY

UNIVERSITY
Indiana 745
Maryland, of 810
N. Carolina, of 809
North Carolina, of 787
Pennsylvania, of 506
Washington Medical, of Baltimore 389
VALLEY
Powl's 110
Sonoma, of 440
WHARF
CAMPBELL's 818,907
Ferry 840
WOODS
Rocky Hock 902

www.ingramcontent.com/pod-product-compliance
Lightning Source LLC
Chambersburg PA
CBHW042358070526
44585CB00029B/2978